Ethnic Factors in Health and Disease

J. K. Cruickshank MSc, MD, MRCP
Senior Registrar, in Medicine and Clinical Epidemiology, Northwick Park
Hospital/Clinical Research Centre, Harrow, Middlesex

D. G. Beevers MD, FRCP
Reader, University of Birmingham Department of Medicine, Dudley Road Hospital,
Birmingham

WRIGHT

Wright
An imprint of Butterworth–Heinemann Ltd
Westbury House, Bury Street, Guildford, Surrey GU2 5BH

 PART OF REED INTERNATIONAL P.L.C.

OXFORD   LONDON   GUILDFORD   BOSTON
MUNICH   NEW DELHI   SINGAPORE   SYDNEY
TOKYO   TORONTO   WELLINGTON

First published 1989
Reprinted 1991

© **Butterworth–Heinemann Ltd, 1989**

British Library Cataloguing in Publication Data
Ethnic factors in health and disease.
  1. Man. Health
  I. Cruickshank, J. Kennedy
  II. Beevers, P. Gareth
  613

  ISBN 0–7236–0916–0

Library of Congress Cataloging in Publication Data
Ethnic factors in health and disease / [edited by] J.K. Cruickshank.
  D. G. Beevers
      p.   cm.
  Includes bibliographies and index.
  ISBN 0–7236–0916–0
  1. Minorities—health and hygiene—Cross-cultural studies.
  2. Minorities—Diseases—Cross-cultural studies. I. Cruickshank,
  J. K. (John Kennedy) II. Beevers, D. G. (D. Gareth)
    [DNLM: 1. Disease—ethnology. 2. Ethnic Groups. 3. Socioeconomic
  Factors. WB 720 E84]
  RA563.M56E84 1989
  362.1'089—dc20

Typesetting by TecSet Limited
Printed and bound by Hartnolls Ltd, Bodmin, Cornwall

Foreword 1

It is neither novel nor profound to restate that there will always be differences between people and many of mankind's blackest hours were as a result of the strife and intolerance which these differences provoked. One of the significant advances of modern times has been the growing conviction that it is more productive to use the diversity in a positive way to contribute to our wellbeing. Jamaica's motto 'Out of many, one people' is a reflection of this desire to focus on the unity which overrides differences.

Ethnicity is one kind of patent difference, and although it is difficult to define it accurately, it does convey the idea of peculiar characteristics assigned to some group of persons who can be easily recognizable and can be differentiated from others. Ethnicity often conjures up the image of the exotic, whether in terms of music, food, dress or even style of cricket! These ethnic differences have been explored in several places, and the roots and origins of much of Caribbean expression and thinking have been fertile fields for musicologists, anthropologists and the ethnologists.

Only occasionally have health professionals examined systematically these ethnic differences, gone beyond the stage of phenomenology and attempted to seek explanations for the differences in disease expression which are found.

This book represents a truly splendid effort by professionals from several parts of the world, and who work in a wide range of health disciplines, to examine the differences in various aspects of health which exist between groups of persons distinguished by their ethnic origins.

It is refreshing to read in the same book fascinating accounts of the sociology of race and health alongside descriptions of the clinical aspects of various interesting diseases. The range of problems addressed is also impressive and although the majority of the authors or the topics have Caribbean connections, there are contributions and perspectives from many other parts of the world.

This book must surely be seen as a first step the intrepid editors have taken in an area which is intrinsically sensitive, but which has to be explored if health care workers in various parts of the world are to deepen their understanding of the significance of their observations not only in the ethnic minority, but also in the numerically dominant majority

George A. O. Alleyne
Area Director, Health Programs Development,
Pan American Health Organization.
Formerly Professor of Medicine,
University of West Indies.

Foreword 2

Medicine does not stand still. New diseases emerge, old diseases fade away, methods of investigation and treatment change constantly. Dr Cruickshank and Dr Beevers have identified a new and important factor in the metamorphosis of medicine, that arises from the movement of populations and the opening up to scrutiny of areas of the world that have not hitherto been easily accessible. The ease of international travel and the (usually enforced) migration of large groups requires all of us to know more about diseases that were once rare in the developed world. Epidemiologists must revel in the new opportunities to study common diseases as they present and evolve in different parts of the world among people of different genetic and environmental backgrounds, and are now greatly assisted in this task by the specificity and certainty of new molecular markers of genetic identity.

In tackling this fascinating topic, the editors have brought together a large and impressive international team. The first quarter of the book provides a general background that highlights ethnic differences and some of the factors that account for them. The rest of the book examines specific topics: infection, blood disorders, psychiatric disease, nutrition (illustrating the particular interests of the editors that must have stimulated them to produce this book) and cardiovascular disease including hypertension and diabetes.

This is an important book. It serves to throw into prominence aspects of medicine that could illuminate some of our darkest areas of ignorance. It is also easy, indeed engrossing, to read.

Raymond Hoffenberg
President, Wolfson College, Oxford.
Recently, President of the Royal College of Physicians, London

Preface

There can be few people in Europe or North America who are not aware of the ethnic diversity of modern society. Communication between ethnic groups is often poor, even without language barriers, and may lead to an unawareness or lack of interest in the lives, aspirations and worries of ethnically different people, living and working no distance away. The domination of the media tends to encourage the majority to put over its ideas to minorities; the reverse rarely occurs. Assimilation into the majority is unusual so that minority groups tend to retain their cultural, religious and hence ethnic identity, as well as their social and health problems. Ethnic diversity will remain a feature of modern society. In the USA, the black, white, Hispanic and Jewish communities have retained their identities after generations of living in close proximity. The ethnic angle to health and disease is not unique to any country but has not yet achieved the understanding or perhaps sympathy of doctors, health-care planners or even patients.

Ethnicity rather than race

We have intentionally used the term 'ethnic' in preference to 'racial' throughout the book. 'Race' and 'racial' not only have inflammatory connotations, but are sloppy terms implying a precision of classification between peoples that has no biological basis. We agree with Cooper [1] who has argued that the concept of 'race' has been based on appearance and degree of melanization (skin pigmentation) rather than on repeatable biological or genetic measures. He suggests the word now has little meaning. How do the Ashanti or Yoruba peoples of West Africa differ from Nilotics of southern Sudan or black Americans or Negrito aboriginal peoples of Melanesia? Are Poles as distinct from Anglo-Saxons as they appear to be from Chinese? More relevant to medical science, how many research workers have bothered to define the 'racial' groups they study? To our knowledge, only Miller (see Chapter 32) has categorized black or Indian groups, whom he studied in Trinidad, by grandparental origin rather than by immediate appearance as a surrogate for 'race'. Hill (see Chapter 5) elegantly describes the limitations to genetic definition of different peoples and the lack of specific genetic markers to identify 'races'. Rather, the frequency of particular genes may be greater in one area than another and differences *within* groups are much greater than *between* groups.

The term 'ethnic' also has a much more appropriate wider context. It includes individual factors shared by groups (which may be genetic) as well as the social, economic, dietary and personal habits that characterize whole societies. By means of experience and education, effort or invitation, people can alter their social class. However, their ethnic origin remains relatively unchanged and may continue to influence their health. Analysis of these factors can lead to advances in our understanding and treatment of disease, as illustrated in the chapters on changes in cancer incidence and cardiovascular disease with migration.

Research results and positive discussion of ethnic factors have clearly benefitted people affected by specific diseases, often after extended efforts by pressure groups. For example, the knowledge and management of sickle cell and thalassaemia syndromes has improved considerably in the last decade. The technical and practical benefits allowed patients and their relatives to become directly involved, as in the development and day-to-day running of community sickle cell centres. There is increasing awareness of appropriate therapy for hypertension in blacks; nutritional supplements are given to susceptible pregnant mothers and their children.

The benefits are not restricted to more effective delivery of health services. Monitoring the epidemic of diabetes among people of Indian and Afro-Caribbean origin is providing clues to its origin. Advances have also come from the study of the interaction between lipids and coagulation factors as a cause of coronary heart disease, with important clues from ethnic differences. The finding that the retrovirus HTLV-I is implicated in spastic paraparesis in Afro-Caribbean and Japanese communities has provided a model for the pathogenesis of multiple sclerosis. We believe these examples represent *clinical epidemiology* at its best – approaching disease in individuals with a population perspective and the appropriate methods.

An important challenge to doctors will be a change in attitude to being questioned. In particular in these special topics, the 'informed-doctor-dispensing-to-ignorant-patient' approach will have to give way to an appreciation that many 'minority' patients will know more of recent developments in their condition than their doctors.

Thus the topics in this book cover much of medicine and international health. They could have been even wider; there is no specific discussion of ethnicity and disease in the South Pacific, in Japanese migrants, native American Indians or South Africa. Some topics (e.g. AIDS) are intentionally omitted as they have their own burgeoning literature. To have included or distilled the results from all potential 'ethnic' areas would have made the book unfocused, but we hope that the expertise of the authors and the breadth they cover will provide a comprehensive outline of how ethnicity affects health and medical practice.

Features of the book are the international contributions from the Caribbean, USA and Singapore where ethnic factors are obvious facts of daily life. These should balance the British perspective and encourage collaboration between colleagues working in the countries of origin and destination of migrant peoples. Unfortunately, the enormous topic of ethnic diversity and health in the Indian subcontinent itself could not be included. We hope, however, that the basic philosophy of the topics chosen will prove relevant.

Our book is aimed at doctors, nurses and health workers and the intention has been to allow any interested person to understand the topics discussed. Perhaps some of the lessons learned over the past 20 years in chronic diseases and how migrant people are affected by them may be of value to developing nations, so that they can avoid at least some of the public health mistakes of industrialized societies.

Other books cover aspects not detailed in this book. Sociological issues are discussed further in *Health, Race and Ethnicity* [2] and an anthropological viewpoint is given in *Culture, Health and Illness* by Holman [3]. Paediatrics does not have its own section here because it was covered recently in a detailed series of articles by Black [4] and its social and educational context was examined in a report on a 1970 UK birth cohort [5]. Finally, an excellently illustrated manual on training and practice for health workers in a multi-ethnic society has been produced by Mares, Henley and Baxter [6].

Ethnic factors in health and disease are likely to become more, not less important. They present a major challenge; this book aims to provide the background with which to face that challenge and to implement the results.

References

1 Cooper, R and David, R. The biological concept of race and its application to public health and epidemiology. *J. Health Politics Policy Law*, **11**, 97–116 (1986)
2 Rathweld, T. and Philipps, D (eds). *Health, Race and Ethnicity*, Croom Helm, London (1986)
3 Holman, C. *Culture, Health and Illness*, John Wright, Guildford, pp.224 (1984)
4. Black, J. *Child Health in Ethnic Minorities*, BMJ Publications, London, pp.72 (1985)
5 Osborn, A. F. and Butler, N. R. *Ethnic Minority Children. A Comparative Study from Birth to Five Years*, Commission for Racial Equality, London (1985)
6 Mares, P., Henley, A. and Baxter, C. *Health Care in Multi-racial Britain*, Health Education Council and National Extension College Trust, Cambridge (1985)

J.K.C.
D.G.B

Contributors

Dr Rachel Abraham
Research Dietician, Northwick Park Hospital, Watford Road, Harrow, Middlesex HA1 3UJ, UK

Professor A. M. Adelstein
Emeritus Professor of Epidemiology, London School of Hygiene and Tropical Medicine, c/o Department of Community Medicine, University College/Middlesex School of Medicine, 66–72 Gower Street, London WC1E 6EA, UK

Dr Elizabeth N. Anionwu
Head, Brent Sickle Cell and Thalassaemia Centre, Willesden Hospital, Harlesden Road, London NW10 3RY, UK

Dr Anne Aukett
Consultant Paediatrician, West Birmingham Health Authority, Dudley Road Hospital, Birmingham B18 7QH, UK

Dr. D. G. Beevers
Reader, University of Birmingham Department of Medicine, Dudley Road Hospital, Birmingham B18 7QH

Dr Milica Brozović
Consultant Haematologist, Central Middlesex Hospital, Acton Lane, London NW10 7NS, UK

Dr Aggrey W. Burke
Senior Lecturer, Department of Psychiatry, Jenner Wing, St George's Hospital Medical School, Tooting, London SW17 0RE, UK

Dr J. K. Cruickshank
Senior Registrar in Medicine and Clinical Epidemiology, Northwick Park Hospital/Clinical Research Centre, Harrow, Middlesex HA1 3UJ

Dr Angus G. Dalgleish
Head, Retrovirus Research Group, Division of Immunological Medicine, Clinical Research Centre, Watford Road, Harrow, Middlesex HA1 3UJ, UK

Dr Patricia Davidson
Assistant Professor, Division of Hypertension, University of Maryland Hospital, 22 South Greene Street, Baltimore, Maryland 21201, USA

Dr Sally C. Davies
Consultant Haematologist, Central Middlesex Hospital, Acton Lane, London NW10 7NS, UK

Dr Charles DeCeulaer
Scientific Staff/Honorary Consultant Physician, MRC Sickle Cell Unit, University of the West Indies, Kingston 7, Jamaica

Dr Nicholas E. Day
Director, MRC Biostatistics Unit, 5 Shaftesbury Road, Cambridge CB2 2BW, UK

Ms Jenny Douglas
District Health Promotion Manager, Sandwell Health Authority, Health Promotion Unit, 8 Grange Road, West Bromwich, B70 8PD, UK

Professor John Fox
Chief Medical Statistician, Office of Population Censuses and Surveys, St Catherine's House, 10 Kingsway, London WC2B 6JP, UK

Dr W. Nigel Gibbs
Recently: Professor of Haematology, University of the West Indies, Jamaica Currently: Chief Medical Officer, Health Laboratory Technology, World Health Organization, 1211 Geneva 27, Switzerland

Dr Gyles R. Glover
Lecturer, Department of Community Medicine, Charing Cross and Westminster Medical School, London SW1P 2AR, UK

Professor Gerald A. C. Grell
Department of Medicine, University of the West Indies, Mona, Kingston 7, Jamaica

Dr Craig L. Hanis
Geneticist, Center for Demographic and Population Genetics, Graduate School for Biomedical Sciences, University of Texas Health Science Center, Houston, Texas 77225, USA

Dr E. Nigel Harris
Departments of Rheumatology and Medicine, University of Louisville, Louisville, Kentucky 40292, USA

Dr Glynn Harrison
Consultant Psychiatrist, Academic Department of Psychiatry, University Hospital, Nottingham NG7 2UH, UK

Joan Henthorn
Chief Medical Laboratory Scientific Officer, Department of Haematology, Central Middlesex Hospital, London NW1 7NS, UK

Dr Adrian V. S. Hill
Wellcome Senior Clinical Fellow, Institute of Molecular Medicine, John Radcliffe Hospital, Oxford OX3 9DU, UK

Dr Liam Hughes
Research Fellow, Department of Cardiology, Northwick Park Hospital, Watford Road, Harrow HA1 3UJ, UK

Mrs S Ganatra
Nutritionist, Milk Marketing Board, Thames Ditton, Surrey, KT7 0EL, UK

Dr Stuart Logan
Department of Paediatric Epidemiology, Institute of Child Health, Guildford Street, London WC1, UK

Dr I. R. McFadyen
Senior Lecturer in Obstetrics and Gynaecology, University of Liverpool, Royal Liverpool Hospital, Prescot Street, Liverpool L7 8XP, UK

Dr Dermot McGovern
Consultant Psychiatrist, Barnsley Hall Hospital, Stourbridge Road, Bromsgrove B61 0EX, Worcestershire, UK

Dr Martin W. McNicol
Consultant Physician, Director of Chest Medicine, Central Middlesex Hospital, Acton Lane, London NW10 7NS, UK

Professor M. G. Marmot
Department of Community Medicine, University College/Middlesex Hospital Medical School, 66–72 Gower Street, London WC1E 6EA, UK

Dr George J. Miller
Senior Scientific Staff, MRC Epidemiology and Medical Care Unit, Northwick Park Hospital, Harrow HA1 3UJ, UK

Dr Bernadette Modell
Consultant in Perinatal Medicine, University College and Middlesex School of Medicine, Department of Obstetrics and Gynaecology, 86–96 Chenies Mews, London WC1E 6HZ, UK

Professor Owen St C. Morgan
Head, Department of Medicine, University of the West Indies, Mona, Kingston 7, Jamaica

Dr Errol Y. St A. Morrison
Consultant Physician and Senior Lecturer, Department of Biochemistry, University of the West Indies, Mona, Kingston 7, Jamaica

Dr Angus Nicoll
Wellcome Lecturer in Tropical Community Health, London School of Hygiene and Tropical Medicine, Keppel Street, London WC2, UK

Dr Paul J. Pacy
Senior Registrar, Nutrition Research Group, Clinical Research Centre, Northwick Park Hospital, Harrow, Middlesex HA1 3UJ, UK

Dr Maggie Pearson
Lecturer in Medical Sociology, Department of General Practice, University of Liverpool, New Medical School, Ashton Street, PO Box 147, Liverpool L69 3BX, UK

Dr Lee Hin-Peng
Associate Professor, Department of Community, Occupational and Family Medicine, National University Hospital, Lower Kent Ridge Road, Singapore 0511

Dr Mary Petrou
Senior Associate, Perinatal Centre, University College and Middlesex School of Medicine, Department of Obstetrics and Gynaecology, 86–96 Chenies Mews, London WC1E 6HX, UK

Dr Neil Poulter
Honorary Senior Lecturer, Department of Community Medicine, University College/Middlesex Medical School, 66–72 Gower Street, London WC1E 6EA, UK

Dr J. H. Richardson
Research Scientist, Retrovirus Research Group, Clinical Research Centre, Harrow HA1 3US, UK

Dr Elijah Saunders
Associate Professor, Chief, Division of Hypertension, University of Maryland Hospital, 22 South Greene Street, Baltimore, Maryland 21201, USA

Professor William J. Schull
Director and Ashbel Smith Professor, Center for Demographic and Population Genetics, Graduate School of Biomedical Sciences, The University of Texas Health Science Center, PO Box 20334, Houston, Texas 77225, USA

Professor G. R. Serjeant
Director, MRC Laboratories, University of the West Indies, Kingston 7, Jamaica

Professor K. Shanmugaratnam
Singapore Cancer Registry, c/o Department of Pathology, National University Hospital, Singapore 0511

Dr Juliet Webster
Research Fellow, Research Centre for Social Sciences, University of Edinburgh, 56 George Square, Edinburgh EH8 9JU, UK

Professor Brian Wharton
Rank Professor of Human Nutrition, University of Glasgow Department of Human Nutrition, Yorkhill Hospitals, Glasgow G3 8SJ, UK

Mrs Pamela Wharton
Lately Research Dietitian, Maternal and Child Health Unit, Sorrento Maternity Hospital, Wake Green Road, Moseley, Birmingham B13 9HE, UK

Contents

Section I

Background issues

Chapter 1

Migration, ethnicity, health and disease

J. K. Cruickshank and D. G. Beevers

Historical background and origins

Substantial numbers of migrant people have settled in Europe and North America over the past 30 years. Most European countries now have sizeable ethnic minority groups, mainly migrants from former colonies. However, Europe and the Americas are not alone. The history of modern nations from India, Malaysia and Singapore in South-east Asia to East Africa and the eastern Caribbean could be summarized as the struggle, peacefully or otherwise, of different ethnic groups to develop together. Several centuries of domination of Asian, Caribbean and latterly African countries by empire builders altered people's identities and produced entirely new political boundaries. The relatively sudden departure of colonial powers in 30 years after the Second World War left behind partly developed or impoverished nations, where premature death is still an everyday occurrence.

Despite prolonged often acrimonious struggles for independence, the departing colonists usually bequeathed their language, economic influence, educational systems and religion as they left. The prosperity of Europe and North America in the 1950s and 1960s and low levels of unemployment meant that many people from Third World nations migrated, often by direct invitation, in search of jobs and a higher standard of living. Thus many Indians, Pakistanis, West Indians, West and some East Africans arrived in Britain. Many Central and North Africans moved to France and Belgium, East Indians moved to the Netherlands and Arabs, in smaller numbers, moved throughout Europe. Turkish migration was not along the usual routes of shared culture, history or language. Here the reasons for migration were purely economic. Sweden and West Germany, the richest countries, now have substantial minorities of Turks. Many were originally 'guest workers' who were supposed one day to go home; their labour conditions remain the poorest in Europe [1]. The prospect of increased standards of living also attracted many Japanese to the USA post-war, and continues to attract Mexicans across their border, while part-time workers from the Caribbean have stayed on in the USA.

Initially migration tended to consist largely of economically active men, prepared to take on unpopular, poorly paid jobs. In Europe, there followed a second period of 'social migration' of wives, fiancees, and elderly dependent relatives. Family units were established, often in poor areas of inner cities. Some migrants were political refugees from Third World countries discriminating against their own ethnic minority groups. Many people of Indian origin who had lived for generations in East Africa came to Britain as refugees from racist policies of their new rulers.

These East African Asians were often of higher social class than those who arrived directly from India. They had been lawyers, teachers, administrators and merchants and soon settled into Britain and Canada to resume their former occupations. Thus the Asian community in Britain is diverse although often naively perceived as simply 'Asian'. Similarly the Vietnamese refugees and boat people tended to be economically active, having had positions of influence and prosperity while South Vietnam was under first French and later American control. They present special problems as most have no historical or linguistic links with the 'host' countries. Further south, in the two hundredth anniversary of white settlement, Australians have only recently been made more aware of the health and social problems of their indigenous black minority group, the Aborigines.

Until the last decade, for 200 years immigration had been officially encouraged by the ethnically diverse USA. Most recently, non-white immigrants, particularly Hispanics, arrived; in part because of language and economic barriers they have experienced discrimination similar to that directed at American blacks and have tended to form a lower social class of poorly paid workers in the south-west and the larger cities. The abolition of American slavery only after the Civil War in 1866, and the slow attrition of racial repression and segregation since, may well have contributed to the excess mortality in blacks from all causes compared with whites. These health problems are now of national concern in the USA, as evidenced by the Minority Health Reports [2]. Are the striking ethnic differences in, for example, hypertension due to genetic factors, to poorer social class, to the stress of racial discrimination or to all of these? Such questions will probably never have precise answers but their careful study allows solutions to evolve.

Limited vital statistics

Estimates of the numbers of migrants in Western European countries are hard to come by. In England and Wales, the population of 48 million includes around 3 million people who were born in the Indian subcontinent, the West Indies or Africa. Some of these are ethnically white as the children of former colonists. Census and death certificate data on ethnic origin in Britain are inadequate as they only code place of birth, rather than ethnic origin. However, their inspection can allow extraction of important data, for instance by distinguishing mortality rates in different subgroups of Indian subcontinent origin by name on the certificate (Gujarati, Hindu, Muslim, Punjabi, etc.) [3].

Many black and Asian children have been born in Britain in the last 30 years, but there is little information in official statistics. The British Census in 1981 did not ask about ethnic origin because the topic was considered to be too sensitive. Some leaders of the non-white communities feared that collection of such data might lead to racial discrimination. Indeed, there is good informal evidence that many young blacks of British and Caribbean birth simply did not register in 1981 and 1971. As Burke points out in Chapter 21, this has serious implications for the use of official statistics in interpreting the high rates of schizophrenia; denominator figures for young blacks are probably gross underestimates in the larger inner cities of England. However, in the USA, ethnic or racial breakdown of health and vital statistics has allowed programmes and preventive efforts to focus on minority health problems. We believe the lack of such data in the British system, far from preventing health and social problems for ethnic minorities, merely perpetuates them. The recent announcement that the 1991 Census will now ask about ethnic origin is therefore welcome.

Ethnic diversity and appropriate terminology

Ethnic minority groups in most countries tend to live in relatively close-knit communities in cities. Thus in Britain, Jamaicans tended to settle in South London and West Birmingham. Muslims travelled to Bradford and the cotton towns of the North of England, Sikhs moved to Birmingham and Southall, London, and Gujarati Hindus moved to Leicester and Wembley. The concept of 'racial integration' as used in the past has largely been abandoned. Most minority communities choose to keep together, and among Asian groups marriages are still arranged, voluntarily or involuntarily, within the same ethnic or religious background. Such 'ghetto-ization' has often been for genuinely social reasons, but it also occurred because of economic necessity and fear of violent discrimination and racial harassment, by no means always from the 'host' population. Thus the minority communities tend to become microcosms of the original home nation, with similar social, marital and dietary habits and often similar occupations. Shops, restaurants, temples or mosques have sprung up and many migrants are employed by members of their own community. Similar health problems remain a feature of these communities even in modern cities. There is a notable absence of newly acquired tropical diseases, except for malaria contracted on visits without prophylaxis to India or Africa.

Within each migrant ethnic group there are marked variations of social class, acculturation, and length of stay in the host country. A black Jamaican carpenter or bus-driver in England for 40 years, or his British-born children, differ in all respects from a recent black Ugandan immigrant or visiting tourist. Most blacks in Britain are either Caribbean or West African in origin but differences in culture, health, language, religion and social class are as great as those between an Anglo-Saxon Londoner and a Russian in the Caucasus. Many West Indians from Trinidad, Guyana and occasionally Jamaica are ethnically Indian or sometimes Chinese; hence the description as Afro- or Indo-Caribbean.

The term 'Asian' is unsatisfactory and too inclusive. To Americans, the term describes people from South-east Asia or Japan; in Britain it refers to people originating from India, Pakistan, Bangladesh or Sri Lanka, with many Indians coming via East Africa. India is culturally very diverse with its panoply of Hindus, Muslims, Sikhs and Christians. Cultural diversity among whites is also enormous. An urban Scandinavian, a Scottish Highland crofter and a south Italian peasant are all white but have almost nothing in common. However, for ease of description in Britain it is simplest to consider health and diverse lifestyles in three main groupings: whites, Afro-Caribbean blacks and Asians from India or Pakistan, defined by religious or geographic subgroup. A major consideration is social class. Clearly a migrant Indian doctor has more in common with a white doctor than with a migrant Punjabi subsistence farmer or his wife although their families may rapidly alter social positions. Health patterns are in general more related to socioeconomic circumstances than to 'race' alone.

Religion has little to do with health or disease. Often, religious practices were related to avoidance of health hazards; for example, the prohibition of pork originated in a period when pigs were frequently infected. While some people's food habits may make them unwell (e.g. strict ovo-lacto-vegetarianism), these habits are more often due to custom than religion. Many devout Sikhs and Hindus eat meat, although many choose not to. Indian-origin women may be kept in strict purdah (seclusion from the outside world and particularly from men), away from sunlight; some develop the psychiatric consequences of loneliness in Western inner cities, while some may develop adult osteomalacia, due at least in part to sheltering from sunlight. Yet devout Muslim women become doctors, teachers and politicians and are no less Muslim. Racial origin or religion cannot be 'blamed' for different disease rates. Rather, adaptive aspects of lifestyle, dietary customs, poverty and overcrowding are more culpable. Modifications that may be necessary, for example the introduction of vitamin D-enriched chapati flour, and possibly the avoidance of clarified butter, require careful sympathetic positive counselling, preferably by Indian-origin dietitians or health workers.

Genetic factors within and between different ethnic groups do have powerful effects. Diabetes, hypertension and coronary heart disease all tend to run in families; such familiality may be partly genetic and partly due to shared environmental influences. It is these environmental factors which need investigation and informed action, because they act upon susceptible genotypes. Genes, particularly those promoting the polygenic chronic disorders, may provide disease markers but will be more difficult, and much more expensive, to influence directly. Diet, urban stress, smoking and alcohol consumption, access to medical care, attitude to health and simple geography (e.g. north vs. south) are the major contributors to disease.

References

1 Wallraff, G. *The Lowest of the Low*, Methuen, London (1988)
2 *Report of the Secretary's Task Force on Black and Minority Health*, vols 1–8, US Department of Health and Human Services, Washington (1985/86)
3 Balarajan, R., Bulusu, L., Adelstein, A. M. and Shukla, V. Patterns of mortality among migrants to England and Wales from the Indian sub-continent. *Br. Med. J.*, **289**, 1185–1187 (1984)

Chapter 2

The changing nature of populations: the British example

Juliet Webster and John Fox

The concept of 'ethnic origin' is not simple. There are fundamental questions of definition of 'ethnicity' to be addressed and any investigation of ethnic groups requires a method to identify their members. For example, does the term include solely immigrants, or also those born in the 'new' country to parents (or grandparents) born overseas? If the latter, is membership of a particular ethnic group restricted to those with both parents born in the same country; how are those of mixed parentage to be assigned? To a great degree the choices to be made rest upon the requirements and orientation of the researcher. Only when the population to be studied has been identified can its size, qualities and the changes it may have undergone be assessed. As Marmot *et al.* [1] have noted, disease and mortality are functions of social culture as well as of class, and different diseases prevail in different cultures. Immigrants may adopt a new lifestyle, but they also retain elements of their country of origin. This is less the case for the second generation born in a 'new' country.

The data source on Britain's ethnic minorities is the decennial census which includes the respondent's country of birth. However, this involves accepting a definition of ethnicity based on immigrant status – that is, being born abroad – since the census does not separate those born to immigrant parents from the 'indigenous' population. Bearing this in mind, some major features of Britain's immigrant population can be identified as well as how these may have changed since largescale immigration to Britain began.

Apart from the Irish, who in 1981 constituted the largest single group of immigrants to the UK, most immigrants are either of Indian subcontinent or West Indian origin, and this is only since the 1950s. The process of commonwealth immigration to Britain was not uniform but was characterized by peaks and troughs in which different groups came in response to differing demands in the British labour market [2] and as a result of immigration controls in the early 1960s [3]. Migration of West Indians and those from India was well under way during the 1950s, and the former made up the bulk of immigrants during that decade; Indian and Pakistani arrivals did not become substantial until the 1960s (Table 2.1).

Paradoxically, the arrival of people from Pakistan was encouraged by legislation intended to restrict entry. Expectation of controls led the Pakistani government to remove restrictions and promote the migration of Mirpuri families dispossessed by the construction of the Nanglen Dam [4]. Similarly, in the week before the 1986 introduction of visas, people from the Indian subcontinent waited in queues at Heathrow airport for days to gain entry to Britain. Well over half the Indian and

Table 2.1 Size of immigrant population to Britain: 1951–1981

	Country of birth		
	India	Pakistan	W. Indies
1951	110 767[*]	11 117[*]	16 188
1961	157 435	30 737	172 379
1971	321 995	139 935	237 035
1981	391 877	236 715[†]	295 179

[*] These figures include non-Indian whites born in India and are an overestimate of the Asian Indian-born population. Deakin puts the total overseas-born black population at no more than 75 000 in 1951 and his figures include West Indians.
[†] Includes Bangladesh for comparative purposes.

three-quarters of the Pakistani immigrants who arrived in Britain prior to control arrived in the 18-month period before the 1962 Commonwealth Immigrants Act [3].

Sex and age structure

Sex composition can also be attributed to a mixture of labour demand and responses to legislation. Among the Indian and Pakistani community, the proportion of women among early settlers was very low, immigrant labour being generally young, male and unmarried. In 1961, when immigration from the Indian subcontinent became significant, only 4818 or 15% of the 39 737-strong Pakistani community were women. This discrepancy can be seen in Figure 2.1 which shows the difference in number and composition of men and women in each immigrant group.

Due to the inclusion of Indian-born whites the sex composition of Indian immigrants is harder to identify from these data (illustrating the case for avoiding country of birth as a measure of ethnicity). However, in a study of Sikhs in Southall in the late 1950s, it was estimated that the proportion of women was as low as 4% [5], this deficiency later rebalanced in the 1970s and 1980s. By contrast, immigration from the Caribbean has always included more women; by 1971 they had overtaken their male counterparts and continued to do so in 1981. The sex composition of each group changed over time; the earlier marked majority of Indian and Pakistani men was reversed as they reacted to the threat of immigration controls by bringing their wives to England. Since the voucher system of regulation was introduced the number of actual voucher holders arriving has been far exceeded by the number of their dependants. Deakin [3] noted that by 1967 over 90% of all Commonwealth immigrants to Britain were dependants. Paradoxically, therefore, the Commonwealth Immigrants Act of 1962 failed to limit the numbers arriving from India and Pakistan, whom the government was most anxious to restrict. In fact, the legislation had unintended consequences:

> The balance of migration since July 1962 shifted in a number of ways; from the Caribbean to India to Pakistan . . . , from the economically active to the

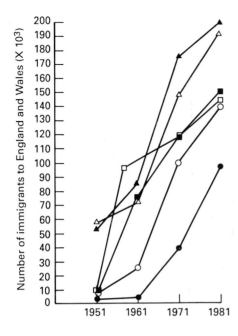

Figure 2.1 New Commonwealth immigration to England and Wales 1951–81. ●————●, Pakistani females; ○————○, Pakistani males; ■————■, West Indian females; □————□, West Indian males; ▲————▲, Indian females; △————△, Indian males. Figures for Indian females and males include white Indian-born. Figures for Pakistan include Bangladesh for comparability

economically inactive, from adults to children and within the small numbers of men still entering from the unskilled to the professionally qualified. (Deakin, 1970, p.49[3]).

The age profiles differ both between and within groups over time. In 1981 most West Indians were over 45, while most Pakistanis were aged 20–29, reflecting the different periods of immigration from the different countries.

Wives and elderly relatives represented the first wave of dependants arriving in Britain, but increasingly the later arrivals have been children. In the 1960s and 1970s, the age structure was weighted towards the under thirties, and in the case of Pakistanis, has become steadily younger over the 1961–1981 period.

Census statistics (Table 2.2) focus only on those born overseas and underestimate the total number of ethnic minorities in Britain. Preliminary calculations using the OPCS Longitudinal Study confirm that the age structure of Britain's black population remains young as ethnic minorities reach child-rearing ages [6] and tend to have larger families [7].

Geographical dispersal of Britain's black immigrants (Table 2.3)

The ethnic minorities are not uniformly distributed across Britain but are concentrated in a small number of electoral wards, so that ethnic groups seem to be relatively numerous in some localities while only constituting a tiny proportion of the national population [7]. Where many of the overseas-born population are found, there are often low proportions of UK-born, underlining also the segregation of Britain's ethnic minorities. Figures collected by the Policy Studies Institute and based on the ethnic origin rather than the country of birth of the respondents show a strong correspondence with census figures [7].

Table 2.2 Country of birth by age for residents of Great Britain: 1961–1981

Age (yr)	West Indies		India		Pakistan	
	No.	%	No.	%	No.	%
1961						
0–4	2 348	1.52	1 613	10.87	390	1.41
5–19	17 730	11.50	22 861	15.55	2 755	9.98
20–29	60 749	39.40	31 959	21.74	8 646	31.32
30–39	45 446	29.48	31 763	21.61	8 989	32.56
40–44	11 799	7.65	11 354	7.72	2 345	8.49
45+	16 081	10.43	47 403	32.25	4 475	16.21
Total	154 143		146 953		27 600	
1971						
0–4	860	0.36	2 900	0.90	4 170	2.97
5–19	48 424	20.43	56 940	17.68	40 015	28.59
20–29	45 065	19.01	69 630	21.62	25 875	18.48
30–39	71 570	30.19	74 485	23.13	38 055	27.19
40–44	28 505	12.02	29 060	9.02	13 085	9.34
45+	42 595	17.97	88 980	27.63	18 750	13.39
Total	237 030		321 995		139 950	
1981						
0–4	822	0.27	1 780	0.45	5 765	3.06
5–19	13 910	4.71	33 808	8.62	37 961	20.17
20–29	63 689	21.57	80 437	20.52	57 873	30.75
30–39	55 305	18.73	85 046	21.70	31 399	16.68
40–44	43 962	14.89	42 674	10.88	16 688	8.86
45+	117 491	39.80	148 129	37.80	38 512	20.46
Total	275 179		391 874		188 198	

Table 2.3 Regional distribution (%) by country of birth

	UK	Caribbean	Bangladesh	India	Pakistan
Greater London	11.93	57.00	46.16	36.35	19.59
Outer South-east	20.58	9.70	12.59	15.55	13.20
East Midlands	7.92	4.96	6.77	5.80	3.89
West Midlands	10.50	14.24	13.77	18.90	21.05
North-west	13.43	4.5	11.10	7.38	11.09
Yorks/Humberside	10.18	4.46	6.77	5.80	20.57
Rest of East and West	25.42	5.11	6.39	7.07	6.07

Source: OPCS (1983) 1981 Census: Country of Birth Tables, HMSO, London.

Both sets of figures show a concentration of black people in Greater London and the West Midlands (and, in the case of Pakistanis, also in the Yorkshire/Humberside region). Geographical distribution largely reflects an occupational segregation of black immigrants following arrival in Britain in response to the available labour market. Overwhelmingly, areas were favoured which provided employment in transport (West Indians), engineering (Pakistanis), labouring (all groups), metal manufacturing (Indians and Pakistanis) and wool and textile production (Pakistanis), serving as a replacement population for whites and moving into second-rate jobs and decayed urban areas [2].

Immigrants vs. ethnic minorities born in the UK

Data collection and analysis on ethnic minorities has to date been concerned either with immigrants (e.g. the Census), or with those who for any reason assign themselves to an ethnic minority group (Labour Force Survey, PS1 Survey). In official statistics, descendants of immigrants (born in the UK) have not yet been considered as a specific group and now need attention as they represent the major demographic change within the ethnic minority population. Country of birth as an indicator of ethnicity seriously and increasingly underestimates the black population and provides an inaccurate picture because it includes overseas-born whites. Distinctions between immigrants and the children of immigrants need to be made to contrast and compare characteristics and social circumstances. The UK-born black population differs in important ways from that which first came to Britain 30 years ago. This issue needs to be addressed if an understanding of Britain's ethnic minorities is to be furthered.

References

1 Marmot, M. Adelstein, A. and Bulusu, L. Immigrant mortality in England and Wales 1970–78. In *Population Trends 33*, Autumn, HMSO, London (1983)
2 Peach, C. *West Indian Migration to Britain: A Social Geography*, Oxford University Press, London (1968)
3 Deakin, N. *Colour, Citizenship and British Society*, Panther Books, London (1970)
4 Saifullah Khan, V. (ed.). *Minority Families in Britain: Support and Stress*, Macmillan, London (1979)
5 Aurora, G. S. *The New Frontiersmen*, Popular Prakashan, Bombay (1967)
6 Webster, J. *Using the OPCS Longitudinal Study to Classify Ethnic Origin*, Social Statistics Research Unit Working Paper No. 41, The City University, London (1986)
7 Brown, C. *Black and White Britain: The Third PSI Survey*, Heinemann, London (1984)

Chapter 3

General approaches to migrant studies: the relation between disease, social class and ethnic origin

M. G. Marmot

Why study disease rates in migrants?

What is a migrant?

A migrant is someone born in one place and living in another. Migration may be from one part of a country to another, or international, where the influences that affect disease rates may vary more. The general principles of study and inference are similar.

Time, place and person

Epidemiological investigation into causes of disease traditionally traces variation with time, place and person. Non-artefactual differences in disease rates between places may be due to differences in environment or in the people who live there, including both acquired characteristics and genetic endowment: nurture and nature. Lifestyle results from an interaction of personal factors with social, economic, cultural and environmental influences. Examination of disease rates in people who migrate has made important contributions to dissecting out these possible influences.

For the major causes of coronary heart disease (CHD) to be genetically determined the low rates of CHD in Japan compared to the USA would have to be due to genetic differences between Japanese and Americans; or, alternatively, to differences in the way diseases are diagnosed, certified and coded. These explanations were shown to be unlikely by the studies of men of Japanese ancestry living in Japan, Hawaii and California [1]. Using standardized diagnostic techniques, CHD prevalence [2] and mortality [3] were higher in Japanese in the USA than in Japan. These changes subsequent to migration led to exploration of the role of cultural and other factors in the aetiology of CHD [4].

Similarly, the patterns of cancer incidence and mortality after migration have strengthened the argument that the majority of cancer deaths are of environmental origin.

Migrants or ethnic groups?

These are overlapping, but not identical, categories. Children of migrants born in the 'new' country may be considered to belong to the same ethnic group as their parents. By contrast, migrants may not necessarily belong to a different ethnic group from the host population. The definition of 'ethnic' is blurred. Should immigrants to England from the Indian subcontinent be considered to be ethnically different from native-born English? What if they were born of English parents? Are migrants to England from South Africa ethnically different from the English? Only if non-white? What if their parents were Portugese?

The term 'ethnic' presupposes cultural differences. If the country of destination is a 'melting pot', ethnic distinctions may become blurred in subsequent generations. Elsewhere ethnic distinctions may remain – Indians in Fiji and Chinese in Malaysia, although born in those countries, are treated as culturally distinct from Melanesians and Malays respectively.

The vagueness of the term 'ethnic', and a similar lack of clarity as to whether migrants are, of necessity, special, does not invalidate this area of study. If two groups, however defined, have different rates of disease, productive aetiological investigations may follow – particularly if disease rates change after migration.

Influences on the disease rates of migrants

Influences of the 'old' and 'new' countries

Disease rates affected both those in the 'old' country and those in the 'new' and will depend, among other things, on age at and years since migration and will vary from disease to disease (Table 3.1, see also Chapter 6). For CHD, mortality rates are intermediate between the rates in the old country and those in England and Wales, whether the immigrants come from a higher rate country (Scotland) or lower rate countries (France and Italy). Rates for lung cancer are more like the old country; for cirrhosis of the liver more like the new country. With both cirrhosis, accidents and violence, persisting influences from the old country can be seen.

` If migrants kept their pattern of disease from the old country this would imply one or more of the following: (a) their pattern of disease was genetically

Table 3.1 Mortality (SMR) by country of birth among immigrants to England and Wales (aged 20+) and in corresponding home country (aged 15–74): 1970–72

	CHD	Lung cancer	Cirrhosis of the liver	Accidents and violence
Scotland				
Home	124	113	161	136
Immigrants	114	113	160	142
E & W	100	100	100	100
France				
Home	30	43	1648	244
Immigrants	85	78	163	176
E & W	100	100	100	100
Italy				
Home	43	56	1466	153
Immigrants	74	68	205	91
E & W	100	100	100	100

E & W, England and Wales
From Marmot et al. [5] with permission

determined; (b) the effects of early environmental influences persist; (c) they bring their lifestyle with them and it is this that determines their persisting disease patterns.

If the disease rates of immigrants change to resemble that of the new country, this suggests the primacy of the environment and/or lifestyle of the new country, or that the differences in rates between old and new countries were all due to differences in diagnosis.

Studies of immigrants have helped to sort out these possibilities. For example: (a) Carefully conducted field studies such as the Japan-Hawaii-California study (see above) have validated diagnoses. (b) The changed rates in the children of immigrants lend weight to an environmental/lifestyle explanation: immigrants to Israel from Europe or North America have higher rates of CHD than immigrants from North Africa and Asia. Both groups in the second generation have CHD rates similar to that prevailing in Israel. (c) The persisting effect of country of origin on cirrhosis mortality, accidents and violence suggests a possible continuation of behaviour pattern established prior to migration.

Age at migration and length of stay

These factors can add to our knowledge of 'incubation' periods of disease and critical ages of exposure. The latter is illustrated by multiple sclerosis. Immigrants from a high to a low rate country apparently take on the rates of the new country if they migrate before age 15. This may relate to a critical age of infection. Like poliomyelitis, infection at a later age may result in a greater likelihood of clinically apparent disease than infection at a younger age. This hypothesis could imply a greater prevalence of the possible infectious agent in low rate countries, and hence infection at an earlier (safer) age.

Earlier age at migration is also likely to be associated with a greater acceptance of the life of the new country. It is difficult to distinguish the effects of age at migration from the length of time since migration, because the two are highly correlated. Occasionally a natural experiment allows some distinction to be made. The Tokelau Island Migrant study [6] followed migrants who left these coral atolls, where mean blood pressures are low, for New Zealand, where blood pressures are higher, during a limited time after a natural disaster on the Islands. Hence people who migrated at different ages had been in New Zealand for similar periods of time. It is therefore interesting that older immigrants show a greater difference in blood pressure from Island dwellers than do younger immigrants (Figure 3.1). This holds promise for elucidating factors acting in adult life that affect blood pressure and, perhaps, a decline with age in adaptability.

Selection of migrants and the process of migration: the 'healthy migrant' effect

For immigrants from most countries, ill-health is likely to limit migration. This may explain why immigrants to England and Wales, in general, had a lower all-cause mortality than that of their old country, or of England and Wales [5]. The exception to this was Ireland where adverse social selection may operate: perhaps the socially disadvantaged may be more likely to leave Ireland for England – hence their higher all-cause mortality.

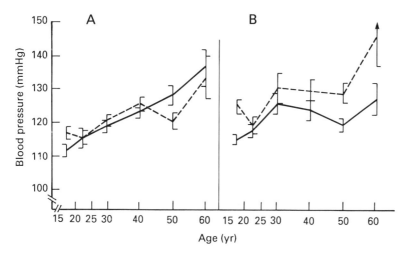

Figure 3.1 Mean systolic blood pressure by age of Tokelauan men comparing non-migrants at two surveys with migrants before and after migration to New Zealand. Non-migrants (A): ———, 1968/71 Tokelau; – – –, 1976 Tokelau. Migrants (B): ———, 1968/71 Tokelau; – – –, 1975–77 New Zealand

The process of migration itself involves major changes which may affect disease risk. Economic and social disruption, breaking down of family ties, changes in smoking, drinking and dietary practices may all occur [5].

Social and cultural influences

Social class, at least in Britain, has served as an indicator of the social forces affecting health and disease [7]. It has a strong association with mortality at every age, with disease incidence and survival, and with a wide range of health behaviours. However, social class, as conventionally defined, cannot explain patterns of disease seen among immigrants. Table 3.2 illustrates this with mortality from all circulatory disease [5]. Immigrants from Ireland show a similar social class gradient to the England and Wales population; but in each social class the standardized mortality rate (SMR) for Irish immigrants is higher than that of all men in England and Wales. Immigrants from the Indian subcontinent show an inverse association between social class and mortality among non-manual but not among manual classes. Immigrants from Africa and the Caribbean actually have higher mortality in non-manual than manual class.

These figures suggest that the forces determining mortality in immigrants are not well summarized by the conventional social class measure. Either this measure is not completely capturing the social position of the immigrants, as possibly in the case of the Irish, or it is not reflecting the environmental and cultural/ethnic influences on disease risks. This is hardly surprising. If, for example, diet plays a role in disease risks, a Bangladeshi man of social class V is likely to have different patterns of diet-related diseases from an Italian man of social class V.

The conclusion must be that while we should pay great attention to the social and economic position of immigrants, these are unlikely to be the only factors that

Table 3.2 Mortality, from all circulatory disease, of male immigrants aged 15–64 by country of birth and social class, and of married female immigrants aged 15–64 by country of birth and social class of husband: 1970–72

Country of birth	Social class I Deaths	I SMR	II Deaths	II SMR	IIIN Deaths	IIIN SMR	IIIM Deaths	IIIM SMR	IV Deaths	IV SMR	V Deaths	V SMR	Total* Deaths	Total* SMR
Males														
All Ireland	120	100	314	103	269	118	1 119	117	925	124	770	123	3 577	113
Indian subcontinent	74	97	191	126	191	145	284	135	313	140	226	115	1 318	123
African Commonwealth	15	164	26	122	26	133	16	70	26	124	12	188		
Caribbean Commonwealth	9	141	29	148	30	160	168	79	123	83	131	92	505	85
Europe (incl. USSR)	145	115	335	92	174	111	659	86	461	93	273	104	2 111	90
Poland	50	113	103	112	61	111	359	100	202	104	135	126	943	104
All countries†	4 424	86	21 323	89	14 708	110	45 749	106	25 791	110	12 664	118	127 138	100
Married females														
All Ireland	24	80	109	103	72	109	361	157	223	139	142	146	960	121
Indian subcontinent	13	92	50	125	36	126	66	179	49	140	33	154	259	123
Caribbean Commonwealth	1	56	11	213	2	57	84	240	61	244	32	161	197	173
African Commonwealth	1	52	4	112	6	190	6	169	4	126	1	134	24	117
Europe (incl. USSR)	19	55	66	57	40	68	128	93	91	102	28	80	395	73
Poland	2	36	10	75	14	182	29	107	21	127	10	110	88	98
All countries†	891	62	5 221	77	3 204	86	14 358	121	7 916	125	3 950	147	36 266	100

* Includes also 'unoccupied'/'unclassified'
† Includes people born in England and Wales.

From Marmot et al. [5] with permission.

determine their pattern of disease. By focusing, in addition, on other cultural/lifestyle features, there is a prospect of a better understanding of disease aetiology and of contributing to disease prevention.

References

1 Syme, S. L., Marmot, M. G., Kagan, H and Rhoads, G. Epidemiologic studies of CHD and stroke in Japanese men living in Japan, Hawaii and California: introduction. *Am. J. Epidemiol.*, **102**, 477–480 (1975)
2 Marmot, M. G., Syme, S. L., Kagan, A. *et al.* Epidemiologic studies of CHD and stroke in Japanese men living in Japan, Hawaii and California: prevalence of coronary and hypertensive heart disease and associated risk factors. *Am. J. Epidemiol.*, **102**, 514–525 (1975)
3 Worth, R. M., Rhoads, G., Kagan, A. *et al.* Epidemiologic studies of coronary heart disease and stroke in Japanese men living in Japan, Hawaii and California: mortality. *Am. J. Epidemiol.*, **102**, 481–490 (1975)
4 Marmot, M. G. and Syme, S. L. Acculturation and CHD in Japanese-Americans. *Am. J. Epidemiol.* **104**, 225–247 (1976)
5 Marmot, M., Adelstein, A. M. and Bulusu, L. *Immigrant Mortality in England and Wales: 1970–1978* (Studies on Population and Medical Subjects: no. 47) (Office of Population, Censuses and Surveys), HMSO, London (1984)
6 Prior, I. A. M. Isolated groups, particular populations and their contributions. In *Cardiology. Proceedings of the VIII World Congress of Cardiology, Tokyo 1978* (International Congress Series 470) (eds S. Hayase and S. Murao), Excerpta Medica, Amsterdam, pp. 131–136 (1979)
7 Department of Health and Social Security, *Inequalities in Health. Report of a Research Working Group* (Black Report), HMSO, London (1980)

Chapter 4

Genetic versus environmental influences on disease: perspectives from obesity in particular populations

William J. Schull and Craig L. Hanis

Information on disease risks from obesity, possibly the most common of all deviations from the 'norm', is often conflicting, but there is persuasive evidence of a significant association with maturity-onset diabetes [1,2], premature myocardial infarction and hypertension [3], gallbladder disease [4], gout [5], cancer of the uterus [6] and possibly fatal cancer of the prostate [7].

Obesity clearly occurs in all ethnic groups as do most, if not all, these diseases. There is a growing literature on its familiality (occurrence in families) as well as attempts at defining truly genetic components. In the context of 'race' or ethnicity (which have no specific genotype), this chapter offers a perspective of how genes may interact with, rather than be an alternative to, environmental stimuli in promoting a chronic disorder. In this respect obesity serves as an example of many other disorders. Idiopathic obesity is discussed, and not that associated with simply inherited genetic syndromes whose public health impact is small.

Strategies to analyse genetic variation

A variety of conventional strategies have been employed to determine the role of genetic variation in obesity. Each has its strengths and limitations. The approaches include the correspondence in weight between monozygous versus dizygous twins; the correlation in weight between foster children and their adoptive and biological parents [8–10], and traditional family investigations (see [11] for a review). They have rarely focused on the process of weight gain itself, and the results have frequently been contradictory. Techniques of measurement have not been well standardized, if at all. Some are based on direct, but single, observations, others on self-reported weight, still others have employed silhouettes. Some used skinfold thickness as measures of corpulence. Few have examined the pattern of fat distribution or the tracking of weight over time; concomitant sources or variation, such as activity or temporal trends, have been poorly controlled or ignored.

This unsatisfactory situation seems likely to persist until more pertinent measurements are used. These include variation in lean body mass, fat distribution and biochemical or physiological measures associated with specific genes. Until recently, this has not been practical. The intention here is to urge a strategy that has been successfully used in the assessment of specific apolipoproteins and their genes in lipid metabolism [12,13], even if the specific mechanisms are not borne out by further research.

Candidates for specific genetic mechanisms

First, there is the apparent role in obesity of the ionic pathways associated with the red blood cell membrane. Four pathways are presently recognized; more exist. They include: (1) the so-called Na–K pump, an active pathway that is inhibited by ouabain, (2) the sodium co-transport system, a passive pathway inhibitable by furosemide, (3) the sodium–lithium countertransport system, another passive pathway inhibited by phloretin and, finally, (4) the 'leak', a minor pathway that seems to reflect a random loss of the ion in question.

An enzymic defect exists in the obese mouse, a common animal model for obesity in man [14]. There is a loss of thyroid-induced sodium- and potassium-dependent ATP; the homozygous obese mouse has reduced levels of sodium-potassium ATPase. This observation prompted De Luise and colleagues [15–17] to look for evidence of reduced energy use in the cells of obese persons since ATP is the principal energy currency of the body. They find the number of sodium-potassium units in the erythrocytes from obese subjects to be reduced by about 22% as compared with non-obese controls, and also report the number of pump units to be significantly and negatively correlated with percentage of ideal body weight. Normally, the sodium pump is responsible for 20–50% of total cellular thermogenesis (some estimates are as high as 70%). The weights of the obese individuals in this study ranged from 147% to 277% above their ideal body weights. They clearly satisfy most operational definitions of obesity but the selection criteria used may inadvertently compromise the inferences which can be drawn, for the causal mechanisms which give rise to extreme measurements in a continuous distribution are often more limited in number than those seen more centrally in the distribution. It has been argued, for example, that some of the effect they observe is attributable to ethnic differences in obesity and the ethnic origin of patient and comparison person was not controlled in De Luise's studies [18]. This caveat notwithstanding, their observations suggest that within these obese individuals there exists some subset where the pump may be defective, cellular utilization of ATP diminished and the 'calories' that would normally find their way to glycolysis are stored.

Given the quantitative nature of the findings of De Luise and his colleagues, one might assume that the $Na^+–K^+$ pump is genetically controlled, but suspect a multifactorial basis for the inheritance of differences. Most enzymic variation appears continuously distributed, however, if measured in terms of activity levels even when the underlying structural differences are known to be simply and discretely inherited. The seemingly continuous nature of the variation in the pump may merely reflect the metric used to assess differences, and not the nature of the genetic variability. While it is too early to know whether these findings will be supported with time, there are observations which suggest they may be. For example, there is evidence that some obese humans have an impaired thermogenetic response to a stimulus such as a rise in circulating catecholamines [19]. Weight gain is a commonly observed phenomenon among manic depressives on lithium therapy where it has been thought that this was due to the known effects of lithium on water balance. While this seems undoubtedly to be one of the mechanisms contributing to weight gain, there is also a gain in weight not attributable to retained water [20]. Lithium impinges on the sodium–potassium pump, and can seemingly do so at lithium concentrations in the range of one milligram per litre of water [21]. Thus, weight gain with lithium therapy, and possibly at still lesser levels of lithium absorption, suggests a change in the sodium–potassium pump, either inherited or directly due to the competitive effects of this metal. These observations aside, a defect in the pump, where it occurs, makes the widespread effects of obesity more easily understood.

Second, there is evidence that sex-hormone-binding-globulin (SHBG), a genetically controlled protein, is instrumental in weight gain and fat patterning. Although the precise functions of this protein are not fully defined, De Moor and Joossens [22] found a significant inverse correlation between SHBG and body weight using an oestradiol binding index constructed from the binding capacity and affinity association constant. This correlation was independent of nine other factors including blood pressure, cholesterol, age and height. Other studies have reported similar effects. Thus, low serum testosterone and SHBG have been found in massively obese men, and in obese women. Kopelman *et al.* [23] reported increased plasma testosterone and decreased SHBG levels compared to lean controls. Two human studies have looked specifically at the relationship between fat deposition and levels of SHBG. Purifoy *et al.* [24] compared levels of serum androgens and SHBG in obese female Pima Indians and normal weight Caucasians. While the Pimas, who have a strong propensity for android obesity, did have decreased SHBG compared to controls, a strong age effect confounded the association. Nevertheless, one can speculate that the females' predisposition for upper trunk adiposity in this ethnic group may involve the action of androgens during development and later life. Evans *et al.* [25], in a study of the relationship of androgenic activity to body fat topography, fat cell morphology and metabolic aberration in premenopausal women, found a decrease in SHBG and an increase in percentage free testosterone to be accompanied by: (1) increasing hip to waist girth ratios, (2) increasing size of abdominal, but not femoral adipocytes, (3) increasing plasma glucose and insulin levels, and (4) diminished *in vivo* insulin sensitivity. They concluded tentatively that in premenopausal women increased tissue exposure to unbound androgens may be partially responsible for fat localization in the upper body and the associated upset of glucose-insulin homeostasis. None of these studies have, however, examined the role of genetic factors in a rigorous or quantitative manner. Presumably this failure to do so has reflected the absence of good methods for visualizing the protein in sera. This situation seems to be changing, and possibly soon methods will be at hand to examine these issues in the context of known genotypes (e.g. see [26]).

Finally, there is other evidence of the role of genetic factors in human fatness. Some of this is of a biochemical nature, such as the apparent functioning of the enzyme, lipoprotein lipase, as the 'gatekeeper' for the entry of lipids into the cell; some is not. Mueller ([11]; see also [27]) has recently reviewed this latter evidence and concludes that there is low to moderate heritability of adult static fatness. He asserts that one-third or so of the variation between individuals in fatness appears ascribable to genetic causes, and further notes that changes in fatness in the course of life as well as the anatomical positioning of fat are important modifiers of the health effects of obesity. Notable is the apparent centripetal distribution of fat seen in diabetes (e.g. see [28]) and the relation of fat distribution to cardiovascular risk factors [29]. While these have focused on static fatness, there is evidence accumulating of a substantial role of genetic factors in the 'tracking' of weight [30]. Such longitudinal family studies permit an assessment of how body mass is associated with other risk factor levels (e.g. blood pressure).

The recent sequencing and cloning of some of the 'satiety' hormones, cholecystokinin [31], glucagon [32] and somatostatin [33] may shed light on the role of their genetic variation in obesity.

Interactions

Patently, the origins of obesity and fat patterning are complex, and there are numerous opportunities for genetic variation. Few if any studies have examined more than one of the numerous interacting factors. It seems unlikely that our knowledge will be materially furthered until a more holistic approach becomes practicable. Such an approach grows progressively more feasible and essential. Collectively, the number of measurable genotypes with apparent effects upon obesity is growing fast enough to apply the strategy used for apolipoprotein genes in lipid metabolism [12], namely to analyse the component of variation in weight, ascribable to variation at specific genetic loci. Although obesity appears to be a characteristic of all human populations under appropriate circumstances, those populations with unusual frequencies of obese individuals may be particularly informative [2].

Specific populations

Among such populations are the indigenous inhabitants of the New World, the islands of the Pacific (e.g. the Nauruans, Samoans, and the like), the blacks of the Americas, and many admixed groups such as the Mexican-Americans of the USA. Prevalence patterns in the latter populations commonly parallel the degree of Amerindian admixture which strongly implicates a genetic mechanism [34,35].

Among Mexican-Americans, a group of particular interest for its size and accessibility, Mueller and colleagues [36] used a cutpoint for body mass index of 30 or greater, which corresponds roughly to the 90th percentile of the HANES distribution [37,38]. The percentage of Mexican-Americans over 20 years who resided in Starr County, Texas and exceeded this cutpoint, ranges from 22 to 53% in females and from 27 to 40% in males. This population is known to have age-specific prevalences of non-insulin-dependent diabetes that are three to five times greater than those seen in non-Mexican-Americans in Texas [39], and this situation seems to prevail generally among Mexican-Americans [40,41].

Age-specific prevalences of gallbladder disease, as revealed by cholecystectomy and ultrasonography, are equally elevated and cases of cholecystitis and cholelithiasis are known to cluster within families ([42]; unpublished observations). Moreover, there is evidence that in females under the age of 45 a significant association between gallbladder disease and diabetes exists that is not explicable by increased body mass alone. Most, if not all of the stones are cholesterol in nature, and the precocity of their appearance is startling. Cases of acute cholecystitis with literally dozens of stones have been seen in females as young as 12. Invariably other close female relatives have exhibited early, if not always equally precocious onset of gallbladder disease. Qualitatively the diets of those individuals appear to have changed little in the recent past although the quantities of the limited number of foodstuffs eaten have increased. Current studies of lipid metabolism, including extensive apolipoprotein genotyping and the use of specific restriction endonucleases, may clarify the situation and the interrelationships of the various disease processes.

A search for variation at the loci responsible for those satiety hormones that have been cloned and sequenced might also be profitable, although the study of the insulin gene has not yet been especially rewarding. Similarly the molecular structure of cholecystokinin, for example, appears to have been highly conserved for at least 500 million years and may, therefore, be a poor candidate for much interindividual variability [43].

A final area in which appreciation of genetic factors may be rewarding is intervention and therapy. By focussing on individuals as the unit of intervention rather than the family one ignores both the existence of genetic factors in the response to intervention as well as the psychosocial role the family may play in the acceptability of the intervention itself. Specific recommendations must await a better understanding of the genetic events involved.

References

1 West, K. M. *Epidemiology of Diabetes and its Vascular Lesions*, Elsevier, New York (1978)
2 Knowler, W. C., Pettitt, D. J., Savage, P. J. and Bennett, P. H. Diabetes incidence in Pima Indians: contributions of obesity and parental diabetes. *Am. J. Epidemiol.*, **116**, 631–642 (1981)
3 Pickering, G. *High Blood Pressure*, Grune and Stratton, New York (1968)
4 Abbruzzese, A. and Snodgrass, P. J. Diseases of the gallbladder and bile ducts. In *Harrisons's Principles of Internal Medicine* 6th edn (eds M. M. Wintrobe, G. W. Thorn, R. D. Adams *et al.*), McGraw-Hill, New York (1970)
5 Wyngaarden, J. B. Gout and other disorders of uric acid metabolism. In *Harrisons's Principles of Internal Medicine*, 6th edn (eds M. M. Wintrobe, G. W. Thorn, R. D. Adams *et al.*), McGraw-Hill, New York (1970)
6 Wynder, E. L., Escher, G. and Mantel, N. An epidemiological investigation of cancer of the endometrium. *Cancer*, **19**, 489–520 (1986)
7 Snowdon, D. A., Phillips, R. L. and Choi, W. Diet, obesity and risk of fatal prostate cancer. *Am. J. Epidemiol.*, **120**, 244–250 (1984)
8 Annest, J. L., Sing, C. F., Biron, P. and Mongeau, J-G. Familial aggregation of blood pressure and weight in adoptive families. I. Comparisons of blood pressure and weight statistics among families with adopted, natural, or both natural and adopted children. *Am. J. Epidemiol.*, **110**, 479–491 (1979)
9 Annest, J. L., Sing, C. F., Biron, P. and Mongeau, J-G. Familial aggregation of blood pressure and weight in adoptive families. II. Estimation of the relative contributions of genetic and common environmental factors to BP correlations between family members. *Am. J. Epidemiol.*, **110**, 492–503 (1979)
10 Stunkard, A. J., Sorenson, T. I. A., Hanis, C. *et al.*. An adoption study of human obesity. *N. Engl. J. Med.*, **314**, 193–198 (1986)
11 Mueller, W. H. The genetics of human fatness. *Yearbook Phys. Anthropol.*, **26**, 215–230 (1983)
12 Sing, C. F. and Davignon, J-G. Role of the apolipoprotein E polymorphism in determining normal plasma lipid and lipoprotein variation. *Am. J. Hum. Genet.*, **37**, 268–285 (1985)
13 Boerwinkle, E. Chakraborty, R. and Sing, C. F. The use of measured genotype information in the analysis of quantitative phenotypes in man. I. Models and analytical methods. *Ann. Hum. Genet.*, **50**, 181–194 (1986)
14 York, D. A., Bray, G. A. and Yukiura, Y. An enzymatic defect in the obese (ob/ob) mouse: loss of thyroid-induced sodium- and potassium-dependent adenosine triphosphate. *Proc. Natl Acad. Sci. USA*, **75**, 477–481 (1978)
15 De Luise and Flier, J. S. Functionally abnormal Na^+–K^+ pump in erythrocytes of a morbidly obese patient. *J. Clin. Invest.*, **69**, 38–44
16 De Luise, M., Blackburn, G. L. and Flier, J. S. Reduced activity of the red-cell sodium–potassium pump in human obesity. *N. Engl. J. Med.*, **303**, 1017–1022 (1980)

17 De Luise, M., Rappaport, E. and Flier, J. S. Altered erythrocyte Na^+-K^+ pump in adolescent obesity. *Metabolism*, **31**, 1153–1158 (1982)

18 Beutler, E., Kuhl, W. and Sacks, P. Sodium–potassium–ATPase is influenced by ethnic origin and not by obesity. *N. Engl. J. Med.*, **309**, 756–760 (1983)

19 Jung, R. T., Shetty, P. S., James, W. P. T. *et al*. Reduced thermogenesis in obesity. *Nature*, **279**, 322–323 (1979)

20 Dempsey, G. M., Dunner, D. L., Fieve, R. R. *et al*., Treatment of excessive weight gain in patients taking lithium. *Am. J. Psychiatry*, **133**, 1082–1084 (1976)

21 Clench, J., Ferrell, R. E., Schull, W. J. and Barton, S. A. Hematocrit and hemoglobin, ATP and DPG concentrations in Andean Man. In *Proceedings of the Seventh International Conference on Red Cell Metabolism* (ed. G. F. Brewer), Alan R. Liss, New York (1981)

22 De Moor, P. and Joossens, J. V. An inverse relation between body weight and the activity of the steroid binding beta-globulin in human plasma. *Steroidologia*, **1**, 129–136 (1970)

23 Kopelman, P. G., Pilkington, T. R. E., White, N. and Jeffcoate, J. L. Abnormal sex steroid secretion and binding in massively obese women. *Clin. Endocrinol.*, **12**, 363–369 (1980)

24 Purifoy, F. E., Koopmans, L. H., Tatum, R. W. and Mayes, D. M. Serum androgens and sex hormones binding globulin in obese Pima Indian females. *Am. J. Phys. Anthropol.*, **55**, 491–496 (1981)

25 Evans, D. J., Hoffman, R. G., Kalkhoff, R. K. and Kissebah, A. H. Relationship of androgenic activity to body fat topography, fat cell morphology, and metabolic aberrations in premenopausal women. *J. Clin. Endocrinol. Metab.*, **57**, 304–310 (1983)

26 Meikle, A. W., Stanish, W. M., Taylor, N. *et al*. Familial effects on plasma sex-steroid content in man: testosterone, estradiol and sex-hormone-binding globulin. *Metabolism*, **31**, 6–9 (1982)

27 Savard, R., Bouchard, C., Leblanc, C. and Tremblay, A. Familial resemblance in fatness indicators. *Ann. Hum. Biol.*, **10**, 111–118 (1983)

28 Joos, S. K., Mueller, W. H., Hanis, C. L. and Schull, W. J. Diabetes Alert Study: weight history and upper body obesity in diabetic and non-diabetic Mexican American adults. *Ann. Hum. Biol.*, **11**, 167–172 (1984)

29 Reichley, K. B., Mueller, W. H., Hanis, C. L. *et al*. Centralized obesity and cardiovascular risk factors in Mexican Americans from Starr County, Texas. *Am. J. Epidemiol.*, **125**, 373–386 (1987)

30 Hanis, C. L., Sing, C. F., Clarke, W. R. and Schrott, H. G. Multivariate models for human genetic analysis: aggregation, coaggregation, and tracking of systolic blood pressure and weight. *Am. J. Hum. Genet.*, **35**, 1196–1210 (1983)

31 Deschenes, R. J., Lorenz, L. J., Haun, R. S. *et al*., Cloning and sequence analysis of cDNA encoding rat preprocholecystokinin. *Proc. Natl Acad. Sci. USA*, **81**, 726–730 (1984)

32 White, J. W. and Saunders, G. Structure of the human glucagon gene. *Nucleic Acids Res.*, **14**, 4719–4730 (1986)

33 Goodman, R. H., Jacobs, J. W., Chin, W. W. *et al*. Nucleotide sequence of a cloned structural gene coding for a precursor of pancreatic somatostatin. *Proc. Natl Acad. Sci. USA*, **77**, 5869–5873 (1980)

34 Weiss, K. M., Ferrell, R. E. and Hanis, C. L. A new world syndrome of metabolic diseases with a genetic and evolutionary basis. *Yearbook Phys. Anthropol.*, **27**, 153–178 (1984)

35 Hanis, C. L., Chakraborty, R., Ferrell, R. E. and Schull, W. J. Individual admixture estimates: disease associations and individual risk of diabetes and gallbladder disease among Mexican-Americans in Starr County, Texas. *Am. J. Phys. Anthropol.*, **70**, 433–441 (1986)

36 Mueller, W. H., Joos, S. K., Hanis, C. L. *et al*. The Diabetes Alert Study: growth, fatness, and fat patterning, adolescence through adulthood in Mexican Americans. *Am. J. Phys. Anthropol.*, **64**, 389–399 (1984)

37 Hamill, P. V. V., Drizd, T. A., Johnson, C. L. *et al*. NCHS growth curves for children birth to 18 years United States, *Vital and Health Statistics*, Series 11, No. 165, Department of Health, Education and Welfare, Washington, DC (1977)

38 Abraham, S., Johnston, C. L. and Najjar, M. F. Weight and height of adults 18–74 years of age, United States 1971–1974. In *Vital and Health Statistics*, Series 11, No. 211, Department of Health, Education and Welfare, Washington, DC (1981)

39 Hanis, C. L., Ferrell, R. E., Barton, S. A. *et al*. Diabetes among Mexican-Americans in Starr County, Texas. *Am. J. Epidemiol.*, **118**, 659–672 (1983)

40 Stern, M. P. Gaskill, S. P., Allen, C. R. Jr *et al*. Cardiovascular risk factors in Mexican Americans in Laredo, Texas. I. Prevalence of overweight and diabetes and distributions of serum lipids. *Am. J. Epidemiol.*, **113**, 546–555 (1981)

41 Stern, M. P. Diabetes in Hispanic Americans. In National Diabetes Data Group, *Diabetes in America*, NIH Publication No. 85–1468, US Department of Health and Human Services, Washington DC (1985)

42 Hanis, C. L., Ferrell, R. E., Tulloch, B. R. and Schull, W. J. Gallbladder disease epidemiology in Mexican Americans in Starr County, Texas. *Am. J. Epidemiol.*, **122**, 820–829 (1985)

43 Vigna, S. R., Thorndyke, M. C. and Williams, J. A. Evidence for a common evolutionary origin of brain and pancreas cholecystokinin receptors. *Proc. Natl Acad. Sci. USA*, **83**, 4355–4359 (1986)

Chapter 5

Molecular markers of ethnic groups

Adrian V. S. Hill

There has been a recent upsurge of interest in molecular comparisons of human populations. Although this is due in part to an increased awareness of the differences in the spectrum of disease seen in various peoples, it stems mainly from the dramatic recent progress in analysis of the human genome. The main goal of these early studies of human DNA has been to elucidate the molecular basis of common single gene disorders such as the thalassaemias and haemophilia. However, such analysis has revealed not only different molecular defects which produce the same condition in different races but also an enormous amount of variation in the non-coding DNA between genes. These DNA polymorphisms represent a huge pool of genetic variation between individuals and ethnic groups that has already substantially increased the number of known molecular markers of particular populations.

In this chapter the traditional blood group, protein and antigen variants will be briefly reviewed prior to discussing some of the results and the potential of DNA studies. Before doing so it may be useful to note some of the applications of molecular markers. A primary goal of molecular population studies has been the quantification of the genetic affinities between various ethnic groups to allow a genetic classification of the races of man. Such data are now fundamental to the study of human evolution and help to reconstruct prehistoric migration routes and colonization patterns. More recently, with the availability of highly specific population markers, more interest has been shown in potential forensic applications of molecular variants. Finally, the value of an understanding at the molecular level of population differences is becoming increasingly apparent in clinical practice [1]. It has long been realized that a knowledge of the racial distribution of genetic disorders such as sickle cell disease and glucose-6-phosphate dehydrogenase deficiency is very useful in differential diagnosis. More recently, it was appreciated that the severity of such disorders appeared to differ in various ethnic groups. Now, an exact molecular definition of the DNA defect in, for example, the thalassaemias may explain such differences in severity, allows a more precise prognosis to be given and permits prenatal diagnosis by direct gene analysis. Clearly, when screening directly for such mutations either pre- or postnatally it is important to appreciate that there may be considerable differences between ethnic groups in the molecular basis of a disorder, as has been demonstrated in the case of the thalassaemias.

Blood group and protein variants

The ABO blood groups were the first genetic markers to be surveyed in many different ethnic groups and their frequencies have been documented in great detail. The least common allele, group B, is absent from American Indian and many Oceanic populations and is found at its highest frequency in Southern Asia. The inferences that may be made about population affinities and early migrations from the ABO and other blood groups have been recently reviewed [2]. Because of the enormous amount of data available it was possible for Mourant to reach many conclusions despite the fact that most blood groups are not population specific and vary only in their frequencies. One notable exception is the Duffy blood group antigen which is absent only in some African populations in which its absence provides protection from *Plasmodium vivax* malaria.

With the advent of techniques for electrophoresis of serum and red cell proteins in the 1960s, large numbers of such electrophoretic variants were reported and some were characterized. The more recent introduction of isoelectric focussing had revealed further diversity. Some of these proteins such as haptoglobin and transferrin have, like the ABO blood groups, more than one allele widely distributed in different racial groups. However, these are exceptional. For most proteins a single type predominates in all populations and uncommon variants are found in certain groups. Some of these variants are useful in that they are population-specific markers, but they are almost invariably found only at low frequency in the population of which they are characteristic. Despite this, analysis of the collected data from worldwide surveys along with blood group results has allowed Nei and Roychoudhury [3] to construct dendrograms of the relationship of human populations which are in reasonable agreement with older morphological classifications. An important conclusion of such work is that the amount of genetic variation within a racial group is considerably greater than the average genetic difference between races. Clearly the genes responsible for the morphological features that allow us to classify individuals into broad racial groupings are atypical and extremely unrepresentative of the true degree of interracial genetic difference.

Variants of haemoglobin illustrate many of the advantages and disadvantages of protein surveys. Ease of collection and the medical importance of haemoglobin have led to thousands of reported population studies [4]. Some variants such as haemoglobin (Hb) C in West Africans show a well-localized distribution, presumably reflecting a single origin for this variant. Hb E, which reaches carrier rates of 50% in parts of Thailand, is a South-east Asian marker but it has been found sporadically in Europeans almost certainly as a result of new mutations. Hence, probably few markers will turn out to be absolutely population specific. Hb S, the best known variant, is found not only in Africans and their descendants but in parts of Southern Europe, Arabia and India. There is good evidence that its elevated frequency in all these populations results from a relative protection of carriers from *P. falciparum* malaria. A longstanding controversy has existed on the question of whether or not the variant in all these areas had a single origin, thereby indicating either a common original population or substantial early migration between these countries [5]. Recently, DNA studies have made the multiple mutation hypothesis by far the more likely. This and other examples of independent origins of the same mutation in different ethnic groups urge caution in the interpretation of population surveys using small numbers of markers. Particular care should be taken with inferences from variants characterized only by their electrophoretic mobility. Several hundred types of glucose-6-phosphate dehydrogenase (G6PD) variants have been reported and alleles with decreased activity are subject to malarial selection [6]. Two such alleles, *Gd A⁻* and *GD^Mediterranean*, are relatively population specific, the former being common in blacks. Because the *Gd A⁻* allele is associated with a lesser degree of enzyme deficiency, oxidant-induced haemolysis in G6PD-deficient individuals is usually milder in blacks than Mediterraneans.

Highly polymorphic antigenic variants

Antigens of the human leucocyte antigen (HLA) and immunoglobulin gene complexes are extremely informative molecular makers which merit special consideration. Recent DNA studies have mapped the genes of the HLA complex on chromosome 6. In the class I region are the HLA-A, -B and -C genes, the products of which are detected by microcytotoxicity assays [7]. DR, DQ and DP antigens are the products of class II genes and their specificities may now be determined by DNA analysis. These loci have been shown to have up to 30 alleles in man so the potential number of combinations of these antigens, or haplotypes, is estimated to exceed 10^5. Not all of the known HLA antigens are found in all populations and some populations have a relatively restricted range of HLA alleles. Some alleles are unique to specific populations and many occasionally reach high frequencies. For example, *HLA-Bw 42* occurs in almost 25% of some African populations but not in non-Africans. Similarly, *HLA-Bw 46* is a high-frequency Chinese marker found in nearly 50% of Cantonese. Furthermore, certain haplotypes exhibit greater population specificity than their component antigens and may be used as highly specific markers. The HLA system is so polymorphic that it has been used alone for constructing dendrograms of human population affinities [8] and tracing prehistoric migration routes [9]. However, because of the strong selective forces that may influence their frequencies HLA antigens are not ideally suited to the quantification of genetic distances between populations. Nonetheless, further analysis of more recently defined HLA antigens, haplotypes and, in particular, their genes should continue to provide very informative molecular markers of different ethnic groups.

Polymorphisms in both the heavy (Gm and Am types) and light chains (Km types) of immunoglobulin molecules constitute another set of useful markers. Linked arrangements of these variants known as allotypes show significant population specificity. These have been extensively reviewed [10] and their use in conjunction with new DNA polymorphisms in the immunoglobulin heavy chain gene cluster should be very valuable in population studies [11].

DNA markers

The introduction of techniques of rapid DNA analysis has led to considerable excitement about the great potential of this technology in detecting new molecular markers for human populations. This enthusiasm is based on three observations. The first of these is that scattered every hundred bases or so throughout the genome are single base changes that represent polymorphisms between individuals and populations. The great majority of these are in non-coding DNA and are thought to be selectively neutral. Many of these single base changes produce sequence differences that alter the recognition sequence for specific restriction endonucleases. Hence these polymorphisms can be detected by simple Southern blot analysis [12]. Point mutations that do not alter a restriction enzyme site may be detected either by using newer oligonucleotide probes or through direct sequencing of cloned or amplified DNA. Just as alleles of linked HLA genes may be grouped as haplotypes, so also closely linked DNA polymorphisms have been put together as restriction enzyme haplotypes [13].

The second important observation is that as well as these point mutations there are numerous regions of length variation within the genome. These are particularly useful as molecular markers both because they are, in principle, always detectable by Southern blot analysis and because they are multiallelic. Some regions of length variation have only a few common length alleles but others, such as the hypervariable region downstream of the α-globin gene complex, have at least 50. The molecular basis of such length heterogeneity has been shown to be variation in the copy number of short tandemly repeated DNA sequences. A striking example of the informativeness of such hypervariable regions is provided by minisatellite DNA probes which simultaneously detect certain regions of length variation in different parts of the genome and thereby produce a genetic fingerprint unique to each individual [14].

Although new DNA polymorphisms continue to be described almost daily the number of these that have been studied in a wide variety of ethnic groups is still limited. Clearly, the most useful DNA polymorphisms for studies of ethnic differentiation will be those that are population specific, sometimes termed 'private' polymorphisms. Although most DNA polymorphisms described to date are 'public' in that they are polymorphic in most ethnic groups, sufficient private polymorphisms are turning up to indicate that the genome as a whole must contain large numbers of population-specific variants.

The first formal DNA study of numerous world populations was of a restriction enzyme haplotype close to the β-globin gene [15]. This indicated a large genetic distance between African and all non-African populations, reinforcing a conclusion suggested by studies of protein variants [3]. Preliminary observations at other loci indicate that there appears to be an excess of population-specific DNA polymorphisms among individuals of African origin. This greater genetic diversity may in part be attributable to the mixed ancestry of North American blacks who have been studied more than native Africans. However, the available data on African individuals also suggest that the largest pool of genetic diversity lies in that continent. This implies that it should be easier to assign African ancestry to an individual on the basis of DNA polymorphism studies than other racial origins.

The third observation that has enhanced the scope of DNA studies for population markers is that of marked heterogeneity in the molecular basis of some common genetic diseases. Thalassaemia is the best studied example. There are over 60 different mutations affecting the β-globin gene which have been shown to produce the phenotype of β-thalassaemia and the majority of these are population specific [13]. Hence, a condition which was known to be distributed throughout the subtropical and tropical 'malaria-belt' of the Old World has been shown to result from a great multiplicity of, presumably local, mutations. It is now clear that Asian Indians, Mediterraneans, African blacks and South-east Asians each have a different spectrum of mutations that may be used as population markers [13] and accumulating information for other loci also suggests substantial molecular diversity and population specificity. A frequent objection to the use of molecular variants such as thalassaemia mutations as markers in population comparison is that they are not neutral variants having been selected by, in this instance, malaria. While this certainly complicates the interpretation of the frequency of a thalassaemia allele, such specific markers are still very useful as qualitative markers for comparing populations and tracing prehistoric migration routes [16a].

Another old problem which DNA studies may help with is the question of whether particular variants in different geographical areas may have had more than one origin. Comparisons of the restriction enzyme haplotypes of the β^s-globin gene have indicated that this mutation probably occurred on several occasions because it is associated with different haplotypes in different countries [16b]. Furthermore, as our understanding of the mechanisms and the probability of occurrence of different molecular types of mutation increases it is becoming possible to identify variants that would be expected to occur very infrequently. For example, it appears that mutations resulting from recombination between completely unrelated DNA sequences, so-called illegitimate recombination events, occur far less often than point mutations and mutants resulting from such events should constitute a highly useful group of molecular markers.

Mitochondrial DNA differs in many respects from nuclear DNA and some of its unique features make it particularly suitable for population comparisons. The 16.5 kilobase mitochondrial genome is present in hundreds to thousands of copies in each cell but does not undergo recombination and, remarkably, is strictly maternally inherited. These features make it very useful for tracing female lineages, the lack of recombination allowing a simple molecular clock to be employed in calculating divergence times between mitochondrial types. Furthermore, the observation that the mutation rate of mitochondrial DNA is about 10 times higher than that of nuclear DNA makes it particularly suitable for comparison of populations that have diverged relatively recently. Results to date agree with other markers in pointing to an African origin for human populations and promise to provide fascinating comparisons of the distribution of female and male (Y chromosome) genetic markers [17].

Genetic disorders and molecular markers

Analysis of the molecular basis of genetic disorders has been the stimulus to the finding of a large number of the known molecular markers of human populations. Despite the recent rapid progress in elucidating the molecular basis of common disorders such as thalassaemia, haemophilia and phenylketonuria, the thousands of monogenic disorders of man listed by McKusick [18] indicate how much remains to come! However, the great majority of those catalogued are rare defects and more useful population markers may become available from a molecular analysis of common phenotypic variants such as pharmacogenetic polymorphisms [19] or inherited lactase deficiency. Here the object would be to discover a gene defect which would be more readily screened for than the phenotype itself.

It is apparent that the genetic disorders best characterized at a molecular level to date are predominantly those of tropical and subtropical populations such as sickle cell disease, G6PD deficiency and thalassaemia. Exceptions are α_1-antitrypsin deficiency and phenylketonuria, both diseases of Europeans in which molecular defects have been identified. The recent localization of the cystic fibrosis gene on chromosome 7 promises that mutations causing this common disorder of North Europeans will soon be identified. Ultimately with detailed information on the distribution of the various molecular forms of such conditions it should be possible to analyse the importance of possible selective pressures, genetic drift and population movements on their current prevalences. At a greater level of complexity it should, in the foreseeable future, be possible to analyse population differences in susceptibility to diseases with polygenic inheritance. The array of highly informative multiallelic markers distributed across all chromosomes that is required for such a comprehensive study is gradually becoming available.

Prospects

A major concern of population genetics has been the measurement of the amount of genetic variation in human populations. Although estimates of this vary, all are agreed that the amount of variation within any ethnic group is much greater than. the difference between groups. Nonetheless, many population-specific genetic variants exist and newer techniques of DNA analysis are providing an efficient way of detecting these. Despite prodigious efforts over the years in determining gene frequencies for blood group and protein variants in many populations, it seems likely that DNA polymorphisms will provide the ultimate method of classifying population groups. Substantial progress has been made in defining the nature of the molecular defect in many single-gene disorders. As well as providing new means of prenatal diagnosis these studies have revealed unexpected heterogeneity between populations both in the nature of the underlying defect and in closely linked DNA polymorphisms. Current searches for highly variable length polymorphisms on different chromosomes for use in linkage analysis appear likely to detect further markers highly suited to detailed population comparisons. With the continuing impetus of rapid advances in molecular genetics the study of molecular markers in different ethnic groups should continue to form a highly productive interface between anthropology and medicine.

References

1 Weatherall, D. J. *The New Genetics and Clinical Practice*, 2nd edn, Oxford University Press, Oxford (1986)
2 Mourant, A. E. *Blood Relations: Blood Groups and Anthropology*, Oxford University Press, Oxford (1983)
3 Nei, M. and Roychoudhury, A. K. Genetic relationship and evolution of human races. *Evolutionary Biol.*, **14**, 1–59 (1982)
4 Livingstone, F. B. *Frequencies of Hemoglobin Variants*, Oxford University Press, Oxford (1985)
5 Hill, A. V. S. and Wainscoat, J. S. The evolution of the α- and β-globin gene clusters in human populations. *Hum. Genet.*, **74**, 16–23 (1986)
6 Luzzatto, L. and Battistuzzi, G. Glucose-6-phosphate dehydrogenase. In *Advances in Human Genetics*, vol. 14, Plenum, New York, pp. 217–329 (1985)
7 Bodmer, W. F. and Bodmer, J. G. Evolution and function of the HLA system. *Br. Med. Bull.*, **34**, 309–316 (1978)
8 Piazza, A., Sgaramella-Zonta, L., Gluckman, P. and Cavalli-Sforza, L. L. The fifth histo-compatibility workshop gene frequency data: a phylogenetic analysis. *Tissue Antigens*, **5**, 445–463 (1975)
9 Serjeantson, S. W. Migration and admixture in the Pacific. *J. Pacific History*, **19**, 160–171 (1984)

10 Steinberg, A. G. and Cook, C. E. *The Distribution of the Human Immunoglobulin Allotypes*, Oxford University Press, Oxford (1981)

11 Migone, M., de Lange, G., Piazza, A. and Cavalli-Sforza, L. L. Genetic analysis of eight linked polymorphisms within the human immunoglobulin heavy-chain region. *Am. J. Hum. Genet.*, **37**, 1146–1163 (1985)

12 Southern, E. M. Detection of specific sequences among DNA fragments separated by gel electrophoresis. *J. Mol. Biol.*, **98**, 503–517 (1985)

13 Antonarakis, S. E. Kazazian, H. H. and Orkin, S. H. DNA polymorphism and the molecular pathology of the human globin gene clusters. *Hum. Genet.*, **69**, 1–14 (1985)

14 Jeffreys, A. J., Wilson, V. and Thein, S. L. Hypervariable 'minisatellite' regions in human DNA. *Nature*, **314**, 67–73 (1985)

15 Wainscoat, J. S., Hill, A. V. S., Boyce, A. *et al.* Evolutionary relationships of human populations from an analysis of nuclear DNA polymorphisms. *Nature*, **319**, 491–493 (1985)

16a Hill, A. V. S. and Serjeantson, S. W. (eds). *The Colonization of the Pacific: A Genetic Trail*, Oxford University Press, Oxford (1989)

16b Pagnier, J., Mears, J. G., Dunda-Belkhodja, O. *et al.* Evidence for the multicentric origin of the sickle haemoglobin gene in Africa. *Proc. Natl. Acad. Sci. USA*, **81**, 1771–1773 (1984)

17 Caan, R. L., Stoneking, M. and Wilson, A. C. Mitochrondrial DNA and human evolution. *Nature*, **325**, 31–36 (1987)

18 McKusick, V. *Mendelian Inheritance in Man*, 7th edn, The Johns Hopkins Press, Baltimore (1986)

19 Kalow, W. Ethnic differences in drug metabolism. *Clin. Pharmacokinet.*, **7**, 373–400 (1982)

Section II

Epidemiology

Chapter 6

The health of migrants in England and Wales: causes of death

A. M. Adelstein and M. G. Marmot

This chapter is a review of the causes of death of immigrants to England and Wales from 1970 to 1978 [1]. Additional mortality figures come from the Office of Population Censuses and Surveys' (OPCS) publications on perinatal and infant mortality. We refer to a number of studies of immigrants in other countries which include emigrants from the UK or from countries which also sent immigrants to the UK. For a discussion of the uses of such studies, see Chapter 2.

The material is considered in two parts: the first deals with methods and analysis of selected causes of death; specific-cause death rates of immigrant groups are compared with their home country and with the corresponding rate in England and Wales. The second part reverses the format, examining the pattern of disease in each immigrant group. Grouping by country of birth allows questions about lifestyle, environment, culture and genes of a particular group that leads to high (or low) rates of different diseases. The 1971 Census showed that 8.6% of the population enumerated in England and Wales was born elsewhere. Major immigrant groups comprise those from Scotland (1.6%), Ireland (1%), the Indian subcontinent (1%), the Caribbean (0.6%), Africa (0.3%) and several European countries.

Methods

An analysis of mortality of immigrants in England and Wales followed the introduction in 1969 of a statement of place of birth on death certificates. From the 1971 Census the numbers of persons born in each country outside England and Wales were available as denominators for calculation of the standardized mortality ratios (SMRs) in 1970–72. Furthermore, specific causes of death of immigrants in the period 1970–78 were analysed by proportional mortality rates (PMRs): that is, ratios for which the denominator is not population but deaths. For this purpose immigrants were regarded as persons born outside England and Wales; it included people born in Scotland or Ireland, although these are not usually thought of as immigrants. This definition is not always equivalent to ethnic origin, especially when referring to people born in the Indian subcontinent, Africa or the Caribbean. A measure of ethnicity was available for the first two by classifying names of the deceased; thus among the deaths of persons born in the Indian subcontinent, British-type names could be distinguished from Indian, and both could be distinguished from Africans among immigrants born in Africa. These subsidiary

Table 6.1 Examples of SMRs (approx 1970–72) in country of birth (aged 15–74) and corresponding migrant group (aged 20+) (England and Wales = 100)

| | Ireland | | France | | Italy | | Caribbean* | | Indian subcontinent | | | |
| | | | | | | | | | All ethnic groups | | Indians[†] (PMR) | |
	M	F	M	F	M	F	M	F	M	F	M	F
All causes												
Home	99	117	96	84	91	92	119	171	–	–	–	–
Migrant	114	109	88	88	77	84	94	117	98	106	–	–
Migrant deaths	16742	13506	419	961	756	668	1545	1163	4352	98	–	–
Tuberculosis												
Home	243	316	244	199	288	189	392	341	–	–	–	–
Migrant	245	215	123	66	49	–	123	299	315	914	510	1673
Migrant deaths	150	53	2	1	2	0	11	11	64	62	50	47
All cancers												
Home	83	103	100	80	95	85	45	8	–	–	–	–
Migrant	109	106	102	87	77	87	79	86	69	90	46	46
Migrant deaths	3759	2982	99	167	162	179	316	262	722	656	190	88
Intestine												
Home	116	133	99	78	84	71	77	51	–	–	–	–
Migrant	118	99	145	74	27	70	65	47	55	80	38	23
Migrant deaths	266	284	10	17	4	13	17	11	38	58	10	3
Trachea, bronchus and lung												
Home	57	90	43	25	56	35	15	19	–	–	–	–
Migrant	111	159	78	54	68	67	40	33	53	86	25	32
Migrant deaths	1537	475	28	10	52	14	61	10	218	65	39	6
Breast												
Home	–	88	–	64	–	67	–	55	–	–	–	–
Migrant	–	88	–	79	–	85	–	73	–	80	–	37
Migrant deaths	–	552	–	29	–	44	–	60	–	131	–	21
Ovary												
Home	–	–	–	–	–	–	–	–	–	–	–	–
Migrant	–	86	–	110	–	71	–	37	–	104	–	53
Migrant deaths	–	181	–	13	–	12	–	10	–	57	–	9

Diabetes												
Home	146	151	169	149	239	293	1081	1310	–	–	–	–
Migrant	82	69	66	97	109	102	321	436	188	146	243	330
Migrant deaths	77	95	2	12	7	9	36	46	55	52	28	18
Hypertensive disease												
Home	111	133	53	62	101	163	357	690	–	–	–	–
Migrant	135	108	85	75	111	80	343	430	128	79	168	103
Migrant deaths	302	244	6	16	16	11	84	63	85	45	41	6
Ischaemic heart disease												
Home	96	118	30	31	43	52	70	120	–	–	–	–
Migrant	104	109	85	89	74	79	51	89	115	115	119	119
Migrant deaths	4669	2796	115	218	209	117	257	113	1533	739	606	53
Motor vehicle accidents												
Home	144	133	206	179	218	135	138	101	–	–	–	–
Migrant	166	134	215	245	119	87	97	96	110	139	107	83
Migrant deaths	390	134	14	17	31	8	61	19	134	45	93	16
Immigrant population (in thousands)	399.3	427.0	9.7	23.4	22.0	22.7	121.4	118.0	213.7	150.7	–	–

Note that SMRs are not directly comparable between sexes.
* Home rates are from Trinidad, while migrant rates are for people of all West Indian islands combined.
Indian refers to all persons born in the Indian subcontinent who have ethnicity of the countries in the Indian subcontinent

ethnic analyses are based on PMRs, there being no corresponding population denominators. Ratios of each cause of death were compared between England and Wales, each specific immigrant group, and its respective home country (if figures were available). A weakness of the study is the absence of a date of entry into England and Wales of each deceased person.

SMRs are a measure of mortality adjusted for age by the indirect method calculated separately for men and women so that, for each sex, ratios for England and Wales are 100. *Therefore mortality for men and women may not be compared directly, but only with respect to how far their mortality ratios deviate from the England and Wales average for that sex.*

Mortality from 'all causes'

Table 6.1 shows mortality ratios (SMR or PMR) for selected causes in some countries and in their respective immigrants in England and Wales for the period 1970–72. Immigrants' SMRs refer to ages '20 and over' and PMRs to ages 20–69, while for home countries SMRs refer to ages 15–74. The text which follows includes discussion of data not shown in the table. For general points (the 'healthy' migrant effect, social class, etc.) see Chapter 2.

Selection and adaptation
The lower mortality of immigrants compared with their respective old countries has been noted in other studies, including those of emigrants from the UK and from Ireland [2]. The immediate effect of selection may gradually wear off, and the rate may be further influenced by the new environment. Examples of selection and late adaptation will be cited in respect of cardiovascular disease and of various cancers in emigrants from the UK.

Possibly, the processes of selection and adaptation have so varied between social classes as to eliminate differences which are presumed to be present in industrialized countries of origin. In countries with little industry, categories of class, based on occupation in industrialized countries, probably have different meanings.

Specific diseases (Table 6.1)

Tuberculosis
SMRs are generally high for immigrants and their respective home countries, with the highest at over 900 for women from the Indian subcontinent. The high ratio is confined to ethnic Indians; people of British background born in the Indian subcontinent have ratios only marginally raised (Table 6.2) as consistently noted in morbidity studies [3]. Raised ratios also occurred in immigrants from Ireland, the Caribbean, Africa and to a lesser extent from Scotland. Countries of origin with high SMRs include Poland, Italy, France and Spain.

Malignant neoplasms
SMRs (all sites combined) are generally low among immigrants and in their home countries (where figures are available); there are large differences in mortality among countries and also among immigrant groups. For example, immigrants from the Indian subcontinent, especially when of Indian background, have very low mortality ratios for a number of cancers including stomach, intestine, rectum,

'trachea, bronchus and lung', breast, ovary (see Table 6.3), cervix and skin. High ratios were found in both ethnic communities born in the Indian subcontinent for primary liver cancer; and elevated ratios were also found for cancers of the buccal cavity and pharynx and for lymphomas in females.

British people born in the Indian subcontinent with British names had ratios between those for England and Wales, and those with Indian names, suggesting either some acquired protection from that environment or less exposure (Table 6.2).

Table 6.2 PMR (number of deaths) of immigrants aged 20–69 from the Indian subcontinent: 1970–72

| Cause of death | Ethnic origin* | | | |
| | Males | | Females | |
	Indian	British	Indian	British
Tuberculosis	510 (50)	145 (10)	1673 (47)	162 (5)
All cancers	46 (190)	85 (370)	46 (88)	92 (316)
Stomach	28 (11)	46 (18)	78 (7)	62 (13)
Intestine	38 (10)	74 (16)	23 (3)	68 (19)
Lung, trachea, bronchus	25 (39)	69 (109)	32 (6)	63 (26)
Breast (F)			37 (21)	90 (110)[†]
Cervix uteri			69 (10)	131 (26)
Ovary			53 (9)	133 (34)
Liver	369 (11)	246 (7)	137 (1)	168 (3)
Ischaemic heart disease	119 (605)	121 (535)	119 (53)	119 (192)
Diabetes	243 (28)	149 (12)	330 (18)	90 (10)

* Determined by name on death certificate.
† Age 20+

High ratios for liver cancer occurred in Caribbean and African immigrants. Low ratios for colon cancer were found in immigrants from the Caribbean and from Italy and Spain. As expected, ratios for cancer of the lung were low in all immigrant groups born outside of the British Isles as was also the case in their own countries.

In contrast with American findings [4], rates for cancers of the intestine, breast and prostate do not appear to have changed in the first generation of migrants. Cancers thought to be caused by a combination of smoking and drinking alcohol (i.e. cancers of the mouth and larynx) were highly in excess in France, Spain and Italy, where the consumption of alcohol is high. Cancer of the oesophagus is high in France. For these three sites, large differences between countries are confined to males, and immigrants have much lower ratios than in their old countries.

The relative influence of the old and new countries varies with different diseases. Haenszel, based on data in the USA 30 years ago [4], produced the following generalizations. For cancer of the stomach immigrants from high-risk areas show some reduction in rates, but still display the characteristic experience of their country of origin. By contrast, for large bowel, breast (female), ovary, corpus uteri and prostate cancer immigrants from low-risk areas attain, in their lifetime, rates prevailing in the host population; the breast cancer experience of Japanese migrants to the USA is an exception to this rule – the increase subsequent to migration occurs in the second generation.

In general this pattern is not observed in England and Wales. Any changes depend to some extent on whether the home rate was relatively low or high. Low rates have generally stayed low, while high rates in the home countries usually declined towards those of the host country. For example, immigrants from some countries with high mortality from stomach cancer (Poland, Italy, Spain) have lower SMRs in England and Wales. Immigrants from countries with low rates of colon cancer (the Indian subcontinent, Italy, Spain, Poland), have low SMRs in England and Wales. Female migrants from the Indian subcontinent also retain their low rates of breast cancer. In respect of other groups of disease (e.g. infections, cardiovascular disease, some cancers and accidents) mortality of immigrants shows a clear and persisting influence of the home country.

For lung cancer the high rates for the UK countries stand out. Immigrants have low rates, usually marginally raised in comparison with their home countries. Ireland is an exception. Rates in Ireland are lower than in England and Wales, but this high rate indicates the high rate of smoking of Irish immigrants, as shown in the General Household Survey conducted by OPCS (General Household Survey, Social Survey Division, Series GHS. Unpublished tables, 1975, 1976, 1978). Cigarette smoking is probably the only relevant environmental hazard for which there are available estimates of exposure in immigrants. OPCS surveys show that immigrants from the Indian subcontinent, the Caribbean and Africa smoke much less than the rest of the UK population. Although immigrants from Europe currently seem to smoke about the same as the indigenous population, figures from their old countries suggest that the amount may have been increased later in life.

Diseases of the nervous system
The main finding is the very low mortality attributed to multiple sclerosis in immigrants born in the Caribbean, Africa and the Indian subcontinent, particularly in those of Indian origin. Mortality ratios for motor neurone disease, looked at as a 'control' for possible selection against nerve diseases, are more or less the same as in England and Wales. These figures supplement studies of hospital admissions by Dean et al. [5], and are in accord with a hypothesis that in poor countries, early infection might protect against the subsequent development of multiple sclerosis.

Diseases of the cardiovascular system and diabetes
International differences in cardiovascular disease rates have made an important contribution to their investigation. There are substantial differences between countries in mortality from hypertension, cerebrovascular and ischaemic heart disease. Studies of migrants such as those from Japan to the USA, and from Europe, North America and the Middle East and Israel, show that mortality and morbidity rates of migrants differ from those prevailing in the old country. In general mortality rates of immigrants are intermediate. Japanese immigrants in the USA, for example, experience a level of mortality from stroke that is substantially lower than the very high rate in Japan, and the mortality of ischaemic heart disease is increased over the low rate in Japan, although not to the high North American levels. Some studies show that members of one ethnic group may have similar rates of disease in different countries. For example, people of African origin, both in the USA and to a lesser extent in the Caribbean, have high levels of blood pressure and of associated mortality; in the UK a similar picture emerges.

Low ratios are noted in immigrants from France, Italy and Spain; high ratios in immigrants from the Indian subcontinent and these are more pronounced among ethnic Indians, who have the highest mortality from ischaemic heart disease. In this respect it is notable that ethnic Indian immigrants have a very low ratio for cancer of the intestine, unlike the usual pattern among countries where rates for these diseases are correlated [6]. Very high mortality ratios for hypertension and stroke and low ratios for ischaemic heart disease occur in immigrants from the Caribbean and from Africa (see Chapter 31).

Mortality from diabetes is very high in immigrants from the Caribbean and from the Indian subcontinent – the high ratio of the latter group being confined to ethnic Indians, among whom there are numerous reports of high mortality from diabetes in the Indian subcontinent and in Indian immigrants in other countries [7] (see Chapter 33).

Diseases of the respiratory system

Mortality from obstructive lung disease is generally relatively low in countries of birth of immigrants born outside the British Isles; the only two exceptions (with sufficient numbers) are for women in the Caribbean and for both sexes in South Africa.

Immigrants retain the low ratio of their countries of origin. The two ethnic groups of immigrants born in the Indian subcontinent are affected about equally. Studies of British immigrants in other countries – Australia, USA, South Africa – show that they retain the high ratio of mortality from bronchitis [8]. These observations of migrants, both into and away from the UK, are in accord with findings which link exposure to hazards in childhood (e.g. air pollution, respiratory infections, passive smoking) with later chronic respiratory disease.

Although called the 'British disease', all the evidence points to the origins of chronic obstructive lung disease being environmental rather than genetic. This is further confirmed by examining the mortality of immigrants from the Indian subcontinent according to ethnic group. As shown before, British born in the Indian subcontinent have higher PMRs for lung cancer than Indians. It is therefore more likely that the respiratory disease in the British is related to smoking, whereas that in the Indians results from infection.

Diseases of the digestive system

All the countries of origin showed high ratios for this group, made up mostly from peptic ulcer and liver cirrhosis. In most countries outside the British Isles there are high ratios of liver cirrhosis, and generally immigrants have lower ratios than are reported in their country of origin. Immigrants born in Scotland or Ireland, however, retain high ratios. There are high ratios for cirrhosis in immigrants from the Indian subcontinent, the Caribbean and Africa.

Diseases of the genitourinary system

Considering genitourinary diseases together (mainly nephritis and nephrosis), the principal features are the high ratios in immigrants from the Caribbean, Africa and the Indian subcontinent, with the last confined to ethnic Indians. These are groups who also have high mortality ratios attributed to hypertensive disease.

Maternal mortality (complications of pregnancy, childbirth and puerperium)
Even after standardizing for the number of births, mortality ratios were very high in women born in the Caribbean, in Africa, and to a lesser extent in the Indian subcontinent (Table 6.3).

Table 6.3 Maternal mortality by country of birth (per million live births): 1970–72

Country of birth	Deaths	Rate
UK	271	134.5
Irish Republic	11	171.9
Indian subcontinent	22	343.3
African Commonwealth	22	1431.3
Caribbean Commonwealth	35	934.1
Australia and New Zealand, Canada	3	422.3
Europe	15	392.0

Analysis of the causes of maternal death by the International Classification of Disease (ICD) shows that they are generally spread over all categories. There is a strikingly high number attributed to abortion. Further analysis during 1973–78 showed a considerable reduction of these deaths, although other causes of maternal deaths still remained high. The improvement of maternal mortality in the UK, and in other industrialized countries since 1950, suggests that these deaths are largely preventable. It is not clear to what extent the improvement is due to better general health or better health services.

High maternal mortality of some groups might be related to general poor health; for example, the SMR for all causes for women from the Caribbean was 131, and even after removing deaths from maternal mortality it was 124, substantially higher than the average for England and Wales. It is likely that the high rate for women from Europe is inflated by cases who come to England and Wales for abortions; deaths are counted in the numerator but cases not counted in the denominator.

Accidents, poisoning and violence (including suicide)
Immigrants, with the exception of the Italian-born, have somewhat high mortality rates, reflecting rates in their home countries, and determined largely by motor vehicle accidents. Deaths due to falls, probably at work, are frequent in immigrants born in Ireland, as also are deaths due to fire. High mortality rates from suicide were found in immigrants from Poland, Germany and the USSR.

Perinatal and infant mortality
The latest analysis published for 1984 shows that perinatal and neonatal death rates are relatively high in children of mothers born in the Indian subcontinent, the Caribbean or Africa [9].

Pattern of mortaility in different immigrant groups

Immigrants from Scotland and Ireland differ from other immigrants in this report, in that they move freely within the UK without language or other cultural impediments. There is no legal restriction that would make ill-health a barrier to immigration.

Immigrants from Scotland

The all-cause mortality of Scottish immigrants is higher than the England and Wales average, but marginally lower than the SMR in Scotland (standardized to England and Wales) – thus indicating that these immigrants bring their risk of disease with them. Lung cancer and ischaemic heart disease contribute greatly to excess deaths in the immigrants, as in Scotland.

There are very few causes of death for which the Scottish immigrants show even a small advantage compared with the England and Wales average: multiple sclerosis in men and women, 'other' forms of heart disease, but this small deficit is swamped by the excess from ischaemic heart disease and respiratory disease.

Immigrants from Ireland (all parts)

Immigration from Ireland to England and Wales has been well established for at least 150 years and the majority of the Irish-born population enumerated in the 1971 Census of Great Britain were long-time residents – 54% had entered the UK earlier than 1955. It is difficult to obtain information on characteristics of Irish immigrants prior to migration. Once resident in England and Wales a disproportionately high number are in semi-skilled or unskilled occupations (classes IV and V).

Ease of migration may account in part for the high all-cause mortality of Irish male immigrants compared with mortality either in Ireland or in England and Wales (Table 6.1). Easy travel from Ireland would make ill-health less of a barrier to migration than, for example, from the New Commonwealth.

Possibly, immigrants from Ireland who become ill may be less likely to return than other immigrants, although this would still leave the question of why some disorders are more affected than others. In addition, economic and social disadvantage might be a spur rather than a barrier to migration from Ireland. If 'economic disadvantage' is the reason for the high mortality of Irish male immigrants, it is not being measured by the conventional index of social class, based on occupation.

Irish immigrants have a high SMR from almost every cause of death – the exceptions being multiple sclerosis, diabetes mellitus, carcinoma of the breast and uterus other than cervix (much of which results from failure to distinguish cervical cancer).

It is likely that the high mortality from alcohol-related diseases – cirrhosis, carcinoma of the buccal cavity and pharynx, larnyx and oesophagus – and accidents and violence reflect not only the cultural patterns, but the poorer than average conditions of Irish immigrants. The high mortality from tuberculosis in Irish immigrants is a reflection of the high rate in Ireland.

Among the biggest differences in mortality between Ireland and England and Wales is that from lung cancer: an SMR of 64 was noted for men living in Ireland. This has been explained, in part, by the higher proportion of the Irish population that is rural, and the urban–rural gradient [10]. However, the SMR from lung cancer among Irish immigrants is higher than the England and Wales level. This is likely to be related to smoking; the prevalence of smoking, particularly heavy smoking (20 or more per day), among Irish immigrants is higher than the England and Wales average.

Immigrants from the Indian subcontinent

Immigration from India and, to a lesser extent, Pakistan occurred largely before 1954 and during the 1960s. The earlier period consisted mostly of British subjects returning from the ex-colonies. It has been estimated that in 1951, of 121 884 residents of England and Wales who were born in India and Pakistan, 86 000 (71%) were white. Subsequent migration was largely of Asians. By 1956, the India- and Pakistan-born population had increased to an estimated 304 340, of whom the white proportion had decreased to 24%. These two groups, white and Asian, would have different mortality patterns as a result of different cultural patterns.

One indication that migration from India and Pakistan may differ is given by the sex ratio of immigrants in the 1971 Census: from India there were 1.17 males for every female; from Pakistan, the ratio was 2.57. Unfortunately it is not possible to make an accurate assessment of the effect such differences might have. Because of inaccuracies on the death certificate, deaths of immigrants from India, Pakistan and Sri Lanka have been considered together.

The all-cause mortality for men is the same as for England and Wales. For women, the SMR of 111 is significantly greater than 100. A high incidence of tuberculosis is reflected in high mortality, although the number of deaths is small.

Among cancers, SMRs for liver cancer in men and women and buccal cavity cancer in men are high. Several other cancers are low. The low mortality from cancer of the trachea, bronchus and lung is consistent with low rates of smoking.

Mortality is also high from diabetes and from homicides. The high mortality from cirrhosis, particularly in women, is probably post-infectious in origin rather than the result of alcohol abuse and may also be related to the high mortality from liver cancer.

Particularly striking is the high mortality from complications of pregnancy, childbirth and the puerperium (see above). In the terms of the Confidential Enquiries into Maternal Deaths, many of these are likely to be 'avoidable deaths'.

PMRs for most cancers of ethnic British born in the Indian subcontinent are higher than those of ethnic Indians born there, but low compared with rates in England and Wales (Table 6.2). Ischaemic heart disease mortality is high both in ethnic Indians and ethnic British, but the high PMRs for diabetes are more marked in the ethnic Indians. These findings point to the greater importance of lifestyle and environment than of genes in determining mortality rates, except perhaps in the case of diabetes.

An unexplained feature of the mortality of immigrants from the Indian subcontinent is the flattening of the inverse relationship between social class and mortality seen so strongly in England and Wales.

Immigrants from the Caribbean Commonwealth

Of the 304 070 residents of Great Britain (1971 Census) born in the Caribbean, over 100 000 arrived in the years 1960–62 and a further 82 780 in the years 1963–71.

The bulk of the remainder arrived between 1955 and 1959. The migration is thus recent and the disease patterns might be expected to be strongly influenced by those of the old country (here taken to be Trinidad whose population is half Indian and half black African origin) and by the process of migration itself.

The all-cause SMR is low in male immigrants from the Caribbean and somewhat higher than average in women. Complications of pregnancy, childbirth and the puerperium, although contributing only a small number of deaths to the overall excess death rate in women, are associated with a dramatically high relative risk (SMR, 659). As with the high mortality in Asian women, better access to medical care and improved conditions of hygiene could reduce this high mortality.

In both men and women there are high SMRs for hypertensive disease and cerebrovascular disease and a high attributable risk. The high mortality from chronic renal disease could be a cause or a consequence of the high mortality associated with hypertension. The magnitude of the excess mortality from hypertensive disease and cerebrovascular disease is too great to be explained simply by the unfavourable social class distribution of Caribbean migrants. (There are other possibilities, particularly competitive mortality and the low rates of ischaemic heart disease; see Chapter 31.) There are high SMRs from venous thrombosis and embolism and diabetes, particularly in women. Mortality is high from primary liver cancer and carcinoma of the prostate. This latter has been reported to be high in blacks in the USA. The high SMRs from blood diseases, observed also in immigrants from Africa, is not explained by sickle-cell disease (see Chapter 12). Mortality from homicide is also very high.

The high mortality from these diseases is offset somewhat by the low mortality from ischaemic heart disease, respiratory disease and from many cancers – oesophagus (in men), intestine, rectum, larynx, lung, skin and breast.

The low mortality from lung cancer is in contrast to the Irish immigrants. Both Irish and Caribbeans come from countries with low mortality rates from lung cancer. In England and Wales, the Irish SMR is greater than 100, whereas the SMR for Caribbeans remains low. Mortality from respiratory disease is also high in Irish immigrants (and in Ireland) but remains low in Caribbean immigrants. The explanation for this pattern may be the lower prevalence of heavy smokers among Caribbean than Irish immigrants. Also relevant is that Caribbean immigration is recent compared to Irish, allowing less time for exposure to the conditions conducive to respiratory disease.

The low respiratory mortality in Caribbean immigrants is the converse of the experience of British migrants to the USA. When migrating from a country (Britain) with a high respiratory disease rate to a country (USA) with a lower rate, the prevalence of respiratory disease among British immigrants remains high. Both patterns indicate that some of the determinants of respiratory disease act early in life.

Immigrants from the African Continent

The 164 000 immigrants (1971 Census) from the African Commonwealth include Africans, Indians born in Africa and British born in Africa. These three different groups cannot easily be distinguished in the census classification 'birthplace Africa'. As with the Caribbean immigrants, the migration is recent – nearly 135 000 since 1960. More of the migrants are in social classes I, II and III non-manual than average.

Immigrants from Africa stand out as having the highest male and female all-cause mortality of any immigrant group. The pattern of causes of death is quite different from England and Wales as a whole. Mortality is high from tuberculosis and whilst overall cancer mortality does not differ greatly from an SMR of 100, the distribution of cancers by site is different. High SMRs are recorded for cancer of the liver, gallbladder and bile ducts, low mortality from carcinoma of the trachea, bronchus and lung. As with Asian and Caribbean migrants the high mortality from liver cancer is associated with high mortality from cirrhosis of the liver, further increasing the speculation that infection plays a role in both diseases.

There are few deaths from blood diseases, but the SMRs are high. More important as a contributor to the absolute number of excess deaths is the high mortality from hypertensive and cerebrovascular disease. As with Caribbean migrants, the mortality from nephritis and infections of the kidney is high.

A subdivision of death certificates according to ethnicity of descendant showed particularly high proportionate mortality ratios from hypertensive and cerebrovascular disease in Africans of African origin, and high PMRs from ischaemic heart disease in those of Indian origin from Africa. This confirms the impression of a high susceptibility to hypertension and its consequences in other immigrants of African origin – from the Caribbean – and a somewhat higher than average susceptibility to ischaemic heart disease of immigrants from the Indian subcontinent.

The high mortality from complications of pregnancy, childbirth and the puerperium observed in Asian and Caribbean immigrants is strongly in evidence here. Mortality in men is high from suicide and suspected suicide, and homicide.

Various studies of immigrants from a common country of origin

The interpretation of studies of disease ratios in immigrants may be taken further by comparing findings between countries that have immigrants from a common source, such as the USA, Australia, and the UK, each of which has received immigrants from the 'same' countries, e.g. Italy [2,4]. In Italian-born immigrants only one major site of cancer (stomach) has a mortality ratio that is higher than for any of the respective host countries. Furthermore, when Italian and British immigrants in Australia are compared, these results are supported, as Italian-born immigrants have a higher cancer rate than British-born only for cancer of the stomach. An important point is revealed when stomach cancer figures for immigrants from England and Wales are subdivided; immigrants from Wales have higher rates than those from England and this reflects the national rates within the UK.

These comparisons between studies in different countries increase our confidence in international and immigrant mortality figures [11].

Further evidence that selection of immigrants as healthier than the population from which they come is discussed in the Australian report [2]. Mortality ratios for some cancers rise shortly after immigration, presumably as a result of loss of the selective effect, and subsequently the rate moves towards that of Australia – presumably as a result of developing a new lifestyle in the new environment.

References

1 Marmot, M. G., Adelstein, A. M. and B̈ulusu, L. *Mortality by Cause in Immigrants in England and Wales 1970–1978.* (Studies on Population and Medical Subjects: no.47) (Office of Population, Censuses and Surveys), HMSO, London (1984)

2 Armstrong, B. K., Woodings, T. L., Stenhouse, N. S. and McCall, M. G. *Mortality from Cancer in Migrants to Australia 1962–1971*, University of Western Australia, Perth (1983)

3 Medical Research Council. Tuberculosis and Chest Diseases Unit. National survey of tuberculosis notifications in England and Wales 1978–9. *Br. Med. J.*, **281**, 895–898 (1980)

4 Haenszel, W. Variation in incidence of and mortality from stomach cancer, with particular reference to the United States. *J. Natl. Cancer Inst.*, **21**, 213–262 (1958)

5 Dean, G., Brady, R., McLoughlin, H. *et al.*, Motor neurone disease and multiple sclerosis among immigrants to Britain. *Br. J. Prev. Soc. Med.*, **31**, 141–147 (1977)

6 Doll, W. R. S. and Peto, R. *The Causes of Cancer: Quantitive Estimates of the Avoidable Risks of Cancer in the United States Today*, Oxford University Press, Oxford (1981)

7 Jackson, W. P. U. Racial and geographic factors in diabetes. *Lancet*, **i**, 601–602 (1971)

8 Reid, D. D. The future of migrant studies. *Isr. J. Med. Sci.*, **17**, 1592–1596 (1971)

9 Office of Population Census and Surveys. *Mortality Statistics, Perinatal and Infant: Social and Biological Factors* (Review of the Registrar General on deaths in England and Wales: Series DH3 no.17), HMSO, London (1984)

10 Ward, J. B., Healy, C. and Dean, G. Urban and rural mortality in the republic of Ireland. *J. Irish Med. Assoc.*, **71**, 3 (1978)

11 Reid, D. D. Studies of disease among migrants and native populations in Great Britain, Norway, and the United States. I. Background and design. In *Epidemiological Approaches to the Study of Cancer and Chronic Diseases* (National Cancer Institute Monograph 19) (ed. W. Haenszel), US Department of Health, Education and Welfare, Public Health Service, Bethesda, Maryland (1966)

Chapter 7

Epidemiological and clinical comparison of cardiovascular disease in blacks and whites in the USA

Patricia Davidson and Elijah Saunders

Introduction

'Black' is a sociological category. It is an ethnic grouping and due to racial admixture in societies such as the USA and Caribbean cannot be considered a genetic classification. It distinguishes a group of people with similar social and historical backgrounds, as well as physical features [1].

Cardiovascular disease includes hypertension and ischaemic heart disease (IHD) which consists of functional myocardial changes resulting from narrowed or occluded coronary arteries and includes angina pectoris, myocardial infarction (MI) and sudden cardiac death.

A high incidence of hypertension with cardiac involvement has been reported in blacks [2,3]. The extent to which hypertensive myocardial changes contribute to coronary heart disease (CHD) in blacks has yet to be determined, but there is no question that the latter is accelerated by the former.

Epidemiology

For years a variety of studies with small sample sizes had suggested that coronary artery disease and MI was different in character and incidence in blacks. Yet a survey from Harlem Hospital in New York analysed 131 cases of acute MI between 1950 and 1954 and concluded there were no racial differences between blacks and whites in symptoms, incidence and mortality [4]

In the 1940s, the black male mortality from CHD was less than in white males but by 1968 it exceeded that of white males, leading Gillum in 1982 to describe CHD mortality in blacks as one of the highest in the world. Subsequently, CHD mortality has declined to similar levels in white and black males. However, sudden death, usually assumed to be due to CHD, remains excessive in blacks compared to whites. Data, although inconclusive, also suggest a greater CHD mortality in black women compared to white women [5].

Specific studies: cohort studies

The Evans County Study was a population-based age-adjusted cohort study in rural Georgia and the first of its kind in the USA. In 1960, 3102 black and white residents

Table 7.1 Prevalence of CHD in blacks and whites aged 15–75 (per 1000 cases): Evans County, Georgia (1960)

Sex and race	Prevalence of CHD			
	Definite	Probable	Possible	Total population
Black males	3	5	11	395
White males	33	11	27	664
Black females	3	2	10	472
White females	3	6	16	685

Modified from McDonough et al. [6].

aged 15–75 were surveyed (Table 7.1). The prevalence of CHD was defined by angina pectoris. MI history, or electrocardiographic (ECG) findings suggestive of MI. There was a lower prevalence, and 7-year follow-up indicated a lower CHD incidence and prevalence, in black compared with white males. There was a similar prevalence and incidence in black and white females [6,7].

Cholesterol levels were lower in black than in white males and also lower in poorer than in higher social class white males who were less physically active, implicating these risk factors as major determinants of CHD prevalence [6].

Twenty-year mortality data displayed a change in the trend leading to comparable survival rates in black males and lower social status white males. These rates were less favourable than higher social status white males [8]. Gillum pointed out the limitations of this study with such a small black sample size [5].

The Charleston Heart Study, South Carolina from 1960 to 1975 followed a cohort of 2775 black and white men and women randomly sampled from the population aged 35 years and older for CHD incidence [9]. A group of high social class black males was later recruited in 1964 and the total group was re-evaluated in 1974. An incident case was defined as death from CHD, non-fatal acute MI, ECG evidence of acute MI or coronary insufficiency, or history of angina pectoris as determined by the Rose questionnaire.

Total CHD incidence was highest in white males. The sudden death rate was higher in black males. With 11 new cases of sudden death in 322 men (a rate of 32/1000) their rate was three times greater than for white males, four times that for white females, and two and a half times the rate in black females. The selected population of 101 black males of high social class exhibited half the incidence of CHD and acute MI compared to all other black males and no cases of sudden death.

An autopsy survey in New Orleans, an extension of the International Atherosclerosis Project, evaluated cardiovascular mortality for black and white males by using standardized criteria in autopsy and hospital records and in physician interviews [10]. In the 2700 autopsies (1433 black subjects), the CHD mortality among black men aged 30–44 years was greater than in white males. The opposite was true for the age-group 45–64. The authors speculated that black men may be on the verge of an epidemic of CHD with future rates in this young male population likely to exceed that in white males.

The New Orleans Community Pathology Study included autopsies on 899 black and 393 white males, aged 26–44 years, and compared the extent of coronary atherosclerotic lesions during the 1960–68 and the 1969–78 period [11,12]. Raised lesions and fatty streaks were greater in the 10–19-year-old blacks than whites but were less extensive in black than white men after age 25. Black women had more extensive involvement than white women. There was a trend for a decrease in raised lesions in young white males who had had more extensive raised lesions in coronary arteries in the initial study [12], but the young black male population displayed no change in the extent of raised lesions [11].

Studies of sudden death and MI: The Baltimore Sudden Death and MI Study examined associated factors, and the epidemiology, pathology and medical care prior to sudden death [13]. The rate of sudden deaths attributed to arteriosclerotic heart disease was greater in men than women and marginally so in black than white men but the incidence of transmural MI was reversed, being greater in whites than blacks for both sexes. These racial differences might have been due to a higher frequency of untreated MIs or silent, painless MIs in blacks [13].

In *Nashville, Tennessee* in 1967 and 1968 a similar study of 167 000 persons aged below 75 years of whom 20% were black evaluated MI and sudden death incidence from hospital records, death certificates and physician interviews [14]. Sudden death (within 24 hours of onset of symptoms) from CHD was marginally greater in black than white males (2.8 versus 2.2/1000). The incidence in black women was twice that of white (1.48 versus 0.7/1000). Again, the reverse was true for MI, with the incidence for white males greater than twice that for black males (5.88 versus 2.12/1000). White women exhibited a slightly higher incidence of MI than black women (1.92 versus 1.11/1000).

The paucity of acute MI in *Newark* blacks was investigated in a small hospital admission survey in 1973, documenting 273 cases with 50 black males and 43 black females [15]. There was no statistically significant difference for age-specific rates between whites and blacks. However, death certificate evaluation revealed a higher 'dead on arrival' rate among blacks in all decades of both sexes (Table 7.2). Total hospital mortality from acute MI was higher in black males compared to white males (32% versus 22%). However, the white female mortality was greater than

Table 7.2 Out-of-hospital deaths attributed to coronary artery disease: Newark (1973)[*]

Sex and race	Age-group (yr)							
	20–29	30–39	40–49	50–59	60–69	70–79	80+	Total
White men	—	3 (34)	11 (109)	28 (278)	44 (577)	44 (1022)	27 (1628)	157
Black men	3 (2)	8 (68)	32 (336)	34 (450)	42 (1138)	18 (1214)	4 (909)	141
White women	—	1 (11)	3 (28)	12 (105)	27 (294)	38 (6201)	28 (1147)	109
Black women	—	3 (19)	13 (111)	18 (246)	38 (827)	29 (1463)	9 (1255)	110

[*] Numbers within parentheses indicate rates per 100 000.
Modified from Weisse, Abiuso and Thind [15].

twice the black female (40% versus 16%). Results were similar in another hospital admission survey in *Patterson, New Jersey* [16].

A *South Carolina* survey in 1978 compared hospital cases of acute MI and all death certificates within a defined rural and urban community [17] (Table 7.3). The prevalence of acute MI among both black females and males in the urban community was higher than in their rural counterparts, the opposite was found for white males, and there was no regional difference among white females. On the other hand, out-of-hospital mortality for urban black males was 2.4 times the white male rate. The mortality rate of rural black males was 40% higher than white males.

In 1961, the incidence of CHD in a population of insured New Yorkers, aged 25–64, was evaluated in *Health Insurance Plan (HIP) of Greater New York* [18]. The MI incidence rate for white men was two-fold greater than black men, and one and a half times greater for angina. Sudden death in black men with MI was 49%, but only 31% in white males.

The more recent *Multicenter Investigation of the Limitation of Infarct Size (MILIS)* reviewed the effects of gender and race on survival, 48 months after MI. The highest cumulative rate was among 63 black women at 48%, then 32% in 163 white women and the lowest in 511 white men at 21% and 23% in 79 black men.

Table 7.3 Out-of-hospital acute MI mortality during 1978 (age-adjusted rates per 1000)

Area	Black males	White males	Black females	White females
Urban	629	349	238	96
	(71)	(30)	(39)	(14)
Rural	404	366	189	50
	(68)	(48)	(40)	(16)

Numbers within parentheses indicate rates per 100 000.
Modified from Keil *et al.* [17].

Angiographic studies

The *Coronary Artery Surgery Study (CASS)*, published in 1986, analysed the small black population from their registry. Angina was the indicator for angiography. There were 578 blacks and 22 781 white participants [20]. Two-thirds of the black men were labourers, compared to 40% of the white males, as were 27% black women and 10.6% of white women. Recreational activity level did not differ but the percentage of smokers was higher in black men and women, although the heaviest smokers were white males and females. Hypertension and diabetes were more prevalent in black men and women than white men and women.

The documented incidence of MI was higher in white men compared to black men. There was no racial difference in women. Angiographic evidence of coronary artery disease was significantly less in blacks, with 47% of black men and 67.3% of black women having normal or minimal disease compared with only 20% of white men and 55% of white women. Left main and three-vessel coronary artery disease was greater in white men. A higher percentage of black participants tended also had normal left ventricles. As the authors pointed out, it is unknown to what extent these participants represented the total black population undergoing angiography. Other studies have also noted more extensive angiographic lesions in white men.

Oberman and associates reported a three-fold greater prevalence of two- or three-vessel disease in white males, after adjustment for risk factors [21].

Conclusions

As demonstrated from these selected examples, the data concerning the prevalence and incidence of CHD in blacks is inconsistent and incomplete. The Report of the Secretary's Task Force on Black and Minority Health attributed the inadequacy of the data to the limited number of blacks in the studies, varying standards of age adjustment, varying diagnostic criteria, and varying length of follow-up [22]. Mortality rates from CHD, although falling in both ethnic groups, may be higher in blacks than whites but the evidence that documented angiographic disease is excessive in blacks is poor, if anything suggesting the opposite. Whether much of the CHD mortality in blacks is confounded by purely hypertensive heart disease remains speculative but possible.

Risk factors

Gillum and Grant reviewed the available data on 'established' risk factors for CHD in blacks [23]. This section outlines recent developments.

Hypertension

The prevalence in blacks is reported to be up to 4 times that observed in whites, with severe elevations (diastolic BP > 115 mmHg) being five to seven times commoner [24]. What is still not conclusive is the impact of hypertension on the development of CHD.

The Evans County Study, as stated previously, had few black cases in 322 black males in a total of 3102 participants. The levels of BP were higher in black males but the risk of CHD compared to white males was lower [7,8,25]. Another study suggesting a lower risk of CHD in black hypertensive men was the screened cohort of the Multiple Risk Factor Intervention Trial (MRFIT) – 23 490 blacks were compared to 325 384 white men. Hypertension was commoner but CHD mortality was lower in black hypertensive males compared to whites [26].

In the Hypertension Detection and Follow-up Program (HDFP), over 5000 participants were evenly divided between both sexes and races. The presence of angina in hypertensive black men was associated with a 5-year mortality of 22.1% versus 13.5% in white males, and 9.8% in white females. While angina was more prevalent in black female hypertensives, the mortality rate was lower at 5.3% [27,28]. The incidence of MI diagnosed by all criteria (ECG evidence of MI and clinical history) was approximately similar in all four race and sex groups.

The Beta-Blocker Heart Attack Trial (BHAT) included a total of 3837 patients, 333 of whom were black [29]. Comparative analysis was difficult with such a disparity in numbers. Black patients had more risk factors including hypertension and angina, with a higher mortality rate in both the placebo (15.9%) and beta-blocker-treated (11.7%) groups compared with 9.8% and 7.2% respectively in non-blacks.

Lipids

Several studies have compared lipid profiles in blacks and whites. The Bogalusa Heart Study found higher alpha-lipoprotein (HDL), lower pre-beta-lipoprotein (VLDL) in black children compared with whites [30]. Similarly, in the Cincinnati Lipid Research Clinic Princeton School Study [31], the Lipid Research Clinics Program Prevalence Study [32] and the Evans County Study [8,33], HDL cholesterol levels tended to be higher in black males with lower low-density lipoprotein (LDL), and triglycerides.

Differences appeared greatest among black juveniles and black male adults but not for HDL cholesterol in black and white females [34]. The loss of this protective factor is possibly due to more obesity in black women because the other factors that tend to reduce HDL cholesterol (smoking, diabetes and antihypertensive drugs) have not, despite greater prevalence in blacks, reduced the HDL advantage in black males.

The Framingham Minority Study compared HDL cholesterol levels in 45 black males and 55 black females with the previously obtained Framingham data [35]. However, these residents were more highly educated than most blacks in previous studies. The authors noted significantly lower HDL levels, conflicting with earlier data of a correlation with HDL and educational achievement [36]. The small sample size may have accounted for these discrepancies.

Evaluation of dietary intake data in the second National Health and Nutrition Examination Survey (NHANES II) collected in 1976–80 showed less total carbohydrate consumption in blacks than whites [37], suggesting that an inverse relationship between dietary carbohydrates and HDL cholesterol may account for the observed HDL differences. There is another genetic hypothesis to account for this: HDL facilitates macrophage immobilization of the trypanosome causing sleeping sickness which is endemic in west and sub-Saharan Africa. A genetic protective factor against sleeping sickness may have evolved that results in higher HDL cholesterol levels in peoples of African descent [34].

Diabetes mellitus

In 1982, Gillum and Grant noted that there had been no prospective cohort studies on diabetes in blacks and their risk of CHD, and this lack of data continues. National statistics demonstrate a higher prevalence of self-reported diabetes in blacks [37,38].

The Chicago Heart Association Detection Project in Industry examined the prevalence of diabetes and associated cardiovascular risk factors in an employed population of 28 895 whites and 2607 blacks [39] (but definitions of diabetes were not standard.) The diabetes prevalence rate for white males was highest, black men and white females were next, with black females having the lowest rates. (These figures are the reverse of those from national probability samples.) The opposite was true for obesity, with black women exhibiting the highest prevalence, followed by white males, black males and white females.

Cardiovascular mortality in 'diabetes' was higher in white males than blacks. However, 'diabetic' black men displayed a higher risk of cardiovascular mortality than non-diabetics.

Possible sources of bias in this study include the unusual definition of diabetes and small numbers of diabetic deaths in black males (9) versus 240 in white males.

Also, only an employed population was examined, excluding diabetics too ill for employment.

MRFIT included a small black population, and there were only seven CHD deaths in black diabetics. They noted the 5-year, age-adjusted, CHD mortality among black diabetics to be 8.5/1000 compared to 4.1/1000 in black non-diabetics. This was less than the non-black diabetic mortality of 14.2/1000 [40].

Smoking

Smoking appears to be more prevalent in black males, but heavy smoking of 25 or more cigarettes per day is greater among white males [41]. Smoking prevalence for women was less, with no racial difference in its importance as a predictor for CHD [25,26,29].

Obesity

Obesity in black women has been described as pandemic. Interestingly in the NHANES II data total caloric intake including carbohydrates was lower in black than thinner white women [37], leading to speculation that obesity may reflect a reduced energy expenditure, or a genetic difference in how white and black females handle calories [37].

ECG abnormalities

In some studies of whites it has been observed that ECG abnormalities are predictive of CHD. The Framingham Study supported the theory that voltage increase with ST- and T-wave changes indicate ischaemic myocardial involvement in left ventricular hypertrophy (LVH). Voltage criteria alone indicated ventricular hypertrophy but without ischaemia [42]. The former is defined as 'definite' ECG-LVH and the latter 'possible' ECG-LVH. After the adjustment for the effects of hypertension, the risk of clinically overt CHD was increased threefold in those with 'definite' ECG-LVH. This grave prognosis was not exhibited in those with just voltage hypertrophy.

There are several studies which included small numbers of blacks who tended to have a greater frequency of ECG abnormalities than whites. Whether the predictive value of these in blacks is the same as in whites remains uncertain, indeed controversial.

The HDFP, MRFIT, Evans County, and Birmingham Stroke studies all indicated a higher prevalence of ECG abnormalities in blacks. In the Birmingham Stroke Study, increased R-wave amplitude and ST–T changes were greater and significantly associated in black men and women [43], but were independent of blood pressure and history of treated hypertension. The normal variant of ST segment elevations consistent with early repolarization was twice as common in younger than in older black males and four times greater than in whites.

Abnormal Q waves are considered to indicate CHD. Their prevalence increased with age but did not differ with race, sex or other risk factors. Left axis deviation (LAD) prevalence was higher in blacks and increased with age in all groups.

The Evans County Study revealed a threefold greater prevalence of ECG-LVH in blacks [44]. Increased QRS voltage with ST changes, prolonged PR intervals, bundle branch block, and sinus tachycardia were associated with a greater incidence of new coronary events in white males [45], but did not carry the same risk in black males. LAD, raised QRS voltage, ST- and T-wave changes all correlated with a higher rate of CHD in white females. Only black females with LAD had more CHD.

In the MRFIT trial of the 7% of over 12 000 males who were black, nearly half had abnormal ECGs (49.4%), compared with 26.3% of white males. There was also a fourfold greater prevalence of major ECG abnormalities in both non-hypertensive and hypertensive blacks [46, 47].

In the HDFP trial of antihypertensive treatment, as expected, the risk of mortality in participants with ECG-LVH was greater than in those without LVH in all races and sexes in either treatment group [48].

Summary
Most studies have shown that the ECG profile differs; the clinical significance of typical changes predictive of CHD in whites appears to be different, with some data implying a more benign nature to apparent ECG abnormalities in blacks.

Left ventricular hypertrophy (LVH)

The echocardiogram (ECHO) is considered a more sensitive indicator of LVH than the ECG [49,50], in which increased R-wave voltage is the major criterion. However, factors other than LVH may affect ECG voltage [50–52].

Comparative studies are few and conflicting. Savage and associates evaluated 68 white and black selected hypertension patients, matched for clinical characteristics. Left ventricular mass, wall thickness and left ventricular chamber dimensions were assessed [51] and were similar for the two groups. Dunn and associates evaluated 60 untreated black and white hypertensives, also clinically matched [51]. Wall thickness measurements were the same in both groups, but left ventricular mass index was increased in blacks. Correlations between posterior ventricular wall thickness, arterial pressure and total peripheral resistance were found only in black patients in whom they hypothesized that arterial pressure played a more dominant role in LVH development. Hammond and associates evaluated a sample of 207 employees. Black hypertensives displayed higher relative wall thickness than their white counterparts. They later noted a twofold greater prevalence of increased left ventricular mass and threefold increase in wall thickness among black participants [54].

One reason for the discrepancies in this small number of studies may be the sample sizes and lack of representativeness of the general black and white population. Another possibility is that the actual blood pressures were not reflected by the study visit in measurements, making matching by blood pressure inaccurate [53,54]. Other possible causes of LVH include neurohumoral factors, ageing, genetic predisposition, increased heart rate and altered myocardial composition that may have contributed to the discrepancies among patients [51,56].

Serum creatine phosphokinase (CPK)

Increased CPK levels in black men compared with white men were noted by Meltzer. Diet and physical activity did not differ [57,58]. Wong and associates confirmed this finding, with a greater than twofold increase for the normal range of CPK in black men and slightly less than twice in black women, compared with whites [59]. This has not had an adequate explanation but the difference has considerable implications in black patients for the diagnosis of acute MI where a rise in CPK is a major criterion. It has been speculated that the CPK sarcolemma membrane is genetically different [58]. Another hypothesis that has not been well accepted is a racial difference in skeletal muscle mass compared to total body mass [59,60].

Thrombogenesis

International studies have compared fibrinolytic activity in African, Caribbean and European subjects [61]. In the American-only study from Evans County [62], an impairment of fibrinolysis in 155 white compared to 182 black men was observed. Plasma fibrinolytic activity was detected in a significantly higher percentage of blacks. There was also a higher plasminogen content and lower antiplasmin levels. The higher incidence of CHD in the white participants correlated with the impairment of fibrinolysis, Szczeklik and associates suggested that the results may be due to cultural and environmental differences, rather than race.

Surgical intervention

Studies of myocardial revascularization have again included only small numbers of black patients.

The Walter Reed Army Medical Center reported a 5.6% operative mortality in only 54 black patients between 1970 and 1982, compared with a 4.2% mortality in 1323 non-black patients [63] treated by coronary artery bypass graph-surgery (CABG).

The University of Alabama Medical Center noted a marked discrepancy in racial origin among patients undergoing cardiac catheterization and CABG [20], of whom only 4% were black. A lower number of black patients with ischaemic symptoms were advised to have the procedure, and, as in the previous study [63], they had a higher prevalence of hypertension, smoking, and lower HDL-cholesterol to total cholesterol ratios.

The 5-year survival rates for black males undergoing surgery over age 50 was lower than in whites but below the age of 50 the estimated survival rates were similar.

The Johns Hopkins University evaluated the results of CABG in 56 black men and women between 1972 and 1980 [64] undergoing CABG. Half had unstable angina with a 15% overall mortality and an operative mortality of 9%. Forty per cent had hypertension, 45% were smokers, with diabetes in 10% and 53% with previous MI. The authors concluded that the high mortality rate was due to the advanced state of the disease at the time of CABG.

Conclusion

Watkins described the state of epidemiology of CHD in the black population as a 'mortality muddle', with Gillum also pointing out the limitations of the data [5,65].

Even though we have come a long way from the days when CHD was considered non-existent in blacks, the preceding inconsistencies leave major questions.

The role of psychosocial factors still needs extensive study. Type A behaviour, associated with a higher risk of CHD in whites [66], has not been studied in blacks.

Sherman James [67] suggested that the reported excess of CHD in black females may be connected with economic disparities. The 'coping style' that enables this population to deal with stress may be manifested as Type A behaviour. He also pointed out the inconsistencies in data on socioeconomic status (SES) and CHD in blacks [68]. Not all studies have found an inverse relationship, as noted in the white population. Possibly, in the early process of urbanization, the risk of CHD is greater in those of higher SES. With time, the risk declines to less than that for the lower social classes. The Charleston cohort study noted a significant decrease in prevalence and incidence in CHD in its 100 high SES black males compared with poorer black males [9].

What we do know is that reduction of risk factors is beneficial. HDFP noted the 5-year incidence of MI and angina was reduced in those in the Stepped Care compared with the Referred Care group [27], most notably in blacks.

Between the first and second NHANES (1971–75 and 1976–80) a decreased prevalence was noted in elevated BP and smoking as well as a reduction in the percentage of black adults with two or more risk factors. This was felt to correlate with the observed CHD mortality decline of 13% for black males and 20% for black females [69].

Continued study of the above questions and larger black samples should help solve the 'mortality muddle' of CHD in the black population.

References

1 Cooper, R. A note on the biologic concept of race and its application in epidemiologic research. *Am. Heart J.*, **108**, 715–723 (1984)

2 Dunn, F. G., Oigman, W. Sungaard-Riise, K. *et al.* Racial differences in cardiac adaptation to essential hypertension determined by echocardiographic indexes. *J. Am. Coll. Cardiol.* **1**, 1348–1351 (1983)

3 Hypertension Detection and Follow-up Program Cooperative Group. Race, education and prevalence of hypertension. *Am. J. Epidemiol.*, **106**, 351–361 (1977)

4 Mihaly, J. P. and Whiteman, N. C. Myocardial infarction in the negro: historical survey as it relates to negroes. *Am. J. Cardiol.*, **2**, 464–474 (1958)

5 Gillum, R. F. Coronary heart disease in black populations: I. mortality and morbidity. *Am. Heart J.*, **104**, 839–851 (1982)

6 McDonough, J. R., Hames, C. G., Stulb, S. C. and Garrison, G. E. Coronary heart disease among negroes and whites in Evans County, Georgia. *J. Chronic Dis.*, **18**, 443–468 (1964)

7 Cassel, J., Heyden, S., Bartel, A. G. *et al.* Incidence of coronary heart disease by ethnic group, social class, and sex. *Arch. Intern. Med.*, **128**, 901–906 (1971)

8 Tyroler, H. A., Knowles, M. G., Wing, S. B. *et al.* Ischemic heart disease risk factors and twenty-year mortality in middle-age Evans County black males. *Am. Heart J.*, **108**, 738–746 (1984)

9 Keil, J. E., Loadholt, C. B., Weinrich, M. C. *et al.* Incidence of coronary heart disease in blacks in Charleston, South Carolina. *Am. Heart J.*, **108**, 779 (1984)

10 Oalman, M. C., McGill, H. C. and Strong, J. P. Cardiovascular mortality in a community: results of a survey in New Orleans. *Am. J. Epidemiol.*, **94**, 546–555 (1971)

11 Strong, J. P., Oalman, M. C., Newman, W. P. *et al.* Coronary heart disease in young black and white males in New Orleans: Community Pathology Study. *Am. Heart J.*, **108**, 747–759 (1984)

12 Strong, J. P., Restrepo, C. and Guzman, M. Coronary and aortic atherosclerosis in New Orleans: II. Comparison of lesions by age, sex and race. *Lab. Invest.*, **39**, 364–369 (1978)

13 Kuller, L. H., Cooper, M. Perper, J. and Fisher, R. Myocardial infarction and sudden death in an urban community. *Bull. N.Y. Acad. Med.*, **49**, 532–543 (1973)

14 Hagstrom, R. M., Federspiel, C. F. and Ho, Y. C. Incidence of myocardial infarction and sudden death from coronary heart disease in Nashville, Tennessee. *Circulation*, **44**, 884–890 (1971)

15 Weisse, A. B., Abiuso, P. D. and Thind, I. S. Acute myocardial infarction in Newark, N. J.: a study of racial incidence. *Arch. Intern. Med.*, **137**, 1402–1405 (1977)

16 Ahmed, S. S., Rozefort, R. and Brancato, R. Incidence of acute myocardial infarction among blacks in an urban community. *J. Med. Soc. N.J.*, **74**, 1058–1060 (1977)

17 Keil, J. E., Saunders, D. E., Lackland, D. T. *et al*. Acute myocardial infarction: period prevalence, case fatality, and comparison of black and white cases in urban and rural areas of South Carolina. *Am. Heart J.*, **109**, 776–784 (1985)

18 Shapiro, S., Weinblatt, E., Frank, C. W. and Sager, R. V. Incidence of coronary heart disease in a population insured for medical care (HIP): myocardial infarction, angina pectoris, and possible myocardial infarction. *Am. J. Public Health*, **59**,(6), 1–44 (1969)

19 Tofler, G. H., Stone, P. H., Muller, J. E. *et al*. MILIS Study Group. Effects of gender and race on prognosis after myocardial infarction: adverse prognosis for women, particularly black women. *J. Am. Coll. Cardiol.*, **9**, 473–482 (1987)

20 Maynard, C., Fisher, L. D., Passamani, E. R. and Pullum, T. Blacks in the Coronary Artery Surgery Study: risk factors and coronary artery disease. *Circulation*, **74**, 64–71 (1986)

21 Oberman, A. and Cutter, G. Issues in the natural history and treatment of coronary heart disease in black populations: surgical treatment. *Am. Heart J.*, **108**, 688 (1984)

22 Henderson, M. J. and Savage, D. D. Prevalence and incidence of ischemic heart disease in United States' black and white populations. *Report of the Secretary's Task Force on Black and Minority Health*, **4**, 347–363 (1986)

23 Gillum, R. F. and Grant, C. T. Coronary heart disease in black populations: II. Risk factors. *Am. Heart J.*, **104**, 852–864 (1982)

24 *Report of the Secretary's Task Force on Black and Minority Health*. Cardiovascular and cerebrovascular disease. **4**, (1), 7, 22, 120, 21 (1986)

25 Kleinbaum, D. G., Kupper, L. L., Cassel, J. C. and Tyroler, H. A. Multivariate analysis of risk of coronary heart disease in Evans County, Georgia. *Arch. Intern. Med.*, **128**, 943–948 (1971)

26 Neaton, J. D., Kuller, L. H., Wentworth, D. and Borhani, N. O. Total and cardiovascular mortality in relation to cigarette smoking, serum cholesterol concentration, and diastolic blood pressure among black and white males followed up for five years. *Am. Heart J.*, **108**, 759–770 (1984)

27 Hypertension Detection and Follow-Up Program Cooperative Group. Effect of stepped care treatment of the incidence of myocardial infarction and angina pectoris. *Circulation*, Suppl., **6**, (2), I–198–206 (1984)

28 Langford, H. G., Oberman, A., Borhani, N. O. *et al*. Black–white comparison of indices of coronary heart disease and myocardial infarction in the stepped-care cohort of the Hypertension Detection and Follow-Up Program. *Am. Heart J.*, **108**, 797 (1984)

29 Haywood, L. J. Coronary heart disease mortality/morbidity and risk in blacks. I. Clinical manifestations and diagnostic criteria: The experience with the Beta Blocker Heart Attack Trial. *Am. Heart J.*, **108**, 787 (1984)

30 Srinivasan, S. R., Frerichs, R. R., Webber, L. S. and Berenson, G. S. Serum lipoprotein profile in children from a biracial community: The Bogalusa Heart Study. *Circulation*, **54**, 309–318 (1976)

31 Morrison, J. A., Khoury, P., Mellies, M. *et al*. Lipid and lipoprotein distributions in black adults: The Cincinnati Lipid Research Clinic's Princeton School Study. *JAMA*, **245**, 939–942 (1981)

32 Tyroler, H. A., Blueck, C. J., Christensen, B. *et al*. Plasma high-density lipoprotein cholesterol comparisons in black and white populations: The Lipid Research Clinics Program Prevalence Study. *Circulation*, Suppl., **62**, (4), IV–99–107 (1980)

33 Heiss, G., Schonfeld, G., Johnson, J. L. *et al*. Black–white differences in plasma levels of apolipoproteins: The Evans County Heart Study. *Am. Heart J.*, **108**, 807 (1984)

34 Glueck, C. J., Gartside, P., Laskarzewski, P. M. *et al*. High-density lipoprotein cholesterol in blacks and whites: potential ramifications for coronary heart disease. *Am. Heart J.*, **108**, 815 (1984)

35 Wilson, P. W. F., Savage, D. D., Castelli, W. P. *et al*. HDL-cholesterol in a sample of black adults: The Framingham Minority Study. *Metabolism*, **32**, 328–332 (1983)

36 Heiss, G., Haskell, W., Mowery, R. *et al*. Plasma high-density lipoprotein cholesterol and socioeconomic status: The Lipid Research Clinics Program Prevalence Study. *Circulation*, Suppl., **62**, (4) IV–108–115 (1980)

37 Gartside, P. S., Khoury, P. and Glueck, C. J. Determinants of high-density lipoprotein cholesterol in blacks and whites: the Second National Health and Nutrition Examination Survey. *Am. Heart J.*, **108**, 641 (1984)

38 *Report of the Secretary's Task Force on Black and Minority Health*. Cardiovascular and cerebrovascular disease, **4**, 22 (1988)

39 Cooper, R., Liu, K., Stamler, J. *et al*. Prevalence of diabetes/hyperglycemia and associated cardiovascular risk factors in blacks and whites: Chicago Heart Association Detection Project in Industry. *Am. Heart J.*, **108**, 827 (1984)

40 *Report of the Secretary's Task Force on Black and Minority Health*. Cardiovascular and cerebrovascular disease, **4**, 120 (1986)

41 *Report of the Secretary's Task Force on Black and Minority Health*. Cardiovascular and cerebrovascular disease, **4**, 21 (1986)

42 Kannel, W. B., Gordon, T., Castelli, W. P. and Margolis, J. R. Electrocardiographic left ventricular hypertrophy and risk of coronary heart disease: The Framingham Study. *Ann. Intern. Med.*, **72**, 813–822 (1970)

43 Riley, C. P., Oberman, A., Hurst, D. C. and Peacock, P. B. Electrocardiographic findings in a biracial, urban population: The Birmingham Stroke Study. *Ala. J. Med. Sci.*, **10**, 160–170 (1973)

44 Beaglehole, R., Tyroler, H. A., Cassel, J. C. *et al*. An epidemiological study of left ventricular hypertrophy in the biracial population of Evans County, Georgia. *J. Chronic Dis.*, **38**, 549–559 (1975)

45 Bartel, A. Heyden, S., Tyroler, H. A. *et al*. Electrocardiographic predictors of coronary heart disease. *Arch. Intern. Med.*, **28**, 929–937 (1971)

46 Connett, J. E. and Stamler, J. Responses of black and white males to the special intervention program of the Multiple Risk Factor Intervention Trial. *Am. Heart J.*, **108**, 839–848 (1984)

47 The Multiple Risk Factor Intervention Trial Research Group (MRFIT). Multiple Risk Factor Intervention Trial. *JAMA*, **248**, 1465–1477 (1982)

48 Tyroler, H. A. Race, education and 5-year mortality in HDFP Stratum I referred-care males. In *Mild Hypertension: Recent Advances*, Gross/Strasser, Raven, pp. 65–176 (1983)

49 Savage, D. D., Drayer, J. I. M., Henry, W. L. *et al*. Echocardiographic assessment of cardiac anatomy and function in hypertensive subjects. *Circulation*, **59**, 623–632 (1979)

50 Dunn, F. G., Chandraratna, P., deCarvalho, J. G. R. *et al*. Pathophysiologic assessment of hypertensive heart disease with echocardiography. *Am. J. Cardiol*, **39**, 789–795 (1977)

51 Dunn, F. G., Oigman, W., Sungaard-Riise, K. *et al*. Racial differences in cardiac adaptation to essential hypertension determined by echocardiograph indexes. *J. Am. Coll. Cardiol.*, **5**, 1348–1351 (1983)

52 Savage, D. D., Henry, W. L., Mitchell, J. R. *et al*. Echocardiographic comparison of black and white hypertensive subjects. *J. Natl. Med. Assoc.*, **71**, 709–712 (1979)

53 Hammond, I. W., Devereux, R. B., Alderman, M. H. *et al*. The prevalence and correlates of echocardiographic left ventricular hypertrophy among employed patients with uncomplicated hypertension. *Am. Coll. Cardiol.*, **7**, 639–650 (1986)

54 Hammond, I. W., Alderman, M. H., Devereux, R. B. *et al*. Contrast in cardiac anatomy and function between black and white patients with hypertension. *J. Natl. Med. Assoc.*, **76**, 247–255 (1984)

55 Devereux, R. B., Pickering, T. G., Harshfield, G. A. *et al*. Left ventricular hypertrophy in patients with hypertension: importance of blood pressure response to regularly recurring stress. *Circulation*, **68**, 470–476 (1983)

56 Frohlich, E. D. and Tarazi, R. C. Is arterial pressure the sole factor responsible for hypertensive cardiac hypertrophy? *Am. J. Cardiol.*, **44**, 959–963 (1979)

57 Meltzer, H. Y. Factors affecting serum creatinine phosphokinase levels in the general population: the role of race, activity and age. *Clin. Chem. Acta.* **33**, 165–172 (1971)

58 Meltzer, H. Y. Black–white differences in serum creatine phosphokinase (CPK) activity. *Clin. Chim. Acta*, **54**, 215–224 (1974)

59 Wong, E. T., Cobb, C., Umehara, M. K. *et al*. Heterogeneity of serum creatine kinase activity among racial and gender groups of the population. *Am. Soc. Clin. Pathol.*, **79** 582–586 (1983)

60 Olerud, J. E., Homer, L. D. and Carroll, H. W. Incidence of acute exertional rhabdomyolysis: serum myoglobin and enzyme levels as indicators of muscle injury. *Arch. Intern. Med.*, **136**, 692–697 (1976)

61 Meade, T. W. Brozovic, M., Chakrabarti, R. *et al.* Ethnic group comparisons of variables associated with ischaemic heart disease. *Br. Heart J.*, **40**, 789–795 (1978)

62 Szczeklik, A., Dischinger, P., Kueppers, F. *et al.* Blood fibrinolytic activity, social class and habitual physical activity – II. A study of black and white men in Southern Georgia. *J. Chronic Dis.*, **33**, 291–299 (1980)

63 Sterling, R. P., Graeber, G. M., Albus, R. A. *et al.* Results of myocardial revascularization in black males. *Am. Heart J.*, **108**, 695 (1984)

64 Watkins, L., Gardner, K., Gott, V. and Gardner, T. J. Coronary heart disease and bypass surgery in urban blacks. *J. Natl. Med. Assoc.*, **75**, 381–383 (1983)

65 Watkins, L. O. Epidemiology of coronary heart disease in black populations: methodologic proposals. *Am. Heart J.*, **108**, 635–640 (1984)

66 Haynes, S. G., Feinleib, M. and Kannel, W. B. The relationship of psychosocial factors to coronary heart disease in the Framingham Study. *Am. J. Epidemiol.*, **3**, 37–58 (1980)

67 James, S. A. Socioeconomic influences on coronary heart disease in black populations. *Am. Heart J.*, **108**, (3: Part 2), 669–672 (1984)

68 James, S. A. Coronary heart disease in black Americans: suggestions for research on psychosocial factors. *Am. Heart J.*, **108** (3: Part 2), 833–838 (1984)

69 Rowland, M. L. and Fulwood, R. Coronary heart disease risk factor trends in blacks between the First and Second National Health and Nutrition Examination Surveys, United States, 1971–1980. *Am. Heart J.*, **108**, (3: Part 2) 771–779 (1984)

Chapter 8

Blood pressure in urban and rural East Africa: the Kenyan Luo Migrant Study

Neil Poulter

Background

In a review of epidemiological approaches to determining the aetiology of essential hypertension, Cassel argued in 1974 that the best advances in our understanding of the aetiology of hypertension may be based on carefully carried out studies of migrant groups [1]. Similar views have been expressed by several other authors [2,3] and yet with the possible exception of the Tokelau Island study, no longitudinal migrant study has been carried out. Several cross-sectional studies of various ethnic groups in different environments have, however, been reported and have demonstrated that when people originating from 'low-blood pressure' populations (i.e. those in which essential hypertension is rare or even non-existent and blood pressures rise little, if at all with age) live in more urbanized or Westernized circumstances, their blood pressures are higher and do rise with age [4,5]. These studies serve to emphasize that some environmental factors are crucial for the rise of blood pressure with age found in all 'Westernized' societies.

A longitudinal study of a migrating low-blood pressure population has several advantages over cross-sectional studies. First, it allows the variable effects of migration on the blood pressures of individuals to be observed. Secondly, a more accurate estimate of the timing of blood pressure changes can be made. Thirdly, it provides a more reliable source of information as to the nature of the environmental agent(s) responsible for the rise in blood pressure seen when populations become acculturated.[*] The great importance of identifying these agents is based on the premise that the factors involved in the aetiology and pathogenesis of essential hypertension are similar to, if not identical to, those responsible for the increase in blood pressure when low-blood pressure populations 'Westernize'. That is, whatever environmental agents associated with acculturation cause the blood pressure profile of a low-blood pressure population to rise with age (see Figure 8.1(a)) are the same as those which shift the blood pressure distribution of such a population to the right (Figure 8.1(b)) and thereby include 'essential hypertensives'.

---

[*]Acculturation: the process or result of adopting factors (artefacts, customs and beliefs) from another civilization.

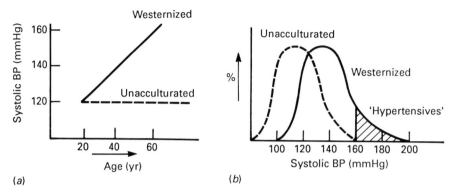

Figure 8.1 Blood pressure patterns of Westernized and unacculturated societies. (*a*) The effect of age on blood pressure. (*b*) Frequency distribution of systolic blood pressure

Pilot studies

In order to carry out a longitudinal study of migrants from a low-blood pressure population, four preliminary objectives have to be achieved:

1. A cooperative low-blood pressure population has to be identified.
2. It has to be determined that from within the identified population, there are sufficient migrants going to an urbanized area over a reasonably short period, such that the study is statistically and logistically viable.
3. It has to be demonstrated that the blood pressure levels of those residents of the urbanized area who originate from the low-blood pressure community are significantly higher than those of the low-blood pressure community and an estimate made as to how quickly the migrants will develop these higher blood pressure levels.
4. A large number of potential migrants from the low-blood pressure population should have blood pressure measurements taken at some stage prior to migration.

Identification of a suitable low-blood pressure population

The second of two rural populations studied in Kenya proved to be a low-blood pressure population. The group studied were randomly selected from a total population of 30 000 living in a geographically defined area on the NE shores of Lake Victoria in Western Kenya. Eighty-five per cent of the adult population of this community are subsistence farmers and over 99% of the population are from the Luo tribe. No cases of essential hypertension were discovered among 861 men and women from this community, and the rise of blood pressure with age was minimal and only significant for systolic pressure. A house-to-house survey of randomly selected homes demonstrated that the migration rate to Nairobi (Kenya's capital) was sufficient to produce meaningful results in a longitudinal study.

The Luo population in Nairobi

No population census of Nairobi is available and so, in order to find Luo residents of Nairobi who originated from the rural study area, contact tracing was utilized. Over a 2-month period, 310 such subjects were traced and studied and their blood pressure levels were shown to be significantly higher than those of their rural counterparts [6]. It also became clear that it was feasible to find migrants from the rural area despite the slum conditions of the overcrowded shanty town areas to which the vast majority of them moved.

Thus we had established that the Luo community in both urban and rural settings were, by virtue of their blood pressure profiles, cooperation (almost 100% response rates), migration rates and ability to be traced, suitable for the proposed longitudinal migrant study.

Premigration data

In order that we would have data on migrants prior to leaving the rural area, the focus of investigation returned to the rural area and by means of letters delivered to every home and 'baraazas' (local village meetings), we recruited a further 1473 male volunteers aged 16–45 years to be studied. Young males were chosen as the optimal subjects since they are most likely to migrate to Nairobi, being in need of work.

The longitudinal study

Design and methods

The basic plan of the study was to try to recruit any person (whether previously studied in the rural area or not) over the age of 15 who, having left the rural study area, arrived in Nairobi with the intention of living there for at least 6 months. These people would be studied as soon as possible after arrival in Nairobi ('0' months), and thereafter at 3, 6, 12, 18 and 24 months after arrival. The cross-sectional data had suggested that 2 years was sufficient to observe changes in blood pressure due to migration and, given the estimated migration rate, that we would need to recruit subjects for 2 years in order to reach a satisfactory study size. Hence the study would last for 4 years and, for logistical reasons, the rural-based controls were to be studied as a cohort in the middle of this period at the same time intervals. These controls were age, sex and geographically matched to the migrants as a group. Unfortunately, an attempted coup in 1982 deferred the ideal onset of the study of controls.

On average it took 1 month for the migrants to be traced and studied after arrival in Nairobi (range 0–60 days), and hence the initial investigation although described '0' months was on average 1 month after migration. The migrants were traced by means of house-to-house surveillance in the rural area whereas the rural field team asked for names and contacts of anyone recently migrating to Nairobi. This information was forwarded to the urban fieldworkers who tried to trace them. Other recent migrants (< 60 days' residence in Nairobi) were found by contact tracing in Nairobi. Once traced, the migrants were studied in their place of residence and each 'study' consisted of completing a questionnaire which was administered by Luo fieldworkers and provided information on the following factors: age; sex; parity and menstrual history; alcohol, smoking and drug ingestion; years of education; housing conditions; duration of previous urban residence; past and present occupation; marital status and location of spouse(s) and family.

In addition, the following measurements were made by one of two observers: ambient temperature; time of day; height; weight; two blood pressure recordings; radial pulse; casual or 'spot' urine samples; 3×12-h or 24-h urine samples; 3×24-h diet histories using a semiquantitative recall method.

Blood pressures were measured using random zero sphygmomanometers [7] by one of the two trained and standardized observers [8] after subjects had been lying for at least 5 min. Diastolic blood pressure was recorded at phase V and the mean of the two readings was used in the analyses. Urine samples were analysed for sodium, potassium and creatinine concentration. A subsample of migrants and controls provided urine samples for analysis of calcium and catecholamine content. In another substudy, 3-day duplicate meal samples were collected from a randomly selected subsample of 20 migrants and controls and these collections were analysed for nitrogen, carbohydrate, fats (saturated and unsaturated), sodium, potassium, calcium, magnesium, fibre, iron and calorific content.

Finally, a further randomly selected subsample of migrants and controls gave a blood sample for analysis of liver functions tests, haemogram, lipid fractions and intracellular electrolytes.

The cohort of controls was studied by the same observers, completed the same questionnaire and underwent the same investigations as the migrants. Since the controls were studied as a cohort, for logistical reasons they had to be studied in one of five 'clinics' in the rural area rather than in their homes. These 'clinics' were in fact classrooms of local schools converted for the purposes of the study.

Results

Pilot studies

Electrolytes and blood pressure
Three populations were investigated during the pilot studies: the rural and urban Luo, and a second rural population (which was found to be unsuitable for the longitudinal study) consisting of Kamba tribespeople. When urinary electrolyte excretion concentrations and ratios (reflecting dietary intakes) of these three populations were compared with the slopes of regression of blood pressures on age, there appeared to be a dose-response relationship between electrolyte excretion and blood pressure (see Table 8.1) [9]. In keeping with other studies of low-blood pressure populations [10,11], the rural Luo population were found to have low salt intakes, but a more surprising finding was that within the rural Luo population significant correlations between blood pressure and urinary electrolytes were found despite collecting only casual urine samples (see Table 8.2) [12]. These findings stimulated two substudies designed to try to explain why we should find correlations between blood pressure and urinary electrolytes within a population (especially using only casual urine samples) when so many other studies had failed to do so. These studies demonstrated a high correlation between electrolyte data from spot urine samples and 7-day samples (e.g. for Na^+/K^+: $r = 0.67:P< 0.01$)

Table 8.1 Slopes of blood pressure regression with age and mean urinary electrolytes in three Kenyan communities

	Rural Luo (n = 861)	Rural Kamba (n = 261)	Urban Luo (n = 310)
Slope of DBP (mmHg/yr)	0.14	0.30	0.57[**]
Na$^+$ (mmol/l)	82.4	89.6	108.6[*]
Na$^+$/K$^+$	1.7	2.5	4.2[***]

Rural Luo vs. rural Kamba vs. urban Luo: [*]$P < 0.05$: [**]$P < 0.01$: [***]$P < 0.001$.

Table 8.2 Blood pressure and urinary electrolytes; correlations within the rural Luo male population (n = 1639)

	Systolic BP (r)	Diastolic BP (r)
Na$^+$/K$^+$	0.05[*]	0.09[**]
Log K$^+$/creatinine	− 0.06[***]	− 0.10[***]

[*]$P < 0.05$: [**]$P < 0.01$: [***]$P < 0.001$.

and a very limited within-individual variation of sodium excretion [12], contrasting greatly with the findings in a Westernized population [13]. We concluded that the relatively low levels of salt intake of this population may be on the steep part of a sodium/blood pressure dose-response curve, thereby making the finding of within-population correlations more likely than for higher sodium intakes, which may be above a threshold level. Furthermore, it may be that the marked lack of variability in the diets enabled these correlations to be 'exposed' even when collecting only casual urine samples.

Socioeconomic factors and blood pressure
Within the rural Luo population, significant associations were demonstrated between years of education and blood pressure, and different occupational groups and blood pressure. However, ANOVA revealed that these apparent associations were explained largely by the higher body weights and urinary electrolyte ratio (Na/K) of those with more education and non-traditional lifestyles (occupations other than subsistence farming) [12].

Longitudinal study

Migrants were traced and recruited into the study at a satisfactory rate, except for the 6 months following the civil unrest of mid-1982. Because it became apparent that important and significant blood pressure differences occurred within the first 6 months of urban residence, the recruitment of migrants was extended until February 1985, which permitted at least 6 months of follow-up on all recruits before the end of the study. In all, 381 migrants were traced, of which 216 were followed up for at least 6 months, but to date, analyses are only available on some of the variables (blood pressure, body weight, pulse rates, urinary electrolytes, age and sex), from some of the migrants and controls.

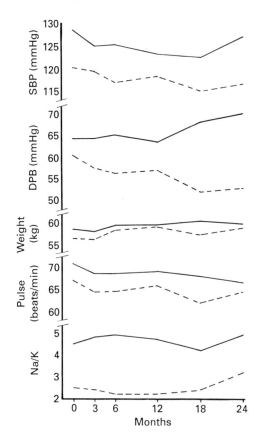

Figure 8.2 Age-adjusted mean variables in rural control (– – –) and urban migrant (———) men. SBP, systolic blood pressure; DBP, diastolic blood pressure

Figure 8.2 shows the mean values of blood pressures, pulse rate, body weight and overnight urinary electrolytes on male migrants and controls over a 2-year period. Migrants have significantly higher blood pressures throughout the study. Control systolic and diastolic blood pressures fall, while migrant diastolic blood pressures rise, and migrant systolic blood pressures remain at a significantly higher level than those of controls (they only rise between 3 and 6 months, and 18 and 24 months).

Migrants have significantly higher urinary Na/K ratios at all stages, and significantly higher body weights at 0 and 3 months. Migrant pulse rates are significantly higher throughout except at 12 and 24 months. ANOVA shows that body weight, pulse rate and Na/K ratio are related to the blood pressure differences shown, although this is not always a statistically significant contribution.

It is of interest to note that at '0' months the blood pressures of the migrants were already significantly higher than those of the controls. One possible explanation of this finding is selective migration (i.e. within the rural area would-be migrants have higher blood pressures than non-migrants). However, a large number of migrants had been studied prior to leaving the rural area, and examination of the premigration data revealed that the migrants were, from a blood pressure viewpoint at least, *not* different from the community from which they migrated. This data, supported by correlations of '0' month blood pressures with duration of urban residence prior to the '0' month study [14], inclined us towards the belief that the '0' month blood pressure differences were real and induced by migration to Nairobi.

Although not consistently significant for males and females at every stage, further within-population correlations between blood pressure and urinary electrolytes were found in migrants and controls (e.g. see Table 8.3) [12].

Table 8.3 Blood pressure and urinary electrolytes; correlations in the Luo migrant study (6-month data)

	Males (n = 140)	Females (n = 94)
Systolic BP	0.24[***]	0.28[***]
Diastolic BP	0.35[***]	0.11

[***]$P < 0.001$.

The early differences between the body weights of migrants and controls gave rise to concern that there had been a systematic measurement bias. However, the premigration data and analysis of some of the dietary data suggest that this increase is real, occurs subsequent to migration and may be due to fluid retention. We have hypothesized that this weight gain may be interrelated with increased pulse rates and dietary sodium intakes in producing the increases in blood pressure shown [15].

Summary

While several important aspects of the study such as diet histories and the effect on blood pressure of reverse (urban–rural) migration remain to be analysed, so far the data has shown:

1. An apparent dose–response relationship between blood pressure and urinary electrolytes in three Kenyan populations [9].
2. Several examples of within-population correlations between urinary electrolytes and blood pressures [12].
3. A further example of a low-blood pressure population having a low mean salt intake [12].
4. The unique observation that blood pressures rise rapidly after migration from an unacculturated low-blood pressure population to a Westernized city [13].
5. That changes in blood pressure consequent upon migration are associated at least in part to changes in dietary electrolyte intake, body weight and pulse rate [13].

Assuming the basic premise that the causes of blood pressure changes upon migration are those responsible for the pathogenesis of essential hypertension, then this study has provided the data which forms the basis of a new hypothesis for the evolution of essential hypertension [15], and is a unique model upon which it is possible to base primary intervention studies. Such studies, preferably carried out in countries where hypertension is increasing rapidly, may in turn bring us as close as we are ever likely to get towards understanding the aetiology and pathogenesis of essential hypertension.

Acknowledgements

The author gratefully acknowledges the support of the Wellcome Trust and the Kenya Medical Research Institute and all the collaborators and fieldworkers of the Wellcome Trust Kenyan/St Mary's Hospital research programme.

References

1 Cassel, J. Hypertension and cardiovascular disease in migrants; a potential source of clues? *Int. J Epidemiol.*, **3**, 204–205 (1974)

2 Sanderson, J. E. In *Cardiology* (eds P. Sleight and J. V. Jones), William Heinemann Medical Books, London, pp. 397–402 (1983)

3 Vaughan, J. P. A review of cardiovascular diseases in developing countries. *Ann. Trop. Med. Parasitol.*, **72**, 101–109 (1978)

4 Sever, P. S., Gordon, D., Peart, W. S. and Beighton, P. Blood pressure and its correlates in urban and tribal Africa. *Lancet*, **ii**, 60–64 (1980)

5 Cruz-Coke, R., Etcheverry, R. and Nagel, R. Influence of migration on blood pressure of Easter Islanders. *Lancet*, **i**, 697–699 (1964)

6 Poulter, N., Khaw, K. T., Hopwood, B. E. C. *et al.* Blood pressure and its correlates in an African tribe in urban and rural environments. *J. Epidemiol. Community Health*, **38**, 181–186 (1984)

7 Wright, B. M. and Dore, F. A random-zero sphygomomanometer. *Lancet*, **i**, 337–338 (1970)

8 Rose, G. Standardisation of observers in blood pressure measurement. *Lancet*, **i**, 673–674 (1965)

9 Poulter, N. R., Khaw, K. T., Mugambi, M. *et al.* Blood pressure patterns in relation to age, weight and urinary electrolytes in three Kenyan countries. *Trans. R. Soc. Trop. Med. Hyg.*, **79**, 389–392 (1985)

10 Sinnett, P. F. and Whyte, H. M. Epidemiological studies in a total highland population – Tukisenka, New Guinea: cardiovascular disease and relevant clinical electrocardiographic, radiologic and biochemical findings. *J. Chronic Dis.*, **26**, 265–290 (1975)

11 Oliver, W. J., Cohen, E. L. and Neel, J. V. Blood pressure, sodium intake and sodium related hormnes in the Yanamano Indians, a 'no-salt' culture. *Circulation*, **52**, 146–151 (1975)

12 Poulter, N. Khaw, K. T., Hopwood, B. E. C. *et al.* Blood pressure and associated factors in a rural Kenyan community. *Hypertension*, **6**, 810–813 (1984)

13 Liu, K., Cooper, R., McKeever, J. *et al.* Assessment of the association between habitual salt intake and high blood pressure methodological problems. *Am. J. Epidemiol.*, **110**, 219–226 (1979)

14 Poulter, N. R., Khaw, K. T., Hopwood, B. E. *et al.* Determinants of blood pressure changes due to urbanisation: a longitudinal study. *J. Hypertension*, **3**, S375–S377 (1985)

15 Sever, P. S. and Poulter, N. R. An hypothesis for the pathogenesis of essential hypertension based on a new human model of migration induced blood pressure elevation. In *Proceedings of the International Symposium on the Early Pathogenesis of Primary Hypertension*, Elsevier, Amsterdam (1987)

Sociology

Chapter 9

Sociology of race and health

Maggie Pearson

The majority of chapters in this book are based on data from health service (usually medical) sources on particular diseases. Doctors' preconceptions and assumptions inevitably play an important part in the diagnostic process, but it is not just in the one-to-one diagnostic enounter that preconceptions affect medical interpretation. Epidemiological analysis is similarly underpinned by concepts in which some of the patients' personal and social circumstances are thought to be more salient than others.

Contemporary clinical practice takes an individualistic approach to health and disease. When significant social differences in health and disease are identified, the emphasis is on the individual's lifestyle rather than on associated social and material conditions. In part, this emphasis may be pragmatic, focusing on issues over which the individual is felt to have some control, and power to change, rather than on larger social structures. An individualistic stance is, however, a consciously 'apolitical' one. Many doctors feel that the political realm of social inequalities in health is forbidden territory. In short, medicine feels able to intervene and exhort change in an individual's life, but not to change the wider social sphere which constrains access to health resources.

This approach has major implications in a society where black or Asian people may be seen by some as inferior and deviant from the white 'norm' [1]. Historically underpinned by spurious 'scientific' theories of biological 'race' [2], medical perspectives on black people's health have emphasized notions of alienness and cultural difference. Although a complex and controversial sociological concept, 'ethnicity' is increasingly invoked in medicine as an 'independent' variable, on the basis of which some epidemiological differences may be explained.

This emphasis has led to some misleading conclusions. A simplistic 'ethnic' dimension implies that the groups defined by 'culture' or 'origins' are socially homogeneous. The impact of other factors such as class and wealth are often not considered when crude 'ethnic' comparisons are made. It is not that cultural norms and values are unimportant, but rather than they are only part of the story of black people's experience. The social and political experience of racial minorities in Britain is categorically excluded. In not addressing the impact of racism on the health of ethnic minorities in a white society, the 'ethnic differences' perspective fails to provide adequate analysis. Moreover, in seeing the relationship between the 'culturally distinct' minorities and white society exclusively in terms of culture, the outcome has been to focus on 'their' culture as alien, deviant, deficient and resistant to change [3].

This chapter attempts to redress the balance of emphasis on 'ethnicity' and black people's culture. First, the social and material conditions of black people and other ethnic minorities* in Britain are described, in the light of which racial inequalities in the risk of illness can be assessed. Secondly, the complex process of becoming ill and seeking help is considered as a person's beliefs, experience and expectations play a major role. Because of the dangers of over-generalizing into gross stereotypes of 'cultural difference' [1,3], the second section discusses the relationship between social circumstances and responses to illness. The last section considers the appropriateness of the NHS for a multiracial population.

Racial inequalities in the risk of becoming ill

For various ethical, political and practical reasons, data on 'race' or ethnic group are not systematically gathered in Britain. While the health of British people born elsewhere can be ascertained from government data which record occupation *and* place of birth, such data cannot be used to identify the health experience of British-born people of black and Asian origin. Studies which identify the relative social and material position of ethnic minorities have an important role to play in suggesting explanations for racial inequalities and 'ethnic' differences in disease. However, the assumption that factors such as occupational class have a homogeneous influence on health may be wrong, as there are frequently gender and other differences. Surrogate data on black people's social circumstances have to be used as a basis for inference about health and disease and are discussed here.

Racial inequalities in social and material conditions

There is ample evidence that racial inequalities persist in Britain in many respects from education to employment, housing and health status. The combined impact of lower job status, unemployment, poor and overcrowded living conditions, with fewer basic amenities are important when assessing racial inequalities or 'ethnic differences' in health and disease. This applies to road traffic accidents in inner-city areas as well as to other conditions such as rickets, respiratory and mental illness and heart disease.

The most comprehensive source of recent data on the relative social situation of black and white people in Britain is the third survey undertaken by the Policy Studies Institute (PSI) in 1982 into 'the circumstances of the British black population'[†], based on interviews with 7264 adults [4]. Brown's results are drawn

* Throughout this paper, the terms 'black' and 'ethnic minorities' are used. Sometimes they are interchangeable and sometimes they are not. *None* of these terms implies that the people to whom they refer are not British. The word 'ethnic' is used intentionally, but not approvingly, for it is precisely within the culturalist framework that data on black people's health have largely been researched and collected. 'Black' refers in the political sense to those whose skin colour is not white, and whose common experience of racism is not differentiated by culture, language or tradition. 'Ethnic minorities' refers to people who may not see themselves as black, but nevertheless experience discrimination and inequality on account of their skin colour, origins, way of life, language or religion.

† The PSI survey defined black people as 'all vulnerable to the prejudice and discrimination based on skin colour' (p.4).

upon heavily in this section. Where the PSI report data are quoted, their definitions of black, 'Asian' and 'West Indian' are employed. *

Occupational status

Occupational class differences in mortality and morbidity were discussed in the Black Report on Inequalities in Health [5], and subsequent government social surveys [6] and mortality reports [7]. Men and single women are classed on the basis of their own occupation (or educational qualifications, training or last job if unemployed or retired); married or widowed women and dependent children are classed according to the occupation of the head of their household.

Racial discrimination in employment is acknowledged to be such a problem that, in April 1984, Parliament approved a Code of Practice for its elimination [8]. The need for such a code is evident not only from individual cases of discrimination in recruitment and promotion, but also from racial inequalities in occupational status not explained by educational disadvantage and differential qualifications. White people are consistently found in jobs of higher status and earnings than black people with the same qualifications [10].

Among respondents in the PSI survey who were in formal employment, 73% of 'Asian' men and 83% of the 'West Indians' but only 58% of white men were in manual occupations [4]. Moreover, within the manual occupations, 'more of the blacks are doing unskilled and semi-skilled manual work than the whites . . . ' ([4], p.157). Seventy per cent of men of Bangladeshi origin were in semiskilled and unskilled manual posts, compared with 16% of white men. Within each socioeconomic category fewer black people were in supervisory posts. Less than 1% of white employees had an immediate superior who was black, compared with 5% of people of West Indian origin, and 12% of people of Asian origin. Nineteen per cent of white people in the survey were employers, managers or in professional posts, compared with only 13% of people of Asian origin and 5% of people of West Indian origin [4].

Inequalities in occupational status are less sharply pronounced among women, partly because fewer are in professional and managerial positions, and manual occupations officially classed as skilled. The proportion of women in professional/managerial positions was 7% among white women, 6% among 'Asian' women, and only 1% among 'West Indian' women.

Income

Inevitably, racial inequalities in occupation are reflected in inequalities in earnings: the median weekly earnings for white men in the PSI survey was £129, compared with £109.20 for 'West Indian' men, and £110.70 for 'Asian' men. The economic differential was lower (and reversed) among women, whose earnings were generally lower than men's. White women's median weekly earnings were £77.50 compared with £81.20 for 'West Indian' women and £73.00 for 'Asian' women [4]. These differentials are notable when one considers that shift work was consistently more common for black employees than for whites.

* The terms 'Asian' and 'West Indian' were used in the PSI report to refer to people with family origins (as defined by the respondents) in the Indian subcontinent and the West Indies respectively. A separate 'African Asian' group was defined in the PSI report.

Unemployment

The adverse impact of unemployment on health has been described in many studies, whether in mortality, mental health problems such as suicide and parasuicide or physical ill-health [11,12]. Black people are vulnerable to unemployment, because of discrimination when seeking work and because they are highly represented in the ailing sectors of the economy which have contracted sharply in the last decade, i.e. 'old' textile, vehicle and heavy manufacturing industries, and the public services.

Racial discrimination in employment opportunities was evident in the government's 1981 Labour Force Survey, in which unemployment was higher among black people than among whites with the same qualifications [10]. Unemployment had risen faster among the ethnic minorities since the mid-1970s than among whites. Where entire plants have not had to close, black people's jobs may be the first to be shed because they are often unskilled. In the PSI survey in 1982, 13% of white men and 10% of white women were unemployed, compared with 25% of 'West Indian' men and 16% of 'West Indian' women, and 20% of 'Asian' men and women [4].

Housing

Most ethnic minorities in Britain live in inner cities, where housing is often poor (Census, 1981). This coupled with the high proportion unemployed or in low paid jobs restricts access to decent housing and mobility in the housing market. There is evidence of discrimination in the allocation of housing. Building societies' mortgage allocation practices have been found to discriminate indirectly against black people [13]. A recent formal investigation by the Commission for Racial Equality found that Hackney Council has discriminated in the standard of housing allocated to black people [14]. Research suggests similar discrimination in local authority housing in Liverpool [5]. Because of the fragmented nature of the privately rented property market, it is more difficult to pinpoint discrimination but many small landlords let property by word of mouth; this often militates against some ethnic minority groups.

Thus the outcome of allocation procedures, whether formal or informal, is that white people live in better housing. Black people are consistently found in older property and in areas of high housing density and less often in detached or semidetached housing. In council property, black people are more likely to live in flats than houses or maisonettes, and in the private sector, black tenants are more likely to be sharing basic amenities, and to be in crowded accommodation [4]. 'Bangladeshi' people were most likely to be living in poor and overcrowded accommodation.

Besides the actual standard of housing, there are racial inequalities in living space. In the PSI survey, white households had, on the whole, twice as much household space per person than 'Asian' households, and over one and a half times as much space as 'West Indian' households. In each sector there were fewer white people per room. Seventeen per cent of 'West Indian' households and 44% of 'Asian' households in inner cities had more than one person per room, compared with only 1% of the white population. This reflects the older age structure of white inner city populations, with a high proportion of lone pensioners, and also the differential mobility of white families as they move away from the inner cities.

Thirty-seven per cent of white households in inner cities comprised only one person, compared with 7% of 'Asian' households and 13% of 'West Indian' households [4].

Household structure

Household size and structure also have a major impact. Isolation as well as overcrowding generate stresses which may predispose to physical and mental ill-health. White households were smaller on average (2.6 people) than 'Asian' (4.6 people) and 'West Indian' households (3.4 people). These averages mask important differences in structure. There were few single-adult 'Asian' households, whereas among white people there were pensioner-households, and among 'West Indians', single parents. Ninety per cent of white and 'West Indian' households contain a single family unit, compared with 80% of 'Asian' households.

Resources and responsibility may be unequally distributed within a household. Child care almost invariably falls to women, who may be isolated from other adult company, although living in a densely populated area. Nurseries are in short supply in inner cities, and single parents who go out to work are often given priority. Other parents, either not working or not alone, may therefore be virtual prisoners of their domestic environment, trying to cope with small children in an overcrowded flat, worrying about financial problems, unable to go out because of poverty or fearing racial abuse. 'West Indian' lone parents were more likely to be living with their children than were white lone parents, who may live with their parents or another adult. While there may be less chance of conflict between children and partner when single parents live alone, isolation and stress can be severe. There is a significant association between social isolation and depression. In South London, clinical depression was found in 16% of housebound women with one or more dependants under the age of 5 [16]. Other studies have shown how rare it is for women with babies and young children to go out without their children, with little respite from the stresses and strains of being marooned in a high-rise flat [17].

Racism as a source of stress

The stress from direct racist abuse, and indirect structural discrimination also has an impact on health. The number of cases of racial discrimination upheld by industrial tribunals, and identified by the Commission for Racial Equality are all testimony of harassment, whether veiled or direct, which black people may face. More obvious instances are physical attacks and threats, which are increasingly documented. Less directly, threatening taunts prey on mental well-being. A recent survey of black people in Bristol quoted many black respondents' concerns about the safety of their families [18].

Becoming ill and seeking help: responses to illness

This section considers the impact of social circumstances, of which racism and cultural differences are integral elements, on people's responses to illness.

Undocumented or unmeasurable morbidity

The epidemiological data in this book are the product of medical interpretations of people's experiences of health and illness. They cannot tell the whole story. Clinical studies require contact with the health service, but illness presenting to doctors may only be the tip of an iceberg. Contact with the NHS is only a part of the complex process of becoming ill, seeking help and becoming a patient, during the course of which the person becoming patient will develop their own beliefs and fears about what is wrong and may seek advice from several sources.

Illness, the individual's subjective experience, is not the same as disease, as defined by doctors. Some people with underlying clinical pathology may be unaware of their disease, while others, despite feeling unwell, may not go to their doctor. Some who are aware of their deteriorating health may never seek help at all. Several studies have shown that the episodes of illness reported to doctors are only a small proportion of the total illness experienced in a population [19,20]. In the 1983 General Household Survey, general practitioners were consulted in less than 20% of episodes of 'acute sickness' which restricted 'normal' activities [7]. Other studies have shown that, on average, 37 symptom-episodes were experienced per patient for each consultation initiated. For some symptoms, such as disturbance of gastric function, changes in energy and headache, which might herald serious disease, over 100 symptom-episodes were experienced for each consultation [21]. Feeling unwell clearly does not necessarily result in a visit to the doctor.

Recognizing illness

There are several components of responses to feeling unwell in which non-medical factors have a major influence. First, there is a recognition that 'something is wrong', followed by a period during which the seriousness of the symptoms is evaluated. Other people may be important at this initial stage. Friends, workmates or relatives may recognize illness before the patient, particularly if it is denied for long because of fear of the consequences. The significance attached by an individual to particular symptoms depends on many factors. These include his/her usual 'baseline' state of well-being; the perceived seriousness of the symptoms; the extent to which the discomfort disrupts what he/she wants (or needs) to do. The prevailing culture will clearly influence this response.

The consultation

There is strong evidence that patients from social, and cultural, circumstances similar to that of doctors consult their general practitioner more often and earlier per symptom-episode than working class patients and have more positive, active input into the consultation, in which professional, middle class values are inevitably paramount [7,22]. Middle class patients participate more, communicate more items of information, and ask more questions during a consultation than do working class patients [23]. Clearly the current social class distribution of most people of black and 'Asian' origin in Britain limits this exchange. In a society in which racism is deeply ingrained, ethnic minorities may have particularly bad experiences and low expectations of doctors and the NHS.

'Learning' to be a patient

Reactions of general practitioners' receptionists and other health service staff to what they perceive to be inappropriate use of services may adversely influence the experience of consultation. People may become aware that they are labelled as 'awkward' if they challenge the submissive culture of being a patient. Black and ethnic minority patients are often so labelled if they do not speak English, or want to do things differently from the accepted 'norm' (see below).

There are many unwritten rules in the health service which the patient has to grasp. This is clearly easier if one is from the same culture as those who design and staff the service.

It is often assumed by the providers that the alien culture is inferior and somehow pathogenic. Assumptions in which one culture imprisons another can only produce barriers to good health care.

The NHS – meeting whose needs?

Even the most gentle suggestion that racism and discrimination are a problem in the NHS often prompts surprise, indignation and disbelief. The employment of ethnic minority staff and that people are treated the same are often proudly quoted to demonstrate the absence of racism in the NHS, in employment or in service delivery. Evidence suggests that racial inequality is as deeply embedded in the health service as it is in education, employment and housing [4]. Several individual cases brought against health authorities for overt racial discrimination have been won in industrial tribunals; there is other, more 'silent' evidence. Often at the heart of the matter is the medical profession: it comes as little surprise that St George's Hospital Medical School was recently found guilty of discriminating against women and ethnic minorities in its admission policy, based on a computer program that correlated highly with what the School has since admitted was entrenched bias and which it is now committed to eliminate. Other medical schools no doubt are yet to be found out [24].

While a walk around many hospitals would reveal a reasonable number of ethnic minority staff, a disproportionate number are in inferior positions. The majority are in low paid, ancillary and manual jobs, working night shifts and at weekends, in the less qualified echelons of nursing or in 'twilight' areas such as geriatrics and psychiatry in the less prestigious non-teaching hospitals [9,25,26]. The public image of black staff in the health service is therefore second class. As service users receiving care, black people and ethnic minorities are also at a disadvantage. The lack of variety of meals in hospital or appropriate food or nutritional advice and the language barrier, are daily problems, while it has taken many years of pressure to develop services such as routine screening for the genetic diseases to which they are particularly at risk.

What constitutes racial discrimination?

Few NHS staff are aware of their legal responsibilities as employers, managers and direct service providers. It is not surprising that many find it difficult to understand the charges of racism levelled at the service, when they feel they are doing their best to treat everyone similarly and never to react with hostility. For professionals whose training and ethics are grounded in the fundamental principle that all patients should be treated equally, no matter who they are, it goes against the grain to take special note of race, skin colour or ethnic background when recruiting staff or providing care. This section therefore briefly considers how discrimination as defined in the Race Relations Act inevitably occurs by 'carrying on as usual' in the NHS unless positive steps are taken.

The Race Relations Act 1976 (a revision of the first Act in 1965) defined as unlawful, discrimination against or segregation of someone on 'grounds of colour, nationality (including citizenship), or ethnic or national origins' (Section 3.1). The Act defines three offences (the relevant section of the Act is given in parentheses):

Direct discrimination in which, on racial grounds, a person treats someone less favourably than others would be treated (Sections 1 and 3). Such discrimination may take the form of segregation, over hostility or abuse, or, in personnel matters, failure to appoint someone on the grounds of their colour, race or nationality or ethnic or national origin.

Indirect (or *institutional*) discrimination, when a requirement or condition is applied equally to all people, but the proportions of people in a particular racial group who can comply with the requirement is unusually small; *and* the requirement/condition is not justifiable *irrespective* of whom it is applied to; *and* is to the detriment of the person who cannot comply with it (Sections 1 and 3). This has been cited in successful cases where female nurses required, by their religion, to wear trousers are required to wear uniform skirts.

Victimisation, when a person is harassed, dismissed or moved to a different workplace solely for bringing actions under the Race Relations Act in good faith (Section 2).

Potential employment discrimination is set out clearly in the Act, and a more detailed Code of Practice for its elimination and promotion of equality of opportunity has since been published [8].

Discrimination in the delivery of care and services is less clearly defined although *positive* special provision 'to meet the special needs of . . . that group in regard to their education, training or welfare or any ancillary benefits . . . ' (Section 35) is allowed, to prevent indirect, institutional discrimination by services which do not address ethnic minorities' needs. This legal provision has permitted some local authorities to employ 'ethnic minority' social workers and schools liaison officers if needs were not being met by the established services. In June 1985, the London Hospital similarly advertised for ' . . . a personal counsellor for Bangladeshi mothers (mainly from Sylhet) of handicapped children . . . '*

---

* Advertisement in *The Guardian*, June 1985.

Discrimination in the NHS

Most complaints of discrimination practices brought against the NHS have been about employment and personnel, rather than in the delivery of services. This may reflect the more clear-cut nature of employment procedures, which have specific outcomes of 'success' or 'failure'. The delivery of care involves many more complex and ill-defined processes, so that 'less favourable treatment' is more difficult to establish on 'hard' performance indicators and outcome measures. Differential waiting lists, times and use of services may highlight some problems. People may be reluctant or unable to complain about the quality of service when they feel ill or vulnerable, lest their chances be further jeopardized by challenging a professional decision. Despite the practical problems of its assessment, quality of care is the subject of debate and major policy changes which highlight the importance of consumer (or 'customer') choice and views in the NHS. If grasped positively, this opportunity would facilitate greater consideration of the ethnic minorities' views and perspectives.

Indirect (or *institutional*) discrimination may not be so easily identified. Any policy or practice based on assumptions which exclude certain minorities may result in less favourable treatment. A closer look behind the veneer of the NHS reveals a web of policies, procedures, and individual attitudes which result in 'less favourable treatment' for ethnic minorities.

The NHS: equality for whom?

The essential ethos of the NHS, that equality of care will be ensured if the same service is provided everywhere, does not ensure equal access to services for those who need them. Difference and diversity are not taken into account, so that 'carrying on as usual' may result in less favourable treatment and/or unequal access. Policies and procedures which assume that a patient or client can speak English, or that they eat a carnivorous diet, or which fail to provide genetic screening services for diseases more common in ethnic minorities all contravene the spirit, if not the *letter* of the law of racial equality.

The oft-encountered disbelief that racism is a problem in the NHS is a symptom of 'Colour-blindness' in which the everyday experiences of black patients and staff are invisible. This problem of 'Colour-blindness' is further compounded by the lowly position of black and other migrant workers within the NHS. The long history of this in the NHS has tended to reinforce attitudes and images of black people as second class. The obviously 'different' minority experiences or needs may be interpreted as awkwardness, intransigence or ignorance [3,26].

Failure to attend for appointments, to adhere to professional advice, or to conform to 'normal' hospital procedures such as accepting male doctors may be misinterpreted if the difficulties are not considered. Black people may have poor access to cars and telephones, which are importance for keeping or rearranging appointments [4,18], especially for people in casual work who are suddenly required to work a different shift. It may be difficult to follow dietary advice if diet sheets only relate to 'normal' English foods, are written only in English, and involve extra expense from an already overstretched family budget.

The image created by the official face of the NHS is that valued professional care is delivered *by* white people *for* white people. The perspectives of women and 'working class' people are often also excluded.

Many official posters and leaflets still have illustrations only of white people, or are written only in English. On arrival at any registration point, whether in a health centre, general practitioner's surgery or a hospital, the reception staff are highly likely to be white. Besides feeling isolated and a problem because of being *black*, additional stresses are created if interpreters have to be called, a young child is expected to interpret to the gynaecologist, a name causes inordinate problems, or being a single parent is seen as deviant.

For inpatients, the feeling of isolation can deepen for example by being the only black patient in the ward, or by the nurse not appreciating that serving egg with the bacon-server to a strict Muslim will cause religious offence. Comments about 'not understanding *their* culture' are often only thinly veiled. The dietician may know nothing about Rastafarian or vegan diets, or the calorific value of sweet potatoes or other foods commonly eaten as part of Caribbean diets.

If hospital staff feel hostility towards black people, and have personal views about 'them always causing problems', it will be all the more difficult for black patients to negotiate concessions to the established routine, which white patients may acquire more successfully. Complaints or opinions may be dismissed as 'awkwardness', which can pose acute risks if the patient does not speak English confidently in the hurried and forbidding hospital atmosphere. It may be difficult for relatives to visit at officially approved times, because of problems with transport or child care. Anxieties expressed by a black person about the results of a sickle cell screening test may be dismissed as 'nothing to worry about' by white health service staff who cannot imagine what it feels like to be at risk of a genetically inherited blood disorder.

Low uptake of services

There is evidence of low uptake of, and poor satisfaction with, services by ethnic minorities, particularly in secondary care [18]. This may reflect racial differentials in general practitioners' referral patterns, although it is difficult to establish the scale of inequalities in access to services without systematic data on race and 'ethnic' group. Local studies of uptake of maternity care in Leicester and Bradford have revealed large differences between 'Asian' and 'non-Asian' women in their uptake of maternity services, which are associated with differences in perinatal mortality rates [27,28]. Other studies have identified low and later uptake of maternity services by Afro-Caribbean women and travellers [29,30].

While antenatal services may have only a partial role in reducing perinatal mortality, surveillance of mothers at risk is agreed to be desirable. In Leicester, only 64% of 'Asian' mothers had over 5 months' antenatal care, compared with 80% of 'non-Asian' mothers. There was a similar difference in Bradford, where 60% of mothers of Asian origin had less than 4 months' registered antenatal care, compared with 20% of 'non-Asian' mothers. Access to good quality general practitioners may be an important factor as Asian mothers in Leicester were more likely to be under a general practitioner without approved obstetric experience.

These studies were not standardized for occupational class, but suggest that any measures taken to improve service uptake should consider the social circumstances of ethnic minority women, their access to transport (and its cost) and child care. Mothers may never have been told the purpose of antenatal surveillance. Community-based antenatal and child health clinics, where a pregnant mother and her children can be seen together, may reduce some of the physical and financial problems of access. Joint clinics of this nature were estabished in Dewsbury, West Yorkshire, partly in response to an acute shortage of health service interpreters [31].

Racial equality: an item for the mainstream agenda

Racism is subtly institutionalized in services which do not recognize minority perspectives or racism as major issues on the general agenda of mainstream services. Ethnic minorities are often described as having 'special needs', which can be met by minor adaptations or additions to existing services. But this marginalizes black people and defines their experience as 'abnormal', outside any 'normal' British experience. It reinforces ideas that change in policy and practice are a special concession, rather than a late and justified response to provide an appropriate service to the multiracial population.

Various projects in the voluntary and statutory sectors have been established, partially filling the gap between the homogeneous statutory services and the ethnic minority communities whom they exclude. They have rarely been taken on in the mainstream NHS services [32,33]. In short, many of these projects let the NHS off the hook by enabling it to 'carry on as usual'. There is also a very real danger that health service initiatives set up on 'soft' money outside the mainstream budget become isolated and are seen by health service staff and by the black communities as a second-rate 'soft' option, neither part of the general services, nor permanent, and vulnerable to changes in temporary or 'special' funding. Community-based projects which challenge the nature of the NHS find it difficult to secure even temporary funding unless they are seen to be encouraging use of the statutory services. This can be a major dilemma if the services are alienating and hostile [34].

A comprehensive approach to overcome institutionalized racism is essential to avoid ineffective piecemeal approaches. Existing services, policies and training need regular review so that they take account of race and racism and no longer exclude black peoples' experience and perspectives. Schemes like this now operate in some health authorities (e.g. Brent in NW London). The direct involvement of black people in the review and development process is crucial if colour-blind, institutionally racist services are to be eliminated. Many practical steps can be taken on these issues which need imaginative and flexible thinking more than extra funding. The elimination of discrimination in employment, with a multiracial staff at all levels, would have a positive effect on services to ethnic minority patients. Not only would the service be more welcoming and considerate to its minority users, but as white staff become more accustomed to seeing black people as their equals and superiors, so attitudes and sensitivity to black and minority patients and clients would inevitably improve.

References

1 Lawrence, E. White sociology, black pathology. *Multiracial Education*, **9**, 3–17 (1982)
2 Husband, C. (ed.) 'Race' the continuity of a concept. In *Race in Britain: Continuity and Change*, Hutchinson, London (1982)
3 Pearson, M. The politics of ethnic minority health studies. In *Health, Race and Ethnicity* (eds T. Rathwell and D. Phillips), Croom Helm, Beckenham (1986)
4 Brown, C. *Black and White Britain. The Third PSI Survey*, Heinemann, London (1984)
5 Townsend, P. and Davidson, N. *Inequalities in Health*, Penguin, Harmondsworth (1982)
6 Office of Population Censuses and Surveys. *General Household Survey 1983*, HMSO, London (1985)
7 Office of Population Censuses and Surveys. *Decennial Occupational Mortality Supplement*, HMSO, London (1986)
8 CRE. *Code of Practice for the Elimination of Discrimination in Employment*, Commission for Racial Equality, London (1983)
9 CRE. *Ethnic Minority Hospital Staff*, Commission for Racial Equality, London (1983)
10 Department of Employment. Unemployment and ethnic origin. *Employment Gazette*, June, 260–264 (1984)
11 Moser, K. A., Fox, A. J., Jones, D. R. and Goldblatt, P. O. Unemployment and mortality: further evidence from the OPCS longitudinal study 1971–81. *Lancet*, **i**, 365–367 (1986)
12 Beale, N. and Nethercott, S. Job-loss and family morbidity: a study of a factory closure. *J. R. Coll. Gen. Pract.*, **35**, 510–514 (1985)
13 CRE. *Race and Mortgage Lending*, Commission for Racial Equality, London (1985)
14 CRE. *Race and Council Housing in Hackney. Report of a Formal Investigation*, Commission for Racial Equality, London (1984)
15 CRE. *Race and Housing in Liverpool. A Research Report*, Commission for Racial Equality, London (1984)
16 Brown, G. and Harris, T. *The Social Origins of Depression*, Tavistock, London (1978)
17 Richman, J., Stevenson, J. and Graham, P. *Preschool: A Behavioural Study*, Academic, London (1982)
18 Fenton, S. *Race Health and Welfare. Afro-Caribbean and South Asian People in Bristol: Health and Social Services*, Department of Sociology, University of Bristol (1986)
19 Wadsworth, M. E. J., Butterfield, W. J. H. and Blaney, R. *Health and Sickness: the Choice of Treatment*, Tavistock, London (1971)
20 Verbrugge, L. Triggers of symptoms and health care. *Social Science and Medicine*, **20**, 855–876 (1985)
21 Banks, M. H., Beresford, S. A. A., Morrell, D. C. *et al.* Factors influencing the demand for primary and medical care in women aged 20–44 years: a preliminary report. *Int. J. Epidemiol.*, **4**, 189–195 (1970)
22 Freidson, E. *Profession of Medicine*, Dodds Meads, New York (1970)
23 Cartwright, A. and O'Brien, M. Social class variations in health care. In *The Sociology of the NHS* (ed. M. Stacey), *Sociological Review Monograph*, **22**, University of Keele, Keele (1976)
24 CRE. *Medical School Admissions. Report of a Formal Investigation into St George's Hospital Medical School*, Commission for Racial Equality, London (1988)
25 Doyal, L., Hunt, G. and Mellor, J. Your life in their hands, *Critical Social Policy*, Autumn (1981)
26 Torkington, P. *The Racial Politics of Health – a Liverpool Profile*, Merseyside Area Profile Group, University of Liverpool (1983)
27 Lumb, K. M., Congden, P. J. and Lealman, G. T. A comparative review of Asian and British born maternity patients in Bradford, 1974–1978. *J. Epidemiol. Community Health*, **35**, 106–109 (1981)
28 Clarke, M. and Clayton, D. G. Quality of obstetric care provided for Asian immigrants in Leicestershire. *Br. Med. J.*, **286**, 621–623 (1983)
29 Larbie, J. *Black Women and Maternity Services*, National Extension College Cambridge for Training in Health and Race, Cambridge (1985)
30 SCF. *The Health of Traveller Mothers and Young Children in East Anglia*, Save the Children Fund, London (1983)

31 Pearson, M. *Racial Equality and Good Practice: Maternity Care*, National Extension College Cambridge for Training in Health and Race, Cambridge (1985)

32 Pearson, M. *Equal Opportunities Policies in the NHS: A Handbook*, National Extension College Cambridge for Training in Health and Race, Cambridge (1985)

33 Ahmed, A. and Pearson, M. *Multiracial Initiatives in Maternity Care*, Maternity Alliance, London (1985)

34 CRE. *Report of a Formal Investigation into St Chad's Hospital, Birmingham*, Commission for Racial Equality, London (1984)

Section IV

Specific medical aspects

Chapter 10

Pregnancy

I. R. McFadyen

Ethnicity has many effects on the mother and fetus. Birthweight and gestational age, the rate of complications during pregnancy, the health of the mother and child after delivery as well as maternal and perinatal mortality: all are related to the parents' ethnic origins. Geography and social factors are important and complicate comparisons between apparently similar ethnic groups. So do differences in basic health, the facilities for health care which are available and the use made of them, and the accuracy of data recorded. Comparisons are confused also by religion and diet, the use of tobacco and other drugs, cultural attitudes to the pregnant mother and her fetus, and migration. Each of these is relevant to the success of the pregnancy. In combination they determine that maternal and perinatal mortality in some poor rural populations are ten times higher than in affluent urban communities [1–3].

Conception

Fertility rates show ethnic differences. Where pelvic inflammatory disease is common many women are infertile. Where infant mortality is high, large numbers of children are conceived to ensure sufficient surviving to support their parents as they grow older [4], although many Third World women would be happy with smaller families [2]. Cultural pressures may also require the delivery of healthy sons, so a sequence of daughters prevents limitation of family size until they have brothers. Such proliferation is counter-productive in many ways, most obviously where a child develops kwashiorkor when taken off breast-feeding to make way for the next neonate. Where life-expectancy is greater, family size tends to be limited but this depends on the methods of contraception used. Breast-feeding is effective only while the serum prolactin is raised; this falls after a few months, particularly as the child is being weaned. There are cultural effects and religious taboos which influence contraception. In a male-dominated society the less efficient condom is used more than an oral contraceptive which is managed by the wife. Even where 'the pill' is used its value is undermined if diarrhoea is endemic (or broad-spectrum antibiotic use is widespread) as this reduces hormone absorption. Many cultures consider that medication is effective only when given by injection and so find intramuscular depot preparations the most acceptable [5]. The intrauterine device is acceptable to some societies provided that advice on its use and the actual fitting are carried out by women. Sterilization of either partner is unacceptable for many cultural and religious reasons, and may lead to disintegration of the marriage even if the spouse initially agreed with it.

Disease also affects fertility. Tuberculosis and other infections of the pelvic organs may prevent conception, as can any general debilitating condition. Salpingitis is associated with infertility but also with ectopic pregnancies. Spontaneous abortion is more likely where there is general disease. It may also be more frequent in marriages between blood relatives, but because it is so common and so much a fact of everyday life for many women they tend not to be reported and accurate data are available for few populations.

Differences which may be genetic or environmental are also relevant to conception. Hydatidiform mole occurs once in 2000 white pregnancies but three to four times as frequently among Chinese. Twinning is twice as common among African blacks as it is in whites but may be different between neighbouring tribes in one area [6]. Migration in Europe reduces the twinning rate, but moving from the Philippines to the USA does not alter the proportion of hydatidiform moles which are conceived [7].

Complications of pregnancy

Malnourished populations have a high incidence of eclampsia, accidental haemorrhage, anaemia and other serious complications of pregnancy. While nutrition is relevant to the mother's increased risk and to her ability to cope with life-threatening problems, lack of antenatal care increases the probability of her developing them. Failure to recognize hypertension and proteinuria makes eclampsia more likely: failure to give prophylactic treatment for malaria leads to this being the commonest cause of anaemia affecting pregnant women in many parts of Africa [8]. Malpresentation and disproportion which are unrecognized increase morbidity and mortality for both child and mother. Hookworm infestation, tropical sprue, and other diseases produce malabsorption and undernutrition. The severity of these depends on the level of health in the population. Among the reasonably nourished, infestation with intestinal parasites is not a major problem [9], but it can produce severe anaemia in those with low stores of nutrients. Chronic undernutrition with calcium deficiency is likely to lead to osteomalacia with the demands of many pregnancies at short intervals [10]. This distorts pelvic shape and produces mechanical difficulties in labour ending in fetal or maternal death. Malnutrition also depresses the immune system [11] which may not only reduce mean birthweight but contribute to the exacerbations of malaria, leprosy and AIDS which are common in pregnancy.

Truly genetic problems such as the haemoglobinopathies (Chapters 12–15) have both geographical and ethnic distributions. Patterns of marriage to relatives increase the probability of fetal abnormality. While antenatal diagnosis is available for some of these conditions it is expensive and therapeutic termination is not acceptable to many cultures. Other diseases which have a hereditary component and may affect the mother are ethnically biased: diabetes mellitus is more common in Indians than whites. The consequences of this and other diseases for the pregnancy may be compounded by synchronous treatment with both traditional and modern remedies, but little information is available because frequently only the patient knows when such treatments are combined. Guar and bittergourd reduce blood sugar effectively [12] but the effects on the pregnancy of combining these with insulin are not known.

Physiological adaptation

The quality of a mother's adaptation to pregnancy may be assessed from changes in her weight and in her circulation, and from the birthweight of her child. The normal ranges of weight gain and circulatory changes show little ethnic variation. Indians, whites and Malaysians all gain about 0.5 kg a week in a healthy pregnancy [13,14]. The total gain in weight is not related to the mother's weight at conception but is directly related to her child's birthweight. Ethnic variation in birthweight is partly explained by this relationship being with the mother's lean body mass rather than her total weight. Thin women have heavier babies than fat women of the same weight [15]. Conception before maternal growth is complete means that the relevant weight in these mothers is that at the end of pregnancy [1].

Changes in blood volume show an apparent ethnic difference which is a consequence of the total increase not being related to the circulating volume before conception. Because of the difference in prepregnancy volumes Africans who gain 1270 ml have increased their plasma volume by 55% whereas whites showing the same increase have increased theirs by only 46% [16]. Anaemia and other pathology may affect these adaptations: the optimum haematocrit at delivery is 0.30–0.35 [1].

Other physiological changes during pregnancy show real ethnic differences. Fasting blood glucose and response to a glucose load are similar in whites and Indians but insulin levels are different [17]. Indians have a higher fasting insulin which rises further following a glucose load: to maintain the same physiological level of glucose as whites requires a higher level of insulin in Indians. Lipid metabolism, however, does not show differences between those two ethnic groups, nor are there differences between meat-eating and vegetarian Indians [18].

Birthweight

Birthweight reflects maternal adaptation to pregnancy. The more physiological the adaptations the closer is birthweight to the optimum. Birthweight has to be adjusted for maternal size and gravidity, as well as gestational age and the baby's sex [19]. Such adjusted birthweights do show ethnic differences. In an affluent population of Indians and whites the mean birthweight to Hindus was 180 g lighter than that of whites, but Muslim babies were not significantly lighter than whites: these differences are maintained even when adjusted for different smoking patterns [20]. Most birthweight data are not adjusted so it is not always possible to differentiate between low birthweight due to prematurity and that due to other causes. Nevertheless, in Singapore Chinese and Malay birthweights are lighter than whites but heavier than Indians: in Africa Gambians have lighter babies than Nigerians: and in Britain English babies are lighter than Irish (reviewed by McFadyen [21]).

Patterns of fetal growth also show ethnic differences. North American blacks have heavier mean birthweights than whites of similar social background up to 34–35 weeks, but after this the whites catch up and by term their babies are heavier [22] even though organ maturation appears to proceed at the same rate [23]. Ethiopian mean birthweight is heavier than Swedish up to 33–36 weeks, but then the Swedes catch up [24]. Longitudinal ultrasound studies have shown Indians and whites also have different patterns of fetal growth [25].

Geography and other factors also affect birthweight. For every 1000 m the mother lives above sea level, mean birthweight is reduced by 100 g [26]. Ambient temperature and humidity affect the incidence of eclampsia [27], but whether they are relevant to birthweight is not certain. Pregnancy during the rainy season (which may be a time of toil) increases the exposure to malaria and other infections which reduce birthweight. Tobacco and alcohol also reduce birthweight [28]. Not only do the consumption of these show ethnic and religious variation but their effects do also: maternal smoking reduces birthweight more in black populations than in whites.

Diet affects birthweight both by its calorie content and by individual constituents. Acute starvation can reduce birthweight by 300–400 g because the fetus lacks fat, not because it is stunted [29]. Lack of individual nutrients may affect fetal growth but their absorption rather than their absence could be the real problem. Not only intestinal disease but also high fibre content can reduce absorption of essential nutrients.

Comparisons of birthweight between populations are of uncertain accuracy because many of the data necessary for adjustment of birthweight are not known or recorded. Gestational age is probably the most important but least certain of these. If they are not sought and recorded other ethnic differences may be missed. Marriage between close relatives reduces mean birthweight even in the absence of fetal abnormality. Migration also can affect birthweight. Jewish mothers who live in North Africa have heavier babies than those who live in Israel, but if they move to Israel mean birthweight falls and the longer they live there the closer it gets to the Israeli level [30]. As with almost all aspects of pregnancy, however, the mother's socioeconomic status is one of the best indices of likely outcome: the lower that is the lighter are her babies likely to be [31,32].

Normal values and reference ranges

Ethnic differences in adaptation mean that normal values and reference ranges must be constructed for each group. A population which routinely takes oral iron has a larger increase in mean corpuscular volume (MCV) than one which does not, and one which has a high prevalence of thalassaemia will have a reduced mean MCV. Hindu vegetarians have a lower vitamin B12 intake and lower serum levels than meat-eating Hindus or whites and, despite this, have no more haematological problems (other things being equal), possibly due to an efficient enterohepatic circulation of B12 [33].

Duration of pregnancy may vary and the mean is not the same in all ethnic groups. Among Asian Indians it is 2–3 days shorter than in whites [20]. This may mean that Asian babies are more mature at 27 weeks than those of whites and be more likely to survive if born so premature: conversely postmaturity may start at an earlier gestational age for Asians. Whether or not this is true is not known, nor is the significance of mean blood pressure being lower in Asians than whites.

Ultrasound measurement of fetal head size does not show significant ethnic variation, but among whites reduction in abdominal circumference relative to the size of the fetal head suggests pathological retardation of growth [25]. Not all races grow at the same rate *in utero*: blacks have heavier mean birthweights until about 34 weeks then whites begin to catch up. There may well be different patterns of physiological growth which require ethnic reference ranges.

Cultural factors affecting outcome

The availability and use of facilities for supervision and treatment show considerable cultural and geographical variation with corresponding variation in the successful outcome of pregnancy. An important determinant of the use made of what is available is the education in the society to which the mother belongs. The acceptance of prophylactic care improves the outcome for mother and child worldwide [1,34].

Family structure and customs are variable to each extreme. In some societies the pregnant mother is pampered, in others little notice is taken of her. Marriage and conception before the menarche is not uncommon. Childbearing before the pelvis is fully grown leads to a high incidence of cephalopelvic disproportion, eclampsia, and other problems which produce a high maternal and perinatal mortality among girl mothers [1]. If she does survive an immature woman is more likely to sustain a vesicovaginal fistula and to be rejected by the family [35,36]. Caesarean section might prevent many of these complications but this solution is rejected by some, and in others the husband's permission is required and he may not be available if the wife has been brought to hospital from miles away.

Religion is relevant to the conduct of pregnancy in many societies. In a Hindu community, rites have to be observed at specific stages of pregnancy to ensure a successful outcome [37], and it may be necessary for the mother to be in her home, or her in-laws' home, for their proper observance. Some days may be ill-starred for delivery so have to be avoided for elective Caesarean section or the induction of labour. Ceremonies after delivery are common and can require physical contact between mother and child which an incubator could prevent. Travel on certain days is unlucky so discharge from hospital on them would not be welcomed. Unless this background is understood it is difficult to manage apparently inexplicable demands for discharge of ill mothers or babies from hospital. Usually they are resolved without difficulty when the nature of the request is discussed. One benefit of such religious observance is that with some beliefs a menstruating woman may not cook or carry out family ceremonies; a situation which means that they know their menstrual history more accurately than most.

The mother-in-law is a powerful person in most families, and in some cultures it is she who determines the conduct of the mother's care and of the new baby. If this produces stresses these may be aggravated if the family has migrated and the mother has absorbed a background which clashes with the previous generation's. Migration away from the traditional family support can lead to isolation within a community, lack of antenatal care and preparation for the baby, and problems in the puerperium which are likely to lead to depression due to lack of contact and inability to deal with the neonate or infant in a new environment without help from relatives.

Mortalities

Maternal mortality shows a wide geographical variation which is not so much ethnic as dependent on nutrition, education and the availability of care. Most deaths are due to haemorrhage, infection, complications of hypertension, obstructed labour or induced abortion [38,39], none of which are truly ethnically determined. While mechanical problems in labour may be related to the size of the pelvis in young girls or in osteomalacic multipara, failure to deal with them is as great a problem: 20%

of maternal deaths in Malawi could be prevented by hospital admission after 12 h in labour rather than after several days [40]. Such prolonged labour supervised by the family or local untrained midwife with few facilities is common in many countries with similar consequences [1].

In developed countries 1% of deaths among women aged 15–49 are directly related to pregnancy. Among women of this age in developing countries the proportion is 25% [2]. The rate of maternal mortality also shows extreme variation. In the UK it is one in every 10 000 recognized pregnancies although a few may not be reported. In Jamaica the rate is 10.8 per 10 000 live births [3], in affluent areas of Egypt 19 per 10 000, and in Africa 16–110 per 10 000 [1,2]. The rates are probably higher in rural areas where many are not dealt with in hospital, and underreporting may be as high as 20–30%. In Jamaica [3], over 30% of maternal deaths are due to hypertension or pre-eclampsia, both causes eminently preventable by antenatal care.

Perinatal mortality also is underreported. Both pregnancies and perinatal deaths may pass unnoticed so comparisons of rates between countries are likely to be inaccurate. That there are differences is not disputed. In England and Wales the rate is 10–11 per 1000 births; these are due to fetal abnormality, prematurity, growth disorders and a few due to mechanical problems. In developing countries the causes are similar but a large proportion is due to obstructed or complicated labour: the total perinatal mortality rate may be over 100 per 1000 pregnancies [1].

Perinatal mortality within a country does show ethnic differences. In England and Wales Indian and Pakistani populations have higher perinatal mortalities than indigenous whites [41]. This is separate from the known effects of social class and may improve as that population's stay lengthens (Figure 10.1). In general these deaths are due to the same causes as in whites and in similar proportions but there are more before the onset of labour [42], and lethal fetal anomaly is commoner, possibly due to marriage between close relatives or to high maternal age [43].

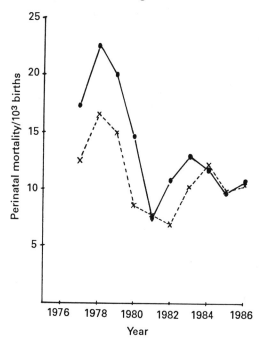

Figure 10.1 An affluent community in London into which equally affluent Indians migrated after 1972 consistently showed a significantly higher perinatal mortality among the Indians, the causes of death being the same in both groups. As the Asian community's stay lengthened the perinatal mortality approached the European without any alteration in obstetric management. x–––––x, White European; ●———●, Indian

Summary

There are maternal and fetal differences in adaptation to and performance during pregnancy which are ethnically determined. These differences are genetic, environmental and cultural. They may be modified or aggravated by migration. The outcome of the pregnancy is determined by the mother's basic health and nutrition, by her age, by endemic disease in the area, by patterns of family custom, and by the availability and quality of care which she receives.

References

1 Harrison, K. A. Childbearing, health and social priorities: a survey of 22774 consecutive hospital births in Zaria, Northern Nigeria. *Br. J. Obstet. Gynaecol.*, Suppl. 5, 1–119 (1985)
2 Rosenfield, A. and Maine, D. Maternal mortality – a neglected tragedy. Where is the M in MCH. *Lancet*, ii, 83–85 (1985)
3 Walker, G. J. A., Ashley, D. E. C., McCaw, A. and Bernard, G. W. Maternal mortality in Jamaica. *Lancet*, i, 486–488 (1986)
4 Ekunwe, E. O. Effect of infant mortality on family formation objectives and behaviour, Shomdie, Lagos. *Nigerian Med. J.*, **13**, 51–56 (1985)
5 Quereshi, B. Family planning and culture. *J. R. Soc. Health*, **1**, 11–14 (1985)
6 Nylander, P. P. S. Ethnic differences in twinning rates in Nigeria. *J. Biosoc. Soc.*, **3**, 151–157 (1971)
7 Jacobs, P. A., Hunt, P. A. A., Matsura, J. S. and Wilson, C. C. Complete and partial hydatidiform mole in Hawaii, cytogenetics, morphology and epidemiology. *Br. J. Obstet. Gynaecol.*, **89**, 258–266 (1982)
8 Fleming, A. F., Harrison, K. A., Briggs, M. D. *et al.* Anaemia in young primigravidae in the guinea savannah of Nigeria: sickle cell trait gives partial protection against malaria. *Ann. Trop. Med. Parasitol.*, **78**, 395–404 (1984)
9 D'Alauro, F., Lee, R. V., Pao-In, K. and Khairallah, M. Intestinal parasites and pregnancy. *Am. J. Obstet. Gynecol.*, **66**, 639–643 (1985)
10 Wilson, D. C. The incidence of osteomalacia and late rickets in Northern India. *Lancet*, ii, 10–12 (1931)
11 Gross, R. L. and Newberne, P. M. Role of nutrition in immunological function. *Physiol. Rev.*, **60**, 188 (1980)
12 Leatherdale, B. A., Panesar, R. K., Singh, G. *et al.* Improvement in glucose tolerance due to *Momordica charantia* (karela). *Br. Med. J.*, **282**, 1823–1824 (1981)
13 Campbell Brown, M., Ward, R. J., Haynes, A. P. *et al.* Zinc and copper in Asian pregnancies – is there evidence for a nutritional deficiency. *Br. J. Obstet. Gynaecol.*, **92**, 875–885 (1987)
14 Sinnathuray, T. A. and Wong, W. P. Physiological weight changes in pregnancy in Malaysian women. *Aust. N. Z. J. Obstet. Gynaecol.*, **12**, 722 (1972)
15 Campbell-Brown, M. and McFadyen, I. R. Maternal energy reserves and birthweight. *Lancet*, i, 574–575 (1985)
16 Harrison, K. A. Blood volume changes in normal pregnant Nigerian women. *J. Obstet. Gynaecol. Br. Cwlth.*, **73**, 717 (1966)
17 Rouse, K. A., Montague, W. and MacVicar, J. Carbohydrate metabolism during pregnancy in groups of women with differing perinatal mortality rates. *J. Obstet. Gynaecol.*, **6**, 24–27 (1985)
18 Rouse, K. A., Montague, W. and MacVicar, J. Cholesterol and triglyceride metabolism during pregnancy in women of different ethnic origins and dietary habits. *J. Obstet. Gynaecol.*, **6**, 28–31 (1985)
19 Thomson, A. M., Billewicz, W. Z. and Hytten, F. E. The assessment of fetal growth. *J. Obstet. Gynaecol. Br. Cwlth.*, **75**, 903–916 (1968)
20 Haines, A. P., McFadyen, I. R., Campbell-Brown, M. *et al.* Birthweight and complications of pregnancy in an Asian population. In *Obstetric Problems of the Asian Community in Britain* (eds I. R. McFadyen and J. R. MacVicar), Royal College of Obstetricians and Gynaecologists, London, pp. 119–126 (1982)

21 McFadyen, I. R. Fetal growth. In *Progress in Obstetrics and Gynaecology*, vol. 5 (ed. J. Studd), Churchill Livingstone, Edinburgh, pp. 58–77 (1985)

22 Freeman, G. M., Graves, W. L. and Thompson, R. L. Indigent Negro and Caucasian birth weight–gestational age tables. *Pediatrics*, **46**, 9–15 (1970)

23 Fujikara, T. and Froelich, L. A. Birth weight, gestational age, and renal glomerular development as indices of fetal maturity. *Am. J. Obstet. Gynecol.*, **113**, 627–631 (1972)

24 Gebre-Medhin, M., Sterky, G. and Taube, A. Observations on intrauterine growth in urban Ethiopia. *Acta Paediatr. Scand.*, **67**, 781–789 (1978)

25 Meire, H. B. and Farrant, P. Ultrasound demonstration of an unusual fetal growth pattern in Indians. *Br. J. Obstet. Gynaecol.*, **88**, 260–263 (1981)

26 McCullough, R. E., Reeves, J. T. and Liljegren, R. L. Fetal growth retardation and increased infant mortality at high altitude. *Arch. Environ. Health*, **32**, 36 (1977)

27 Agobe, J. T., Good, W. and Hancock, K. W. Meteorological relationships of eclampsia in Lagos, Nigeria. *Br. J. Obstet. Gynaecol.*, **88**, 706–710 (1981)

28 Thomson, A. M., Billewicz, W. Z., Thompson, B. and McGregor, I. A. Body weight changes during pregnancy and lactation in rural African (Gambiacs) women. *J. Obstet. Br. Cwlth*, **73**, 724 (1966)

29 Hytten, F. E. Nutrition in pregnancy. In *Perinatal Medicine* (eds O. Thalhautier, K. Baunigarten and A. Pollak), Thiewe, Stuttgart, pp. 34–43 (1979)

30 Yudkin, P. L., Harlap, S. and Baras, M. High birthweight in an ethnic group of low socioeconomic status. *Br. J. Obstet. Gynaecol.*, **90**, 291–296 (1983)

31 Rahimtoola, R. J., Mir, S. and Baloch, S. Low birth weight, the 'small for dates' syndrome and perinatal mortality in a low family income group. *Acta Paediatr. Scand.*, **57**, 534–536 (1968)

32 Butler, N. R. and Alberman, E. D. Maternal factors affecting duration of pregnancy, birthweight and fetal growth. In *Perinatal Problems* (eds N. R. Butler and E. D. Alberman), Churchill Livingstone, Edinburgh, pp. 53–67 (1969)

33 Abraham, R., Campbell-Brown, M., Haines, A. P. *et al.* Diet during pregnancy in an Asian community in Britain – energy, protein, zinc, copper, fibre and calcium. *Hum. Nutr. Appl. Nutr.*, **39a**, 23–35 (1985)

34 Baird, D. and Thomson, A. M. Reduction of perinatal mortality by improving standards of obstetric care. In *Perinatal Problems* (eds N. R. Butler and E. D. Alberman), E. and S. Livingstone, Edinburgh, pp. 255–282 (1969)

35 McFadyen, I. R. Vesico-vaginal fistula. *Br. Med. J.*, **ii**, 1717–1720 (1962)

36 Tahzib, F. Epidemiological determinants of vesico-vaginal fistulas. *Br. J. Obstet. Gynaecol.*, **90**, 387–391 (1983)

37 Abraham, R. Cultural and dietary variation in the Harrow Asian population. In *Obstetric Problems of the Asian Community in Britain* (eds I. R. McFadyen and I. R. MacVicar), Royal College of Obstetricians and Gynaecologists, London, pp. 25–29 (1982)

38 Hartfield, V. J. Maternal mortality in Nigeria compared with earlier international experience. *Int. J. Obstet. Gynecol.*, **18**, 70–75 (1980)

39 Rochet, R. W., Kramer, D., Senanayake, P. and Howell, C. Induced abortion and health problems in developing countries. *Lancet*, **ii**, 484 (1980)

40 Bullough, C. H. Analysis of maternal deaths in the Central Region of Malawi. *East Afr. Med. J.*, **58**, 25–36 (1981)

41 Marshall, T. Perinatal mortality and race – a national view. In *Obstetric Problems of the Asian Community in Britain* (eds I. R. McFadyen and J. R. MacVicar), Royal College of Obstetricians and Gynaecologists, London, pp. 13–17 (1982)

42 Terry, P. B. and Condie, R. G. Ethnic differences in the distribution of normally formed singleton stillbirths. *Postgrad. Med. J.*, **59**, 659–660 (1983)

43 Barnes, R. Perinatal mortality and morbidity rates in Bradford. In *Obstetric Problems of the Asian Community in Britain* (eds I. R. McFadyen and J. MacVicar), Royal College of Obstetricians and Gynaecologists, London, pp. 81–87 (1982)

Chapter 11

Viral infections of pregnancy and childhood

Angus Nicoll and Stuart Logan

Our knowledge of ethnic differences in viral disease is largely based on the seroepidemiology of women in antenatal clinics which provides prevalence rather than incidence data. We have little idea of differences, if any, in natural history between ethnic groups.

Even less is known of the source of variation in disease. Ethnic minorities, particularly in Britain, tend to have been recent immigrants, often living at social disadvantage. Furthermore, distinct gene-pools are associated with different social practices.

Differing susceptibility and vulnerability

Once social factors are controlled there is little evidence of genetically determined variation between ethnic groups in either susceptibility or vulnerability to infection, except possibly for hepatitis B. The few established differences relate to specific genetic defects, e.g. the haemaglobinopathies or Down's syndrome, and then mostly bacterial infections. Little is known of the effects of acquired characteristics on infections in pregnancy. Similarly, apart from the deleterious effects of bottle-feeding in circumstances of poor hygiene [1], acquired susceptibility to infection in childhood is poorly understood.

Vulnerability of children to viral illness is better understood, with malnutrition playing a major role in developing countries [2]; to what extent this is important in Europe or Northern America is unknown.

Differing exposure and protection

Recently arrived migrants usually encounter new disease patterns. Movement between countries can result in the sudden exposure of susceptibles in the newly arrived group or the indigenous population. An example of the former was the exposure of West Indian women to rubella in the UK in the 1950s and 1960s (see below), and of the latter the importation of measles to isolated communities [3].

Cultural patterns frequently differ between ethnic groups resulting in higher or lower transmission rates according to the particular disease. First-generation Asian women in Britain have high cytomegalovirus (CMV) seropositivity, probably because they were predominantly breast-fed as infants. However, the same women have low titres for herpes type II, presumably due to their conservative sexual patterns.

Poverty and social deprivation are widespread among ethnic minority groups, with overcrowding inevitably leading to increased exposure to infectious disease. Asian women entering Britain also had low rates of rubella seropositivity but rapidly acquired the disease (at considerable risk to their pregnancies) presumably from living in overcrowded conditions.

Uptake of immunization among ethnic minority children is generally good [4] but depends on both an appreciation of the need for protection and the availability of appropriate health services.

General viral illnesses

Respiratory tract infections and gastroenteritis are the most important worldwide causes of childhood mortality [5,6]. Except for infant 'cot deaths' their epidemiology is under-researched and little is known about interracial differences. American studies have reported ethnic risk factors for incidence and severity of childhood lower respiratory infections [7], probably the result of social conditions. An excess of deaths due to respiratory tract infections and 'cot death' in British lower social class families is well described [8]. Boys are more vulnerable than girls to respiratory infections [7], and to hepatitis B [9], presumably through a genetic mechanism.

There is a higher hospital presentation rate for gastroenteritis among Asian babies in East London [1]. It is unclear whether this represents a difference in incidence, presentation to hospital or diagnostic labelling. In an almost unique prospective community study, black American babies had a higher occurrence of enteroviruses (both symptomatic and non-symptomatic) compared with whites [10], a finding again explicable through different social conditions.

Specific viral illnesses

Rubella

In the UK rubella is endemic with superimposing epidemics. The majority of children acquire immunity through natural infection. Present immunization strategy is to immunize girls in secondary school so that all women enter pregnancy immune to infection. It has been consistently found that Asian women in antenatal clinics are more often seronegative for rubella than the indigenous population [11–13]. One extensive survey in Manchester, Leeds and Luton in 1984–85 [14] found that the difference was most marked in nulliparous women (Figure 11.1). Since most of these women were first-generation migrants a simple explanation was that many had missed the school immunization programme and later were exposed to rubella from their children. Support for this hypothesis came from the similarity in the age/serology relationship of indigenous males and Asian women (Figure 11.2).

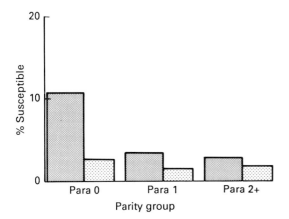

Figure 11.1 Proportion of Asian and non-Asian antenatal patients susceptible to rubella according to parity (Manchester, Leeds and Luton 1984/85). Because of selective antenatal screening in Leeds, data from parous women tested by this laboratory have been excluded. ▨ , Asians;▨ , non-Asians.

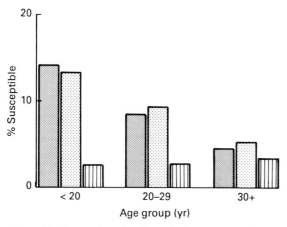

Figure 11.2 Proportion of males and of nulliparous Asian and non-Asian antenatal patients susceptible to rubella according to age (Manchester, Leeds and Luton 1984/85). ▨, Males;▨ , Asian, para 0; ▥, non-Asians

The study could not rule out the possibility that rubella has a lower incidence in India and Pakistan. Certainly the disease exists in the subcontinent and surveys have found a smaller prevalence of positive serology in unimmunized white males [14–16]. However, Miller *et al.* [14] also found that the women were less likely to seek antenatal advice on rubella status, possibly because some Asians are unaware of the dangers of rubella during pregnancy [17]. In adults the illness is mild and in some Asian languages there is no separate word for the disease. This ethnic difference is not academic since a disproportionate number of Asian women have babies damaged by rubella, a fact only partially explained by differential use of pregnancy termination services [14].

There is no similar serological short-fall among women of West Indian origin [13]. Most individuals are now second generation and are as likely as whites to have had rubella or to have been immunized at school. However, there are good reasons to believe that the first-generation mothers would have been highly susceptible, more so than present-day Asians. The Caribbean islands are small and even Jamaica's population is insufficient to maintain endemic rubella [18]. Hence adults are more frequently seronegative than in the Indian subcontinent or the UK [19–21]. Until 1978 there was no schoolgirl immunization programme in the Caribbean and that which exists now is not yet as effective as in the UK [20]. Hence fetal damage is relatively common and occurs in epidemics [18,22,23]. There is insufficient data on whether babies born to Caribbean mothers in Britain were more affected by congenital rubella than those of indigenous mothers during the peak years of immigration in the 1950s and 1960s. One impression of an excess was noted in the early 1960s in Birmingham during an epidemic [24]. Routine Department of Education statistics for 1970–72 (the only years that pupils' country of origin was coded) show an excess of West Indians in schools for hearing-impaired children (Table 11.1).

Table 11.1 West Indians as a percentage of all immigrant* children in ordinary and certain categories of special schools in England and Wales: 1970 [25]

Primary schools	Secondary schools	Schools for the hearing impaired	Schools for children with physical impairment†
45.0%	35.3%	60.6%	50.2%

* Defined as children born outside the UK or in the UK to parents whose countries of origin were abroad after 1 January 1960.
† Combining schools for blind and partially sighted, physically handicapped, and delicate and physically handicapped.

Cytomegalovirus

Virtually everyone acquires cytomegalovirus (CMV) infection some time in their lives. The median age of infection however varies in different populations; in the Ivory Coast nearly all children are seropositive by the age of 10 [26], while the figure is 60% for women of child-bearing age in the UK [27].

Postnatally acquired infection is of little importance except in immunodeficiency. However, primary or recurrent infection may result in transmission to the fetus. Overall 10% of fetuses so infected are handicapped; half with deafness, half with neurological complications [28,29]. In England and Wales some 200 babies (1 per 3000 live births) are affected annually [28].

Differences in both age-specific maternal seropositivity and congenital infection rates in different ethnic groups in the UK have been demonstrated [30] and can be accounted for by social factors (Table 11.2).

The major routes of transmission are thought to be breast-feeding (mother to child) and sexual contact (adults). Hence high rates of breast-feeding in developing countries lead to early CMV immunity. This applies for first-generation black and Asian women and still includes almost all Asian women of child-bearing age [31]. High rates of acquisition of CMV infection among second-generation black women probably reflect culturally different sexual activity.

Table 11.2 Seropositivity and infection for cytomegalovirus

	Caucasians	Blacks	Asians
Maternal antenatal seropositivity (%)	55	82	90
Congenital infection rate (per 1000 live births)	2.5	8.1	1.9

The difference in congenital infection rates are less easy to explain. Populations with high seropositivity rates have been reported to have high rates of congenital infection with recurrent infection playing a major role. It is unclear why this was so for black women but not for Asians in Preece's study [30].

The practical implications are few. Neither an effective treatment nor a vaccine are yet available. The risk to any individual pregnancy is low so that the benefit of any proposed intervention needs careful examination.

Poliomyelitis

India has the world's highest rate of polio but early childhood cases tend to be milder than those in the UK earlier this century [32]. With international travel, families returning to South Asia are at risk of exposure and need protection. Fortunately when services are available Asian families have good immunization uptake [4], but inflexibility in immunization services and lack of appreciation of the dangers among Asian people themselves mean that each year some unprotected individuals contract polio [33] while visiting India.

Small polio epidemics still take place in the West Indies, reflecting incomplete implementation of immunization [34]. Hence first-generation migrants may be susceptible but with low levels of circulating polio virus in Europe this does not represent a significant problem.

Herpes simplex

Herpes simplex type I is a ubiquitous virus which virtually everybody catches during their lives. Although primary infection may be unpleasant, the virus is seldom of major clinical significance. In Western countries the median age of primary infection is increasing while in the developing world it remains a disease of early childhood [35]. Little is known of its epidemiology among migrants from the latter to the former.

Genital herpes, usually caused by type II virus, as well as being unpleasant may lead to devastating neonatal disease. While primary genital infection at the time of delivery carries the highest risk, some cases are infected from recurrences which may be subclinical [36]. Rates of neonatal infection vary from 1 : 7500 deliveries (USA) to 1 : 30 000 (UK) [37]. A recent seroepidemiological survey of pregnant women attending a London hospital found widely varying rates of past infection between ethnic groups (A. Ades and C. S. Peckham, 1988, personal communication) (Table 11.3).

Table 11.3 Seropositivity for herpes simplex type II (total n = 3342)

Asian	White (UK born)	Black (UK born)	Black African	Black Caribbean
3.5%	7.3%	14.7%	36.8%	32.1%

What remains unclear is the risk to any baby born to a seropositive woman and how birth should be managed. In the USA it is recommended that all women with a history of genital herpes have regular viral cultures from 32 weeks and are delivered by caesarean section if shedding virus [36]. In view of the high rates found among black women in the UK and the low rate of neonatal herpes infection it is questionable whether such an excess of caesarean sections would be justified.

Hepatitis B

The high prevalence of chronic carriage of HBsAg in most Asian and African countries results in considerable morbidity from liver disease and an excess incidence of hepatocellular carcinoma [38]. In Western Europe and North America hepatitis B is rare and transmission by contaminated blood products or needles and sexual activity becomes important. In China, parts of Africa and Asia, where carrier prevalence is up to 20%, vertical transmission from mother to baby is the major route of infection, closely linked to the mother's e-antigen status [39]. There are major ethnic differences in the rates of e-antigen expression which seem to have a genetic basis [40]. Virtually no white women are positive and consequently their babies rarely become carriers. On the other hand, most Chinese women are positive and 60–70% of their babies become carriers [41], irrespective of where the mothers are resident.

There remains debate about the risk to Afro-Caribbean babies in the UK who are HBsAg positive. Transmission rates of zero and 30% are quoted [41,42]. As carriage rates of up to 4% have been reported among women in the Caribbean [43] this may be a significant problem and requires further investigation. For women from the Indian subcontinent there is again limited information about e-antigen carriage or vertical transmission. Prevalence rates of HBsAg of 1.5–5% have been reported in India [44–46].

Vaccination of babies born to HBsAg antigen mothers prevents most from acquiring the virus. Women from the Far East should undoubtedly be screened, with babies of carriers receiving immunization from birth. Whether this screening should be extended to African, West Indian and Asian women requires further information [40].

Conclusions and practical issues

Cytomegalovirus and herpes show clear ethnic differences among pregnant mothers but without any clear excess risk to their babies. Whether the herpes excess, or the pattern of sexual activity it reflects, puts black women more at risk of carcinoma of the cervix is controversial. In the light of prevalence and vertical transmission rates there is a strong case for screening all Oriental women for HBsAg during pregnancy and vaccinating babies of those found positive. The case diminishes in strength for black and Asian women.

For rubella, there are several practical issues. Lack of appreciation of the dangers of the disease remains important among the Asian community. Experience suggests that given the knowledge families will seek protection, and services should be sensitive not only to language and cultural needs but also to the practical problems of immunizing individuals outside of the prescribed ages. Women from countries without rubella immunization programmes will usually be seronegative.

Hence their babies will be particularly vulnerable while Britain fails to eradicate the disease.

Although these specific conditions are important, it is also likely that non-specific viral infections are responsible for a far greater excess morbidity. These are unlikely to stem from constitutional factors but rather the conditions of social deprivation in much of the ethnic minority population.

References

1 Cullinan, T. R. and Treuherz, J. *Ill in East London 1979–81*. Available from Department of Environmental and Preventative Medicine, St Bartholomews Hospital Medical College, London (1983)

2 Morley, D. The severe measles of West Africa. *Proc. R. Soc. Med.*, **57**, 846–849 (1964)

3 Brincker, J. A. H. A historical, epidemiological and aetiological study of measles. *Proc. R. Soc. Med.*, **30**, 807–828 (1938)

4 Baker, M. R., Bandaranayake, R. and Schweiger, M. S. Differences in rate of uptake in immunisation amongst ethnic groups. *Br. Med. J.*, **244**, 1073–1078 (1984)

5 World Health Organization. *Viral Respiratory Diseases*, WHO Technical Report Series No. 642, WHO, Geneva (1980)

6 Robinson, M. J. and Lee, E. L. *Paediatric Problems in Tropical Countries*, Churchill Livingstone, Edinburgh (1978)

7 Glezen, W. P. and Denny, F. W. Epidemiology of acute lower respiratory disease in children. *New Engl. J. Med.*, **288** 498–505 (1975)

8 Golding, J., Limerick, S. and Macfarlane, A. *Sudden Infant Death*, Open Books, Shepton Mallett, Somerset (1985)

9 Wheeley, S. M., Boxall, E. H. and Tarlow, M. J. What happens to hepatitis B carrier children. In preparation.

10 Jenista, J. A., Powell, K. R. and Menegus, M. A. Epidemiology of neonatal enterovirus infection. *J. Paediatr.*, **104**, 685–690 (1984)

11 Peckham, C. S., Tookey, P., Nelson, D. B. *et al*. Ethnic minority women and congenital rubella (letter). *Br. Med. J.*, **287**, 129 (1983)

12 Collier, L. H., Hellyar, A., Cefai, C. and Withers, M. Ethnic minority women and congenital rubella (letter). *Br. Med. J.*, **287**, 498–499 (1983)

13 Tookey, P., Johnson, C., Ades, T. and Peckham, C. Racial differences in rubella immunity among pregnant women. *Public Health*, **102**, 57–62 (1988)

14 Miller, E., Nicoll, A., Rousseau, S. A., *et al*. Congenital rubella in babies of South Asian women in England and Wales: an excess and its causes. *Br. Med. J.*, **294**, 737–739 (1986)

15 Seth, P., Manjunath, N. and Balaya, S. Rubella infection; the Indian scene. *Rev. Inf. Dis.*, Suppl. 1, **7**, S64–S67 (1985)

16 Rawls, W. E. World Health Organization collaborative study on the sero-epidemiology of rubella. *Bull. WHO*, **37**, 79–88 (1967)

17 Morgan, S., Stanford, R., Nicoll, A. Knowledge concerning infectious diseases and immunisation amongst some Asian and white parents. Personal communication (in preparation).

18 Miller, C. G. and Thorburn, M. J. An outbreak of congenital rubella in Jamaica. *West Ind. Med. J.*, **15**, 177–188 (1966)

19 Persad, K., Raj Kumar, G., Diggory, P. and Hull, B. Immunity status in a pregnant population in Trinidad. *West Ind. Med. J.*, Suppl., **33**, 43 (1984)

20 Baxter, D. N. Control of congenital rubella syndrome in Jamaica. *West Ind. Med. J.*, **35**, 50–54 (1986)

21 King, S. D. Rubella antibody levels in Jamaican women. *West Ind. Med. J.*, **21**, 82–86 (1972)

22 Ali, Z., Hull, B. and Lewis, M. Neonatal manifestations of congenital rubella following an outbreak in Trinidad. *West Ind. Med. J.*, Suppl., **33**, 44 (1984)

23 Karmody, C. S. Asymptomatic maternal rubella and congenital deafness. *Arch. Otolaryngol.*, **89**, 720–726 (1969) [describes epidemic of CRS in Trinidad]

24 Parsons, C. G. West Indian babies with multiple congenital defects. *Arch. Dis. Child.*, **38**, 454–458 (1963)
25 Department of Education and Science. *Statistics of Education*, vol. 1, *Schools 1970*, HMSO, London (1971)
26 Schopfer, K., Lauber, E. and Keech, U. Congenital cytomegalovirus infection in newborn infants of mothers infected before pregnancy. *Arch. Dis. Child.*, **53**, 536–539 (1978)
27 Peckham, C. S. Cytomegalovirus infection in pregnancy; preliminary findings from a prospective study. *Lancet*, **i**, 1352–1355 (1983)
28 Preece, P. M., Pearl, K. N. and Peckham, C. S. Congenital cytomegalovirus infection. *Arch. Dis. Child.*, **59**, 1120–1126 (1984)
29 Stagno, S. Congenital cytomegalovirus infection. The relative importance of primary and recurrent maternal infection. *New Engl. J. Med.*, **306**, 945–949 (1982)
30 Preece, P. M., Tookey, P., Ades, A. and Peckham, C. S. Congenital cytomegalovirus infection: predisposing maternal factors. *J. Epidemiol. Community Health*, **40**, 205–209 (1986)
31 Immigrant Statistics Unit, Office of Populations, Censuses and Surveys. New Commonwealth and Pakistan population estimates, *Population Trends*, vol. 9, HMSO, London, pp. 4–7 (1977)
32 Aasaad, F. and Kjungars-Esteves, K. World overview of poliomyelitis: regional patterns and trends. *Rev. Inf. Dis.*, Suppl. No. 2, **6**, S302–S307 (1984)
33 Communicable Disease Surveillance Centre. Communicable Disease Report, Weekly Edition 86/41, Public Health Laboratory Service, London (1986)
34 Persaud, V. Poliomyelitis in Jamaica. *West Ind. Med. J.*, **31**, 101–102 (1982)
35 Corey, A., Adams, H. G., Brown, Z. A. and Holmes, K. K. Genital herpes simplex virus infection: clinical manifestations, course and complications. *Ann. Intern. Med.*, **98**, 958–972 (1983)
36 Whitley, R. J., Nahmias, A. J., Visintine, A. M. *et al.* The natural history of herpes simplex virus infection of mother and newborn. *Paediatrics*, **66**, 489–494 (1980)
37 Marshall, W. C. and Peckham, C. S. The management of herpes simplex in pregnant women and neonates. *J. Infect.*, Suppl. 1, **6**, 23–29 (1983)
38 Szmuness, W. Hepatocellular carcinoma and the hepatitis B virus: evidence for a causal association. *Prog. Med. Virol.*, **24**, 40–69 (1978)
39 Okada, K. e antigen and anti-e in the serum of asymptomatic carrier mothers as indicators of positive and negative transmission of hepatitis B virus to their infants. *N. Engl. J. Med.*, **294**, 746–749 (1976)
40 Flewett, T. H. Can we eradicate hepatitis B? *Br. Med. J.*, **293**, 404–405 (1986)
41 Derso, A., Boxall, E. H., Tarlow, M. J. and Flewett, T. H. Transmission of HBsAg from mother to infant in four ethnic groups. *Br. Med. J.*, **1**, 949–952 (1978)
42 Godley, M. J., Laidler, P. W. and Banatvala, J. E. Hepatitis B in a West Indian population in the United Kingdom. *Br. Med. J.*, **292**, 375 (1986)
43 Hull, B., Spence, L. and Williams, M. C. Hepatitis B in Trinidad. *West Ind. Med. J.*, **27**, 31–35 (1978)
44 Sebastian, M., Sarin, S. K., Salkan, R. N. *et al.* Incidence of Hepatitis B surface antigen in and around Delhi. *J. Commun. Dis.*, **18**, 22–27 (1986)
45 Joshi, S. H., Baxi, A. J. and Bhatia, H. M. Prevalence of Hepatitis B surface antigen by rapid passive haemagglutination inhibition technique. *Ind. J. Med. Res.*, **69**, 978–980 (1979)
46 Shanmugam, J., Balakrishnan, V., Venugopalon, P. and Sukumaran, C. Prevalence of Hepatitis B surface antigen in blood donors and pregnant women from South Kerala. *Ind. Med. Res.*, **68**, 91–96 (1978)

Chapter 12

Haematological and clinical aspects of sickle cell disease in Britain

Milica Brozović, Sally C. Davies and Joan Henthorn

Introduction

Until recently sickle cell disease (SCD) was considered to be rare and of little significance in Britain [1]. The great majority of cases in the UK are British born of West Indian or African extraction and are permanently domiciled in Britain (M. Brozović and E. Anionwu, 1985, unpublished observations). About 5% are temporarily resident in the UK as students, visitors, diplomats and businessmen from Africa and some 10% are their children. Most cases are under the age of 30; over 20% live in the boroughs of Brent and Lambeth in London and in Birmingham, the remainder reside in other London boroughs, the Midlands and Merseyside [1].

Patients are thus seen by relatively few haematologists, physicians and paediatricians, predominantly in deprived inner city districts, hardest hit by the reduction and redistribution of NHS funds. A coordinated effort to organize comprehensive care for SCD has never taken off [1]. Individual units, hospitals and districts have attempted to run local programmes but most are foundering for want of staff and funding.

As children with SCD grow up and new cases are born, its very variable manifestations are becoming apparent to British doctors, most of whom lack relevant training. Even those familiar with the Jamaican, North American or African experience are on uncertain ground because SCD varies with climate, geographical location, general health and socioeconomic factors. In the UK we must build our own expertise to provide optimum care for British patients.

Epidemiology

The prevalence of SCD in Britain is not accurately known. In a postal survey of haematologists in England and Wales in 1979, 1367 cases were identified [2]: 862 were in London; 58.5% had sickle cell anaemia (SS), 29.9% had haemoglobin SC disease (SC) and the remainder had sickle thalassaemia syndromes and other haemoglobin S interactions with variant haemoglobins. The true number of cases in Britain was probably twice as large. In 1984 Weddell (personal communication) estimated the number of patients living in London to be 1836 cases based on the 1979 National Dwelling and Housing Survey [3] in an estimated population of

288 000 West Indians and 65 000 Africans. Weddell's estimate held true for the London Borough of Brent where the number of registered cases was as predicted [4].

As there are some 600 000 West Indians and 100 000 Africans currently living in the UK we can estimate the total number of SCD cases. In Jamaica the prevalence of SCD per 1000 births is 5.6 : 3.1 for SS, 2.0 for SC, 0.34 for sickle β^+ thalassaemia (S β^+), and 0.16 for sickle β^0 thalassaemia (Sβ^0)[5]. The prevalence is higher in Africa, especially in the sub-Saharan Region, and may be as high as 16 per 1000 births in Nigeria [6]. If we estimate 5 SCD births per 1000 for the West Indies and 10 per 1000 for Africa, then for:

> 600 000 West Indians: 5 cases of SCD per 1000 = 3000 cases
> 100 000 Africans at 10 SCD cases per 1000 = 1000
>   Total number of cases in UK = 4000

Thus the minimum estimate is about 4000. This does not include SCD arising in Mediterranean populations, Arabs or Indians [7] nor new cases born each year. In Brent the incidence of SCD per 1000 Afro-Caribbean births is 12.1 : 7.7 for SS, 4.3 for SC and 0.14 for Sβ^+[8], compared with 11 per 1000 births in Camberwell: 4.0 for SS, 5 for SC and 2.0 for Sβ^+[9]. The exact number of births to black mothers now living in London is not available but from the Brent and Camberwell figures 50–55 babies with SCD are born every year in inner London alone [9]. A total of 100 to 150 births with SCD should be expected in the UK every year.

Thus, around 6000 cases of SCD will be living in Britain by the year 2000 providing there are no major population shifts.

Haematological features of SCD in Britain

The data presented here are from Brent. Haematological variables were measured with a Technicon H-6000 blood counter in 107 adults in the steady state who were aged 16–35 years, and had no evidence of renal impairment. None had received blood transfusions in the previous 6 months. The patients' genotype are shown in Table 12.1, and the blood count data for SS and SC patients only in Table 12.2.

These findings are similar to those of Hayes et al. from Jamaica [10] , which is not surprising as the Brent patients consisted of 80 West Indians, 26 Africans (all but one from West Africa) and one Indian.

Table 12.1 Genotypes and sex of the adults with SCD studied

Genotype	Male	Female	Total no.
SS	20	21	41
SS$\alpha^- \alpha^-$ *	1	1	2
SBβ^0 *	4	4	8
SBβ^+ *	4	4	8
SC	14	24	48
Total no.	53	54	107

* On the basis of family studies and measurement of globin chain synthesis ratio. No gene mapping was carried out.

Table 12.2 Haematological variables in Brent patients with SCD (mean ± s.d.)

Genotype and sex	RBC (× 10¹²/l)	Hb (g/dl)	PCV	MCV (fl)	MCH (pg)	MCHC (g/dl)	RDW (%)	Retic. (× 10⁹/l)	WBC (× 10⁹/l)	Plt (× 10⁹/l)
SS										
Male (n = 20)	3.08 ± 0.44	8.39 ± 0.63	25.9 ± 2.7	84.6 ± 4.9	27.1 ± 2.9	32.4 ± 1.7	20.4 ± 2.5	468 ± 143	11.9 ± 4.0	400 ± 93
Female (n = 21)	2.94 ± 0.31	8.30 ± 0.96	25.9 ± 3.0	86.5 ± 4.5	27.8 ± 2.7	32.2 ± 1.3	19.5 ± 3.2	485 ± 128	10.5 ± 2.7	453 ± 108
SC										
Male (n = 24)	4.76 ± 0.61	12.9 ± 1.1	39.4 ± 3.6	83.4 ± 5.6	27.9 ± 2.1	33.6 ± 0.7	17.6 ± 1.7	238 ± 96	8.2 ± 3.2	272 ± 148
Female (n = 24)	4.32 ± 0.60	11.7 ± 0.9	35.6 ± 2.8	81.1 ± 6.7	27.2 ± 2.2	32.7 ± 1.23	16.7 ± 1.2	193 ± 51	7.6 ± 2.9	242 ± 126

Iron status was studied in 37 Brent patients with SCD in the steady state [11]. There was no evidence of previous iron loading in those not transfused. Five of eight men were iron deficient and all had proven peptic ulceration. It appears that patients with SCD, unlike many other chronic haemolytic states, do not become iron overloaded unless given multiple transfusions, presumably because they have effective erythropoesis rather than dyserythropoesis.

Clinical features of SCD in Britain

Children under 5 years old

Problems rarely present before the second or third month of life because fetal haemoglobin interferes with the sickling phenomenon. Thereafter infective complications and vaso-occlusion occur with increasing frequency. The first 3 years of life are the period of highest risk for mortality and morbidity [5,12,13] (see Table 12.5).

The incidence of *acute splenic sequestration* and *severe infections* in children born in Britain is unknown because few children have been followed from birth. In a group of 171 children followed on average 4.7 years in South London [14] there were six episodes of acute splenic sequestration (all in children under 21 months) and five episodes of pneumococcal meningitis. In 96 Birmingham children with SCD (none under the age of 3 years) studied between 1969 and 1979 [15], there were only two episodes of pneumococcal infection, both in the same child, and no episodes of splenic sequestration.

In Brent all children with SCD have received once daily prophylactic oral penicillin since 1979. There have been no episodes of pneumococcal infection since, in a clinic of 43 children with 21 followed since birth. In the decade prior to 1979 three episodes of pneumococcal meningitis and one fulminant pneumococcal septicaemia with hepatic sequestration and an associated stroke had occurred in 30 children known to the hospital. Two episodes of acute splenic sequestration have occurred since 1979, both were fatal: one in an 18-month-old child newly arrived from Africa, the other in a Brent child followed by another hospital. Neither child was receiving penicillin; autopsy confirmed the presence of pneumococci in the blood of the second child.

Admissions for *painful crises* increase in frequency as children grow older. In 12 months, 19 of 27 admissions in children under 5 were for painful vaso-occlusive episodes. The pain was localized to the limbs in 12 and trunk pain occurred in only seven episodes [16].

Clinical features in schoolchildren (aged 5–16 years)

In older children and adolescents the main morbidity is due to *vaso-occlusive episodes* (or painful crises). The pain is increasingly localized to the trunk – chest, spine, abdomen, pelvis or scapulae. Of 63 acute admissions in children between 5 and 16 during 1 year, 55 were for a painful episode and in 32 (58%) the pain was in the trunk [16]. Nearly 20% of such episodes are associated with *visceral sequestration*, defined as the loss of function or acute enlargement of a visceral organ (lungs, liver, spleen, gut), associated with severe systemic upset, a fall in haemoglobin concentration and often the platelet count. Four visceral syndromes are recognized: acute splenic sequestration [17,18], hepatic sequestration [19], the chest syndrome [20,21] and the 'girdle' syndrome [22]. The last was first recognized during a systematic study of abdominal pain in SCD and is the most severe form. The syndrome consists of simultaneous, or consecutive, sickling and sequestration in the blood supply to the gut and the liver with the lung bases frequently being involved. This 'girdle syndrome' is characterized by a silent distended abdomen, in over 50% of cases associated with severe lumbar spine pain and frequently a rapid clinical deterioration with a low Po_2. Severe cases require exchange transfusion and carry a significant mortality.

Another vaso-occlusive manifestation common in this age-group is *stroke*. Mann [15] in Birmingham observed two cases of hemiplegia, both with a low IQ and epilepsy, as well as two cases of subarachnoid haemorrhage. Murtaza *et al.*[14] encountered six CNS manifestations in 171 children. In Brent, five of 43 children with SS followed for 10 years developed strokes between the ages of 3 and 11; six of 25 children with SS who had CT scans had multiple infarcts and/or cerebral atrophy; two children with abnormal CT scans were clinically neurologically intact [23].

Infective episodes (Table 12.3) are relatively uncommon in this age-group but may be life threatening. *Aplastic crises*, predominantly due to parvovirus infection, are most frequent in schoolchildren [24,25].

Table 12.3 Infective episodes in 211 cases of SCD during one year in Brent (1984–85)

Age (yr)	Genotype	Episode	Organism
3.5	SS	Meningitis	*H.influenzae*
4	SS	Osteomyelitis, elbow	*S.enteritidis*
13	SS	Aplastic crisis	Parvovirus
14	SS	Vaso-occlusive crisis Febrile illness	Q fever
14	SC	Aplastic crisis Pneumonia	Parvovirus *M.pneumoniae*
16	SS	Aplastic crisis	Parvovirus
20	SS	Urinary tract inf.	*E.coli*
25	SS	Urinary tract inf.	*E.coli*
29	SC	Splenic abscess	*S.virchow*
30	SC	UTI postpartum	Pseudomonas

Clinical features in adults (over 16 years)

There is a paucity of data published on the problems of adults with SCD in Britain [4,26]. Of 135 cases living in Brent, 59 have SS, 54 have SC, six have $S\beta^0$, 12 have $S\beta^+$ and four have other forms of SCD. Only 25 patients (six with SS, 15 with SC, two with $S\beta^+$ and two with other forms of SCD) are over 35 years of age. Thirty-two (23%) of 135 adult Brent patients required 72 acute admissions in 1 year [16]. Sixty-eight of these admissions were for *painful crisis*, mainly with trunk pain. Nineteen of the crises culminated in a *visceral sequestration syndrome* (seven chest syndromes, 12 girdle syndromes) and one 19-year-old boy with the girdle syndrome died despite emergency exchange transfusion and intensive resuscitation.

Five of the Brent adults (aged 17–23 years) with SCD were found to have had major *CNS complications*: a dense hemiplegia and a hemianopia in SS disease; convulsions during a crisis with multiple old cerebral infarcts shown later on CT scan in $S\beta^0$; acute vertigo and unsteadiness due to cerebellar infarction in HbSC; a 19-year-old woman with SS died from a massive intraventricular haemorrhage in the 39th week of her first pregnancy, and a 49-year-old woman with SC developed septicaemia, bilateral chest syndrome followed by a stroke and died despite intensive treatment. In six neurologically normal adult patients with SS, PET and CT scans showed cerebral atrophy and areas of infarction in three [27]. In Brent 10 men (eight with SS, two with SC) have presented with episodes of *priapism* [4]. The youngest was nine and the oldest 30. Four patients remained impotent and three have silicone penile prostheses implanted.

Severe *infective episodes* are less frequent (Table 12.3); there were three episodes of salmonella infection (two cases of osteomyelitis and one splenic abscess) during a period of 5 years. Only three patients in Brent with SS have to date developed *renal impairment*: two with the nephrotic syndrome, one with amyloid and the other following a *streptococcal* glomerulonephritis now in remission. A third with SC developed transient impairment postpartum due to severe urinary tract infection (Table 12.4)

Avascular necrosis of bones is evident in 18.5% of SS patients, 19.0% of SC patients and 20.8% of $S\beta^+$ patients in Brent [28a], similar to the incidence reported from other parts of the world. Twenty-four had unilateral femoral head involvement and seven bilateral, 12 had unilateral involvement of the head of the humerus and 14 bilateral. In younger patients with Perthe's type disease six of the eight cases were female; seven had SS. Other major SCD-related events were seen in 66% of the affected patients including the chest syndrome, retinopathy, priapism, etc.

Flattening of the vertebral bodies often with vertebral end-plate depression was seen in 14.7% of Brent patients. This leads to low back pain and morning stiffness. In the affected group the level of HbF was significantly lower.

Osteomyelitis is well recorded in SCD with 5.6% of the Brent patients having documented episodes. The site is most commonly metaphyseal, mainly affecting the long bones (70%), and 90% of cases are caused by salmonella species [28a].

Eye disease is common in SCD, with tortuosity of retinal vessels visible in most patients with SS and proliferative retinopathy (PSR) well described. It is thought that the development of PSR depends on the balance between the haematocrit and the red blood cell deformability with the highest incidence occurring in SC patients, up to 40% in Jamaica [5]. In Haringey, North London [28b], 41% of SS patients and 85.7% of SC patients examined had evidence of PSR; the Brent experience is similar [4]. The most severe complication of PSR is retinal detachment – 15 cases were seen at Moorfields Eye Hospital over the period 1976 to 1985 [29], 13 underwent surgery with 11 maintaining or improving their visual acuity following treatment.

Sexual development is delayed in SCD but the relationship between weight and menarche appears to be maintained [30]. In Brent the average age at menarche was 14.4 years for girls with SS and 13.6 years for those with SC ([4], M Brozović, 1989, personal communication). Women with SCD are normally fertile unlike the men in whom subfertility is frequent [31].

Pregnancy is associated with major pathology for both mother and fetus. In 1983, Tuck reviewed 125 pregnancies in SCD women from a number of British centres

[32]: 38% had vaso-occlusive crisis in the antenatal period and 22% in the postnatal period, with 48% suffering from pre-eclamptic toxaemia. During 24% of deliveries there was evidence of fetal distress, 13% of deliveries were preterm and 20% of the babies were light for date. While there was no maternal mortality, the stillbirth rate was 40/1000 and the neonatal death rate was 8/1000. Severe splenic sequestration during pregnancy, frequent in Nigeria and Ghana, does not appear to be a feature in Britain.

In Brent almost all 26 pregnancies reviewed in 1984 (M. Brozović, 1989, personal communication) suffered some SCD complication. These included a maternal death from stroke at 39 weeks, a stillbirth following a fulminant abdominal sickling crisis at 29 weeks, splenic infarction in the second and third trimesters and rapidly progressive aseptic necrosis of the hip and sickle retinopathy. An important feature was the postpartum cluster of pulmonary thromboembolic events (sickle 'chest syndrome') in patients with SC which had been abolished by the use of prophylactic twice daily subcutaneous heparin from 36 weeks to 6 weeks postpartum.

Adequate hypertransfusion (HbS < 20%) can prevent some of these complications if started sufficiently early in pregnancy. There are however problems associated with this treatment; the most important is alloimmunization [33] with potential haemolytic disease of the newborn, as well as iron overload, infection and the risk of precipitating labour with sudden blood volume alterations. The role of transfusion in pregnancy has not been fully evaluated but in some patients is lifesaving.

Renal disease is common in pregnancy, particularly an increased incidence of *urinary tract infection*. Of eight pregnancies in 1986 in Brent, three of the SS patients developed *renal papillary necrosis* while hypertransfused and another SC patient developed a transient impairment of creatinine clearance associated with pseudomonas infection.

Comparison of clinical features of SCD in Brent and Jamaica

The severity of SCD is affected by genetic and environmental factors which include cold climate, leg trauma, exposure to infections, availability of health care, economic and social factors. Table 12.4 compares some of the clinical features of SCD in Brent and Jamaica [4].

Admissions for painful crises were commoner in SS patients in Brent than in Jamaica: by contrast, fewer patients with SC needed admission for painful crises. Similar percentages of patients with SS in both locations were admitted with the chest syndrome, but in the SC patients this was less common in Brent than in Jamaica. Leg ulcers were rare in Brent but common in Jamaica. Splenomegaly was found in 14% of SS patients in Brent and Jamaica but was more frequent in Jamaican SC patients than in Brent.

There were fewer pregnancies in Brent women than in their Jamaican counterparts, probably reflecting altered social and reproductive patterns as well as the relatively young age in Brent (21.9 years for SS and 26.3 for SC women).

Thus, the general impression is that patients with SS in Britain have more painful and more severe crises but experience fewer chest problems and have virtually no leg ulcers. Patients with SC seem to be less severely affected in Britain. The accuracy of these observations can only be confirmed by long-term studies of cohorts followed from birth. Such cohort studies are neither available nor planned in Britain.

Table 12.4 Comparison of some clinical features in Brent and Jamaica

Clinical feature	SS		SC	
	Brent	Jamaica	Brent	Jamaica
Patients studied (no.)	68	88	71	90
Patients requiring admission for painful crises (no.)	63 (92%)	35 (39%)	16 (22.5%)	35 (39%)
Patients admitted with chest syndrome (no.)	18 (26%)	30 (37%)	6 (8%)	26 (29%)
Leg ulcers	3 (4%)	40 (45%)	0 (0%)	18 (20%)
Splenomegaly	10 (14%)	12 (17%)	23 (32%)	51 (57%)
Priapism (cases/men)	7/31	5/40	2/31	4/44
Retinopathy (cases/examined)	2/10	36/306	14/21	101/282
Aplastic crises	5	6	3	Not known
Pregnancies (no.) per women over 16	12/23	46/30	38/23	72/21
Fetal loss per pregnancy	(0.52) 3/12	(1.53) 9/46	(1.65) 5/38	(3.1) 7/72

Taken with permission from Brozović and Anionwu [4].

Mortality in SCD

In the Jamaican cohort study, Serjeant has shown a mortality of 10% in the first year of life, 5% in the second and 3% in the third [34]. He suggested that by the age of 5 years the child may have survived the highest risk and that the prognosis improves with age and he states: ' . . . by the age of 20 years survival to 30 or 40 years may not be uncommon' [5].

The principal causes of death in Jamaica are acute chest syndrome (in the second and third decade), splenic sequestration, renal failure, meningitis and cerebrovascular disease at all ages [24]. In children under 2 years old the main causes of death are pneumococcal septicaemia and acute splenic sequestration [13,34,35]. These complications may cause death before the diagnosis of SCD. In a longitudinal study of 422 children in Los Angeles, Powars [35] calculated a 10% death rate during the first decade and 5% during each subsequent decade of life. She draws attention to the large number of 'cot deaths' in whom autopsy disclosed SS and pneumococcal septicaemia.

Few data are available from Britain. In the 1979 postal survey [2] there were seven deaths in children aged 2 years or less: four could be described as sudden or 'cot deaths', one was due to meningitis (organism unknown), one to massive pulmonary infarction and no details were available in one. In Brent two children under the age of 2 years are known to have died between 1979 and 1966, both from acute splenic sequestration.

An analysis of all reported deaths in Britain according to age is shown in Table 12.5. Sudden deaths with unhelpful coroner's reports such as 'acute sickling', 'acute sickle cell anaemia' and 'pallor of all organs' account for 12 deaths. Acute chest syndrome, CNS deaths and other causes follow closely. The pattern is probably similar to that in Jamaica and the USA but without reliable autopsy reports and careful follow up from birth, no firm conclusions can be reached.

Table 12.5 SCD deaths in Britain – compiled from references

Cause of death	0–2 SS	0–2 SC	3–10 SS	3–10 SC	11–20 SS	11–20 SC	21–30 SS	21–30 SC	>30 SS	>30 SC	Total SS	Total SC
Acute splenic sequestration	2		2	1		1					6	2
Acute chest syndrome		1	1		4						5	1
Pneumococcal infection			1								1	
Other infections	1		1		1			1			3	1
CNS deaths			2		2		1			2	5	1
'Sudden' deaths	4		5	1	2						11	1
Renal failure									1		1	0
Pregnancy related					3*			2			3	2
Other			2				1		1		4	
Not known	1				1	2			1		3	2
Total	9	1	13	2	13	3	2	3	3	2	39	11

Column group header: Age (yr)

* Two deaths due to massive PE (? chest syndrome); one death due to intraventricular haemorrhage.

The mortality in the Brent group followed from 1975 to 1985 is 4.7% per decade (10 deaths among a group of 211 patients), similar to that described by Powars [35] for Los Angeles.

Conclusions

SCD, with at least 4000 cases, is one of the commonest inherited diseases in Britain and in some urban areas accounts for up to 40% of all haematological hospital admissions [4]. SCD also causes significant morbidity and mortality in Jamaica and the USA. Little is known about SCD in British-born patients and there is an urgent need for a good epidemiological study of the natural history of SCD in Britain to establish the prognosis, the pattern of morbidity and life expectancy as well as to plan the appropriate health care. British-born babies with SCD must be diagnosed at birth and protected from fulminant pneumococcal infections by daily oral prophylactic penicillin [36,37].

The management of both the acute and the chronic manifestations of SCD are discussed at length elsewhere [22,38,39]. Care is too often haphazard with poor interdisciplinary cooperation and little or no coordination of effort, a situation reminiscent of haemophilia 25 or 30 years ago. Although there are some promising antisickling agents being developed, none will be available in the near future, or be curative.

It is increasingly important to establish guidelines for the comprehensive care of SCD patients in Britain. The health, educational and social needs of sufferers should be identified, recognized and then met as in other inherited debilitating diseases.

References

1 Prashar, U., Anionwu, E. and Brozović, M. *Sickle Cell Disease – Who Cares?* The Runnymead Trust, London (1985)

2 Davies, L. R., Huehns, E.R. and White, J. M. Survey of sickle cell disease in England and Wales. *Br. Med. J.*, **283**, 1519–1521 (1981)

3 Department of Environment (Government Statistical Service), National Dwelling and Housing Survey, HMSO, London (1979)

4 Brozović, M. and Anionwu, E. Sickle cell disease in Britain. *J. Clin. Pathol.*, **37**, 1321–1326 (1984)

5 Serjeant, G. R. Observations on the epidemiology of sickle cell disease. *Trans. R. Soc. Trop. Med. Hyg.*, **75**, 228–233 (1981)

6 World Health Organization Hereditary Diseases Programme. Update of the Progress of Haemoglobinopathy Control, WHO, Geneva (1985)

7 Serjeant, G. R. *Sickle Cell Disease*, Oxford, Oxford University Press, pp. 19–24 (1985)

8 Henthorn, J., Anionwu, E. and Brozović, M. Screening cord blood for sickle haemoglobinopathies in Brent. *Br. Med. J.*, **289**, 479–480 (1984)

9 Horn, M. E. C., Dick, M. C., Frost, B. *et al.* Neonatal screening for sickle cell disease in Camberwell: results and recommendations of a two year pilot study. *Br. Med. J.*, **292**, 737–740 (1986)

10 Hayes, R. J., Beckford, M., Grandison, Y. *et al.* The haematology of steady state sickle cell disease: frequency distributions, variation with age and sex, longitudinal observations. *Br. J. Haematol.*, **59**, 369–382 (1985)

11 Davies, S. C., Henthorn, J. and Brozović, M. Iron deficiency in sickle cell anaemia. *J. Clin. Pathol.*, **36**, 1012–1014 (1983)

12 Rogers, D. W., Clance, J. M., Cupidore, L. *et al.* Early deaths in Jamaican children with sickle cell disease. *Br. Med. J.*, **1**, 1515–1516 (1978)

13 Serjeant, G. R. *Sickle Cell Disease*, Oxford, Oxford University Press, pp. 344–348 (1985)

14 Murtaza, L. N., Stroud, C. E., Davies, L. R. and Cooper, D. J. Admissions to hospital of children with sickle cell anaemia: a study in South London. *Br. Med. J.*, **282**, 1040–1050 (1981)

15 Mann, J. R. Sickle haemoglobinopathies in England. *Arch. Dis. Child.*, **56**, 676–683 (1981)

16 Brozović, M., Davies, S. C. and Brownell, A. Acute problems in sickle cell disease. A study of acute admissions in 211 patients with SCD during one year. *Br. Med. J.*, **294**, 1206–1208 (1988)

17 Tomlinson, W. J. Abdominal crises in uncomplicated sickle cell anaemia. A clinicopathologic study of 11 cases with a suggested explanation of their cause. *Am. J. Med. Sci.*, **209**, 722–741 (1975)

18 Seeler, R. A. Deaths in children with sickle cell anaemia. *Clin. Pediatr.*, **10**, 418–419 (1972)

19 Hatton, C. S. R., Bunch, C. and Weatherall, D. J. Hepatic sequestration in sickle cell anaemia. *Br. Med. J.*, **290**, 744–745 (1985)

20 Charache, S., Scott, J. C. and Charache, P. 'Acute chest syndrome' in adults with sickle cell anaemia. *Arch. Int. Med.*, **139**, 67–69 (1979)

21 Davies, S., Winn, A. A., Luce, P. J. *et al.* Acute chest syndrome in sickle cell disease. *Lancet*, **i**, 36–38 (1984)

22 Yardumian, A. and Davies, S. C. Clinical management of severe sickle cell disease. *Acta Haematol.*, **78**, 193–197 (1987)

23 Hindmarsh, P., Brozović, M., Brooks, C. G. D. and Davies, S. C. Incidence of overt neurological damage in children with sickle cell disease. *Postgrad. Med. J.* **63**, 751–753 (1987)

24 Pattison, J. R., Jones, S. E., Hodgson, J. *et al.* Parvovirus infection and hypoplastic crises in sickle cell anaemia. *Lancet*, **i**, 664–665 (1981)

25 Brownell, A. I., McSwiggan, D. A., Cubbitt, W. D. and Anderson, M. J. Aplastic and hypoplastic episodes in sickle cell anaemia and thalassaemia intermedia. *J. Clin. Pathol.*, **39**, 121–127 (1986)

26 Anionwu, E., Walford, D., Brozović, M. and Kirkwood, B. Sickle cell disease in a British urban community. *Br. Med. J.*, **282**, 283–286 (1981)

27 Herold, S., Brozović, M., Gibbs, J. *et al.* Measurement of regional cerebral blood flow, blood volume, and oxygen metabolism in patients with sickle cell disease using Positron Emission Scanning. *Stroke*, **17**, 692–698, (1986)

28a Taylor, L. J. Sickle cell disease in Britain: a review. Royal College of Surgeons, Jacksonian Prize Winning Thesis (1985)

28b Kehinde, M. O., Marsh, J. C. W., and Marsh, E. G. Sickle cell disease in North London. *Br. J. Haematol.*, **66**, 543–547 (1987)

29 Brazier, D. J., Gregor, Z. J., Blach, R. K. *et al.* Retinal detachment in patients with proliferative sickle cell retinopathy. *Trans. Ophthalmol Soc. UK*, **105**, 100–105 (1984)

30 Platt, O. S., Rosenstock, W. and Espoland, M. A. Influence of sickle haemoglobinopathies on growth and development. *N. Engl. J. Med.*, **311**, 7–12 (1984)

31 Osegbe, D. N., Akinyanju, O. and Amaku, E. Fertility in males with sickle cell disease. *Lancet*, **ii**, 275–276 (1981)

32 Tuck, S. M., Studd, J. W. W. and White, J. M. Pregnancy in sickle cell disease in the UK. *Br.J.Obstet.Gynaecol.*, **90**, 112–117 (1983)

33 Davies, S. C., McWilliam, A. C., Hewitt, P. E. *et al.* Red cell alloimmunization in sickle cell disease. *Br. J. Haematol.*, **63**, 241–245 (1986)

34 Serjeant, G. R. *Sickle Cell Disease*, Oxford, Oxford University Press, pp. 344–398 (1985)

35 Powars, D. R. Natural history of sickle cell disease. The first ten years. *Semin. Hematol.*, **12**, 107–126 (1975)

36 Gaston, M. H., Verter, J. L., Woods, G. *et al.* Prophylaxis with oral penicillin in children with sickle cell anaemia. *N. Engl. J. Med*, **314**,1593–1599 (1986)

37 Editorial. Penicillin prophylaxis for babies with sickle cell disease. *Lancet*, **ii**, 1432–1433 (1986)

38 Charache, S., Lubin, B. and Reid, C. D. (eds). *Management and Therapy of Sickle Cell Disease*, NIH Publication No. 84–2117, US Department of Health and Human Services, Public Health Service, National Institutes of Health, Washington (1984)

39 Brozović, M. and Davies, S. C. Management of sickle cell disease. *Postgrad. Med. J.*, **63**, 605–609 (1987)

Chapter 13

Thalassaemia screening: ethics and practice

Bernadette Modell and Mary Petrou

The haemoglobinopathies are common medical problems in the ethnic minorities in European countries and will be handed on indefinitely to later generations (Table 13.1). They are also unique among inherited diseases because heterozygous carriers can be detected cheaply with nearly 100% accuracy. Carriers can therefore be advised *prospectively* that, if by chance they mate with another carrier, they have a 1 in 4 risk in each pregnancy of producing a child with a major haemoglobinopathy. Prenatal diagnosis is now available in the second trimester by fetal blood sampling [1], and in the first trimester by chorionic villus sampling and DNA analysis [2].

When fetal diagnosis was possible only at 18 weeks' gestation, most British couples of Mediterranean or Indian origin at risk for having children with thalassaemia major requested fetal testing, and decided to abort affected

Table 13.1 Frequency of haemoglobinopathy traits detectable by routine 'haemoglobinopathy screening' in ethnic minorities in the UK

Population	% of population carrying:								
	Thalassaemia traits			Abnormal haemoglobins				Total	
	β	α^0	Homozygous α^+	HbE	HbS	HbC	HbD	All	Pathological
Mediterranean									
Cypriots	16	1	2	0	1	0	0	20	18
Others	1–10	0–1	?2	0	+	0	0	1–14	1–12
South Asians									
Sindi	10	0	6	?	?	0	+	16	10
Gujarati	6	0	6	+	+	0	+	12	>6
Other Indians	3	0	6	+	+	0	+	9	3
Pakistani	5–6	0	6	0	?	0	+	12.5	6.5
East Asians[*]									
e.g. Hong Kong	3	3	?	+	0	0	0	6	6
West Indians	1–2	0	?5	0	6–12	1–3	+	>16	>11
Africans	1–2	0	?5	0	12–20	0–15	0	>25	>20
'Native' British	0.1–0.2	+	0	0	0	0	+	0.1–0.2	0.1–0.2

[*] 'Oriental'.

pregnancies. However, there was a relatively small demand from British Pakistanis at risk and also from couples at risk for sickle cell disease, due to unacceptability of at termination of pregnancy at 20 weeks; first-trimester prenatal diagnosis has changed this and it is now more acceptable. Our experience of prenatal diagnosis for sickle cell disease is still limited, so the main emphasis in this chapter is thalassaemia.

If adequate population screening and appropriate counselling are provided, prevention by fetal diagnosis is acceptable and the birth rate of affected children can be greatly reduced. This has now occurred in many areas in the Mediterranean region, where thalassaemia is an important public health problem [3].

Ethically, one of the following explanations must apply for each birth of a thalassaemic child that occurs: ignorance on the part of the patient or the doctor; an error in diagnostic testing of the carrier or the fetus; or the informed choice of the couple not to accept testing or not to terminate a pregnancy known to be affected. As only the last of these explanations is ethically acceptable, so it is an important responsibility for the medical profession to ensure community education, and to provide screening and appropriate counselling. However, to deliver such information and services when they are needed, i.e. before a couple has started to reproduce, it is necessary to move outside a traditional medical context, and make contact with the healthy community.

Community information – how to generate the request for testing?

Before they can request heterozygote testing, people need to be informed of risk in a way that they can understand; to grasp the point that the problem could affect *them*; that severe consequences can be avoided; and that testing is freely available.

In England the diversity of the ethnic groups that need to be targeted creates practical problems in communication. Ways of reaching the ethnic minorities may be:

1. To develop groups within the different communities concerned with information, screening and genetic counselling (e.g. Sickle Cell Centres, Thalassaemia Societies. Relevant addresses are appended to Chapter 14).
2. To provide informative posters and leaflets available at places of first medical contact such as general practitioners' surgeries, family planning clinics and antenatal clinics. A suitable poster and leaflets are now available from the UK Thalassaemia Society (address appended).
3. To encourage education about human genetics in schools to include the principles of recessive inheritance, using the haemoglobinopathies and other inherited diseases such as cystic fibrosis as examples. Improved genetics teaching in schools is important to help to break through the psychological 'invulnerability barrier' of healthy young people.

The educational approach is still in its infancy. It will be slow and difficult, but it is particularly important for ethical reasons.

Laboratory testing for thalassaemia carriers: screening for genetic counselling

The objectives of carrier diagnosis are: to provide advice about genetic risk, give information about how risk may be avoided, and offer contact with a specialist resource for advice and social support; to help avoid iatrogenic disease; and to increase community awareness by creating a nucleus of informed individuals within each group at risk.

As each ethnic minority carries a different combination of haemoglobinopathy traits (Table 13.1) it is not acceptable only to test blacks for sickle cell trait, and Cypriots and Asians for thalassaemia, because a minority in each group carries the other form of haemoglobinopathy. The only practical approach is to consider all members of all the ethnic minorities as potential carriers of one or another trait, and to test all in the same way.

Not all haemoglobinopathy traits carry a reproductive risk. For instance, Hb D trait and α^+-thalassaemia trait are usually harmless, but cannot be ignored. Accurate diagnosis and advice is needed to avoid people being told they have a serious genetic risk when they do not. In a mixed population such as now exists in Northern Europe, complex combinations can occur, and expert genetic counselling may be needed.

The basic laboratory investigations for a haemoglobinopathy 'screen' are:

red cell indices, to detect microcytosis associated with thalassaemia traits;
electrophoresis to detect abnormal haemoglobins and an elevated haemoglobin F;
sickle test specifically to identify Hb S.

α- and β-thalassaemia trait are first indicated by a microcytic blood picture. The normal mean cell haemoglobin (MCH) is 27–32 pg. In α-zero or β-thalassaemia trait it is typically 18–23 pg, and nearly always below 25 pg. When the Hb value is in the normal range this picture always indicates one or another form of thalassaemia trait. Children under 4 years old often have rather small red cells, which can confuse the diagnosis. The distinction between α- and β-thalassaemia traits is made by measuring the Hb A_2 level. A value above 3.5% indicates β-thalassaemia trait and the carrier can be given clear genetic information. A value below 3% suggests an α-thalassaemia trait.

The technical difficulty of screening for thalassaemia differs with the ethnic group concerned. For instance, β-thalassaemia trait is by far the commonest cause of marked microcytosis among Cypriots, who are rarely iron deficient. By contrast, between 6% and 11% of Indian- and Pakistan-origin people have an MCH below 25 pg, but only half of these have β-thalassaemia trait. The remainder have one or other form of α-thalassaemia trait, or iron deficiency, or a combination. In many more the MCH is between 25 and 27 pg: these may have α-plus thalassaemia and/or iron deficiency. Screening Asian populations is therefore more difficult and expensive, since HbA_2 estimation has to be done in a larger proportion of cases, in order to detect reliably all carriers of the thalassaemia traits.

Incidental screening for thalassaemia

Since Coulter counters are now routine in most haematological laboratories in the UK, and since the microcytosis associated with the significant thalassaemia traits is so marked, carriers can be identified automatically whenever a haemoglobin estimation is requested for any reason. If an MCH of less than 25 pg is found, that blood sample should be sent for Hb A_2 estimation. Patients who definitely carry thalassaemia trait should be appropriately counselled. Such incidental testing is exceptionally cheap.

Incidental screening where there are few or no representatives of the ethnic minorities is important, since 1–2/1000 native British are thalassaemia carriers. It is particularly indicated to detect and advise them, because the risk of iatrogenic disease associated with thalassaemia trait is highest for North Europeans, due to the infrequency of the condition. Thalassaemia carriers can be over-treated for non-existent iron-deficiency anaemia with iron, which can lead to iatrogenic haemochromotosis, especially in males.

One problem when carrying out incidental screening on people who have not requested testing is that carriers then need to be correctly informed. At present many haemoglobinopathy carriers are detected and the information is put in their notes for medical purposes, but the genetic implications are not communicated to the person most concerned, i.e. the patient. This is partly because doctors in so many specialities are involved and even if they are aware of the genetic implications of the diagnosis they rarely have time to give genetic counselling. Now that simple information booklets are available, this problem can be overcome if the haematology laboratory supplies a counselling booklet to the requesting doctor – to be passed on to the patient – with every positive diagnosis.

Genetic risk of thalassaemia trait

The genetic risk for a thalassaemia carrier differs with ethnic group. In most populations, if a carrier marries within the same ethnic group, the risk of marrying another carrier is equal to the frequency of β-haemoglobinopathy traits in that ethnic group. For instance, a Cypriot with β-thalassaemia trait has a 16% chance of marrying a carrier of β-thalassaemia and a 1% chance of marrying a carrier of Hb S, while a Sikh with β-thalassaemia trait has only a 3% chance of making an at-risk marriage. Although 3% of Chinese carry α-zero thalassaemia trait and 3% carry β-thalassaemia trait, the chance of making an at-risk marriage is only 3%, since only marriage to a carrier of the same class of disorder creates a genetic risk.

However, certain ethnic groups favour consanguineous marriages. In such populations, when a thalassaemia carrier is identified he or she must be considered as at exceptionally high genetic risk. For instance, among British Pakistanis first cousin marriages are common [4]. The frequency of thalassaemia trait is around 6% [5], so a carrier who marries an unrelated person has a 6% risk of making an at-risk marriage. However, if he or she marries a first cousin, then the chance of making an at-risk marriage is about 18%. This detectable high risk underlines the importance of screening partners of pregnant women who are found to carry thalassaemia, and of following up the parents of children who carry thalassaemia.

Genetic counselling for the haemoglobinopathies

The objective of identifying heterozygotes is to provide genetic counselling. The ethical principles underlying genetic counselling have been studied, and summarized as 'the autonomy of the individual or the couple, their right to full and complete information, and the preservation of the highest standard of confidentiality' [6]. These principles indicate the extent to which genetics practice depends on satisfactory communications: a point of particular significance in counselling the ethnic minorities.

The counselling of single heterozygotes is relatively simple. They must be given a clear understanding of the meaning of thalassaemia trait, but the message conveyed is not excessively worrying, being a potential, rather than an actual problem. Because of this simplicity, and the large numbers involved, such information would best be given at the primary health care level. However, as few doctors, apart from specialist geneticists, have adequate time, this might best be provided by trained nurses or health visitors, and aids in the form of leaflets in relevant languages are needed. It is also important to have appropriate expert counsellors to whom carriers with special problems and at-risk couples can be referred. Although these needs are now clear, the development of the appropriate service structure has barely begun.

Counselling at-risk couples is much more complex, and needs to be done by a specialist. The genetic counselling should be non-directive and should leave people free to choose from the options available. The counsellor's role is to ensure that the couple are fully informed, and to accompany them in their decision making, taking into account their social and religious position, and to reach a conclusion that they will be able to live with for the rest of their lives. The amount of information to be conveyed, the need to ensure that it has really been understood, and the life-long consequences of these decisions mean that the counsellor must spend adequate time with the couples. Differences of language, culture and religion require even more care.

It is important to have a counselling structure within an at-risk community to make contact and to develop, for example, a network of sickle-cell centres. An army of specialist counsellors is not needed, but enough are necessary to permit health visitors, midwives, nurses and general practitioners to integrate sickle cell counselling into their daily work, and to refer to a specialist centre when necessary.

The main strategy for the haemoglobinopathies in the UK is testing pregnant women (of 'not North European origin'). When a pregnant carrier is found, her husband is sent for. If both prove to be carriers, they are informed of their risk and offered the possibility of prenatal diagnosis. This strategy has worked well for Cypriots and Indians, but it is no longer appropriate alone as those detected cannot take advantage of firsst-trimester prenatal diagnosis. This is also true for couples at risk for sickle-cell disease, and for most Muslims, because first-trimester testing by chorionic villus sampling is the only form of prenatal diagnosis that they generally accept. In fact, no systematic effort has yet been made to provide Britain Pakistanis with education, screening and counselling, and this is now the most important issue in thalassaemia screening in the UK.

Screening British Pakistanis for thalassaemia traits

The 1983 Labour Force Survey located 383 000 people of Pakistani origin in the UK. One result of migration has been an increase in consanguineous marriages from about 30% in Pakistan to about 50% in the UK [4]. Consequently the birth rate of infants with recessively inherited disorders, such as thalassaemia major, is higher than it would be if mating were 'random'.

Many British Pakistanis are still first generation immigrants from rural areas. They are devout Muslims and believe that the soul enters the fetus at around 12–16 weeks of fetal life (14–18 weeks of gestation). Termination of pregnancy after 'ensoulment' is not generally accepted, although termination of pregnancy in the first trimester may be. Thus, only a small proportion of British Pakistani couples with one or more thalassaemic children accepted the offer of prenatal diagnosis in subsequent pregnancies, giving an impression of lack of interest in the prevention of genetic disease. However, now that first-trimester prenatal diagnosis is available there is interest, but the requirements for communicating genetic information to this group have not been met.

Many British Pakistani women do not speak English and live primarily in the extended family and the home. Trained female counsellors who speak the language, and preferably share their religion, are necessary. Counselling for important decisions like requesting fetal diagnoses or termination of pregnancy, is best carried out in the home. The facilities for providing this service do not exist in Britain yet, but in many cities there are Urdu- or Punjabi-speaking health workers who could incorporate basic genetic counselling into their work. To achieve this a few specialist centres are needed to produce literature and other educational aids in the appropriate languages, and provide training for other health workers.

As a new generation educated in England undergoes social change, the requirements for genetic counselling will change.

Ethical aspects

The existing thalassaemia control programmes have provided answers to some questions with moral overtones, such as whether people usually want to know if they carry an inherited disease. The success of these programmes, even in underdeveloped and Catholic areas of Italy [7], shows that most people *do* wish to know if they risk transmitting a severe disease to their children. Table 13.2 lists the choices available to couples who know that they have a high genetic risk; all these choices have important moral implications. If the information comes to light during

Table 13.2 Possibilities open to carriers of inherited diseases, to avoid bearing affected children

Time of knowing risk	Possible action
Before marriage	1. Not to marry 2. Not to marry another carrier 3. Marry in the usual way
After marriage	4. Not to reproduce 5. 'Take the chance' 6. Reproduce with fetal diagnosis 7. Reproduce with a substitute partner 8. Divorce and reproduce
After birth of an affected child	9. Accept infant and treatment 10. Accept infant but not treatment 11. Reject infant

pregnancy, the choice is limited to whether to accept prenatal diagnosis and selective abortion. If the risk is discovered before reproduction, more choices are open.

People at risk for having thalassaemic children in general are not prepared to alter their marriage behaviour as a result of genetic information, but may be prepared to modify their reproductive behaviour. Few couples found to be at risk prior to marriage decide not to marry: very few couples divorce for genetic reasons, and few reproduce with a surrogate partner (i.e. make use of artificial insemination by donor, or of egg donation). Most couples appear to want their partner's genetic children, and the two commonest choices are to take the risk, or to request prenatal diagnosis.

The evolution of heterozygote screening is well illustrated by the Cypriot thalassaemia prevention programme [8]. It was expected that screening and counselling prior to marriage would alter people's choice of partner but, as elsewhere, this proved to be mistaken. An initial effort to discourage carriers from marrying each other 'resulted in non-cooperation' and had to be abandoned. In fact, trying to alter such an important piece of social behaviour amounts to 'objective' stigmatization of carriers, since the aim would be to limit their freedom to behave like other people. Such stigmatization is unacceptable, and would make it impossible to run a screening programme.

In Cyprus, a programme of public information, population screening, and genetic counselling was started before prenatal diagnosis for thalassaemia was possible. When it became available in England soon afterwards, many at-risk couples travelled there for diagnosis at their own expense, and plans were made to set up the service in Cyprus. The most marked effect of screening in the absence of prenatal diagnosis, but with the knowledge that it would become available, was a fall in the birthrate of thalassaemic infants, because the couples at risk refrained from reproducing (or terminated their pregnancies indiscriminately) until testing became available locally. Once prenatal diagnosis was freely available, the fraction of the fall in thalassaemic births due to refraining from reproduction rapidly diminished, while that due to prenatal diagnosis with selective abortion has increased progressively (Table 13.3). The message is clear. Most couples wish to have their own family, and take advantage of prenatal diagnosis to do so.

There has been considerable evolution in the Cypriot programme, as to when it is best to provide genetic information. Screening could be offered in childhood, prior to marriage, or during pregnancy. Initially, because the social implications of screening in school or prior to marriage were uncertain, and because of limited laboratory resources, screening was offered only to those at most immediate risk, i.e. to pregnant women. But when opening the new Thalassaemia Centre, the Archbishop of Cyprus pointed out that this form of screening did not allow couples the full range of choices; he felt that, for moral reasons, knowledge should be available prior to marriage, and he instituted an ecclesiastical ruling that every couple to be married should present a certificate that they had been screened, and suitably advised, at the laboratory. (This certificate does not give the diagnosis, which is confidential to the couple.) Since there is no civil marriage in Cyprus, this is tantamount to a law requiring premarital screening. The possibility of introducing such a civil law had been considered, and ruled unconstitutional. Since premarital screening has become a regular practice, only 2% of the couples who are both carriers have decided not to go ahead with the marriage: the majority proceed with the marriage and plan to use prenatal diagnosis in due course.

Table 13.3 Effects of counselling and fetal diagnosis* on the incidence of thalassaemia major in Cyprus

Year	Total births	Thalassaemia major births			Homozygous fetuses aborted		Fall in birth rate due to refraining from conception (%)
		Expected (no.)	Found (no.)	Difference (%)	No.	% expected	
1974	8594	64	51	20	0	—	20
1975	8039	59	47	20	0	—	20
1976	9295	69	34	50	0	—	50
Prospective genetic counselling started →							
1977	9188	68	34	50	3	4	46
1978	9644	71	21	70	6	9	61
1979	10372	77	18	77	18	23	54
Fetal diagnosis started →							

* Fetal diagnosis was available only by going abroad to London, Athens or Jerusalem, until May 1981, when it was started in Nicosia. Modified from Angastiniotis and Hadjiminas [8]

It has become clear that it is to the advantage of the whole population to provide adequate screening and counselling, rather than to continue to allow unforeseen births of thalassaemic children with the heavy financial consequences for the community that this implies [2].

The most important issue is inadequate provision of screening and counselling, and there is clear evidence that at-risk couples need and want it. In the UK, because of the large population, and the diversity of ethnic minorities, there is a long way to go before we can offer screening and counselling to all in need of it. The situation is already better than it was a few years ago, and we now know what we should be doing, and the necessary educational aids are becoming available.

For addresses of relevant self-help groups, see Appendix 1 to Chapter 14.

References

1 Matsakis, M., Berdoukas, V. A., Angastiniotis, M. et al. Haematological aspects of antenatal diagnosis for thalassaemia in Britain. Br. J. Haematol., 45, 185–197 (1980)
2 Old, J. M., Fitches, A., Heath, C. et al. First trimester fetal diagnosis for the haemoglobinopathies: report on 200 cases. Lancet, ii, 763–767 (1986)
3 Update of the Progress of Haemoglobinopathies Control. Report of the Third and Fourth Annual Meetings of the WHO Working Group for the Community Control of Hereditary Anaemias. Unpublished Report of WHO: HMG/WG/85.8. Can be obtained from Hereditary Diseases Programme, WHO, Geneva (1985)
4 Darr, A. and Modell, B. The frequency of consanguineous marriage among British Pakistanis. J. Med. Genet., 25, 186–190 (1986)
5 Buckley, M. E., Brassington, P. E. and Long, M. J. Abnormal haemoglobins in South-East Staffordshire. Lancet, ii, 82 (1975)
6 Fletcher, J. C., Berg, K. and Tranoy, K. E. Ethical aspects of medical genetics. A proposal for guidelines in genetic counselling, prenatal diagnosis and screening. Clin. Genet., 27, 199–205 (1985)
7 Cao, A., Furbetta, M., Galanello, R. et al. Prevention of homozygous β-thalassaemia by carrier screening and prenatal diagnosis in Sardinia. Am. J. Hum. Genet., 33, 592–605 (1981)
8 Angastiniotis, M. A. and Hadjiminas, M. G. Prevention of thalassaemia in Cyprus. Lancet, i, 369–370 (1981)

Chapter 14

Running a sickle cell centre: community counselling

Elizabeth N. Anionwu

Introduction

The Brent Sickle Cell and Thalassaemia Centre opened in October 1979 to provide information, screening and counselling for inherited haemoglobin disorders such as sickle cell disorders (SCD) and thalassaemia major. There are about 5000 patients in Britain with SCD, about the same number as are affected by haemophilia and cystic fibrosis [1].

The centre, based at Willesden Hospital, counsels affected patients and their families and offers screening and counselling services to those who wish to know if they are at risk of having affected children. If both parents carry a trait there is a 1 in 4 risk that each child could inherit the illness. There are thousands of at-risk couples, as sickle cell trait is found in 1 in 10 of the Afro-Caribbean population and in higher frequencies in West Africans (1 in 4 Nigerians). In addition, the sickle gene is found in the Asian, Eastern Mediterranean and Middle East populations [2].

The centre is also concerned with thalassaemia, particularly in the Asian and Mediterranean communities. Thalassaemia trait is present in 1 in 20 Asians, 1 in 6 Cypriots, 1 in 50 Afro-Caribbeans as well as 1 in 1000 of the white British population [3].

The frequencies cited above for both the sickle and thalassaemia gene mean that they are significant health issues in a district like Brent where the 1981 Census recorded 83 023 people (33.5% of the population) living in households headed by someone born in the New Commonwealth, which compared to 14.5% in Greater London as a whole. No other London Borough has such a high black ethnic minority population [4].

Sickle cell disorders and thalassaemia major are both inherited in a recessive fashion (i.e. both parents pass on the gene to the child). There is also a 3 out of 4 chance that each child is unaffected either because they inherit the trait (one affected gene only) or the usual haemoglobin type. In some families all children are affected, in others it is just one or two while there will be some parents who may not even know they are at risk because none of their children inherit the illness.

Recently the counselling needs of such families and communities in Britain have been highlighted [1,5–8], and voluntary organizations for both SCD and thalassaemia (Appendix 1) have started to improve awareness in the community and among professionals and policy-makers. The Sickle Cell Society's report 'Sickle Cell Disease: the Need for Improved Services' [7] made 24 recommendations for better services. Printed in 1981 and revised in 1983, the report's recommendations provided the basis of the Runnymede survey in 1984 which investigated the provision of screening and counselling services for SCD in 101 English Health Authorities [6].

Case study

The need for community counselling provisions is amply demonstrated by the following extract of a taped interview with the parent of a young girl with sickle cell anaemia, conducted in 1981 by the author at the Brent Sickle Cell Centre.

> It started just over a year ago, when Julie was about 2 years of age. She had a temperature and I took her to the doctor. He said, 'It's natural for a child of her age to have a temperature'. But I insisted that she should have a blood or urine test. So he sent me down (for the blood test) and he diagnosed sickle cell anaemia. He said, 'It's sickle cell, which the majority of coloured people, black people have and there is no cure'. He just told me that. He said, 'They can't do anything about it; but if she gets any funny symptoms, I should try giving her Junior Disprin or aspirin and try to keep her warm', and that's about it. But she keeps on going in (to hospital) very often with swollen legs and hands and pain in her tummy, which I couldn't understand, which they didn't really explain.
>
> Sickle cell anaemia can cause great pains, and it's all different ways. She's off her food, she has pains in her joints and she gets urine infection pretty regular, or sometimes she passes blood with her urine. These are her symptoms. When she is getting the attacks she goes very quiet, doesn't play with her sister, she just lies and wants to go to sleep and sometimes she wants water. Just water all the time. She doesn't want to eat or anything. Then the temperature begins and I know she's going funny.
>
> (Before that) I had never heard anything about sickle cell anaemia. It was only after the diagnosis that I was reading in the West Indian World paper about your Sickle Cell Centre in London. So my sister here in London advised me to come and get more advice about it, and I put it off, I said I can't do anything because here is Dr G. telling me one thing and different people tell me another – finally they persuaded me. If I didn't come to London my child would probably die on me, and I would probably be blamed by the Welfare for not taking care of her.
>
> They should explain better how you can deal with it, and where you can get advice. The doctor says there is nothing to worry about, but you do worry. You could scream. You could feel like hitting them over the head, if you know what I mean, but when you have the child 24 hours and they 'Oh, Mummy I'm this and that' it really gets you down.
>
> I have had to come 60 miles to hear more about it (from the Sickle Cell Centre) which I don't think is right. I think it should be the GP that you should turn to really.
>
> Now I'm going to go and see my doctor and have a word with him. I know you don't really think about these things until your child is ill, but it's really terrible. You say, 'It couldn't be me, because I'm never ill', and my husband says 'it couldn't be him', and we're blaming each other, but there is none of us to blame really, it's just traits, we can't help it.

Identification of counselling services required

The emotional turmoil of anger, guilt and fear experienced by this mother came tumbling forth at this, her first counselling session. Her demand for information about the illness, the genetics, prenatal diagnosis and many other issues had not been adequately met by her local health service. In addition, they had either not been aware of, or not put her in touch with the various voluntary and health agencies that could have offered more support and information.

Details from her case identified the following gaps in health service provision that have exacerbated the stress to the family, and withheld various choices open to them, and had left their daughter vulnerable to severe and possible fatal complications in early childhood before the diagnosis was made.

1. In both of her pregnancies the mother was not informed that she had sickle cell trait. After the diagnosis of her daughter she discovered that like other black women, she had been routinely screened during her pregnancies but the information that she had sickle cell trait was not passed on to her and no effort was made to screen her partner. It was thus not possible for the couple to discuss various options available to them, including prenatal diagnosis.
2. Although it was noted that the mother had sickle cell trait no effort was made to test the baby at birth or to recall the child at a later stage. There is still a mistaken view, even among some paediatricians, that it is not possible to test a baby at birth. The views of those involved with this child were not known as the mother was not even made aware that she carried the sickle gene. The failure to screen such children at an early age leaves them extremely vulnerable, after the age of 6 months, to sudden death due to overwhelming infection and other complications [9].
3. The mother was very angry at the lack of specific information and counselling that could assist her in coping with her child's illness. It was through her own efforts that she discovered the existence of the Brent Centre, the only one in existence in the health service at that time.
4. The mother also revealed professional ignorance and the need for doctors to be more informed about the illness.

Research undertaken in Brent [10,11] had highlighted similar experiences of local families and the need for community screening and counselling services alongside normal medical follow-up.

Brent Sickle Cell Centre activities

The centre is part of the Haematology Department of the Central Middlesex Hospital, although based at Willesden Hospital. It used to be financed through a variety of sources including grants from Joint Funding, Urban Aid and the Local Health Authority. Mainstream funding is now allocated from the Regional Health Authority and the Local Health Authority. Since January 1988 the North West Thames Regional Health Authority has financed the first regional neonatal screening programme.

The staff of the centre comprises five health visitors trained in haemoglobino-pathy counselling and three clerical staff. One of the counsellors, who is Gujarati speaking, specializes in thalassaemia and improving awareness amongst the large Asian community in Brent.

The following comprehensive services have been developed over the past 9 years to meet the needs of affected patients and their families, the community, and professionals from all disciplines.

Counselling patients with SCD

There has been a significant increase in the number of patients recorded on the register at the Brent centre since the original 70 who were known in 1979. In 1988 there were 382, of whom 112 were under the age of 16 years.

The haemoglobinopathy counsellors attend the weekly adult and paediatric sickle clinic at the Central Middlesex Hospital, they visit patients when they are admitted and accompany the haematologist on a weekly ward round. This regular contact allows patients and their families the opportunity to discuss their condition and any problems that may worsen their condition. These include childcare arrangements, housing, school, welfare rights, employment, pregnancy and birth control. The counsellor can provide information, advice and referral to relevant agencies. Liaison with the latter is important to ensure that staff from the various disciplines (e.g. teachers and housing officers) fully comprehend the nature of the illness and factors that can trigger off a crisis.

Bereavement counselling is an important aspect of this work as experience in Brent has been that one patient dies per year. These deaths are usually sudden, e.g. due to chest syndrome in a young adult, and the grief experienced by the family can be overwhelming. In addition, because of the closeness of the black community, the news of such a death travels fast and rekindles fears held about the illness. The centre encounters numerous enquiries from relatives, friends and other local patients. This area of work can be emotionally draining for the staff of the centre and a close working relationship between the counsellors, doctors and nurses can provide mutual support.

Intensive counselling is also offered to parents of newly diagnosed children at their time of shock and anxiety. Other emotional responses can include anger, blame, guilt and denial, together with an overwhelming fear that their child will die young. The counsellor liaises with health visitors and general practitioners and this might also include joint home visits. A handbook on SCD [12] was produced in collaboration with the Sickle Cell Society to meet the demands for information from parents of newly diagnosed children. A local parents group has been established which has close links both with the centre and the Sickle Cell Society whose headquarters are based in Brent.

Information, screening and counselling at the centre

Over 3500 individuals have visited the centre for information and blood tests and over 50% have referred themselves. The remainder came through a variety of sources such as general practitioners, health visitors, family planning and well-woman clinics. Others come for family studies after a member of their family has been found to have a trait through routine screening in an antenatal clinic or through the cord blood screening programme at the Central Middlesex Hospital.

As described in the Runnymede report [6], 53% of those attending the centre for screening were found to have the usual haemoglobin type (Hb AA); the remaining 47% required counselling because they had a haemoglobin variant such as sickle cell or thalassaemia trait. These figures are higher than expected in the at-risk populations due to the selective nature of attendance. Some had previously been informed that they had 'sickle cell' or were 'sickle positive' but were not given accurate information whether they had sickle cell trait or a type of sickle cell disorder. Others came because there was a history of sickle cell in the family.

People who are told that they have sickle cell trait may react in a variety of ways, which is influenced by their level of knowledge, and the myths and feelings of stigma attached to a genetic issue associated mainly with the black community. They may be very upset in the mistaken view that they have a mild form of SCD. This view may be encouraged by previous incorrect management and advice of doctors and other health workers, e.g. prescribing folic acid, refusing to prescribe oral contraceptives and advising that it is dangerous to fly or have anaesthetics. Stigmas can be engendered by emphasizing the frequency of the sickle gene within the black community without explaining its origin and evidence of the protection offered by sickle cell trait against falciparum malaria in early childhood. Finally, clients often express their anger at doctors whose sole concern appears to be to tell them that they should not have children with partners who also have the trait.

The counsellors at the centre adopt a non-directive approach and concentrate on providing information, answering subsequent queries, discussing available options, and offering to arrange family screening. They also encourage discussion of the emotional impact on the individual and his or her relatives. Throughout the sessions there is a constant monitoring of what the client has understood, particularly in genetic counselling when dealing with concepts of risk and chance. The objective of the counselling session is to provide information that will enable individuals to make whatever decisions are most appropriate for them.

The centre also provides information for those who write, telephone or call in, including leaflets, articles, reading lists, a portable exhibition and videos.

Specialist counselling

Other areas include counselling women (and their partners) with sickle cell trait or disease in the antenatal clinic, as well as the parents of children identified by neonatal screening.

In a 4-year review 335 women were identified and 71% of their partners attended for a blood test. A total of 43 couples had been identified antenatally in 47 pregnancies as being at-risk of producing a child with a serious haemoglobinopathy [13]. Follow-up sessions allowed the couples to discuss the implications in detail and antenatal diagnosis was offered to 16 couples in 21 pregnancies. Fifty per cent of such couples accepted the test in 12 pregnancies and one affected fetus was aborted. Several follow-up counselling sessions were arranged for this particular couple who in a later pregnancy underwent tests which correctly predicted an unaffected child.

All those counselled in the antenatal period are informed of the neonatal screening policy in Brent. This involves the midwife taking a sample of blood from all neonates (for their haemoglobin type), at the time she takes a sample for PKU; usually 6–8 days. The counsellor arranges counselling for all parents of children with serious haemoglobinopathies as well as those found to have a trait.

Professional education
Since 1982 the Brent Sickle Cell & Thalassaemia Centre has run 5-day counselling courses particularly developed for would-be counsellors. It is one of two courses currently available in Britain and the demand for places is high as health and community workers become interested in specializing in this area. Some attend the course to provide them with more information and insight for their own contact with affected individuals (e.g. ward sisters and midwives). (130 people have attended the course to date.)

The centre also collaborates closely with the Sickle Cell Society in various events aimed at professionals, a recent example being the publication of *Pain in Sickle Cell Disease* [14] which includes the proceedings of a joint conference concerned with the management of the painful crisis.

Conclusion

By 1988, there were 12 sickle cell centres in Britain based in Brent, Hackney, Haringey, Islington, Lambeth, Newham, Waltham Forest, Birmingham, Cardiff, Liverpool, Manchester and Nottingham (Appendix 2), and their development, funding and activities have been described elsewhere [6]. They all have a common feature in dealing with SCD and other haemoglobinopathies, in particular thalassaemia. The positive role of sickle cell counsellors in Britain has recently been recognized:

> Sickle cell counsellors have been of immsense value in providing support and advice for patients and their families and education and screening for the community. They are also ideally placed to tackle educational and employment problems in both the school and the workplace. Probably one counsellor will be needed for every 50 sufferers and financial support is required urgently to establish these posts nationally. [15]

The Runnymede survey [6] uncovered the ad hoc and patchy nature of services in this country. The authors argue that:

> the provision of care for sickle cell disease can no longer be left to agencies outside the health service. If phenylketonuria with an estimated incidence of about 10–12 cases in London every year can be covered by a central newborn screening and follow-up programme, and haemophilia, with between 4000 and 5000 sufferers in Britain, can be provided through the National Health Service, then sickle cell disease, with at least 4000 sufferers in Britain, must be offered equal treatment.

They conclude that Sickle Cell Centres should be established in areas with high incidence of SCD (a minimum of 50–100 patients).

References

1 Davies, S. Comprehensive care for sickle cell disease. THS Vol 111, (X11), 7 (1986)
2 Lehmann, H. and Huntsman, R. G. *Man's Haemoglobins*, Elsevier/North Holland, Amsterdam (1974)
3 Modell, B. and Berdoukas, V. *The Clinical Approach to Thalassaemia*, Grune & Stratton, New York (1984)

4 London Borough of Brent. Race Relations Unit Information Pack (1984)
5 Anionwu, E. and Beattie, A. Learning to cope with sickle cell disease – a parent's experience. *Nurs. Times*, **77**, 1214–1219 (1981)
6 Prashar, U., Anionwu, E. and Brozovic, M. *Sickle Cell Anaemia – Who Cares?* Runnymede Trust, London (1985)
7 Sickle Cell Society. *Sickle Cell Disease – The Need For Improved Services*, 2nd edn, Sickle Cell Society, London, (1983)
8 Choiseul, M. and May, A. Sickle cell anaemia and thalassaemia: symptoms, treatment and effects on lifestyle. *Health Visitor*, **61**, 212–215 (1988)
9 Editorial. Early infant death in sickle cell disease. *Lancet*, **i**, 1141–1142 (1983)
10 Anionwu, E., Walford, D., Brozovic, M. and Kirkwood, B. Sickle cell disease in a British urban community. *Br. Med. J.*, **282**, 283–286 (1981)
11 Anionwu, E. N. Health Education and Community Development for Sickle Cell Disorders in Brent. PhD Thesis, University of London (1988)
12 Anionwu, E. and Jibril, H. *Sickle Cell Disease – A Guide For Families*, Collins, London (1986)
13 Anionwu, E., Patel, N., Kanji, G. *et al.* Counselling for prenatal diagnosis of sickle cell disease and beta thalassaemia major. A four year experience. *J. Med. Genet.*, **25**, 769–772 (1988)
14 Baughan, A. (ed.) *Pain in Sickle Cell Disease*, Sickle Cell Society, London (1986)
15 Franklin, I. M. Services for sickle cell disease: unified approach needed. *Br. Med. J.*, **296**, 592 (1988)

Appendix 1

Sickle cell organizations

Sickle Cell Society
Green Lodge
Barretts Green Road
London NW10 7AP
Tel: 01 961 7795

OSCAR (Organization for Sickle Cell Anaemia Research)
22 Pellatt Grove
Wood Green
London N22 5PC
Tel: 01 889 3300

SCAR
4th Floor
Parkway House
Sheen Lane
London SW14 8LS
Tel: 01 878 8627/8

Thalassaemia organization

UK Thalassaemia Society
107 Nightingale Lane
London N8
Tel: 01 348 0437

Appendix 2

Sickle cell and thalassaemia centres in the UK

Brent
Willesden Hospital
Harlesden Road
London NW10 3RY
Tel: 01 459 1292 ext. 4235

City and Hackney
St Leonard's Hospital
Nuttal Street
London N1 5LZ
Tel: 01 739 8484 ext. 4674
    01 601 7762

Haringey
St Anne's Hospital
St Anne's Road
London N15 3TH
Tel: 01 809 1797

Lambeth
Swan Mews
2 Stockwell Road
London SW9 9EN
Tel: 01 737 3588

Islington
St David's Wing
Royal Northern Hospital
Holloway Road
London N7
Tel: 01 272 7777 ext. 351

Newham
Shrewsbury Road Health Centre
Shrewsbury Road
Forest Gate
London E7 8QR
Tel: 01 470 1311 ext. 38
    01 472 3011 (answer machine)

Waltham Forest
Leyton Green Clinic
Leyton Green Road
London E10
Tel: 01 539 8646

Birmingham
Carnegie Centre for Community Services
Hunters Road
Birmingham B19 1DB
Tel: 021 554 3899 ext. 236

Cardiff
Butetown Health Centre
Loudoun Square
Docks
Cardiff CF1 5UZ
Tel: 0222 488 026

Liverpool
Abercromby Health Centre
Grove Street
Liverpool 8
Tel: 051 708 9370

Manchester
Moss Side Health Centre
Monton Street
Manchester 14 4PG
Tel: 061 226 8972
    061 225 5031 ext. 213/214

Nottingham
Victoria Health Centre
Glass House Street
Nottingham NG1 3LW
Tel: 0602 480 500

Chapter 15

Sickle cell screening and its value in Jamaica

G. R. Serjeant

Sickle cell screening in Jamaica developed from the need for a representative sample of patients with sickle cell disease in order to study its natural history. Previous observations suggested a variable natural history in Jamaica as patients seen in hospital and sickle cell clinics were biased towards those with severe symptoms. Understanding the determinants of this variability could contribute to knowledge of the disease's pathophysiology and to its therapy.

A cord blood screening programme to define a representative sample of patients was therefore initiated at Victoria Jubilee Hospital (the main Government Maternity Hospital) in Kingston, Jamaica. This hospital delivers approximately two-thirds of Kingston births, and one-quarter of all island births, with an annual delivery rate of 13 000–15 000 births. During the $8\frac{1}{2}$-year period from June 1973 to December 1981, 100 000 consecutive deliveries were screened.

Procedure of cord blood screening

Blood samples from the cut end of the umbilical cord were collected into a 10-ml tube containing lithium heparin and were checked against the delivery room records; capillary blood samples were taken from infants without cord samples. At the laboratories rapid haemolysates were made using tetrasodium EDTA [1]. All samples were screened initially by electrophoresis on cellulose acetate membranes with a Tris-EDTA-borate buffer at pH 8.4 [2] and stained with benzidine, allowing the detection of all haemoglobins travelling in the positions of HbA, HbF, HbS, HbC, and Hb Barts. Small amounts of HbA could not always be distinguished from HbF: for this reason and to confirm the identity of HbS and HbC, all electrophoretically abnormal samples were confirmed by citrate agar gel electrophoresis [2] where Hbs, F, A, S and C have characteristic mobilities. The wider separation of HbA from HbF allowed the detection of small amounts of HbA and the distinction of the sickle cell trait from an SS phenotype.

The combination of both electrophoretic techniques should allow the differentiation of the sickle cell trait, sickle cell–haemoglobin C disease, unusual variants, and the SS phenotype. The latter includes SS disease, sickle cell–β^0 thalassaemia, and cases of S/hereditary persistence of fetal haemoglobin which must be differentiated by family study, or the evolution of red cell indices, and of HbA_2 and HbF levels. Sickle cell–β^+ thalassaemia may remain a diagnostic problem, although the amount of HbA is always less than that of HbS, in contrast to the sickle cell trait.

Occasionally it may be necessary to follow such cases for several months before the diagnosis becomes apparent.

Choice of method

Cord blood screening as described above was cost effective, the entire programme being performed by one part-time technician in 4 h daily. Apart from this the most expensive component is the cellulose acetate membrane, although most screening procedures allow the analysis of 14–15 samples per sheet. Agar gels are expensive to buy commercially although very simple and cheap to produce.

The Jamaican study used both methods because of an interest in the frequency of rarer haemoglobin variants. A cheaper screening programme for only clinically significant sickle cell disease can use agar gel alone [3].

Other screening methods have included iso-electric focussing and microcolumn chromatography [5].

Prevalence of genotypes in Jamaica

A summary of the results obtained in the Jamaican screening programme (Tables 15.1, 15.2) confirms that there is close agreement between the observed frequencies of sickle cell disease and that expected from the gene frequency [6], supporting the accuracy of the diagnostic procedures. Furthermore, the analysis of the intervals between births also showed a close proximity to a random model in SS disease [7].

Table 15.1 Principal beta chain phenotypes among Jamaican population sample

Genotype[*]	Observed (O)	Expected (E)	O − E[†]
'AA'	85603	85594	+ 9
AS	10049	10069	− 20
AC	3591	3586	+ 5
A Variant	111	114	− 3
SS	315	299	+ 16
SC	201	213	− 12
S-β^+ thal.	33	33	0
S-β^o thal.	14	14	0
'CC'	62	58	+ 4
Others	21	20	+ 1
Total	100000	0	

Expected values are derived from observed gene frequencies.
[*] 'AA' and 'CC' refer to phenotypes
[†] None of the differences (O − E) reach statistical significance.

Table 15.2 Rare haemoglobin variants among Jamaican population sample

Alpha chain		Beta chain		Gamma chain	
G Philadelphia	44	Korle Bu	35	F Port Royal	35
Fort Worth	14	Osu Christiansborg	21	F Texas I	6
Shimonoseki	5	O Arab	16	F Victoria Jubilee	4
Spanish Town	1	Ocho Rios	10	F Kingston	1
Handsworth	1	D Punjab	9	F Hull	1
		E	7		
		D Iran	6		
		Dhofar	3		
		Caribbean	3		
		K Woolwich	1		
		Lepore-Boston	1		
Total	65		112		47

Based on 224 identified variants of a total of 256 detected.

Sickle cell cohort study

All children with clinically significant sickle cell disease were followed prospectively along with age-sex matched controls with a normal AA genotype in special clinics. The evolution of haematological and clinical changes has been documented with the principal clinical complications and causes of mortality (data reviewed by Serjeant [8]). It became apparent that there were early causes of morbidity and mortality which could only be treated effectively or prevented by early recognition of the underlying sickle cell disease genotype. Cord blood screening therefore changed from an academic approach to sickle cell disease to a practical procedure, essential to satisfactory management. These early complications included acute splenic sequestration, pneumococcal septicaemia, and the aplastic crisis.

Acute splenic sequestration

This is a life-threatening event in which sudden sequestration of red cells within an acutely enlarged spleen may cause severe anaemia and death. Attacks occur as early as 3 months and have been fatal at 4 months [9]. Most attacks occur between 6 months and 1 year and in Jamaican children with SS disease the cumulative probability of an attack was 0.255 by 2 years [10]. There were 13 deaths in the Jamaican study, 11 during the first episode. Events were recurrent, tending to recur at decreasing intervals. Acute splenic sequestration was the commonest cause of death in young children in the Jamaican cohort study.

Prevention of mortality in the first episode depends on parental education and in subsequent episodes on prophylactic splenectomy. Parental education to test for pallor and splenomegaly, significantly reduces mortality, and should commence before the age of 3 months [10].

Pneumococcal septicaemia

Pneumococcal septicaemia may also lead to early mortality in SS disease. The highest risk period is the first 3 years but events are unusual before 6 months.

Prophylaxis must therefore start at this time. There is evidence that parenteral long-acting penicillin gives better protection than pneumococcal vaccine at this age [11].

Aplastic crises

Aplastic crises are well-defined manifestations of chronic haemolytic anaemias in which there is a sudden cessation of intense erythropoietic activity, disappearance of reticulocytes from the peripheral blood, and a rapid progressive fall in haemoglobin level. The prognosis is uniformly good if peripheral oxygen delivery is maintained by transfusion, since bone marrow activity always resumes after 7–10 days. Attacks are rare before the age of 6 months and infrequent after the age of 15 years [12]. In Jamaica they occur in epidemics which last 18–24 months and are almost always attributable to the human parvovirus. Attacks rarely, if ever, recur.
    Education of patients and doctors, and awareness of the existence of an epidemic, may allow early diagnosis and transfusion and avoid the mortality of aplastic crises. A human parvovirus vaccine is currently under development, and when available, will need to be given to susceptible patients before the age of 6 months.

Timing of screening

In addition to the above three specific complications, the general prognosis of sickle cell disease can be improved if families and doctors are aware of the diagnosis early in life. This permits proper immunization, regular monitoring in sickle cell clinics, education of the family and of the doctor, and earlier diagnosis and therapy of complications.
    Thus arguments in favour of the early diagnosis of sickle cell disease are overwhelming. Neonatal screening has been most widely used, having advantages of relative cheapness, simplicity, and the accessibility of the population. The disadvantage is the occasional diagnostic difficulty, requiring the child to be followed up for a few months. Screening at later ages avoids this diagnostic confusion but has the disadvantage of the inaccessibility of the population, and loses its prophylactic function if performed after the age of 6 months.
    Antenatal diagnosis has recently become more widespread, providing the option of termination of an affected pregnancy. The mid-trimester procedure requires fluid obtained by amniocentesis under ultrasound guidance. This is a simple and common procedure, usually performed between 14 and 16 weeks of pregnancy, and has a fetal mortality rate of approximately 1%. However, amniotic fluid may provide only small amounts of fetal DNA and fibroblast culture may necessitate a 2-week delay in diagnosis. Chorionic villous sampling usually performed between 8 and 10 weeks of pregnancy is a more recent procedure in which a small plastic catheter is introduced through the cervix or transabdominally and some of the trophoblast fronds are aspirated. Substantial samples of fetal DNA may be obtained but there is a 3–4% chance of fetal mortality in experienced centres.
    Analysis of the fetal DNA relies on relatively sophisticated but widely available recombinant DNA technology. The restriction enzyme Mst II recognition site is lost in HbS and different restriction fragment lengths are produced. The diagnostic

procedures should be complete within 2 weeks of obtaining a satisfactory sample and chorionic sampling may allow a first trimester termination.

It is too early to assess the parental responses to antenatal diagnosis of sickle cell disease in Jamaica. In Europe and the USA families at risk for homozygous β-thalassaemia differ strikingly in their attitude to termination from families at risk for SS disease [13]. Homozygous β-thalassaemia is a consistently severe, transfusion-dependent condition and termination was requested in all 287 affected pregnancies studied during the period 1984–85. Homozygous SS on the other hand, is extremely variable and 65% of families elected to continue an affected pregnancy reflecting the inability to predict the clinical course. In such a situation, this decision will be influenced heavily by experience with cases of sickle cell disease already within the family.

In the future there is likely to be a progressive shift from neonatal to antenatal diagnosis, because this allows more options and also because there is more time for education and preparation for the parents of an affected child.

References

1 Schneider, R. G. Developments in laboratory diagnosis. In *Sickle Cell Disease: Diagnosis, Management, Education, and Research* (eds H. Abramson, J. F. Bertles and D. L. Wethers), C. V. Mosby, St Louis, pp. 230–243 (1973)

2 Serjeant, B. E., Forbes, M., Williams, L. L. and Serjeant, G. R. Screening cord bloods for detection of sickle cell disease in Jamaica. *Clin. Chem.*, **20**, 666–669 (1974)

3 Pearson, H. A., O'Brien, R. T., McIntosh, S. *et al*. Routine screening of umbilical cord blood for sickle cell diseases. *J. Am. Med. Assoc.*, **227**, 420–421 (1974)

4 Galacteros, F., Kleman, K., Caburi-Martin, J. *et al*. Cord blood screening for hemoglobin abnormalities by thin layer isoelectric focusing. *Blood*, **56**, 1068–1071 (1980)

5 Powars, D. and White, L. Rapid diagnosis of sickle cell disease at birth by microcolumn chromatography. *Pediatrics*, **55**, 630–635 (1975)

6 Serjeant, G. R., Serjeant, B. E., Forbes, M. *et al*. Haemoglobin gene frequences in the Jamaican population: a study of 100 000 newborns. *Br. J. Haematol.*, **64**, 253–262 (1986)

7 Hayes, R. J. and Serjeant, G. R. Testing for the random occurrence of sickle cell disease in a study of 100 000 Jamaican newborns. In preparation. (1987)

8 Serjeant, G. R. *Sickle Cell Disease*, Oxford University Press, Oxford (1985)

9 Walterspiel, J. N., Rutledge, J. C. and Bartlett, B. L. Fatal acute splenic sequestration at 4 months of age. *Pediatrics*, **73**, 507–508 (1984)

10 Emond, A. M., Collis, R., Darvill, D. *et al*. Acute splenic sequestration in homozygous sickle cell disease; natural history and management. *J. Pediatr.*, **107**, 201–206 (1985)

11 John, A. B., Ramlal, A., Jackson, H. *et al*. Prevention of pneumococcal infection in children with homozygous sickle cell disease. *Br. Med. J.*, **288**, 1567–1570 (1984)

12 Serjeant, G. R., Topley, J. M., Mason, K. *et al*. Outbreak of aplastic crises in sickle cell anaemia associated with parvovirus-like agent. *Lancet*, **ii**, 595–597 (1981)

13 Alter, B. P. Prenatal diagnosis of hematologic disease. 1986 update. *Acta Haematol.*, **78**, 137–141 (1987)

Chapter 16

Rheumatic disorders and systemic lupus erythematosus

E. N. Harris and C. DeCeulaer

The decline of rheumatic fever and its cardiac sequelae in developed countries has been a remarkable feature of modern medical history [1–6]. However, its blight continues throughout the poorer nations of the world and the disease illustrates how ethnic variation may be secondary to varying social conditions. The flitting arthritis of sickle cell disease may often be its mimic [7,8], but available evidence does suggest that other rheumatic disorders, such as the spondylarthropathies, occur less frequently in non-Caucasians [9,10].

Rheumatic disorders are often chronic and disabling, ranging from joint deformity in rheumatoid arthritis to renal and central nervous system damage in systemic lupus erythematosus (SLE). These complications have particularly severe consequences in countries where medical and social services are limited or non-existent. Non-white patients in developed countries often suffer socioeconomic deprivation and a chronic disease may prove an added burden. Loss of employment may occur earlier and be higher in manual workers. Education of a child with juvenile rheumatoid arthritis may be difficult anywhere but particularly in deprived populations. Access to expensive physiotherapy and rehabilitation programmes is difficult both in underdeveloped and developed countries.

Understanding rheumatic disease patterns in non-white patients may help in diagnosis and management. Limping in an asymptomatic adolescent of African origin may suggest aseptic necrosis of the femoral head, secondary to haemoglobin SC disease. A systolic murmur in an Indian student may suggest rheumatic heart disease; unexplained periorbital oedema in a young woman from the Caribbean may be the first sign of SLE.

Sociocultural factors may determine a patient's attitude to his disease, and attitudes may vary widely among different ethnic groups. Understanding these cultural factors will improve the patient's insight into his disease and compliance with the prescribed treatment.

The following discussion is a brief description of the presentation, frequency and outcome of the major rheumatic diseases in non-white people.

Rheumatic fever

Undoubtedly one of the most common rheumatic disorders in developing countries is rheumatic fever [3], it is associated with a high morbidity because of progressive valvular heart disease and not because of damage to the joints. It mainly affects children of 4–14 years old, classically with a migratory polyarthritis: major and minor clinical criteria link rheumatic fever to other features including chorea, which may not occur simultaneously with the arthritis. At least 40% of patients have evidence of carditis during their first attack of rheumatic fever. A formal set of major and minor clinical criteria links rheumatic fever to previous streptococcal infection [11]. These criteria may be difficult to ascertain where trained medical personnel and laboratory facilities are limited. Even under optimal conditions, a definite diagnosis may be difficult, especially in adolescents. Wilson and Hughes reported that 26% of patients with culture-positive gonococcal arthritis in Jamaica fulfilled the Jones criteria for rheumatic fever [12]. Gonococcal arthritis may be distinguished from rheumatic fever because of the dramatic response to penicillin [12]. Distinction of juvenile rheumatoid arthritis from rheumatic fever may be difficult. Involvement of the cervical spine, splenomegaly and lymphadenopathy suggest juvenile rheumatoid arthritis, while a dramatic decrease of joint pains with aspirin points to rheumatic fever. A diagnosis of rheumatic fever in patients with sickle cell disease is also difficult because both diseases share symptoms and signs, such as joint pains, non-specific cardiomegaly and heart murmurs. Fortunately, rheumatic fever appears to be extremely rare in children with sickle cell disease [8].

Overcrowding is an important contributor to streptococcal pharyngitis, but in most developing countries and certain urban areas in the developed world, a solution to the problem of overcrowding is unlikely. Thus health workers attempt to prevent either the initial (primary prevention) or recurrent attacks (secondary prevention) by prophylatic antiobiotics. Primary prevention is difficult, because infections are often asymptomatic. Some centres institute primary preventative measures by treating all respiratory tract infections with benzathine penicillin [5,6]. Although this results in the inappropriate treatment of large numbers of children with viral pharyngitis, some of these programmes have resulted in a substantial reduction in the incidence of rheumatic fever in endemic areas [6]. Most authorities recommend secondary prevention for rheumatic fever or rheumatic heart disease with monthly benzathine penicillin [13–16]. In underdeveloped countries, identification and follow-up have proved difficult, only about half of affected patients receiving adequate prophylaxis [16].

Research developments in rheumatic fever have been exciting [3–6]. The finding that patients with rheumatic fever frequently have the B-cell alloantigen 883+ [3] may, if substantiated, help identify those at greatest risk of recurrent episodes who may benefit most with prophylactic therapy.

Rheumatoid arthritis

Rheumatoid arthritis is a symmetrical inflammation of synovial joints, particularly the small joints of hands and feet, with exacerbations and remissions, leading to progressive joint destruction. Rheumatoid factor, although positive in over 70% of patients with rheumatoid arthritis, is not specific being positive in other rheumatic and chronic inflammatory diseases, viral infections, neoplasms and in healthy elderly persons [17].

Using clinical criteria [18,19] the prevalence of definite rheumatoid arthritis has been estimated as 1%. The disease spares no continent nor any racial group, and is as frequent in tropical as in temperate climates. J. S. Lawrence and co-workers in a survey of Jamaicans in the Lawrence Tavern Community estimated the prevalence of definite rheumatoid arthritis to be 1.7% compared to 1.4% in Britain [20]. Reports from Southern Africa suggest that rheumatoid arthritis is more frequent in urban than rural communities [21]. The disease is probably as frequent in Asia and in Latin America, as it is in Africa, Europe and North America [12,20–27]. Chang reported that rheumatoid arthritis was 'quite common' in clinical practice in the Peoples Republic of China [10]. The peak age of onset is the fourth decade in all racial groups. Female predominance and the pattern of joint involvement also appear to be the same. However, disease severity, based on American Rheumato-logical Association (ARA) criteria for functional and radiological class, has been reported to be less in Chinese populations [27]. Data regarding severity in African populations are conflicting. Although it is generally said that rheumatoid arthritis is less severe in blacks, Wilson and Hughes noted that rheumatoid arthritis appeared to be as severe in 'dark-skinned Jamaicans' as it was in Europe [12]. A report from Lesotho described a high incidence of severe rheumatoid arthritis and the presence of advanced disease in young people [28]. Such data are difficult to interpret in countries with inadequate medical facilities and transportation, as some cases may not be treated nor included in epidemiological studies. Of the extra-articular manifestations of rheumatoid arthritis only dermal vasculitis [12] and Felty's syndrome [29] have been reported to be rare in blacks.

An association between HLA-DR4 and seropositive rheumatoid arthritis has been established in various populations [30–33]. The Dw4 subtype may be increased in frequency in DR4-positive Caucasian patients, whereas the Dw13 subtype may be more frequent in DR4 non-Caucasian Americans with rheumatoid arthritis [32].

Rheumatoid arthritis constitutes a heavy economic cost to the community. In North America the average life-time cost for a patient was estimated to be $20 412 in 1977 dollars [34]. Patients with less flexibility over their pace and activities at work are more likely to give up work altogether [35,36]. Workers in underdeveloped countries and in urban areas of developed countries are less likely to be able to control their pace of work and are more likely to lose their jobs.

Numerous drugs have become available for the medical treatment of rheumatoid arthritis, all more acceptable in effect and with fewer side-effects than aspirin. However, the newer non-steroidal anti-inflammatory agents are often expensive and availability in developing countries may be limited. The use of gold and penicillamine for immunosuppressive therapy may also be difficult due to deficient laboratory facilities for monitoring doses and toxicity.

Systemic lupus erythematosus (SLE)

This systemic disorder primarily affects young women and presents frequently as non-erosive polyarthritis or with photosensitive skin rashes, alopecia, pleurisy, pericarditis or rarely peritonitis. Life-threatening situations mainly occur with renal, central nervous system or haematological involvement. Only two groups of autoantibodies are considered to be specific for systemic lupus erythematosus: antibodies against double-stranded DNA and antibodies against Sm, a fraction of ribonucleoproteins. Unfortunately, these antibodies are not always present and sometimes may not appear until after the onset of the disease.

Like rheumatoid arthritis, SLE follows a course of exacerbations and remissions. The reasons for the exacerbations are not clear, but the negative effect of sunlight exposure, medications (including oral contraceptives), pregnancies and some dietary factors have been well documented [17].

As in rheumatoid arthritis, criteria for the classification of SLE has been devised [36] and revised [37], enabling comparable studies in various countries. SLE is present in most areas in the world, although variations may exist due to genetic differences. In the USA, SLE is more frequent in blacks. Siegel and Lee, in a study of four regions, estimated the incidence and prevalence rates to be 14.0 and 90.9/100 000 black females, compared with 3.8 and 27.6/100 000 white females in New York City [38]. Fessel suggested that the prevalence of SLE in black women in the USA exceeded 1 in 250 [39]. In a Jamaican hospital survey, with most patients of African descent, SLE was second only to rheumatic fever in inpatients with rheumatic disorders [12] and was seen nearly as frequently as rheumatoid arthritis in the outpatient department. A subset of Jamaican patients with systemic lupus appears to have a deficiency of the T4 epitopes on T-helper/inducer cells [43]. The disease is also prevalent in Chinese and Indians and their descendents who migrated to other countries [10,40–42].

SLE appears to occur earlier in people of African descent in North America and the Caribbean [12,38,39], and to be associated with greater morbidity and mortality, but is less commonly reported in Africa [23,26] except South Africa [40]. The peak age of onset of SLE was a decade earlier in Jamaican patients compared to a series of white patients [12]. In a series comparing clinical features under and over 55 years, 59% of those less than 55 years were black, compared with 20% of those over 55 [44]. In the USA mortality for black patients with SLE exceeds that of whites [45,46]. At the University of the West Indies in Jamaica we have found a 65% and 55% survival at 5 and 10 years respectively [14], compared with a 98% and 77% reported survival at 5 and 10 years in the UK [47]. Mortality may be a function of socioeconomic factors rather than race. Among 1103 SLE patients in the USA, no significant influence of race and ethnic origin on mortality was found after data were corrected for socioeconomic status [48].

Although steroids may favourably alter the overall prognosis of severe SLE [49], indiscriminate use of high doses of these drugs for prolonged periods is to be discourged in mildly affected patients [50]. In Jamaica mortality from SLE was mostly commonly due to bacterial infection and renal disease, and the incidence of infection correlated with the extended use of steroids [14]. In the majority of patients, SLE is a mild disease and most patients can be managed with low-dose or no corticosteroids. High-dose steroid therapy should be reserved for acute relapses. Antimalarials are useful therapeutic agents in mildly affected patients and may enable treatment without steroids.

Other collagen vascular disorders

Polymyositis/dermatomyositis is an inflammatory autoimmune disorder of skeletal muscle, with or without skin involvement. Objective findings include raised serum muscle enzymes and inflammatory lesions on muscle biopsy. A particular heliotrope skin rash occurs in patients with dermatomyositis. The age at onset of disease shows a bimodal pattern, one group between 5 and 14 years of age, the other between 45 and 64 years [17]. Polymyositis is more frequent in women and may be more severe in non-Caucasian populations. Recently from the USA a 3.5-fold mortality increase was reported in young non-white females compared with whites, so that female sex and non-Caucasian origin might be synergistic determinants of mortality [51].

Mixed connective tissue disease, scleroderma, Sjögren's syndrome and vasculitis have been reported worldwide. There is little evidence to suggest differences in clinical characteristics, although mortality from scleroderma may be higher in blacks [51]. Anti-Ro antibodies may be more frequently found in black patients

[52]. These antibodies are prominent in Sjögren's syndrome and associated with congenital heart block and neonatal SLE in babies born to anti-Ro-positive mothers [53,54].

Polymyalgia rheumatica and temporal arteritis have been reported to be rare in black Americans [55]. However, temporal arteritis may not be uncommon in black patients and should not be missed because without appropriate treatment, blindness may occur in up to 55% of cases [56].

Spondylarthropathies

A major step forward in their understanding occurred with the discovery that 90% of patients with ankylosing spondylitis possess the histocompatibility antigen HLA-B27 [52]. Up to 20% of persons with HLA-B27 have some of the features of ankylosing spondylitis, in particular sacroiliitis [57]. Patients with ankylosing spondylitis who are HLA-B27 positive also appear to have more disease [58].

The HLA-B27 antigen occurs less frequently in non-white populations, hence these disorders occur less frequently in blacks [59,60]. In a survey of Veterans Administration Hospitals in various cities in the USA, ankylosing spondylitis was four times more common in white than black Americans [9]. When the latter were tested for HLA-B27 they were frequently negative [59,60]. The disease is also thought to be less severe in black Americans. Although ankylosing spondylitis, Reiter's disease and psoriatic arthritis have all been described in Jamaica and the Caribbean [12], it is our experience that these diseases are uncommon in this area as they are in Africa and China [10]. In India, ankylosing spondylitis has been reported to be as common as in Europe, but peripheral arthritis occurs more frequently and earlier [61].

Sickle cell arthropathies

Acute joint pain is one of the most characteristic manifestations of SCD [7,8]. The pain is not arthritic in origin, but is due to localized necrosis after small blood vessel obstruction by sickled red blood cells. This painful crisis may involve extremities, back, chest or abdomen: misdiagnosis of rheumatic fever may occur. Primary involvement, however, is in the juxta-articular metaphyseal bone. Careful examination reveals a point of maximal tenderness overlying the bone, not the joint space.

Another complication of avascular sickle cell bone necrosis is dactylitis, commonly called 'hand-foot' syndrome [62]. The affected child presents with acute painful, non-pitting swelling of the extremities, usually subsiding in a few weeks, but often recurring. Dactylitis occurs between 6 months and 2 years of age and is rarely seen after 5 years. Because SCD is usually asymptomatic before the age of 6 months, dactylitis often represents the first symptom but radiological changes appear in the affected bones only after 7–14 days. Complete recovery is usual, but rarely necrosis of the central epiphysis can result in premature fusion and bone shortening [8].

When avascular necrosis occurs close to the articular surface, joint function becomes impaired, most commonly affected are the hips, the shoulders and other peripheral joints. Continued weightbearing on an affected hip causes more destruction, with significant discomfort and impairment of gait. The frequency of hip involvement may differ in various areas: it seems infrequent in Nigeria [63], while in Jamaica it occurs in 15% of sickle cell patients [64]. The complication is as common in patients with the SC haemoglobin as in homozygous sickle cell disease (SS). Since many SC patients are only occasionally symptomatic, aseptic hip necrosis may be the presenting feature. Treatment is still unsatisfactory. Early detection with radioisotopes (because of the delay in radiological changes), followed by immediate immobilization and bedrest, may limit the damage. In practice, however, patients present much later, when significant changes have already occurred and for some patients only total hip arthroplasty can alleviate their symptoms [65,66].

During an episode of painful crisis an acute asymmetrical polyarthritis may occur. The joints may be swollen, warm and tender, suggesting gout or infection. The joint aspirate however reveals a clear sterile and non-inflammatory effusion, in which crystals are absent [7,8]. This type of arthritis has been atributed to occlusion of small blood vessels of the synovium, leading to ischaemia and reactive synovitis [7,8]. Also common is a monoarthritis of the ankle, appearing shortly after the development of a spontaneous malleolar ulcer. Its course seems to parallel the evolution of the leg ulcer, but pain and limitation of ankle movement can be improved with non-steroidal anti-inflammatory drugs [8].

Gouty arthritis is a relatively infrequent complication, despite the 40% incidence of hyperuricaemia in patients with the homozygous form of the disease [67]. In a large group of Jamaican patients, the frequency of gouty arthritis was estimated to be 1% [8]. In a survey of 65 black patients with gout, none had sickle cell disease [68].

Infectious arthritis appears to be uncommon. However, since the susceptibility of sickle cell patients to infections has been well documented, it is important that any type of arthritis should be investigated and infection excluded with appropriate diagnostic techniques.

Degenerative joint disease

All people are subject to degenerative joint disease in later years of life. Radiological surveys in England have estimated the overall prevalence of osteo-arthrosis as 52%, but at ages over 55 years, over 85% had signs of osteoarthrosis in one or more joints [17], including hands, wrists, hips and knees [69,70]. In Caucasians the sex incidence is equal before 54 years of age, whereafter more women are affected.

Osteoarthrosis in Third World countries has been less well documented. However, in a study of 600 adults aged 35–64 in Jamaica the prevalence of osteoarthrosis was similar to that in Wensleydale, in the UK [71]. Differences exist in the distribution of involved joints. The Jamaican population had more frequent involvement of the distal interphalangeal joints, knees, and cervical disc degeneration. In contrast, the Wensleydale community had more abnormalities of the first metatarsophalangeal joints and a greater frequency of Heberden's nodes. Differences in joint pattern have been noted in other populations. Arthrosis of the hips is thought to be less frequent in Chinese and Indian populations than in Europeans. In Nigerians osteoarthrosis of the knees in persons less than 50 years is significantly more common than in Caucasians, apparently not related to trauma [72], but multiple joint osteoarthrosis appears to be less common. In a rural South African community, no sex difference in incidence of osteoarthrosis was found [73]. It is likely that the different patterns of osteoarthritis reflect sociocultural differences rather than true genetic variations. Of interest is the equal distribution of neck pain between men and women of a Philippine village, despite the fact that only women carry loads on their heads. In addition to structural abnormalities, other factors such as muscle strength and posture may significantly influence the occurrence of osteoarthrosis.

Summary

Studies of rheumatism in non-white populations, particularly in underdeveloped countries, are rare. Since rheumatic disorders appear to be as frequent in non-whites as in whites, and the morbidity associated with these disorders is similar, investigators in both developed and underdeveloped countries should devote more attention to the study and treatment of these disorders in Africa, Asia and Latin America. Particular clinical care is necessary in sickle cell arthropathies in black patients.

References

1 Padmavati, S. Rheumatic fever and rheumatic heart disease in developing countries. *Bull. WHO*, **56**, 543–550 (1978)
2 Greenwood, B. M. Autoimmune disease and parasitic infections in Nigerians. *Lancet*, **ii**, 380–381 (1968)
3 Zabriske, J. B. Rheumatic fever: the interplay between host, genetics, and microbe. *Circulation*, **71**, 1077–1086 (1985)
4 Editorial. Decline in rheumatic fever. *Lancet*, **ii**, 647–648 (1985)
5 Bisno, A. L. The rise and fall of rheumatic fever. *JAMA*, **254**, 539–541 (1985)
6 Markowitz, M. The decline of rheumatic fever: a role of medical intervention. *J. Pediatr.*, **106**, 545–550 (1985)
7 Schumacher, H. R., Andrews, R. and McLaughlin, G. Arthropathy in sickle-cell disease. *Ann. Intern. Med.*, **78**, 203–211 (1973)
8 de Ceulaer, K., Forbes, M., Roper, D. and Serjeant, G. R. Non-gouty arthritis in sickle-cell disease: report of 37 consecutive cases. *Ann. Rheum. Dis.*, **43**, 599–603 (1984)
9 Baum, J. and Ziff, M. The rarity of ankylosing spondylitis in the black race. *Arthritis Rheum.*, **14**, 12–18
10 Chang, N. C. Rheumatic disease in China. *J. Rheumatol.*, Suppl. (10), 4–45 (1983)
11 St John Sutton, M. G. and Rubenstein, D. Rheumatic fever. *Br. J. Hosp. Med.*, November, 691–704 (1974)
12 Wilson, W. A. and Hughes, G. R. V. Rheumatic disease in Jamaica. *Ann. Rheum. Dis.*, **38**, 320–325 (1979)
13 Strasser, T. and Rotta, J. The control of rheumatic fever and rheumatic heart disease: an outline of WHO activities. *WHO Chronicle*, **27**, 49–54 (1973)
14 Hassell, T. A., Renwick, S. and Stuart, K. L. Rheumatic fever and rheumatic heart disease in Barbados: detection and prophylaxis. *Br. Med. J.*, **3**, 387–389 (1972)
15 Hassell, T. A. and Stuart, K. L. Rheumatic fever prophylaxis: a three-year study. *Br. Med. J.*, **2**, 39–40 (1974)
16 Strasser, T., Dondog, N., El-Kholy, *et al*. The community control of rheumatic fever and rheumatic heart disease: report of a WHO international cooperative project. *Bull. WHO*, **59**, 285–294 (1981)
17 McCarty, D. J. *Arthritis and Allied Conditions: Textbook of Rheumatology*, Lea & Febiger, Philadelphia (1985)
18 Ropes, M. W., Bennett, G. A., Cobb, S. *et al*. 1958 revision of diagnostic criteria for rheumatoid arthritis. *Bull. Rheum. Dis.*, **9**, 175–176 (1958)
19 Kellgren, J. H., Jeffrey, M. R., Ball, J. (eds). *The Epidemiology of Chronic Rheumatism*, vol 1., F. A. Davis, Philadelphia (1963)

20 Lawrence, J. S., Behrend, T., Bennett, P. H. *et al.* Geographical studies on rheumatoid arthritis. *Ann. Rheum. Dis.*, **25**, 425–431 (1966)

21 Solomon, L., Robin, G. and Valkenburg, H. A. Rheumatoid arthritis in an urban South African negro population. *Ann. Rheum. Dis.*, **28**, 128–135 (1969)

22 Mendez-Bryan, R., Gonzalez-Alcover, R. and Roger, L. Rheumatoid arthritis: prevalence in a tropical area. *Arthritis Rheum.*, **7**, 170–176 (1964)

23 Greenwood, B. M. Polyarthritis in Western Nigeria 1. Rheumatoid arthritis. *Ann. Rheum. Dis.*, **28**, 488–496 (1969)

24 Bagg, L. R., Hansen, D. P., Lewis, C. and Houba, V. Rheumatoid arthritis in Kenya. I. Clinical observations. *Ann. Rheum. Dis.*, **38**, 23–25 (1979)

25 Kanyerezi, B. R., Baddely, H. and Kisumba, D. Rheumatoid arthritis in Ugandan Africans. *Ann. Rheum. Dis.*, **29**, 617–621 (1970)

26 Lutalo, S. K. Chronic inflammatory rheumatic diseases in black Zimbabweans. *Ann. Rheum. Dis.*, **44**, 121–125 (1985)

27 Moran, H., Chen, S., Muirden, K. D. *et al.* A comparison of rheumatoid arthritis in Australia and China. *Ann. Rheum. Dis.*, **43**, 40–43 (1984)

28 Moolenburgh, J. D., Moore, S., Valkenburg, H. A. and Erasmus, M. G. Rheumatoid arthritis in Lesotho. *Ann. Rheum. Dis.*, **45**, 40–43 (1984)

29 Termini, J. D., Binndo, J. J. and Ziff, M. The rarity of Felty's syndrome in blacks. *Arthritis Rheum.*, **22**, 999–1005 (1979)

30 Griffin, A. J., Wooley, P., Panayi, G. S. and Batchelor, J. R. HLA-DR antigens and disease expression in rheumatoid arthritis. *Ann. Rheum. Dis.*, **43**, 218–221 (1984)

31 Alarif, L. I., Ruppert, G. B., Wilson, R. and Barth, W. F. HLA-DR antigens in blacks with rheumatoid arthritis and systemic lupus erythematosus. *J. Rheumatol.*, **10**, 297–300 (1983)

32 Alarcon, G. S., Koopman, W. J., Acton, R. T. and Berger, B. O. DR antigen distribution in blacks with rheumatoid arthritis. *J. Rheumatol.*, **10**, 57–583 (1983)

33 Zoschke, D. and Segall, M. Dw subtypes of DR4 in rheumatoid arthritis: evidence for the preferential association with Dw4. *Hum. Immunol.*, **15**, 118–124 (1986)

34 Stone, C. E. The lifetime economic costs of rheumatoid arthritis. *J. Rheumatol.*, **11**, 819–827 (1984)

35 Yelin, E., Meenan, R., Nevitt, M. and Epstein, W. Work disability in rheumatoid arthritis: effects of disease, social and work factors. *Ann. Intern. Med.*, **93**, 551–556 (1980)

36 Cohen, A. S., Reynolds, W. E., Franklin, A. C. *et al.* Preliminary criteria for the classification of systemic lupus erythematosus. *Bull. Rheum. Dis.*, **21**, 643–648 (1971)

37 Tan, E. M., Cohen, A. S., Fries, J. S. *et al.* The 1982 revised criteria for the classification of systemic lupus erythematosus. *Arthritis Rheum.*, **25**, 1271–1277 (1983)

38 Siegel, M. and Lee, S. L. The epidemiology of systemic lupus erythematosus. *Semin. Arthritis Rheum.*, **3**, 1–54 (1973)

39 Fessel, W. J. Systemic lupus erythematosus in the community: incidence, prevalence, outcome and first symptoms; the high prevalence in black women. *Arch. Intern. Med.*, **134**, 1027–1035 (1974)

40 Frank, A. O. Apparent predisposition to systemic lupus erythematosus in Chinese patients in West Malaysia. *Ann. Rheum. Dis.*, **39**, 266–269 (1980)

41 Malaviya, A. N., Misra, R., Banerjee, S. *et al.* Systemic lupus erythematosus in North Indian Asians: a prospective analysis of clinical and immunological features. *Rheumatol. Int.*, **6**, 97–101 (1986)

42 Feng, P. H. and Boey, M. L. Systemic lupus erythematosus in Chinese. The Singapore experience. *Rheumatol. Int.*, **2**, 151–154 (1982)

43 Stohl, W., Crow, M. K. and Kunkel, M. G. Systemic lupus erythematosus with deficiency on T helper cells. *N. Engl. Med.*, **312**, 1671–1678 (1985)

44 Ballou, S. P., Khan, M. A. and Kushner, I. Clinical features of systemic lupus erythematosus: differences related to race and age of onset. *Arthritis Rheum.*, **25**, 55–60 (1982)

45 Kaslow, R. A. and Masi, A. T. Age, sex, and race effects on mortality from systemic lupus erythematosus in the United States. *Arthritis Rheum.*, **21**, 473–479 (1978)

46 Lopez-Acuna, D., Hochberg, M. C. and Grittelson, A. M. Mortality from discoid and systemic lupus erythematosus in the United States, 1968–1978 (abstract). *Arthritis Rheum.*, Suppl. **25**, 580 (1982)

47 Grigor, R., Edmonds, J., Lewkonia, R. *et al*. Systemic lupus erythematosus – a prospective analysis. *Ann. Rheum. Dis.*, **37**, 211–218 (1978)

48 Rosner, S., Ginzler, E. M., Diamond, H. S. *et al*. A multicenter study of outcome in systemic lupus erythematosus II. Causes of death. *Arthritis Rheum.*, **25**, 612–617 (1982)

49 Dubois, E. L. *Lupus Erythematosus*, University of Southern California Press, Los Angeles (1976)

50 Hughes, G. R. V. The treatment of SLE: the case for conservative management. *Clin. Rheum. Dis.*, **8**, 299–313 (1982)

51 Hochberg, M. C., Lopez-Acuna, D. and Grittelson, A. M. Mortality from polymyositis and dermatomyositis in the United States 1968–1978. *Arthritis Rheum.*, **26**, 1465–1471 (1983)

52 Wilson, W. A., Scopelitis, E. and Michalski, J. P. Association of HLA-DR7 with both antibody to SSA(Ro) and disease susceptibility in blacks with systemic lupus erythematosus. *J. Rheumatol.*, **11**, 653–657 (1984)

53 Kepshot, D. C., Hood, A. F., Provost, T. T. *et al*. Neonatal lupus erythematosus. New serologic findings. *J. Invest. Dermatol.*, **77**, 331–333 (1981)

54 Scott, J. S., Maddison, P. J., Taylor, P. V. *et al*. Connective tissue disease, antibodies to ribonucleoproteins, and congenital heart block. *N. Engl. J. Med.*, **209**, 209–212 (1983)

55 Healey, L. A. and Wilske, K. R. Manifestations of giant cell arteritis. *Med. Clin. North Am.*, **61**, 261–270 (1977)

56 Love, D. C., Rapkin, J., Lesser, G. R. *et al*. Temporal arteritis in blacks. *Ann. Intern. Med.*, **105**, 387–389 (1986)

57 Wright, V. Seronegative polyartheritis: a unified concept. *Arthritis Rheum.*, **21**, 619–633 (1978)

58 Khan, M. A., Kushner, I. and Braun, W. T. Comparison of clinical features in the HLA B27 positive and negative patients with ankylosing spondylitis. *Arthritis Rheum.*, **20**, 909–912 (1977)

59 Khan, M. A., Braun, W. E., Kushner, I. *et al*. HLA B27 in ankylosing spondylitis: differences in frequency and relative risk in American blacks and caucasians. *J. Rheumatol.*, Suppl. 3, **4**, 39–43 (1977)

60 Good, A. E., Kawanishi, H. and Schultz, J. S. HLA-B27 in blacks with ankylosing spondylitis or Reiter's disease. *N. Engl. J. Med.*, **294**, 166–167 (1976)

61 Prakash, S., Mehra, N. K., Bhargava, S. *et al*. Ankylosing spondylitis in North India: a clinical and immunogenetic study. *Ann. Rheum. Dis.*, **43**, 381–385 (1984)

62 Watson, R. J., Burko, H., Megas, H. *et al*. The hand-syndrome in sickle cell disease in young children. *Pediatrics*, **31**, 975–983 (1963)

63 Iwedu, C. G. and Fleming, A. F. Avascular necrosis of the femoral head in sickle-cell disease: a series from the Guinea savannah of Nigeria. *J. Bone Joint Surg.*, **67B**, 29–32 (1985)

64 Ennis, J. T., Sergeant, G. R. and Middlemiss, J. H. Hip involvement in sickle cell disease in Jamaica. *Br. J. Radiol.*, **46**, 943–950 (1973)

65 Chung, S. M. K. and Ralston, E. L. Necrosis of the femoral head associated with sickle-cell anaemia and its genetic variants: a review of the literature and study of thirteen cases. *J. Bone Joint Surg.*, **51A**, 33–59 (1969)

66 Washington, E. R. and Root, L. Conservative treatment of sickle cell avascular necrosis of the femoral head. *J. Pediatr. Orthop.*, **5**, 192–194 (1985)

67 Morgan, A. G., De Ceulaer, K. and Sergeant, G. R. Glomerular function and hyperuricaemia in sickle cell disease. *J. Clin. Pathol.*, **37**, 1046–1049 (1984)

68 Talbot, J. H., Gottlieb, N., Grendelmeier, P. and Rodriquez, Z. E. Gouty arthritis in the black race. *Semin. Arthritis Rheum.*, **4**, 204–209 (1975)

69 Lawrence, J. S. *Rheumatism in Populations*, 1st edn, William Heinemann, London (1977)

70 Valkenberg, H. A. Osteoarthritis in some developing countries, *J. Rheumatol.*, Suppl., **10**, 20–22 (1983)

71 Bremmer, J. M., Laurence, J. S. and Miall, W. E. Degenerative joint disease in a Jamaican population. *Ann. Rheum. Dis.*, **27**, 326–332 (1968)

72 Ebong, W. W. Osteoarthritis of the knee in Nigeria. *Ann. Rheum. Dis.*, **44**, 682–684 (1985)

73 Brighton, S. W., De la Harpe, A. L. and Van Staden, D. A. The prevalence of osteoarthritis in a rural African community. *Br. J. Rheumatol.*, **24**, 321–325 (1985)

74 Harris, E. N., Williams, E., Shah, D. J., Dey Ceulaer, K. Mortality of Jamaican patients with systemic lupus erythematosus. *Br. J. Rheumatol.*, **28**, 113–117 (1989)

Chapter 17

Cancer in migrant populations: a study in Singapore

K. Shanmugaratnam, Lee Hin-Peng and N. E. Day

Cancer occurrence in migrant populations contributes important information on the respective roles of heredity and environment in the development of cancer. Patterns often differ from those in their countries of origin, generally in the direction of those in the country of adoption. These epidemiological findings emphasize the importance of environmental factors in cancer aetiology, but they do not by themselves provide a means of identifying the risk determinants. Some, like air pollution and solar radiation, are almost immediately effective. Others, related to changes in occupation, socioeconomic status, diet and personal habits, occur more gradually. Changes begin with the first generation of migrants and become progressively more marked in succeeding generations born in the host countries. The latter may also undergo genetic changes following intermarriage between migrants and the host populations.

Important sources of error affect the validity of such comparisons. The comparability of data from the country of origin with that of adoption may be affected by availability of medical care that may lead to underdiagnosis, and by variations in the classification of diseases. Since migration is usually selective, the migrant population may not be representative of the country as a whole. Within-country variations in the incidence of cancers of specific sites exist; these may be considerable in large countries like China and India. Data in the host country may be affected by inaccuracies in migration statistics; population censuses do not always identify migrants by social class or province of origin.

This chapter summarizes some of the salient findings in selected populations and presents an analysis of cancer trends among the migrant populations in Singapore.

Evidence from the USA and other countries

Studies in the USA have compared cancer risks among migrants with those of native-born Americans. Risks for *oesophageal cancer* were higher among Asian immigrants from Japan [1] and China [2,3], and European immigrants from Ireland, Poland, Czechoslovakia, USSR and Sweden (females) [4,5]. *Stomach cancer* risks were higher among Asian immigrants from Japan [1,6] and China [2,3], Central American immigrants from Puerto Rico [7] and Mexico [8], and European immigrants from Poland, Czechoslovakia, Hungary, Yugoslavia, USSR, Sweden and Finland [4,5]. *Liver cancer* risks were higher among immigrants from China [2,3] and Mexico [8]. The risks of *nasopharynx cancer* were higher in immigrants

145

from China [2,3,9]. On the other hand, the risks for *colorectal cancers* were lower for immigrants from Japan [1,10,11], China [2,3], Puerto Rico [7], Mexico [8] and Poland [12]. For *cancers* of the *breast* and *prostate*, the risks were lower among immigrants from Japan [1,13], China [2,3] and Mexico [8].

Migrant populations elsewhere have also shown significant site-specific differentials for gastrointestinal cancers. High risks for stomach cancer and low risks for colorectal cancer have been observed among European immigrants to Canada [14], Polish immigrants to England and Wales [15], and Southern European immigrants to Australia [16,17]. In Israel, Jewish immigrants from Europe and America have high risks for colorectal cancer, those from Eastern Europe for stomach cancer, and those from Iran for oesophagus cancer [18]. Incidence levels have generally been intermediate between those in their countries of origin and the host countries. The risks for colorectal cancer change rapidly to resemble those in the host country within one or two generations, while those for cancers of the stomach change more gradually.

Migrant studies in Singapore

The Singapore Cancer Registry, which has maintained a comprehensive population-based register of all cancers diagnosed in Singapore since 1968, has provided an opportunity to study changes in cancer risks following migration of Asian populations within Asia. The Singapore population is composed almost entirely of migrants and the descendants of migrants from China, the Malaysian Archipelago and India. A total of 2413 945 persons (1231 760 males and 1182 185 females) were enumerated in the 1980 Census [19] comprising Chinese (76.9%), Malays (14.6%), Indians (6.4%) and others (2.1%). Foreign-born residents comprised 21.8% of the total population. The proportions of foreign-born persons increase markedly with age, being 4.6% for the age-group 0–14 years, 15.0% for 15–34 years, 41.9% for 35–64% and 78.9% for those aged 65 years and above.

The Chinese in Singapore are mostly derived from the south-eastern Chinese provinces of Fukien and Guangdong, and comprise the following specific communities or dialect groups:

Hokkiens (43.1%) from Fukien province.
Teochews (22.0%) from the Swatow district of Guangdong province adjoining Fukien.
Cantonese (16.5%) from other parts of Guangdong.
Hakkas (7.4%) who are of northern Chinese origin, although most of those in Singapore had migrated from southern China.
Hainanese (7.1%) from the island of Hainan off the southern Chinese coast.
Others (3.9%)

The subgroups of the Malay population were not clearly defined or distinguished in the Cancer Registry. The population categorized as 'Indian' in the Singapore Census denotes all persons derived from the indigenous populations of not only India, but also of Pakistan, Bangladesh and Sri Lanka. This 'Indian' population comprised mainly Tamils (63.9%) and Malayalees (8.1%) from southern India, Punjabis (7.8%) and others (20.2%).

A total of 44 945 cancers were diagnosed among all Singapore residents during the period 1968–82 (Table 17.1) with several significant changes in cancer risks

Table 17.1 Ten most frequent cancers in Singapore (1968–82)

Males			Females		
Site	Nos	ASR	Site	Nos	ASR
1. Lung	5 738	56.1	1. Breast	2 737	22.7
2. Stomach	3 575	35.1	2. Colo-rectum	2 314	20.2
3. Liver	3 011	28.2	3. Lung	2 048	18.4
4. Colo-rectum	2 485	23.9	4. Cervix	2 033	17.4
5. Nasopharynx	1 941	14.9	5. Stomach	1 801	16.2
6. Oesophagus	1 361	14.3	6. Ovary	890	6.9
7. Skin	796	8.0	7. Nasopharynx	816	6.3
8. Larynx	697	6.9	8. Liver	803	7.3
9. Leukaemias	674	4.6	9. Skin	721	6.5
10. Bladder	617	6.3	10. Thyroid	554	4.1
Others	4 821		Others	4 512	
All	25 716	242.0	All	19 229	163.6

ASR, Age-standardized rate per 100 000 per year, standardized to the world population.

Table 17.2 Trends in cancer incidence among all Singapore residents, 1968–82

Site	Average annual change (%)	
	Males	Females
Oesophagus	− 3.6***	− 6.1***
Stomach	− 2.3***	− 1.5**
Colon	+ 2.8***	+ 5.0***
Rectum	+ 2.5***	+ 4.1***
Lung	+ 2.4***	+ 2.3***
Skin (excl.melanoma)	+ 2.5***	+ 3.4***
Breast		+ 3.1***
Ovary		+ 3.4***
Prostate	+ 4.9***	
Bladder	+ 2.5*	
Non-Hodgkin's lymphoma	+ 4.0***	
All sites	+ 0.4**	+ 1.3***

* $P < 0.05$, ** $P < 0.01$, *** $P < 0.001$.

during this 15-year period (Table 17.2). The major trends are the increasing incidence of cancers of the colon, rectum, lung and skin, and decreasing incidence of cancers of the oesophagus and stomach in both sexes; there was increasing incidence of cancers of the prostate, bladder and non-Hodgkin's lymphoma in males and of cancers of the breast and ovary in females. No significant trends were identified for cancers of the nasopharynx, liver, larynx or cervix uteri [20].

Ethnic group variation in Singapore

There are considerable differences between the major ethnic groups in Singapore. Among males, the Chinese have the highest rates for cancers of the nasopharynx, oesophagus, stomach, colon, rectum, liver, lung, skin, bladder and 'all sites'. The

Malays have the lowest rates for most sites, but have higher rates than Indians for cancers of the nasopharynx, liver and lung. The Indians have the highest rates for cancers of the tongue, mouth, oropharynx and hypopharynx. Among females, the Chinese and Indians have roughly comparable rates for 'all sites' while the rates for Malays are considerably lower; the Chinese have the highest rates for cancers of the nasopharynx, lung and thyroid, the Malays for cancer of the ovary and the Indians for cancers of the tongue, mouth, oropharynx, hypopharynx and cervix.

There are equally impressive differences in cancer risks among the major Chinese dialect groups in Singapore. Hokkiens and Teochews, whose patterns are closely similar, have markedly higher risks for cancer of the oseophagus and stomach in both sexes; they also have higher risks for cancers of the lung in males and for the cervix in females. The Cantonese have significantly higher risks for cancer of the nasopharynx in both sexes, for cancer of the colon and prostate in males and for cancers of the lung and breast in females. The Hainanese and Hakka of both sexes have lower risks for most cancers. Such differences in cancer risks between subgroups of Chinese, derived from specific provinces in China, should be taken into account in any study of the effects of migration. The incidence rates in Singapore are therefore not directly comparable with those now available in China or elsewhere.

Singapore Chinese and other Chinese migrants

The incidence rates for selected cancers among Singapore Chinese by dialect group [20], and in Hongkong, Shanghai and the Chinese population of San Francisco Bay area [21] are given in Table 17.3. The population of Hongkong and the Chinese in San Francisco are predominantly Cantonese, while those in Shanghai are of northern Chinese origin. As expected, the rates in Hongkong are roughly similar to those in the Cantonese in Singapore. Both these populations have the highest rates for nasopharynx cancer in both sexes. However, Hongkong Chinese have higher rates for cancers of the oesophagus (both sexes), bladder (males) and cervix (females), and lower rates for cancer of the colon (females). The rates for lung cancer in female Chinese are especially high among the Cantonese in Singapore and the predominantly Cantonese populations in Hongkong and San Francisco. The Chinese in San Francisco have higher rates than both Hongkong Chinese and Cantonese in Singapore for cancers of the colon (both sexes), rectum (males), prostate (males) and breast (females), and lower rates for cancers of the nasopharynx, stomach and liver (both sexes). Incidence rates in China are not available for Fukien province or the Swatow district of Guangdong province from which the Hokkiens and Teochews respectively are derived, or in Singapore for the Shanghainese who form only 0.8% of the Chinese population.

Singapore Indians and other Indian populations

Cancer incidence rates among Singapore Indians are not comparable with those in India because, unfortunately, the Singapore Cancer Registry has not distinguished subgroups of the population by province of origin in India or by ethnicity. The majority of Indians in Singapore are Tamils from southern India. Incidence rates in the Singapore Indian population [20] and from the population-based Cancer Registries in Madras, Bangalore and Bombay [22] are given in Table 17.4. Compared with data from these registries in India, Singapore Indians have

Table 17.3 Cancer incidence in Singapore Chinese by dialect group compared with Hongkong, Shanghai and the Chinese population of San Francisco Bay Area (age-standardized rates per 100 000 persons per year[*])

Sites	Singapore Chinese				Hongkong	Shanghai	San Francisco Bay area
	All	Hokkien	Teochew	Canton			
Males							
Nasopharynx	19.9	17.7	16.6	33.6	32.9	5.6	14.6
Oesophagus	17.4	24.0	29.1	3.8	18.6	24.7	6.9
Stomach	42.9	52.6	50.8	23.8	22.5	55.7	14.7
Colon	14.0	13.3	15.6	15.8	15.0	6.7	25.8
Rectum	13.7	13.9	12.9	12.7	11.6	9.0	17.9
Liver	31.1	35.6	27.4	30.7	34.4	31.7	18.1
Larynx	7.1	10.0	6.6	7.0	11.2	4.0	3.4
Lung	66.2	76.6	73.2	57.1	55.5	51.2	57.0
Skin	8.3	11.9	8.6	5.2	5.8	3.2	—
Prostate	4.2	2.7	3.6	6.8	5.1	0.8	18.6
Bladder	6.7	7.2	9.3	6.8	17.1	7.5	10.6
All sites	275.3	310.6	298.4	245.7	295.2	241.9	253.8
Females							
Nasopharynx	7.4	6.1	6.5	11.2	14.4	2.5	7.7
Oesophagus	4.1	5.3	6.6	1.5	5.5	8.0	2.1
Stomach	17.8	21.2	19.1	13.1	10.3	21.0	7.1
Colon	12.9	12.5	11.4	17.4	11.6	6.0	20.5
Rectum	8.2	8.5	8.1	9.1	8.7	5.7	10.2
Liver	7.2	7.2	8.3	7.6	8.9	9.1	3.6
Lung	19.9	16.6	15.2	29.9	23.4	18.1	25.1
Skin	5.8	8.0	4.9	4.5	3.2	1.6	—
Breast	22.4	22.6	17.3	29.4	31.1	19.6	56.8
Cervix	18.3	22.1	14.7	17.5	30.4	22.1	12.6
Ovary	5.8	5.4	4.9	7.9	5.8	4.4	11.0
Thyroid	3.8	3.5	3.4	3.5	4.4	7.4	9.6
All sites	167.3	174.3	150.4	188.5	210.9	160.3	234.4

[*] Years of registration: Singapore, 1973–77; Hongkong, 1974–77; Shanghai, 1975; San Francisco, 1973–77.

markedly higher rates for cancers of the colon, rectum, lung and 'all sites' (both sexes), liver (males) and stomach (females). Compared with data from Madras and Bangalore, female Indians in Singapore have higher rates for cancer of the breast and lower rates for cancer of the cervix.

Relative risks, comparing locally born Singaporeans with respective foreign-born migrants

A more reliable indication of the effects of migration is provided by analyses of the relative risks among Singapore residents according to place of birth. The relative risks for selected cancers for the foreign-born, as compared with the Singapore-born, among Singapore residents by ethnic group, are given in Table 17.5 and among Singapore Chinese by dialect group in Table 17.6 (see table notes for significance levels).

**Table 17.4 Cancer incidence in Singapore Indians compared with
Madras, Bangalore and Bombay (age-standardized rates[*])**

Sites	Singapore Indians	Madras	Bangalore	Bombay
Males				
Tongue	4.6	4.1	5.0	7.1
Mouth	4.4	8.1	4.5	5.8
Hypopharynx	3.6	4.1	5.4	9.9
Oesophagus	8.7	7.8	9.3	11.9
Stomach	15.6	13.5	12.2	7.5
Colon	8.0	1.8	2.2	2.7
Rectum	6.4	3.0	3.4	4.4
Liver	14.1	2.1	4.5	4.0
Larynx	8.2	5.1	5.0	7.1
Lung	21.3	5.7	5.9	14.0
Prostate	8.9	3.1	4.9	5.7
Bladder	5.8	2.1	3.7	3.7
All sites	156.5	90.8	110.8	123.7
Females				
Tongue	3.3	2.1	1.2	3.1
Mouth	9.5	9.9	15.8	4.6
Hypopharynx	1.6	1.2	1.4	2.2
Oesophagus	3.9	3.6	8.2	9.1
Stomach	16.5	6.6	6.8	5.8
Colon	19.9	0.5	1.8	2.5
Rectum	9.3	1.3	2.9	2.6
Liver	2.8	0.7	1.5	2.8
Lung	6.5	1.1	1.6	3.6
Breast	27.4	20.2	19.5	22.9
Cervix	27.9	45.2	40.1	19.0
Ovary	4.3	4.2	5.6	6.0
All sites	174.6	117.6	146.7	117.5

[*] Years of registration: Singapore, 1978–82; Madras, Bangalore and
Bombay, 1982.

There are no significant differences in cancer risks between Singapore-born and
foreign-born Malay males. Singapore-born Malay females have higher risks for
cancers of the stomach, skin, breast and 'all sites' and lower risks for cancer of the
cervix.

Differences in cancer risks between Singapore-born and foreign-born Indians
(Table 17.5) are not clear cut on account of the relatively small size of the
populations at risk (154 632 persons in the 1980 Census; 57 967 foreign-born and
96 665 Singapore-born of all ages and only 38 726 foreign-born and 11 153
Singapore-born aged 35 years and above). Singapore-born Indian males have
higher risks for cancers of the stomach, colon, rectum, larynx, lung and 'all sites'.
Singapore-born Indian females have higher risks for cancers of the colon, breast
and 'all sites'.

Singapore-born Chinese males have higher risks for cancers of the nasopharynx
(Hokkiens and all groups), colon (Hokkiens, Teochews and all groups), rectum

Table 17.5 Relative risks according to place of birth (foreign-born versus local-born) among Singapore residents, by ethnic group, 1968–1982

Sites	Chinese		Malays		Indians	
	RR	95% CI	RR	95% CI	RR	95% CI
Males						
Nasopharynx	0.76	0.68–0.84	0.95	0.58–1.57	0.47	0.07–3.32
Oesophagus	2.80	2.32–3.39	0.90	0.32–2.49	1.00	0.40–1.59
Stomach	1.19	1.09–1.30	1.02	0.69–1.50	0.57	0.37–0.87
Colon	0.68	0.59–0.79	0.74	0.42–1.29	0.43	0.21–0.87
Rectum	0.85	0.72–0.99	0.59	0.35–1.02	0.40	0.20–0.79
Liver	1.12	1.02–1.36	0.77	0.58–1.02	0.79	0.46–1.37
Larynx	0.90	0.73–1.11	1.48	0.58–3.75	0.40	0.19–0.82
Lung	1.14	1.06–1.22	1.04	0.82–1.33	0.60	0.38–0.95
Skin	0.64	0.51–0.81	0.78	0.39–1.57	0.39	0.13–1.17
Prostate	0.71	0.53–0.95	0.71	0.39–1.31	0.68	0.24–1.87
Bladder	0.78	0.62–0.98	1.04	0.54–2.01	0.72	0.24–2.13
All sites	1.02	0.99–1.06	0.95	0.85–1.06	0.58	0.49–0.68
Females						
Nasopharynx	0.83	0.70–0.98	1.27	0.45–3.63	0.18	0.02–2.04
Oesophagus	2.48	1.83–3.34	0.85	0.36–1.99	1.25	0.45–3.47
Stomach	0.80	0.71–0.90	0.58	0.35–0.96	1.24	0.64–2.40
Colon	0.68	0.59–0.78	1.04	0.57–1.92	0.35	0.17–0.72
Rectum	0.91	0.77–1.08	1.17	0.64–2.13	0.82	0.35–1.92
Liver	0.96	0.80–1.15	0.98	0.55–1.75	0.73	0.27–1.96
Lung	0.99	0.89–1.11	0.98	0.59–1.63	1.02	0.39–2.70
Skin	0.79	0.62–1.00	0.20	0.05–0.88	0.75	0.20–2.77
Breast	0.65	0.59–0.72	0.59	0.43–0.82	0.51	0.34–0.76
Cervix	0.67	0.60–0.74	1.58	1.11–2.24	0.72	0.48–1.07
Ovary	0.54	0.45–0.66	0.89	0.59–1.34	0.51	0.21–1.21
Thyroid	0.93	0.71–1.21	0.63	0.32–1.26	1.16	0.39–3.45
All sites	0.79	0.76–0.82	0.85	0.74–0.96	0.73	0.62–0.87

If 95% CI does not include 1, then RR significantly different from 1 with $P < 0.05$.

(all groups), skin (all groups), prostate (Teochews and all groups) and bladder (all groups) and lower risks for cancers of the oesophagus (Hokkiens, Teochews and all groups), liver (Hokkiens and all groups), larynx (Hokkiens), lung (Hokkiens, Teochews, Cantonese and all groups) and 'all sites' (Hokkiens and Teochews). Singapore-born Chinese females have higher risks for cancer of the nasopharynx (Cantonese and all groups), stomach (all groups), colon (Hokkiens, Teochews, Cantonese and all groups), lung (Teochews), breast (Hokkiens, Teochews, Cantonese and all groups) cervix (Cantonese and all groups), ovary (Teochews, Cantonese and all groups), and 'all sites' (Hokkiens, Teochews, Cantonese and all groups) and lower risks for cancer of the oesophagus (Hokkiens, Teochews and all groups).

Studies in the USA comparing US-born and foreign-born Chinese have shown that Chinese born in the USA have higher mortality rates for cancers of the colon, lung and breast and lower rates for cancers of the nasopharynx, oesophagus and

Table 17.6 Relative risks according to place of birth (foreign-born versus local-born) among Singapore Chinese, by dialect group, 1968–82

Sites	Hokkien		Teochew		Cantonese	
	RR	95% CI	RR	95% CI	RR	95% CI
Males						
Nasopharynx	0.74	0.60–0.91	0.77	0.59–1.01	0.85	0.68–1.06
Oesophagus	3.34	2.60–4.29	3.85	2.60–5.68	2.18	0.95–4.99
Stomach	1.35	1.19–1.54	1.49	1.22–1.82	0.77	0.58–1.02
Colon	0.55	0.43–0.72	0.65	0.47–0.90	0.77	0.55–1.08
Rectum	0.92	0.72–1.18	0.70	0.50–1.00	0.76	0.52–1.13
Liver	1.24	1.07–1.42	1.13	0.90–1.42	1.04	0.83–1.29
Larynx	1.41	1.04–1.90	1.01	0.62–1.65	0.78	0.46–1.31
Lung	1.25	1.13–1.38	1.44	1.22–1.71	1.21	1.01–1.45
Skin	0.84	0.59–1.19	0.92	0.52–1.62	0.57	0.30–1.11
Prostate	0.74	0.43–1.25	0.47	0.24–0.89	0.78	0.42–1.46
Bladder	0.71	0.49–1.02	0.93	0.59–1.47	1.05	0.57–1.96
All sites	1.15	1.10–1.21	1.20	1.11–1.30	0.96	0.88–1.04
Females						
Nasopharynx	0.87	0.63–1.21	1.09	0.73–1.65	0.61	0.45–0.82
Oesophagus	3.16	2.12–4.72	4.46	2.26–8.80	0.84	0.38–1.90
Stomach	0.88	0.74–1.04	1.07	0.82–1.40	0.76	0.56–1.02
Colon	0.72	0.58–0.91	0.66	0.48–0.91	0.71	0.53–0.94
Rectum	0.94	0.71–1.25	1.15	0.78–1.70	0.71	0.50–1.02
Liver	1.00	0.76–1.33	1.22	0.82–1.82	0.96	0.66–1.39
Lung	0.99	0.83–1.19	0.69	0.53–0.90	1.05	0.85–1.29
Skin	1.01	0.68–1.49	1.24	0.63–2.45	0.95	0.52–1.75
Breast	0.80	0.67–0.96	0.58	0.44–0.75	0.65	0.53–0.80
Cervix	1.05	0.88–1.25	0.82	0.63–1.08	0.58	0.45–0.74
Ovary	0.82	0.59–1.12	0.43	0.27–0.68	0.51	0.35–0.75
Thyroid	0.98	0.58–1.65	0.81	0.43–1.50	1.20	0.64–2.25
All sites	0.93	0.88–0.99	0.87	0.79–0.95	0.76	0.70–0.82

If 95% CI does not include 1, RR is significantly different from 1 with $P < 0.05$.

liver [3]. Not all of these changes are similar in direction to those observed in Singapore; among the Chinese in the USA, it is the foreign-born who have higher risks for nasopharyngeal cancer and lower risks for lung cancer.

Implications of cancer trends

The unequivocally higher risks for oesophageal cancer among foreign-born Chinese and the rapidly declining incidence of this cancer in Singapore are strong indications that the aetiological factors are related to the environment and lifestyles in China. On the other hand, the remarkably higher risks in the Singapore-born for cancers of the colon (Chinese and Indians of both sexes) and rectum (Chinese and Indian males), and the rapidly increasing incidence of these cancers in Singapore, are probably related to the dramatic socioeconomic changes occurring in Singapore, associated with a change in dietary habits supported by a marked per capita increase in the supply of meat, eggs and animal fats [23]. These changes are also probably related to the increasing risks for cancers of the breast and prostate.

The rapidly increasing incidence of breast cancer and its higher risks among the Singapore-born of all racial and dialect groups are no doubt related to extraordinary changes in reproductive habits that have occurred among Singapore-born women who have later marriages and rapidly declining fertility rates. The declining rates for stomach cancer and the increased rates for lung cancer in Singapore have not been associated with consistent risk differentials by nativity; the higher risks for these tumours among the foreign-born are observed only among Chinese males.

An increase in risks for cancers of the large bowel, breast and prostate, and a reduction in risks for cancers of the oesophagus and stomach have also been observed among Chinese emigrants to the USA [3]. Of these changes, the most striking has been for cancers of the large bowel for which the incidence levels, low in China, have increased rapidly among the emigrant Chinese to equal and even exceed the levels among native white populations in the USA [21].

The changes in cancer risks in migrant populations begin during the lifetime of the migrants, i.e. from exposure in adult life after arriving in the country of adoption, and become progressively more marked in generations born in the host countries. These changes emphasize the role of environmental factors, especially those related to diet and lifestyles, but the specific risk factors involved in each situation can only be identified through case-control studies, laboratory investigations and intervention trials. The potential value of the demonstration of cancer risk differentials among Asian migrants can be fully realized only if such studies are undertaken systematically in the countries of origin and the countries of adoption.

References

1 Haenszel, W. and Kurihara, M. Studies of Japanese migrants. 1. Mortality from cancer and other diseases among Japanese in the United States. *J. Natl Cancer Inst.*, **40**, 43–68 (1968)

2 King, H. and Haenszel, W. Cancer mortality among foreign- and native- born Chinese in the United States. *J. Chronic Dis.*, **26**, 623–646 (1973)

3 King, H., Li, J. Y., Locke, F. B. *et al.* Patterns of site-specific displacement in cancer mortality among migrants: the Chinese in the United States. *Am. J. Public Health*, **75**, 237–242 (1985)

4 Haenszel, W. Cancer mortality among the foreign-born in the United States. *J. Natl Cancer Inst.*, **26**, 37–132 (1961)

5 Lilienfeld, A. M., Levin, M. L. and Kessler, I. I. *Cancer in the United States*, Harvard University Press, Cambridge, Massachusetts (1972)

6 Haenszel, W. Kurihara, M., Segi, M. and Lee, K. C. Stomach cancer among Japanese in Hawaii. *J. Natl Cancer Inst.*, **49**, 969–988 (1972)

7 Warshauer, M. E., Silverman, D. T., Schottenfeld, D. and Pollack, E. S. Stomach and colorectal cancers in Puerto Rican-born residents of New York City. *J. Natl Cancer Inst.*, **76**, 591–595 (1986)

8 Menck, H. R., Henderson, B. E., Pike, M. C. *et al.* Cancer incidence in the Mexican-American. *J. Natl Cancer Inst.*, **55**, 531–536 (1975)

9 Buell, P. Nasopharynx cancer in Chinese of California. *Br. J. Cancer*, **19**, 459–470 (1955)

10 Correa, P. and Haenszel, W. The epidemiology of large-bowel cancer. *Adv. Cancer Res.*, **26**, 1–141 (1978)

11 Shimuzu, H., Mack, T. M., Ross, R. K. and Henderson, B. E. Cancer of the gastrointestinal tract among Japanese and white immigrants in Los Angeles County. *J. Natl Cancer Inst.*, **78**, 223–228 (1987)

12 Staszewski, J. and Haenszel, W. Cancer mortality among Polish-born in the United States. *J. Natl Cancer Inst*, **35**, 291–297 (1965)

13 MacMahon, B., Cole, P. and Brown, J. Etiology of human breast cancer: a review. *J. Natl. Cancer Inst.*, **50**, 21–42 (1973)

14 Newman, A. M. and Spengler, R. F. Cancer mortality among immigrant populations in Ontario, 1969 through 1973. *Can. Med. Assoc. J.*, **130**, 399–405 (1984)

15 Adelstein, A. M., Staszewski, J. and Muir, C. S. Cancer mortality in 1970–1972 among Polish-born migrants to England and Wales. *Br. J. Cancer*, **40**, 464–475 (1979)

16 McMichael, A. J., McCall, M. G., Hartshorne, J. M. and Woodings, T. L. Patterns of gastrointestinal cancer in European migrants to Australia: the role of dietary change. *Int. J. Cancer*, **25**, 431–437 (1980)

17 McMichael, A. J. and Bonnet, A. Cancer profiles of British and southern-European migrants: exploring South Australia's cancer registry data. *Med. J. Aust.*, **1**, 229–232 (1981)

18 Steinitz, R. and Costin, C. Cancer in Jewish immigrants. *Isr. J. Med. Sci.*, **7**, 1413–1436 (1971)

19 Khoo, C. K. Census of Population 1980. Release No. 2, Department of Statistics, Singapore (1981)

20 Lee, H. P., Day, N. E. and Shanmugaratnam, K. *Trends in Cancer Incidence in Singapore 1968–1982*, International Agency for Research on Cancer, Lyon (1988)

21 Waterhouse, J., Muir, C., Shanmugaratnam, K. and Powell, J. (eds). *Cancer Incidence in Five Continents*, vol. IV, IARC Scientific Publications No. 42, International Agency for Research on Cancer, Lyon (1982)

22 Indian Council of Medical Research. National Cancer Registry, Annual Report 1983, ICMR, New Delhi (1986)

23 Lee, H. P. and Gourley, L. Food availability in Singapore from 1961 to 1983: Implications for health research. *Food Nutr. Bull.*, **8**, 50–54 (1986)

Chapter 18

Human retroviruses: human T-cell leukaemia lymphoma virus (HTLV-I) and disease

A. G. Dalgleish, J. H. Richardson and J. K. Cruickshank

Retroviruses are enveloped RNA viruses which replicate via a DNA intermediate which is synthesized by a virally encoded enzyme, reverse transcriptase. The viral DNA is inserted into a chromosome of the host cell, from where it directs the synthesis of new viral proteins and viral RNA (Figure 18.1). Being physically incorporated into a chromosome, the viral DNA (provirus) is replicated alongside the host cell DNA at cell division.

Integration of the proviral DNA can in some circumstances alter the biology and function of the cell by perturbing cellular gene expression. Mechanisms for this include disruption, activation or deregulation of adjacent cellular genes (e.g. oncogenes) and the modulation of non-adjacent cellular gene expression by virally encoded transcription factors, the 'transactivator' proteins. The transactivator protein of HTLV-I, for example, is known to up-regulate a variety of cellular genes including growth factors, growth factor receptors and oncogenes. Retroviruses with cancer-inducing potential are termed 'oncoviruses'. Another group of retroviruses

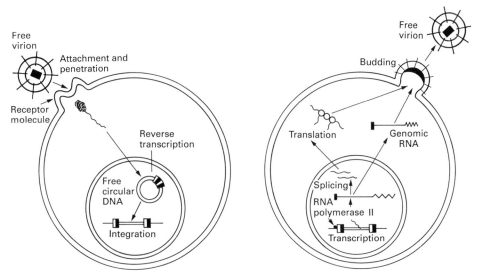

Figure 18.1 Lifecycle of a retrovirus showing attachment, penetration, integration, translation and budding stages

are the non-oncogenic lentiviruses known to cause neurological, rheumatological, and haematological diseases in sheep, goats and horses [1]. The first pathogenic human retrovirus (HTLV-I) remained unreported until as recently as 1980 [2]. The list now includes HTLV-II, HIV-1 and HIV-2. The link between the Epstein–Barr virus (EBV) and Burkitt's lymphoma in central Africa, and with nasopharyngeal cancer in China revealed important geographical and ethnic factors in oncogenesis [3]. The association between the high prevalence of hepatitis B virus (HBV) and hepatoma or cancer of the liver in Africa, Asia and China was a similar landmark; indeed HBV is probably one of the commonest causative factors of cancer in the world [4]. However, whereas EBV and HBV are not uncommon in the Western hemisphere, the relationship to malignancy is much less obvious, if present at all. The disparity highlighted the importance of co-factors in disease development, such as malaria in Burkitt's lymphoma, and possibly a genetic propensity in the presence of a virus in certain populations. Such a 'cluster' of a specific T-cell malignancy in Japan ultimately led to the isolation and characterization of HTLV-I and proof of the causative role of a retrovirus in human malignancy [5].

The adult T-cell leukaemia/lymphoma syndrome (see also Chapter 19)

In 1977 a new disease entity was reported from Southern Japan: an adult T-cell leukaemia and/or lymphoma (ATLL) [6]. The T cells possessed convoluted nuclei and immunofluoresced with autologous serum. The causative viral agent was isolated from a black patient with apparent mycosis fungoides in the USA [2]. A second isolate was made from a black patient with Sezary's syndrome. In retrospect both these patients probably had misdiagnosed ATLL. Cellular, serological and molecular studies have shown that the American and Japanese isolates from ATLL patients are identical and all isolates from ATLL are now referred to as HTLV-I.

Widespread serological screening showed that the virus was endemic in Southern Japan and also in the Caribbean but not in the USA. (For worldwide distribution see Figure 18.2.)

Among patients of Afro-Caribbean origin the clinical features of ATLL (see Chapter 19) were first described in the West in six black patients in Britain, in whom hepatosplenomegaly, skin and bone lesions (not dissimilar from those seen in sarcoidosis) and hypercalcaemia were reported [7]. All patients were positive for HTLV-I, leading to extensive Caribbean studies.

Apart from these two major endemic areas (Japan and the Caribbean), HTLV-I and related clinical disease have been reported worldwide with varying but generally low prevalence including Italy, Alaska, Africa, Taiwan and tropical America.

HTLV-I and its transmission

HTLV-I causes disease in only a minority of people that it infects (1–4%) with an apparent incubation time of up to 30 years [8,9]. Studies in Japan confirmed the likely aetiological association of HTLV-I and ATLL by the following observations:

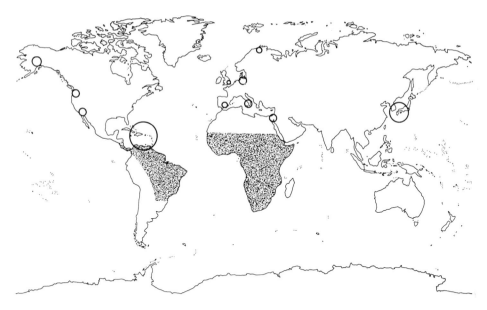

Figure 18.2 Worldwide distribution of HTLV-I where circles indicate endemic areas (large) or disease clusters (small) and shaded areas represent areas of low endemicity

1. Geographically the areas of high incidence ATLL correspond closely with those of HTLV-I infection in seroepidemiological surveys.
2. All individuals with ATLL have evidence of HTLV-I infection.
3. The ATLL tumour cells carry HTLV-I proviruses whereas non-tumourous cells from the same person are not invariably infected.
4. HTLV-I transforms human and animal T-cells *in vitro*.
5. HTLV-I appears to be oncogenic in experimental animals.

Seroepidemiological studies in Japan and the Caribbean using immuno-fluorescence (IF) and enzyme-linked immunoabsorbant assays (ELISA) recently supplemented by a cheaper, sensitive but perhaps less specific particle agglutination (PA) method from Japan [10] have shown that many healthy adults in endemic areas are seropositive and children in endemic areas are usually seronegative unless they have received an infected blood transfusion or are born of seropositive mothers. Cord blood is positive in some 15% of offspring by 12–24 months of age [11]. The 'rate' of seropositivity rises roughly linearly with age, especially in women. There is a strong familial disposition [12]; transmission of the virus is more likely to pass from the father to mother and from the mother to children than vice versa [13,14].

Migrant studies also suggest a long latency period as seen in Caribbean migrants who have been resident in the UK for as long as 30 years prior to developing disease [15–17]. (This is of course assuming that infection did not occur in the UK.)

In vitro studies show that HTLV-I has very low cell-free infectivity, even when harvested from virus-producing cells in culture; viable cell-to-cell contact appears necessary for infection. Thus only intimate body contact with exposure to lymphocytes could be responsible for HTLV-I transmission such as by: (1) blood exchange including trauma and transfusions; (2) exchange of body fluids containing cells such as semen and breast milk. The latter may account for some of the familial transmission but it is clearly not an efficient mechanism as less than 20% of infants remain seropositive in studies so far [11].

Intravenous drug abuse and shared needles have also been associated with transmission [18,19]. Iatrogenic transmissions from blood and related products account for a large number of 'seroconversions' in parts of Japan where up to 8% of blood donors may carry antibodies to HTLV-I [20]. Donor screening in Japan by the PA method, confirmed by immunofluorescence, has dramatically reduced seroconversion [21].

It is not clear whether HTLV-I is transmitted transplacentally or perinatally; the mechanism of such transmission from mother to infant needs to be clarified before public health restrictions in Caribbean countries (e.g. stop seropositive mothers breastfeeding infants) are introduced. As usual, establishing a balance of risks is required.

Ethnic factors

Why is HTLV-I endemic in two such diverse parts of the world as Japan and the Caribbean? Are these peoples genetically particularly susceptible to the virus or are there shared socioeconomic factors which explain this geographical distribution?

There are no clear answers. No genetic, particularly HLA, susceptibility is obvious within the limitations of the studies so far performed [22]. Viruses from infected persons can infect cells from uninfected relatives with comparative ease *in vitro*. Possible co-factors in HTLV-I infection include helminths and protozoa, and in particular *Strongyloides stercoralis*, but the links are tenuous [23]. Opportunistic infections may afflict HTLV-I carriers; whether these co-exist because of the immunosuppression associated with HTLV-I infection remains unproven.

Lessons from bovine leukaemia virus may give some insight into the factors influencing distribution of HTLV-I. Bovine leukaemia virus is a transforming retrovirus of cows. As few as 900 lymphocytes are required for reliable transmission of the virus, a number which could easily be transmitted by insects such as the larger varieties of mosquitos and flies (A Burny, 1988, personal communication). Could mosquitos be vectors of HTLV-I transmission? The relative rarity of HTLV-I in Africa's malaria belt makes this unlikely unless there are marked differences in the species and habits of the mosquitos.

Trinidad, where there are black, white, Indian, Chinese and mixed populations, has been a natural laboratory in which to study ethnic factors in the spread of HTLV-I [24]. A recent study by Miller *et al.* [25] showed that individuals of African descent had a higher seropositivity for HTLV-I (7%) than those originating from India (1.4%), Europe (0%) or subjects of mixed descent (2.7%). Women were infected more frequently than men, and the rates increased with age in both sexes. Poor socioeconomic groups, defined mainly by condition of housing and proximity to water-courses (drains, streams and rivers), was associated with HTLV-I infection. Women living in poor-quality housing or near water-courses were more likely to be seropositive than those living further away. Indeed, seropositivity rates of as high as 30% were seen in a small group of women living in 'yards' near to a water-course. Sexual transmission could easily account for the results.

Within endemic areas strong associations exist between HTLV-I seropositivity and exposure to arthropod-transmitted diseases such as filariasis, malaria and equine encephalitis. These relations may imply human transmission by mosquitos. Indeed in spite of an anti-malaria programme which has all but eradicated the anopheles mosquito, a mosquito of intensely domestic habit such as *Aedes aegypti* has a limited dispersal from its breeding sites in closely populated urban areas in Trinidad. This might also explain the limited seropositivity of peoples of Indian descent in areas of poor housing where people of African origin had a higher incidence of seropositivity. Animal transmission studies have shown bovine leukaemia virus (BLV) in mosquitos which have fed on BLV-infected cows. Mice can also be infected by mosquitos which have fed on mice infected with another retrovirus, the Friend leukaemia virus.

It is possible that mosquito-borne transmission may account for the higher rates of positivity seen in women in Japan and Venezuela as well as in the Arctic regions [26]. It is not clear how the virus entered this community and assay results need confirmation.

HTLV-I and neurological disease (see also Chapter 20)

HTLV-I was first linked to a chronic neurological disease when Gessain and colleagues [27] were screening blood donors during a study of ATL and HTLV-I in Martinique in the West Indies. They found that 10 out of 17 cases of tropical spastic paraparesis (TSP) had antibodies to HTLV-I as tested by both ELISA and Western blot methods. Since then more than 75% of TSP cases worldwide have antibodies to HTLV-I from Jamaica, Colombia, Trinidad, the Seychelle Islands, Japan and British resident Caribbean-born patients [28]. In the British series all 24 so far tested have been positive [17].

In Japan the association between HTLV-I and TSP is recognized in the disease name, HTLV-I-associated myelopathy ('HAM'). In a large series, of over 300 definitive cases, the great majority were positive for HTLV-I antibodies [29]. TSP was first described in Jamaica where it is the commonest neurological problem after stroke. The association between a 'slow' human retrovirus and TSP has particular relevance to multiple sclerosis (MS), especially as HTLV-I has been spuriously linked to MS, unsubstantiated by other workers [30]. Reactivity to HTLV-I core antigens in some MS sera from Japan occurred in a high HTLV-I endemic area. Such reactivity has also been seen in other neurological conditions such as Guillian–Barré syndrome. These 'reactions' are only seen with concentrated virus antigens and relatively undiluted sera, which suggests a non-specific cross-reactivity.

AIDS and HIV

The acquired immune deficiency syndrome (AIDS) which was first recognized in New York and San Francisco homosexuals in 1980–81, has now been shown to be caused by a human retrovirus, the human immunodeficiency virus (HIV) previously HTLV-III. This virus, while bearing many similarities to HTLV-I and HTLV-II (all are T-lymphotropic retroviruses), differs in that it is more similar to the lentiviruses which cause encephalitis, demyelination and arthritis in sheep and goats, none of which are transforming viruses like HTLV-I or HTLV-II [31].

AIDS was first recognized as a heterosexually transmitted disease in Africa where the male/female ratio is roughly equal [32]. Sexual promiscuity and 'prostitutional tourism' (the migration of large numbers of young women from different parts of the sub-Saharan continent to 'meet' troop-ships at large tourist ports – Mombassa, Abidjan, etc. [33]) have had devastating effects on the rate of spread of AIDS in Africa as among homosexuals in the West. Careful interpretation of seroepidemiological results and the use of at least one and possibly two different tests to confirm HIV-positive results are essential in African (and Pacific) studies. False-positives on screening tests, probably because of high titres of other immunoglobulins, have been common.

AIDS was first recognized in sub-Saharan Africa among heterosexually active 'middle class' inhabitants of urban communities in expanding African cities. This was followed by the recognition of the disease in poor rural areas where it is known as 'Slim disease' [32]. It may be significant that these poor rural peoples first developed evidence of the disease after widespread social upheavals following troop movement in countries such as Uganda and Tanzania, so that AIDS became endemic across equatorial Africa.

The association with the malarial belt suggested that mosquito transmission may be important. However, a large study in Uganda (where mosquito-transmitted malaria appears to be an important cofactor in EBV-related Burkitt's lymphoma), conducted in association with the Institute of Cancer Research in London, failed to find evidence of mosquito transmission, although it could not be ruled out [32]. The association of infection with heterosexually active persons in marked contrast to the complete absence in sexually immature people suggests this route to be much more important and provides evidence against insect-borne transmission. Moreover, most diseases that are transmitted by mosquitos undergo replication within the mosquito and there is no evidence that this is the case for HIV.

Ethnic studies on HIV infections suggest that no group is immune, although there appear to be lower rates of infection among peoples of Chinese origins living in San Francisco, and HIV is as yet rare in Japan and in the Indian subcontinent. Transmission studies of HIV show that casual contact is extremely unlikely to transmit the virus and that only sexual and blood-product transmission are likely modes of infection. Unlike HTLV-I, HIV is more infectious in body fluids where it may be transmitted in a cell-free environment. It still appears to be less infectious than HBV which has a virtually identical mode of transmission. It may be difficult to differentiate between sociocultural factors, such as sexual activity, and genetic susceptibility and at present there are not enough data to draw meaningful conclusions. Cultural factors such as ritualistic blood exchange or use of non-disposable needles may play a significant role in the transmission of the virus.

The T4 molecule or CD4 antigen is now accepted as being the HIV receptor. Polymorphisms of T4 epitopes are known to be common in Japanese and African peoples, although a recent study has shown that these polymorphisms are not protective against infection with HIV [34,35]. No obvious human leucocyte antigen association has been shown

A distinct retrovirus not detected by screening techniques used to detect HIV was isolated by Montaignier and his colleagues at the Pasteur Institute in Paris. The virus is now called HIV-2 and appears to be associated with AIDS [37].

References

1 Teich, N. Taxonomy of retroviruses. In *RNA Tumour Viruses* (eds R. A. Weiss, N. Teich, H. Varmus and J. Coffin), Cold Spring Harbour Laboratories, Cold Spring Harbour (1985)

2 Poiesz, B. J., Ruscetti, F. W., Gazdar, A. F. *et al*. Detection and isolation of type C retrovirus particles from fresh and cultured lymphocytes of a patient with cutaneous T-cell lymphoma, *Proc. Natl. Acad. Sci. USA*, **77**, 7415–7419 (1980)

3 De Thé G. Demographic studies implicating the virus in the causation of Burkitt's lymphoma: prospects for nasopharyngeal carcinoma. In *The Epstein Barr Virus* (eds M. A. Epstein and B. G. Achong), Springer, Berlin (1979)

4 Szmuness, W. Hepatocellular carcinoma and hepatitis B virus. Evidence for a causal association. *Prog. Med. Virol.*, **24**, 40 (1978)

5 Gallo, R. C., Essex, M., Gross, L. (eds). *Human T-cell Leukaemia Lymphoma Virus*, Cold Spring Harbour Laboratories, Cold Spring Harbour (1984)

6 Takatsuki, K., Uchiyama, T., Ueshima, Y. and Hattori, T. Further clinical observations and cytogenetic and functional studies of leukaemic cells. *Jpn J. Clin. Oncol.*, **9**, 312–324 (1979)

7 Catovsky, D. E., Greaves, M. F., Rose, D. *et al*. Adult T-cell leukaemia-lymphoma in Blacks from the West Indies. *Lancet*, **i**, 639–643 (1982)

8 Murphy, E. L., Harchard, B., Figueroa, J. P. *et al*. Modelling the risk of adult T-cell leukaemia/lymphoma in persons infected with HTLV-I in Jamaica. *Int. J. Cancer*, **43**, 250–253 (1989)

9 Tokudome, S., Tokunaga, C., Shimamoto, Y. *et al*. Incidence of adult T-cell leukaemia/lymphoma among HTLV-I carriers in Saga, Japan. *Cancer Res.*, **49**, 226–228 (1989)

10 Ikeda, M., Fujino, R., Matsin, T. *et al*. A new agglutination test for serum antibodies to adult T-cell leukaemia virus. *Gann*, **75**, 845–848 (1984)

11 Kusuhara, K., Sonoda, S., Takahashi, K. *et al*. Mother to child transmission of HTLV-I: a fifteen year follow-up in Okinawa, Japan. *Int. J. Cancer*, **40**, 755–757 (1987)

12 Kajiyama, W., Kashiuagi, S., Ikematou, H. *et al*. Intrafamilial transmission of adult T-cell leukaemia virus. *J. Infect. Dis.*, **154**, 851–857 (1986)

13 Tajima, K., Tominaga, S., Suchi, T. *et al*. Epidemiological analysis of the distribution of antibody to ATLV-antigen: possible horizontal transmission of ATLV. *Gann*, **73**, 893–901 (1982)

14 Komura, A., Hayami, H., Fujii, H. *et al*. Vertical transmission of adult T-cell leukaemia virus. *Lancet*, **i**, 240 (1985)

15 Newton, M., Cruickshank, J. K., Newell, A. *et al*. HTLV-I antibody in UK patients with spastic paraparesis. *Lancet*, **i**, 415–416 (1987)

16 Cruickshank, J. K., Knight, J., Porter, J. *et al*. Prevalence of HTLV-I Abs in relatives in Britain and Jamaica of Tropical Spastic Paraparesis patients in Britain. **75**, Suppl. 19:2p, *Clin Sci.*, (1988)

17 Cruickshank, J. K., Rudge, P., Dalgleish, A. G. *et al*. Tropical Spastic Paraparesis and HTLV-I in the United Kingdom. *Brain*, August, (in press) (1989)

18 Tedder, R., Shawson, D., Jeffries, D. *et al*. Low prevalence in the UK of HTLV-I and HTLV-II infection in subjects with AIDS, extended lymphadenopathy and at risk of AIDS. *Lancet*, **ii**, 125–128 (1984)

19 Chiengsong-Popov, R., Weiss, R. A., Dalgleish, A. G. *et al*. Prevalence of antibody to HTLV-III in AIDS and AIDS risk patients in Britain. *Lancet*, **ii**, 477–480 (1984)

20 Sato, H. and Okochi, K. Transmission of human T-cell leukaemia virus (HTLV-I) by blood transfusion. *Int. J. Cancer*, **37**, 395–400 (1986)

21 Inaba, S., Sato, H., Okochi, K. *et al*. Prevention of transmission of HTLV-I through transfusion, by donor screening with antibody to the virus. *Transfusion*, **29**, 7–11 (1989)

22 The T and B cell Malignancy Study Group. The third nationwide study on adult T-cell leukaemia/lymphoma (ATL) in Japan: characteristic patterns of HLA antigen and HTLV-I infection in ATL patients and their relatives. *Int. J. Cancer*, **41**, 505–512 (1988)

23 Neva, F. A., Murphy, E. L., Hanchard, B. *et al.* Antibodies to *Strongyloides stercoralis* in healthy Jamaican carriers of HTLV-I. *New Engl. J. Med.*, **320**, 252–253 (1989)

24 Bartholomew, C., Cleghorn, F., Waveney, C. *et al.* ATL/L and TSP in Trinidad and Tobago. In *HTLV-I and the Nervous System* (eds G. C. Roman, J-C. Verrant and M. Arame), Alan R. Liss, New York, pp. 183–188 (1989)

25 Miller, G. J., Pegram, S. M., Kirkwood, B. R. *et al.* Ethnic composition, age, sex and the location and standard of housing as determinants of HTLV-I infection in an urban Trinidadian community. *Int. J. Cancer*, **38**, 801–808 (1986)

26 Robert-Guroff, M., Clark, J., Lanier, A. P. *et al.* Prevalence of HTLV-I in arctic regions. *Int. J. Cancer*, **36**, 651–655 (1985)

27 Gessain, A., Barin, F., Vernant, J. C. *et al.* Antibodies to HTLV-I in patients with tropical spastic paraparesis. *Lancet*, **ii**, 407–409 (1985)

28 Anonymous Editorial. *Lancet*, **i**, 217–219 (1988)

29 Osame, M., Matsumoto, M., Usuku, K. *et al.* Chronic progressive myelopathy associated with elevated antibodies to HTLV-I and adult T-cell leukaemia like cells. *Ann. Neurol.*, **21**, 117–122 (1987)

30 Dalgleish, A. G., Fazerkely, J. and Webb, J. Can HTLV-I and similar viruses induce autoimmunity in patients with multiple sclerosis? *J. Neuropathol Neurobiol.*, **13**, 241–250 (1987)

31 Haase, A. T. Pathogenesis of lentivirus infections. *Nature*, **322**, 130–136 (1986)

32 Serwadda, D., Mugerwa, R. D., Sevankambo, N. K. *et al.* Slim disease: a new disease in Uganda and its association with HTLV-III infection. *Lancet*, **ii**, 849–852 (1985)

33 Konotey Ahulu, A. and Beverley, P. C. L. HIV-2 in West Africa. *Lancet*, **i**, 553 (1989)

34 Dalgleish, A. G., Beverley, P. C. L., Clapham, P. The CD4 (T4) antigen is an essential component of the receptor for the AIDS virus (HTLV-3). *Nature*, **312**, 763–767 (1984)

35 Sattentau, Q., Dalgleish, A. G., Weiss, R. A. *et al.* Epitopes of the CD4 antigen and HIV infection. *Science*, **234**, 1120–1123 (1986)

36 Kanki, P. J., Barin, F., M'Boup, S. *et al.* New human T-lymphotropic retrovirus related to Simian T-lymphotropic virus type III (STLV-III$_{AGM}$). *Science*, **23**, 238–243 (1986)

37 Clavel, F., Guetard, D., Brun-Vezinet, F. *et al.* Isolation of a new human retrovirus from West African patients with AIDS. *Science*, **233**, 343–346 (1986)

Chapter 19

HTLV-I-associated lymphomas/leukaemias: the Jamaican experience

W. N. Gibbs

During the last decade, evidence has accumulated that the human T-cell lymphotropic virus type I (HTLV-I) is involved in the pathogenesis of a subset of non-Hodgkin's lymphomas (NHLs) and, perhaps, in the evolution of chronic lymphocytic leukaemia (CLL). This chapter reviews the relationship between HTLV-I, and NHL and CLL, with particular reference to the findings in Jamaica.

Prevalence of NHL and CLL in Jamaica

The annual age-standardized incidence of 'lymphosarcoma' and 'other reticuloses' in males in Jamaica for the period 1973–77 was 3.8 and 1.6 per 100 000 of population, 1.9 and 0.6 for females, respectively [1]. These rates are generally lower than those in the USA, and higher than those in Japan [1]. It is assumed that the term 'lymphosarcoma' and 'other reticuloses', which are used here refer to cases of NHL. It is more difficult to compare rates of CLL, because this is included in the group of 'lymphatic leukaemia'. However, CLL and other varieties of lymphatic leukaemia are less prevalent among males and females in Jamaica (1.2 and 0.7 per 100 000, respectively) than in the USA, but are more prevalent than in Japan.

HTLV-I

The structure of HTLV-I and its role in the pathogenesis of adult T-cell leukaemia/lymphoma (ATLL) have been extensively reviewed elsewhere [2,3]. HTLV-I is a retrovirus, with a tropism for OKT4 lymphocytes, and it can induce proliferation or may cause suppression of infected cells [2,3]. The mechanism is uncertain, but there is evidence suggesting that a gene in the long open reading frame region encodes for a protein, which probably transforms cells by exerting control on gene expression through interaction with subsets of non-adjacent viral and cellular promoters.

HTLV-I and NHL

The association between HTLV-I infection and a subset of NHL patients followed the clinical recognition of an aggressive lymphoproliferative malignancy, adult T-cell leukaemia/lymphoma (ATLL), in Japan [4]. As initially described, this disease had the following features: onset in adults; lymphadenopathy and hepatosplenomegaly characteristic of NHL; high frequencies of hypercalcaemia, leukaemia and skin infiltration, without mediastinal involvement.

Convincing seroepidemiological evidence has accumulated, linking HTLV-I with adult T-cell leukaemia/lymphoma (ATLL) in subsequent studies of patients in Japan [5–7], in people of West Indian origin living in Britain who had ATLL [8,9] and in ATLL patients living in the South-eastern USA [9].

Molecular studies of ATLL patients strengthened the evidence for the relationship between HTLV-I infection and ATLL. All patients with typical ATLL studied had HTLV-I provirus integrated into malignant cells [10]. A few cases which were negative for circulating antibody had integrated provirus in the malignant cells [11].

HTLV-I has also been isolated from malignant cells, and can be transmitted *in vitro* by co-culturing infected cells with cord blood lymphocytes, human bone marrow T cells and adult human peripheral blood T cells [12]. Such infected cells have some features similar to those of neoplastic T cells; they have the indefinite growth potential and many of the functional and morphological changes found in the circulating neoplastic cells of ATLL patients.

HTLV-I, NHL and ATLL in Jamaica

A report from the University Hospital of the West Indies, Jamaica, based on a retrospective study of NHL patients, had indicated important differences between Jamaican NHL patients and NHL patients in the USA and Europe [13]. The disease was diffuse in 95% of Jamaican patients, and hypercalcaemia, leukaemia and skin involvement were unusually prevalent. The prognosis was very poor, the median survival being about 30 weeks. It was suggested that the differences in presentation and behaviour of NHL in Jamaica, compared with North America or Europe, could be due to inclusion of ATLL patients among Jamaican NHL patients. In addition, a preliminary study from Jamaica [14] had indicated a high prevalence of HTLV-I antibody positivity in NHL patients, most with features of ATLL.

A prospective study of NHL in Jamaica was started in February 1982 to try to define the relationship between HLTV-I infection, NHL and ATLL. This chapter describes the first 95 patients entered into the study, aged 10–80 years old, nearly all with advanced disease: 78% in clinical Stage IV, 12% Stage III, 8% Stage II and 2% Stage I. Seventy-five per cent had constitutional symptoms.

Fifty-two patients (55%) were HTLV-I antibody positive, significantly more than in the general population in which the prevalence is about 8% ($P < 0.05$). Although the mean age of HTLV-I antibody-positive patients (41 years) was significantly lower than the mean age of antibody-negative patients (48 years; $P < 0.05$), all of the antibody-positive patients were more than 20 years old.

Nearly all patients had generalized lymphadenopathy (Figure 19.1). Hepatomegaly was detected in 55%. Sixty-three per cent had abnormal liver

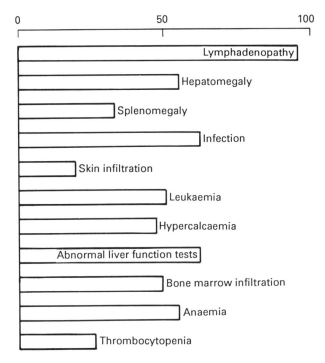

Figure 19.1 Proportions of NHL patients with clinical and laboratory abnormalities

function tests (LFTs). About one-third had splenomegaly, 56% were anaemic and 27% were thrombocytopenic (Figure 19.1). HTLV-I antibody positivity was demonstrated in 42–67% of these patients. Septicaemia was the most common infection and the causative organisms were usually pyogenic: streptococcus, staphylococcus, *E. coli*, proteus or pseudomonas. In contrast with the experience among Japanese patients, systemic opportunistic infections were rare, detected in only two patients.

Skin infiltration (20% of the patients), hypercalcaemia (48%) and leukaemia (51%) were unusually prevalent (Figure 19.1) compared with North American or European patients. There was a strong association between HTLV-I antibody positivity and these disorders ($P < 0.02$ in each case). All but one of the patients with skin infiltration had multiple lesions which were usually papulonodular, but small numbers of patients had large plaques with ulceration, generalized erythroderma, poikiloderma, papulosquamous lesions or diffuse alopecia.

The leukaemic cells (Figure 19.2(a)) were usually small or medium sized, but large cells were seen in all patients and predominated in a few. The nucleus was usually polylobulated. Nucleoli were inconspicuous in the smaller or medium sized cells in which the nuclear chromatin was condensed, but were often prominent in the larger cells in which the nuclear chromatin was more evenly distributed. The cytoplasm was scanty and basophilic. In half of the patients, the bone marrow was infiltrated by cells resembling the leukaemic cells. The infiltration was diffuse in all cases, and was never paratrabecular.

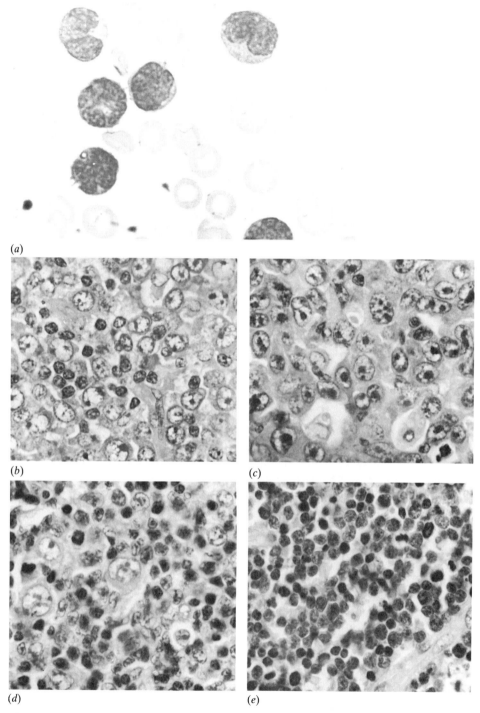

Figure 19.2 Malignant cells in peripheral blood and infiltrating lymph node. (*a*) Peripheral blood, polylobulated medium-sized and large cells. (*b*) Lymph node, large cell lymphoma. (*c*) Lymph node, pleomorphic lymphoma. (*d*) Lymph node, mixed cell lymphoma. (*e*) Lymph node, medium-sized cell lymphoma. ((*a*) Wright's stain, × 1465, reduced to 44% on reproduction; (*b*)–(*e*) H & E, × 1100, reduced to 52% on reproduction)

All patients had diffuse disease. Lymph node architecture was obliterated, sometimes with a paracortical distribution suggesting a T-cell origin of the tumour. The infiltrating cell was pleomorphic. No histopathological scheme is sufficiently precise for classification of Jamaican NHL patients, but the scheme recommended by the Lymphoma Study Group (LSG), Japan [15] is the most useful. Most of the patients had large cell (36%, Figure 19.2(b)), pleomorphic (23%, Figure 19.2 (c)) or mixed cell lymphoma (19%, Figure 19.2(d)), but a smaller number had medium sized cell lymphoma (11%, Figure 19.2(e)) and the remainder was unclassified. There was no correlation between the histopathological subtype and HTLV-I serology.

As noted above, skin infiltration occurs in a relatively high proportion of Jamaican NHL patients. In some patients epidermotropism is demonstrable, but the clinical course of the patients with these figures is characteristic of ATLL rather than of cutaneous T-cell lymphoma. Twenty-seven patients had ATLL, defined here as T-cell NHL associated with skin infiltration, leukaemia or hypercalcaemia, or with combinations of any two or all of these three abnormalities. Twenty-four (89%) patients were HTLV-I antibody positive, emphasizing the strong association between ATLL and HTLV-I infection. Integrated provirus was detectable in tumour cells of HTLV-I antibody-positive Jamaican ATLL patients, but not in tumour cells of HTLV-I antibody-negative patients. Further analysis of antibody-negative ATLL cases with molecular probes and tissue culture is underway to try to determine the reasons.

Median survival of the ATLL patients was 17 weeks, confirming previous reports [4,10] that this disorder has a poor prognosis. However, the spectrum of clinicopathological features is broad, including a subgroup of patients with a median survival of 81 weeks. Skin involvement is prominent in this group, and this feature and the similarity in histopathological appearances between ATL and cutaneous T-cell lymphoma suggest an overlap between these two disorders. Further work is required to define the relationship between them.

The most important prognostic determinant is hypercalcaemia: the median survival of hypercalcaemic ATLL patients (12.5 weeks) was significantly shorter ($P < 0.05$) than the median survival of normocalcaemic ATLL patients. None of the other variables affected prognosis. This effect of hypercalcaemia probably partially reflects the effect of the tumour load, and is partially due to the metabolic effects of the hypercalcaemia itself.

HTLV-I and CLL

An unusually high prevalence of HTLV-I antibody positivity has been detected in Jamaican CLL patients (Table 19.1). One of these six patients had an atypical clinical course, presenting with ascites and jaundice and dying within 1 month of

Table 19.1 HTLV-I serology in Jamaica

	No. tested	No. antibody positive
Foodhandlers	7000	574(8)
NHL patients	95	52(55)
CLL patients	22	6(27)

Figures in parentheses indicate percentages.

diagnosis, but there was no significant difference in clinical and haematological features when the remaining HTLV-I antibody-positive and -negative patients were compared (Table 19.2). The features were also similar to those reported in other groups of CLL patients [16].

No patient had any of the features suggesting ATLL. None of the patients was hypercalcaemic and the leukaemic cells in the blood and the cells infiltrating the bone marrow were small lymphocytes.

HTLV-I provirus was detected in the cultured T-cells, but not in the leukaemic B cells, of one of the HTLV-I antibody-positive patients [17]. An indirect mechanism for the pathogenesis of CLL has been proposed.

Table 19.2 Clinical and haematological characteristics of CLL patients

	HTLV-I antibody*	
	Positive	Negative
Lymphadenopathy	4(67)	14(88)
Hepatomegaly	4(67)	10(63)
Splenomegaly	4(67)	7(44)
Skin involvement	1(17)	3(19)
Hypercalcaemia	0	0
Leukaemia	6(100)	16(100)
Bone marrow infiltration	6(100)	16(100)
Anaemia	5(83)	10(63)
Thrombocytopenia	4(67)	8(50)

* Numbers of patients showing the characteristic, figures in parentheses are percentages

Acknowledgements

This work has been supported by the National Cancer Institute, Bethesda, Maryland, USA (Contract no. NO–CP–31006).

I thank my colleagues at the University of the West Indies, Kingston, Jamaica, and at the National Cancer Institute, Bethesda, Maryland, USA, who have allowed me to use data collected during the study.

References

1 Brooks, S. E. H., Persaud, V., Cowan, I. and Wolff, C. Cancer incidence in Kingston and St Andrew. In *Cancer Incidence in Five Continents*, vol. IV (eds J. Waterhouse, C. Muir, K. Shanmungardrun and J. Powell), IARC Scientific Publications No. 42, Lyon, pp. 764, 768, 772 (1982)
2 Gallo, R. C. and Wong-Staal, F. Retroviruses as etiologic agents of some animals and human leukemias and lymphomas and as tools for elucidating the molecular mechanism of leukemogenesis. *Blood*, **60**, 545–557 (1982)
3 Gallo, R. C. and Blattner, W. A. Human T-cell leukemia/lymphoma viruses: ATL and AIDS. In *Important Advances in Oncology* (eds V. T. DeVita, S. Hellman and S. A. Rosenberg), Lippincott, London, pp. 104–138 (1985)
4 Takatsuki, K., Uchiyama, J., Sagawa, K. and Yodoi, J. Adult T-cell leukemia in Japan. In *Topics in Hematology* (eds S. Seno, K. Takaku and S. Irino), Excerpta Medica, Amsterdam, pp. 73–77 (1977)

5 Gallo, R. C., de The, G. B. and Ito, Y. Kyoto Workshop on some Specific Recent Advances in Human Tumour Virology. *Cancer Res.*, **41**, 4738–4739 (1981)
6 Robert-Guroff, M., Nakao, Y., Notake, K. *et al*. Natural antibodies to human retrovirus HTLV in a cluster of Japanese patients with adult T-cell leukemia. *Science*, **215**, 975–978 (1982)
7 Kalyanaraman, V. S., Sarngadharan, M. G., Nakao, Y. *et al*. Natural antibodies to the structural protein (p. 24) of the human T-cell leukemia (lymphoma) retrovirus found in sera of leukemic patients in Japan. *Proc. Natl. Acad. Sci. USA*, **79**, 1653–1657 (1982)
8 Catovsky, D., Greaves, M. F., Rose, M. *et al*. Adult T-cell leukemia/lymphoma in Blacks from the West Indies. *Lancet*, **i**, 639–642 (1982)
9 Blattner, W. A.,, Kalyanaraman, V. S., Robert-Guroff, M. *et al*. The human Type-C retrovirus, HLTV, in Blacks from the Caribbean region, and relationship to adult T-cell leukemia/lymphoma. *Int. J. Cancer*, **30**, 257–264 (1982)
10 Blayney, D. W., Jaffe, E. S., Fisher, R. I. *et al*. The human T-cell leukemia/lymphoma virus (HTLV), lymphoma, lytic bone lesions, and hypercalcemia. *Ann. Intern. Med.*, **98**, 144–151 (1983)
11 Wong-Staal, F., Hahn, B., Manzari, V. *et al*. A survey of human leukemias for sequences of a human retrovirus, HLTV. *Nature*, **302**, 626–628 (1983)
12 Popovic, M., Sarin, P. S., Robert-Guroff, M. *et al*. Isolations and transmission of human retrovirus (human T-cell leukemia virus). *Science*, **219**, 856–859 (1983)
13 Lofters, W. S., Gibbs, W. N., Campbell, M. *et al*. Clinical features of non-Hodgkin's lymphoma in Jamaica. *West Indian Med. J.*, **33**, 71–75 (1984)
14 Blattner, W. A., Gibbs, W. N., Saxinger, C. *et al*. Human T-cell leukemia/lymphoma virus-associated lymphoreticular neoplasia in Jamaica. *Lancet*, **ii**, 61–64 (1983)
15 Hanaoka, M., Sasoki, M., Matsumoto, H. *et al*. Adult T-cell leukemia: histological classification and characteristics. *Acta Pathol. Jpn.*, **29**, 723–738 (1979)
16 Boggs, D. R., Sofferman, S. A., Wintrobe, M. M. and Cartwright, G. E. Factors influencing the duration of survival of patients with chronic lymphocytic leukemia. *Am. J. Med.*, **40**, 243–254 (1966)
17 Clark, J. W., Hahn, B. H., Mann, D. L. *et al*. Molecular and immunologic analysis of a chronic lymphocytic leukemia case with antibodies against human T-cell leukemia virus. *Cancer*, **56**, 495–499 (1985)

Chapter 20

Tropical myeloneuropathies. The Jamaican experience

Owen St C. Morgan

Introduction

Diseases of the nervous system have been known to occur in Jamaica since its capture in 1655 from the Spanish who had virtually eliminated the original Arawak inhabitants. Reports of epidemic outbreaks of strange palsies among settlers and slaves were noted by Dunn in 1675; multiple peripheral neuritis [1], and of 'the Spanish Town Epidemic' – probably a postinfectious acute sensory neuropathy – among labourers on a sugar plantation [2] are prominent in the medical literature.

The most important of the endemic illnesses to have been recognized, however, was the Jamaican Neuropathy, described in a paper to the *West Indian Medical Journal* by Cruickshank [3]. This original account of the first 100 cases of 'A Neuropathic Syndrome of Uncertain Origin' was followed by a series of articles describing further details of the syndrome in the Caribbean [4], Africa [5–10], South India [11], the Seychelle Islands [12], Colombia [13] and Martinique [14].

The similarity of these diseases originating in a tropical environment led Cruickshank [15] to regard them as the tropical myeloneuropathies (TMN), of which two distinct clinical groups were identified:

1. Tropical ataxic neuropathy (TAN) – a syndrome of posterior column and peripheral nerve signs presenting as proprioceptive disorder, sometimes with pyramidal tract signs, occurring in endemic form.
2. Tropical spastic paraparesis (TSP) – an upper motor neurone disorder with some sensory signs in the lower limbs, occurring in either endemic or epidemic forms.

In practice, neither syndrome appears in its pure form as there is often overlap of clinical features.

Several attempts have been made to determine the aetiology of TMN. Nutritional deficiency, infectious agents especially the treponemata, toxic substances (including cyanide) and certain environmental factors have all been incriminated. In every instance suitable objections have resulted in rejection of these hypotheses.

The discovery of IgG antibodies to the human T-lymphocytic virus (HTLV-I) in the sera of patients with TSP from Martinique [14] was a most important observation. Sera and CSF from Jamaican and Colombian patients with this disorder have also been shown to contain antibodies to HTLV-I [16], and further confirmation of these findings has come from Trinidad [17], the Seychelles [18], the Ivory Coast [10], Japan [19] and in West Indian-born patients in Britain [20]. These findings suggest that the human T-lymphocytic virus, HTLV-I, plays an important role in the pathogenesis of TSP.

Observations will now be presented on 78 new TSP patients and one with TAN studied at the University Hospital of the West Indies, Jamaica between 1983 and 1987. The main purpose of the investigation was to document the clinical, epidemiological, laboratory and histological findings in this recently studied group.

Diagnostic criteria and patients studied

The diagnosis of TSP was accepted if patients had the following features: history of back pain or discomfort; no family history of neurological diseases; frequency, hesitancy and precipitancy of micturition; spasticity and hyperreflexia of the lower limbs; normal mental status; normal myelographic findings. Other symptoms and signs included: burning sensation in the legs; impaired vibration perception; optic atrophy; sensorineural hearing loss.

Fifty-nine were female and 20 male and they originated from the Kingston, St Andrew and St Catherine areas. With the exception of two patients of mixed origin, all were of negro extraction. Ages ranged from 17 to 65 years (mean 46 years). None was malnourished. They had a wide range of occupations, including school teachers, small farmers, nurses' aides, businessmen, domestic helpers and telephone operators. Many were unemployed by virtue of their illness.

Clinical features

Onset of the disease was gradual in the majority of patients, although in some instances it was abrupt. Low back pain was a significant and early complaint and antedated leg weakness by several months. Urinary disturbances such as hesitancy, precipitancy and frequency of micturition were invariably present and in some instances antedated the appearance of leg weakness. A variety of sensory complaints was noted and consisted of cramps, numbness and burning sensations in the feet. Sexual incompetence was a major problem among the males.

The general medical examination was normal in all cases, and in particular no skin lesions, lymphadenopathy or evidence of reticuloendothelial system involvement were found.

Dementia was never present and the only cranial nerve abnormality observed was sensorineural hearing loss in four patients. As in previous reports weakness progressed gradually over 6 months to 1 year and thereafter tended to remain static. Few patients became paraplegic. Spasticity, leg cramps and spasms were particularly distressing. All had difficulty in walking due to spasticity. Pyramidal tract signs in both the upper and lower limbs were readily demonstrable on examination. Vibration perception was impaired in the lower limbs in some cases. Evidence of cerebellar dysfunction was never observed.

Laboratory data

Routine haematological and biochemical tests were normal, except in the one instance where cleaved and trifoliate lymphocytes were present in the peripheral blood smears and an abnormal clone of lymphocytes in the bone marrow of a patient with established TSP.

Chest and cervical spine X-rays were normal. Myelographic studies showed no obstructive lesions and the magnetic resonance scan of the one patient studied was normal. The VDRL test for syphilis (or yaws) was positive in 10% (5/53) of sera and 5% (1/21) of CSF samples tested.

Methods

HTLV-I serological studies

Serum and CSF samples were collected from TSP patients, together with sera from control patients with unrelated neurological illnesses. Samples were coded and shipped on dry ice from Jamaica to the National Institute of Health Laboratories, Bethesda, and stored at $-70°C$. They were tested for IgG antibodies to HTLV-I, using the HTLV-I (ELISA) kit, and disrupted HTLV-I virions as antigen. An optical density of reading equal to or greater than the mean of the positive controls was regarded as positive. Immunoblots of positive and borderline samples were done on serum and CSF using the Biotech Western Blot Kit for the detection of antibodies to the major proteins of HTLV-I. The presence of specific HTLV-I immunoglobulins was indicated by *in situ* labelling of HTLV-I-specific proteins.

IgG antibodies to HTLV-I were present in 87% (41/47) of sera and 83% (40/48) of CSFs. Levels in serum were always higher than those in the CSF. Thirteen per cent of neurological controls were positive for HTLV-I antibody in serum.

Oligoclonal bands – isoelectric focusing

CSF albumin and IgG concentrations were determined on eight patients and serum to CSF ratios calculated. Serum and CSF samples collected and run simultaneously were separated by agarose isoelectric focusing and blotted onto nitrocellulose paper. Immunoblots were performed with antihuman IgG antiserum to demonstrate oligoclonal bands.

Serum/CSF albumin ratios were normal in all patients tested, indicating that the blood–brain barrier was intact. The serum to CSF index indicated intrathecal IgG synthesis. In most patients tested immunoblots with antihuman IgG antiserum demonstrated oligoclonal banding, with some bands common to serum and CSF and others exclusively present in CSF.

Viral isolation

Heparinized blood and CSF were collected and lymphocytes immediately separated on follicol-paque gradients. Cells shipped on wet ice to the NIH were co-cultivated with human umbilical cord blood lymphocytes within 24 h. Viral isolation was attempted on over 30 samples of freshly separated blood lymphocytes. Virus has since been isolated from the CSF in one patient with TSP, and a virus resembling HTLV-I identified by electron microscopy in fixed spinal cord sections of another.

Electrophysiology

Motor and sensory conductions, F-wave latencies and needle electrode examination of the muscles were performed in 21 patients with TSP and one with TAN.

The one ataxic patient showed a general diminution in the amplitudes of the compound motor and sensory nerve action potentials, and motor units were enlarged (due to denervation followed by reinnervation) on needle electrode examination. Motor and sensory conduction velocities and F-wave latencies were all normal.

All 20 patients in the spastic group had substantially normal EMGs.

Discussion

There have been some significant changes in the pattern of TSP in Jamaica since it was first described in 1956. More patients from a higher socioeconomic group are now encountered, and a female–male preponderance of 3 : 1 is observed.

Here the majority of patients appeared to originate from Kingston, St Andrew and St Catherine. Earlier studies had shown that TSP was widely distributed throughout the island, being particularly prevalent in those areas in which yaws was once present. It would be improper to suggest that the geographical distribution of the disease has changed. Patients from outlying areas are known to register the address of their relatives in Kingston as their own. Furthermore, it is probable that many patients residing in the interior of the island have not yet had a medical opinion. Transportation is expensive and by virtue of their slowness of movement and bladder incontinence, these patients depend heavily on the more expensive private taxis, rather than on public transport. A careful survey of the island is planned to determine not only the geographical location of the illness but also its true prevalence and incidence.

Another feature of the study was the striking alteration in the treponemal antibody status of our patients. Only 10% of sera and 5% of CSF specimens were VDRL positive compared with 60% of sera and 6% of CSF specimens in earlier studies [4]. The incidence of yaws has declined sharply in Jamaica. However, there has been no parallel decrease in the number of TSP cases. These observations provide evidence that the positive treponemal status of patients in earlier studies reflected exposure to yaws and not to syphilis, and a treponemal aetiology for TSP is thus most unlikely.

Support for the role of TSP as a retroviral-induced disease is provided by the following observations:

1. The clinical descriptions and serological results of patients from Jamaica, Martinique, Trinidad and Tobago, the Seychelles, Japan and West Indians in Britain.
2. The isolation of a retrovirus from one of our patients with TSP.
3. The identification of viral particles by electron microscopy in fixed spinal cord sections of another.

4. The demonstration of a chronic inflammatory infiltrate with demyelination in the brain and spinal cord of an HTLV-I-positive TSP subject.

Furthermore, such findings could indicate that direct invasion of the CNS had taken place evoking a local as well as a systemic antibody response.

HTLV-I can be transmitted by sexual intercourse, blood transfusions and vertically from mother to child in cases of adult T-cell leukaemia. Zaninovic et al. [13] have shown that the prevalence of HTLV-I is greater than was expected in spouses and first-degree relatives of patients with TSP. It is important that the modes of transmission of this virus be established if the public health aspect of the disorder is to be addressed. Accordingly, studies to evaluate this claim have been commenced in Jamaica.

It has been suggested that HTLV-I may be associated with other neurological diseases, notably facial palsies and ataxic neuropathies.

Data from our controls with neurological disease yielded unexpected information which may link HTLV-I to other neurological diseases. Sera from the seven patients with polymyositis in this group all contained antibodies to HTLV-I in high titres. A larger number of sera is therefore being examined to determine the validity of these results, and efforts are being made simultaneously to recover virus from the muscle biopsy specimens.

The significance of the abnormal lymphocytes in the blood and bone marrow of one TSP patient will now be considered. It has been known for some time that HTLV-I virus is associated with lymphoreticular neoplasia in Jamaica [21]. From Trinidad Bartholomew et al. [17] reported the development of non-Hodgkin's lymphoma in a patient with TSP of several years' duration. Adult T-cell leukaemia-like cells are consistently present in blood and CSF of patients with HTLV-I-associated myeloneuropathy in Japan [19]. Thus in each instance indirect evidence of a causative relationship between HTLV-I, lymphoma and TSP is provided. The presence of abnormal clones of cells in the case under discussion is likely to represent an early stage in the development of the adult T-cell lymphoma syndrome and suggests that the virus possesses distinct neurotropic properties.

Few electrophysiological investigations have been undertaken in the tropical myeloneuropathies [22,23]. We have conclusively shown that the EMGs were substantially normal in the larger spastic group of patients, although the sensory nerve conduction was abnormal in two. The only explanation we can offer for this is that in these two cases there was overlap in the two clinical types of disease.

The studies on the single ataxic patient suggest that TAN is a central peripheral distal axonopathy. Neurones such as the sensory one in the dorsal root undergo degeneration of their distal axonal processes, not only those extending peripherally from sensory end-organs, but also those extending centrally. In contrast to the Nigerian TAN where changes of demyelination were observed, this Jamaican case appears to be primarily axonal. We cannot however categorically state that this is either representative or characteristic of all cases of TAN and the paucity of new cases may prevent this observation from ever being made.

In conclusion it should be stated that TSP poses major socioeconomic, public health and therapeutic problems. The retrovirus HTLV-I has emerged as the pre-eminent aetiological agent for the disease. Much remains to be accomplished if our understanding of the disease is to advance. Further strategies must not only address the development of vaccines and antiviral agents but must devise measures capable of limiting the transmission of the virus in order that control of this disabling disorder may be achieved [24].

References

1 Strachan, H. On a form of multiple neuritis prevalent in the West Indies. *Practitioner*, **59**, 477–484 (1888)
2 Scott, H. H. Investigation into an acute outbreak of central neuritis. *Ann. Trop. Med. Parasitol.*, **41**, (12), 109–196 (1918)
3 Cruickshank, E. K. A neuropathic syndrome of uncertain origin. *West Indian Med. J.*, **5**, 147–158 (1956)
4 Montgomery, R. D., Cruickshank, E. K., Robertson, W. B. and McMeremey, W. Clinical and pathological observations on Jamaican neuropathy, a report on 206 cases. *Brain*, **87**, 425–462 (1964)
5 Money, G. I. Endemic neuropathies in the Epe district of southern Nigeria. *W. Afr. Med. J.*, **8**, 3–17 (1959)
6 Cosnett, J. E. Unexplained spastic myelopathy: 41 cases in a non-European hospital. *S. Afr. Med. J.*, **39**, 592–595 (1964)
7 Makene, W. J. and Wilson, J. Biochemical studies in Tanzanian patients with ataxic tropical neuropathy. *J. Neurol. Neurosurg. Psychiatry*, **35**, 31–33 (1972)
8 Casadei, E., Jansen, P., Rodriques, A. *et al.* Ministry of Health, Mozambique: 1. Mantakassa: an epidemic of spastic paraparesis associated with chronic cassava antoxication in a cassava staple area of Mozambique. 2. Nutritional factors and hydrocyanic content of cassava products. *Bull. WHO*, **62**, 485–492 (1984)
9 Carton, H., Kayembe, K., Kabeya, O. Epidemic spastic paraparesis in Bandundu (Zaire). *J. Neurol. Neurosurg. Psychiatry*, **49**, 620–627 (1986)
10 Gessain, A., Francis, H., Sonan, T. *et al.* HTLV-I and tropical spastic paraparesis in Africa. *Lancet*, **ii**, 698 (1986)
11 Mani, K. S., Mani, A. J. and Montgomery, R. D. A spastic paraplegic syndrome in South India. *J. Neurol. Sci.*, **9**, 179–199 (1969)
12 Kelly, R. and Demot, B. Paraplegia in the islands of the Indian Ocean. *Afr. J. Neurol. Sci.*, **1**, 5–7 (1982)
13 Zaninovic, V., Biojo, R., Arango, C. Paraparesis espastic del Pacific. *Colombia Med.*, **12**, 111–117 (1981)
14 Gessain, A., Barin, F., Vernant, J. C. *et al.* Antibodies of human T-lymphotrophic virus type-I in patients with tropical spastic paraparesis. *Lancet*, **ii**, 407–411 (1985)
15 Cruickshank, E. K. Neurological disorders in Jamaica. In *Tropical Neurology* (ed. J. D. Spillane), Oxford University Press, Oxford, chap. 33 (1973)
16 Rodgers-Johnson, P., Gajdusek, D. C., Morgan, O. St C. *et al.* HTLV-I and HTLV-II antibodies and tropical spastic paraparesis. *Lancet*, **ii**, 1247–1248 (1985)
17 Bartholomew, C., Cleghorn, F., Charles, W. *et al.* HTLV-I and tropical spastic paraparesis. *Lancet*, **ii**, 99–100 (1986)
18 Roman, G., Spencer, P. S., Schoenberg, G. S. *et al.* Tropical spastic paraparesis: HTLV-I antibodies in patients from the Seychelles. *New Engl. J. Med.*, **1**, 316 (1987)
19 Osame, M., Matsumoto, M., Usukuy, K. *et al.* Chronic progressive myelopathy associated with elevated antibodies to human T-lymphotropic virus type-I and adult T-cell leukemia-like cells. *Ann. Neurol.*, **21**, 117–122 (1987)
20 Newton, M., Cruickshank, J. K., Miller *et al.* Antibody to HTLV-I in West Indian born UK residents with spastic paraparesis. *Lancet*, **i**, 415–416 (1987)
21 Blattner, W. A., Gibbs, W. N., Saxinger, C. *et al.* Human T-cell leukaemia/lymphoma virus-associated lymphoreticular neoplasia in Jamaica. *Lancet*, **ii**, 61–64 (1983)
22 Osuntokun, B. O. An ataxic neuropathy in Nigeria. A clinical, biochemical and electrophysiological study. *Brain*, **91**, 215–248 (1968)
23 Arimura, K., Rosales, B., Osame, M. and Igata, A. Clinical electrophysiological studies of HTLV-I associated myelopathy. *Arch. Neurol.*, **44**, 509–512 (1987)
24 Morgan, O. St C., Montgomery, R. D., Rodgers-Johnson, P. The myeloneuropathies of Jamaica: an unfolding story. *Q. J. Med.*, (new series) **67**, 273–281 (1988)

HTLV-I and tropical spastic papaparesis in Britain

J. K. Cruickshank

Tropical spastic paraparesis (TSP) has become closely associated with the retrovirus HTLV-I worldwide, as reviewed in the first section of this chapter by Morgan from Jamaica where the original condition was described [1]. The causal role of this virus in producing the disease has now been almost proven rather than just thought to be highly likely. This short account reviews the experience in Britain of TSP in patients of Caribbean origin who had migrated to the UK. Details are available from the references of our group's work [2–7]. Of 26 cases seen up to 1989 and examined in detail in our series, all 24 tested have been HTLV-I antibody positive by several methods. The clinical features were described in the original 1964 paper from Jamaica [1]. The important investigation for distinguishing TSP from progressive spastic paraparesis occasionally found in multiple sclerosis is magnetic resonance scanning (MRI). In TSP the MRI abnormal signs were non-specific [2,4], rare in the brainstem, unlike multiple sclerosis [4] and not seen in the spinal cord which was atrophied (Figure 20.1). Antibody titres to HTLV-I can be assessed by a variety of methods, including particle agglutination, Western blot, pseudotype neutralization and antibody-directed cell-mediated cytotoxicity [5,6]. In all the British cases, antibody titres are considerably higher than in HTLV-I-related acute T-cell leukaemia patients or in relatives of the TSP cases, except in one healthy spouse. In the CSF some but not all of the IgG oligoclonal bands that are found are directed against HTLV-I [4].

A study of viral transmission among relatives that we have recently carried out showed that 60 of 64 first-degree relatives of the Jamaican-born patients in the series were traced in the UK and Jamaica; 20–30% of those born in the Caribbean had antibodies to HTLV-I, irrespective of their present place of residence, while none of those born in the UK, who were the children of the patients, had antibodies, suggesting that in later adulthood perhaps sexual transmission is much more important than that from breast-feeding. The newer technique of polymerase chain reaction (PCR) applied to DNA from apparently uninfected people may reveal genome-integrated virus without antibodies, but has not done so in our series of relatives. Negative serology was mirrored by negative PCR results, and results were positive in TSP patients and seropositive relatives. Minor sequence variation has been found in the 'pol' sequence of the HTLV-I gene [7], and more recently in the 'env' gene.

Review of the original pathological material (it remains very scarce worldwide), together with data such as the above, and animal models, particularly visna in sheep which shares both clinical and pathological features with TSP, suggest that TSP is due to an HTLV-I-infected lymphocyte/macrophage-mediated inflammatory response in the spinal cord.

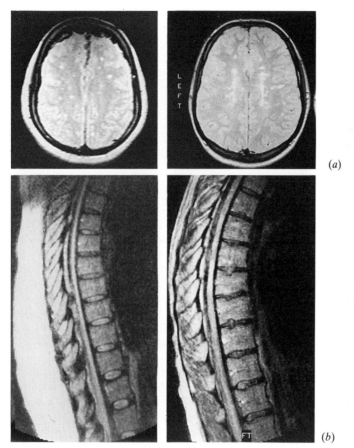

Figure 20.1 MRI scans (a) of cerebrum, (b) of spinal cord. Comparing patients with TSP (left panels) and multiple sclerosis (MS) (right panels). Note high density signals indicating lesions throughout white matter in MS and within spinal cord. In TSP the lesions are not localized and are non-specific. The cord may be atrophied. (Courtesy of Dr A. Kermode)

References

1 Montgomery, R., Cruickshank, E. K., Robertson, W. B. and McMeremey, W. H. Clinical and pathological observations in Jamaican myelopathy. *Brain*, **87**, 425–462 (1964)
2 Newton, M., Cruickshank, J. K., Miller. D. *et al*. Antibodies to HTLV-I in West Indian-born, UK-resident patients with spastic paraparesis. *Lancet*, **i**, 415–416 (1987)
3 Editorial. HTLV-I comes of age. *Lancet*, **i**, 217–219 (1988)
4 Cruickshank, J. K., Rudge, P., Dalgleish, A. *et al*. TSP and HTLV-I in the United Kingdom. *Brain*, August (in press) (1989)
5 Dalgleish, A., Richardson, J., Matutes, E. *et al*. HTLV-I infection in TSP: lymphocyte culture and serologic response. *AIDS Retrovirus Res.*, **4**, 475–485 (1988)
6 Sinclair, A., Habeshaw, J., Muir, L. *et al*. Antibody dependent cell mediated cytotoxicity in patients infected with HTLV-I and HIV. *AIDS*, **2**,465–472 (1988)
7 Bangham, C. R., Daenke, S., Bell, R. E. L., Cruickshank, J. K. *et al*. Enzymatic amplification of exogenous and endogenous retroviral sequences from patients with tropical spastic paraparesis. *EMBO J.*, **7**, 4179–4184 (1988)

Chapter 21

Psychiatric practice and ethnic minorities

A. W. Burke

Introduction

Psychiatry identifies those factors contributing to child, adolescent and personality development, mature adult functioning, to mental health in general and in its absence to the manifestations of mental incapacity, impairment and illness. Its scope is wide and complex – a discipline of *language and communication*, and understanding of crucial inter-relationships with causative factors in the psychological (*psychodynamic*), social (*sociodynamic*), and medical (physical illness) spheres. Like physical medicine it employs a system of disease categories identified by symptoms called phenomenology. The ethnic dimension and the significance of psychiatric practice among black populations in Britain is the subject of this chapter.

For migrant populations, attitudes to illness and utilization of facilities show marked variation in the country of origin and in the country of settlement. Migration itself also has inconsistent effects on morbidity, prior to leaving home [1,2], on arrival in the new environment [3,4] and finally on return home [5]. Before migration Asians and West Indians rely on home practices and traditional healers rather than medical staff for a wide range of physical and emotional problems [6,7]. After arrival, these effects largely depend to a great extent on the continued use of traditional remedies [8,9] and methods [10]. In Britain, Johnson found that the choice of general practitioner by black and white groups is positively associated with the same ethnic group of the practitioner. Afro-Caribbean and Asian patients in this and another West Midland study used their general practitioners more than white cases [11]. The public reporting of therapy satisfaction by black patients has been questioned by Donovan. Often black patients were unwilling to pronounce public dissatisfaction even though privately they were willing to do so. Clearly this issue of reporting is one of language and communication [11]. There the suggestion was that miscommunication was marked between black patients and white therapists. This and other evidence supported the view that racism had an important role in help seeking and general practitioner response.

The lag period in adjustment to health services in the West will be extended if communication problems between doctor and patient persist. Perception of susceptibility to and seriousness of illness may be culturally determined. Services will not be used if perceived benefits are small or the barriers to action are great [12]. Stigma of specific disorders, fear of illness and of personnel providing services, should be considered. The negative attitude of stigma may be as important as the emotion of fear. Therapists from different language, culture and race groups may evoke withdrawal and lead to lower utilization. Intuitive and empathic or professional knowledge should also be considered. Both facilitate communication – the former is culturally determined, the latter likely to be blocked by negative attitudes to race (prejudice) which result in discrimination. The importance of language to communication, particularly among the old or for the family group, in ethnic minority health has been stressed by Malik [13]. Therefore the psychiatry of old age and psychotherapy in families will be most affected.

Physical illness, social conditions and psychological status

Data from Third World countries suggest that prevailing social conditions may contribute to a high prevalence of physical and mental disorders. In one psychiatric sample, epilepsy was common, syphilis and its consequences significant, infections including tuberculosis notable, and hypertension was frequently associated with depression [5]. Poverty-stricken conditions are prevalent in such settings and in ghetto conditions here in the West. As a result effective treatment may not be available.

In Britain there is now a considerable literature on the association of health with inequalities of socioeconomic status, poverty and unemployment. Townsend and colleagues [14] have confirmed previous findings from the Black Report [15] in a sophisticated analysis of conditions in the North of England. Three key dimensions – premature mortality, chronic sickness and disablement, and delayed development were incorporated in an Overall Health Index which correlated highly (0.82) with an Overall Deprivation Index. In the latter, factors highly associated with being black and of minority ethnic status included percentages of unemployed households with more persons than rooms, no car, not owner occupied, and head of household a manual worker [16]. Among 136 electoral wards in the North of England the best 20% were compared with the worst 20%: mortality among males in social classes I and II was 2.5/1000 and 5/1000, while in social classes IV and V the rates were 3.7 and 8.9. For all classes suicide was twice as great in poor compared with better-off wards (57.8 : 29.2/100 000). The authors offer two main explanations; first, the good conditions in some wards; secondly, the varied make-up of persons in different areas. Other possibilities include working conditions, length of residence and previous health status before migration. As poorer health status is associated with concentration of ethnic minorities, racism may surely be important also.

A Black Health Workers and Patients Group [17] have alleged adverse racism-related effects of any policy with community care implications for the black population, including housing and employment. Townsend and colleagues found that while mortality from all causes is markedly increased, the standardized mortality ratios for mental disorder in social classes I, II, IV and V were 35, 48, 97 and 342 for males and for females, 50, 57, 83 and 144 respectively. Similar data are not available for the black populations living there. However, excesses in perinatal mortality among Asians, West Indians and Africans [18,19] have not been explained adequately and nor have the marked excesses of mortality for a wide range of disorders among Asians [20] and for hypertension among all groups [21]. Interpersonal factors, support [22] and unexpressed anger [23] are associated with hypertension and support the view of the present author that high morbidity for hypertension may be an outcome of racism [11].

Racism and its effects

The postulate that racism causes physical and mental illness cannot be accepted without considering the role of migration. The relative importance of social selection, protection (network) and stress in the causation of disorder, for example suicide, must be considered [24]. Selective migration is a crucial consideration in all epidemiological studies: some migrate because of sickness; others for care and others away from poor or towards good housing or labour facilities [25]. If racism is active these selective factors would grossly overestimate morbidity and mortality of a small population, actively mobile and exposed to relocation in ghetto-like areas. Indeed, three-quarters of the black population live in areas with substantial black populations, but only 10% of whites live in those areas. High levels of social stress results, mainly because of bad conditions but also because of strained relationships.

Factors which lead to normal personality development include a high tolerance to external stress, good feelings about oneself and the likelihood of realizing one's worth [26]. Race may not be a relevant variable in the study of personality theory [27] but it is probable that social factors associated with race do have a bearing on self-realization. Specifically, racism which relegates one broad category (black) to inferior status compared with white would restrict opportunity. In Britain clinical evidence suggests an increase in the use of somatic presentations by Asians [28], with eruptive patterns of behaviour among Afro-Caribbean hospital patients [29]. In Trinidad and Tobago, rates of mental disorder in one of the few hospital facilities were similarly distributed by race [2], thus suggesting that sociocultural factors are important in illness behaviour. Social selection is also an important variable in the use of psychiatric services [30], and migrant status, social stress and unintegrated social networks increase the tendency to seek help. In America [31] and in Britain blacks are less tolerant of mental illness than whites but little is known of Asian/West Indian differences in this regard.

Child development and adolescent adjustment

The socioeconomic conditions encountered by the black population may be the most important factor contributing to obstacles to child development and adolescent adjustment [32]. The well-known association of parental insecurity with emotional problems in the child may be greater among Afro-Caribbean families who experience far higher levels of interpersonal difficulty than matched whites. This is a consequence of residence in a hostile society [11] with inevitable disruption of and/or impaired function in family units [16]. Among Asians and Afro-Caribbean groups there may be much variation in rates of family stress according to country of origin [33], the period of settlement, the socioeconomic status of the individual/group, its use of English as first language, the family size and age-group distribution. A half of Bangladeshis are aged less than 17 with almost three-quarters less than 30 years [34]. Pakistanis, Indians, West Indians and Africans are slightly older but whites are much older with 60% over 30.

An increased rate of mental retardation may be one of the inevitable sequelae of deprivation in sectors of Britain's black population. In Camberwell a register of live births and all psychiatric contacts has allowed a careful evaluation of early and late difficulties 'in childhood and adolescence. Wing [35] reported that among 136 children aged 0–14 and with an IQ of less than 50, 42 (30%) were black, twice the number expected. Among 42 of these cases with severe language impairments 22 were black, five times expected. An organic cause was identified in nine of ten whites but only six blacks. Causes might include maternal rubella, infantile spasms, encephalitis, congenital blindness and brain injury, and the author speculated about the greater susceptibility of immigrants to 'a variety of virus infections which may affect the developing foetus'. It seems likely, however, that poor living conditions consequent on institutional factors are more plausible explanations.

An undiagnosed example was seen recently. The patient (now 34 years of age) was born into a household in which five older siblings had died in infancy. Both parents worked, having migrated here years earlier. Three years after the patient's birth his mother, by then diagnosed hypertensive, died in childbirth from a cerebrovascular accident. There was no organic diagnosis given for the patient's hyperactive, destructive, aggressive behaviour which started about the time of mother's death. Behaviour disorder led to detention in hospital during his third year of life and he has remained there since. On examination the patient was well adjusted, stabilized on drugs and without obvious disturbance, yet he was one of a group of black patients making up half the most disturbed patients at that London hospital.

Is behaviour disturbance more prevalent among black than white mentally retarded patients? The increased prevalence of West Indian single-parent households in zones of deprivation [16] may well be an important factor. In Brent almost 4000 live births annually include 10% of West Indian origin, but 46% of 425 children in care are of this ethnic group. For Asians the respective rates are 15% and 1%, supporting the view that intact social support systems are of crucial importance in preventing care orders [85]. The care procedure predisposes to weakening household integrity and its consequences include short-term displacement, categorization as educationally subnormal [36] and long-term maladjustment and identity confusion [37].

There have been several reports on increased behaviour disturbance among West Indian girls and boys in child guidance clinics [38], junior schools [39] and the community [40]. However, in a careful follow-up study Earls and Richman [41] have shown that behaviour disturbance in a matched white working class population was no less than the West Indian rate despite the larger family size and much greater prevalence of a working mother in the latter. Robins [42] has shown that race is not a factor in the adult outcome of behaviour disturbance in childhood. Together, these findings do suggest that with ghetto-like residence in unsupported social networks there will be a continued build-up of unhappy frustrated restless West Indian-origin youngsters in Britain. The vector once again is primarily the social disadvantage of racism.

A study of child-care decision making

In an attempt to deal with the increase in numbers of West Indian children in care, a number of strategies have been adopted by statutory agencies. Child-care practice among well-functioning black families with undoubted behaviour disturbance in the child has mental health implications. (In this section the term 'black' includes Asian, African and West Indian.) In a carefully investigated sample of 20 black child placements the present author found that among 29 parents, two were Asian, two white, the rest were of African/West Indian background. Six pairs were married or cohabitating, other pairs were separated but in regular contact; only nine were employed.

The findings suggested that statutory workers systematically underplayed the strengths of the family network in half the cases, and, contrary to popular opinion, opted for transracial placements in eight; they wrongly alleged [43] sexual abuse in all three identified cases, were more sympathetic in their disposal of cases of alleged physical abuse/neglect (five) and varied in their dealings with 12 cases of emotional neglect. It was unusual to provide effective support psychotherapy for the family or parent(s) and unfortunately these workers negatively highlighted probable deficits resulting from the parents' own child care among eight cases. Poor housing/living and employment conditions [44] among the parents were simply ignored, little concern was shown about the likely damage of such conditions to the children themselves. Care decisions for children in this sample may well have been influenced by race by ascribing behaviour to ethnic status and by witholding assistance and facilities to struggling, sometimes poverty stricken, but often vulnerable persons. In the USA statutory workers have been more inclined to decide for child care among black rather than white respondents [45]. In the present sample florid psychiatric illness among 14 of 29 parents and four of 20 index children seemed less important in reaching a decision regarding child care than race. By contrast, among white cases, psychiatric illness and personality disturbance together with social disadvantage are the pertinent factors in reaching a child-care decision.

Emotionally disturbed children may present to the clinic when parental disruption is evident but intractable. This pattern will be seen in Asian 'two-parent' families and West Indian/African unsupported 'one-parent' families. Among such Asian families multiple presentation of family members is not unusual. Mother may present with physical complaints, father with emotional problems, the child with developmental delay, learning difficulty and emotional problems. In effect the two-parent unit may be undergoing strain and may not be functioning. Underachievement at school may be more frequently found among Asian [46] and West Indian children than whites and this may be associated with higher rates of developmental problems [47]. Although parental absence and/or disruption may be important, this study highlighted the difficulties which arise when hard-pressed mothers (doing shift, as well as long hours of, work) strive to interact with their offspring. Children are more likely to show delayed language development and subsequently may perform poorly at school. This problem may be exaggerated if dialect or language style varies from home to school [49].

Behaviour disturbance in adolescents and adults

Social disadvantage and deprivation predict maladjustment, hospitalized psychiatric disorder and delinquency [50]. Environmental factors interact with cultural ones [51] and causative factors in delinquency may have persisted among West Indians at home and on migration to Britain [52,53]. Delinquency springs from multiple trauma leading to adjustment problems. Parental deviance was uncommon in male and female cases in Jamaica and London respectively. In Britain separation experiences are common but this is not true in the Caribbean.

Thus environmental factors as well as peer group pressure promote the poor opportunity structure in inner city settings [54]. Yet this is not an adequate explanation for prison statistics in 1984 which revealed among men and women that African, West Indian and mixed race groups make up 10% to 15% respectively of all cases. In the remand population there is a 30% increase for both sexes of similar ethnic status. Young offenders aged 14–20 follow the same pattern as adult offenders. Hall and co-workers [55] have argued that cohesive factors based on culture and family distinguish Afro-Caribbean and Asian groups. The data support this view. For males and females Asians make up 2.8% and 1.8% respectively, but there is no marked increase among remand cases. Furthermore, young offender Asians are notable by their absence [56]. The 'mother-present' Asian household may thus protect against visible unrest, behaviour disorder, delinquency, and detention in facilities.

Material on special hospital admissions, inpatients and discharges is not available by race. However, it is known that there is a disproportionate number of Afro-Caribbean cases among admissions and inpatients, with fewer discharged than expected. It is probable that the true rates for Afro-Caribbean admissions and inpatients is, as in prison data, between 10 and 15%.

Workers in Birmingham have reported on the nature of Mental Health Act activity in the admission of patients to one hospital (see pp. 190–194). A quarter of patients aged 16 to 44 are admitted compulsorily and there is no marked difference by race. In the community served by the hospital Asians (11%) and Afro-Caribbeans (6%) were minority groups identified. Among compulsory admissions (age-group 16–44) over 4 years the proportions by contrast were 14 and 37% respectively, and by and large this was unrelated to admission via the police [57]. There was an excess number of schizophrenics among black patients – particularly Afro-Caribbean as noted [58,59]. However, in a London study which found 20% of police admissions under Section 136 to be Afro-Caribbean, schizophrenia and unspecified psychoses were equally distributed by race [60].

Together these data indicate that compulsory detention for child care, delinquency, adult criminality and mental illness may be the outcome of the same deprivation indices most frequently found among Afro-Caribbeans and more so than among Asians. Poor living conditions, salary below the poverty-line and single unsupported parenthood and the attitude of society seem to be salient factors.

Limitations of epidemiology: race and mental illness

Epidemiological studies of ethnic factors in Britain have depended on grossly inaccurate census data and therefore are quite unreliable. To overcome this workers have used material from small area statistics or the Labour Force Survey [34]. Unfortunately both methods lack precision and for small populations are unlikely to be useful. For example, in the Labour Force Survey, people were asked to give their self-perceived ethnic origin; almost a million refused to answer this question; 1.8 million confessed to being West Indian or Asian but little is known about responses for half such populations born in Britain. Respondents may well have been suspicious and fearful of this survey. Therefore, these findings, like those in the census, cannot be relied on for epidemiological analysis. A further problem is the relative mobility of ethnic groups of different age structures. Black populations are young, increasing and are being relocated to run-down areas; whites are older, stable in numerical terms and move out of the inner cities for jobs and better living conditions. The effects are underenumeration with a concentration of vulnerable blacks, while for whites a more stable population base of large size coexists with a dilution effect for the vulnerable.

A third problem is the ascertainment of cases and the crude index given by hospital statistics. For example, there is a marked excess of cirrhosis of the liver in Asians in mortality statistics [20], however, except in suicide data [61]. Asian alcoholism is not a remarkable finding. In the USA evidence supports the view that eating disorders may be more prevalent in lower socioeconomic groups [62], but here in Britain specialist facilities report few cases [63,64]. Studies elsewhere confirm that the concept of illness [65], motivation to use medical services, appropriate staffing of such services, preference for therapists [66] and the ease of access and the likelihood of not meeting racism are crucial factors in seeking help.

There is a further issue which touches on the deprivation indices noted earlier and on service utilization. These are the *nosocomial* factors of psychiatry. The foregoing material on detention and its correlation with ecological structure pinpoints the varied paths taken by deprived and advantaged groups. Marital status and housing class of patients are well-known variables, so too is the class- and race-related ecological variable [67]. Stigma before migration [6], or to illness with migration failure and repatriation [68], lead to underutilization of facilities and a poor outcome [69]; communication facilities should take account of culture, racism, language deficit of patient and staff and the migration/refugee process. In Britain psychiatric services have simply ignored these factors. Therefore it should not be surprising to find the Asian population underrepresented in mental hospital/clinic material [70,71].

Epidemiological findings

The author has identified a similar prevalence of depression [11] but different precipitants of this condition among West Indians and whites in Birmingham. Merrill and Owens [72] replicated earlier work by others on attempted suicide among black and white groups in the same city. Black groups also have a lower rate of attempted suicide but young female Asians more frequently present than Afro-Carribbean and whites [11,72]. Suicide presents major problems of ascertainment but, as with attempted suicide, may be underrepresented in official statistics [73]. The difficulty is compounded by community stigma and high rates of accidental death in deprived areas. Despite low rates in countries of origin, the North American experience of high rates of suicide appears not far off [74].

Mental hospital admission data suggest increased rates for schizophrenia among black males and females and depressive psychosis among females but lower rates for neuroses and drug dependence for black groups. These findings by Dean and co-workers have been commented on by Glover [75] (see also Chapter 22). Clearly such findings only describe the nature of hospital activity by race. In the USA earlier findings showed that high-status migrant West Indians fared well when compared with low-status native blacks there [76]. In this area it is surprising to find epidemiological reports which are poor in methodology, based on small numbers and which fail to take account of basic epidemiological principles. For example, one set of workers decided to increase numbers of Afro-Caribbean subjects ethnicity by including 3 years' admission data in addition to the 1 year of the study (see Chapter 22). They used only the four inner city wards of drifting disadvantaged populations for this purpose. This might have grossly inflated the numbers of cases simply because vulnerable individuals drift into such areas. It is clear from their findings that social drift of younger black populations into areas of residence by settled older white populations was taking place. They failed to note this fact. In Manchester 3-year data were employed for epidemiological purposes. The 102 black cases (six African, 41 West Indian and 55 Asian) were used for comparison with 1159 British patients and the authors concluded that the immigrant rate (27.9/10 000/year) is twice that of the British rate of 13.5 [77]. The 10% census of 1974 was used to give the population base but little mention was made of its limitation. The Manchester group simply ignored the ecological factor, while the Bristol group mentioned it without stressing that relocation to bad areas is often based on race [78]. Hence the higher admission rate is a racial outcome rather than caused by race. Like Carpenter and Brockington [77], workers in Bradford found paranoid symptomatology more common in migrants than locals [79]. Their study of Poles and Russians used the technique of boosting the migrant rate by increasing the study period. The interpretation of such data is impossible. Nonetheless, these studies do confirm that Afro-Caribbeans and Asians are likely to come for help later than whites and when admitted or forcibly brought in (especially among Afro-Caribbean patients) are more likely to have schizophrenia.

Alcoholic behaviour has attracted recent attention and has been studied among Asians and West Indians in the community [80,81]. Alcohol abuse is not unusual in Asian and West Indian populations in the community here in Britain or in home environments abroad. Hospital data show that alcoholism itself shows a marked excess among migrant Asians as compared to West Indians [71]. The rates are low and it is probable that the data understate the true prevalence in both populations.

The cultural dimension

During the past decade transcultural psychiatry has shifted its concern with the exotic in the international setting to a pragmatic approach focussing on deprivation and disadvantage consequent on racism and other indignities [11,82]. The Black Health Workers and Patients Groups [17] allege that in psychiatry in Britain black patients do not have any rights. They have carefully investigated written material slanted against blacks and pointed to its limitations and dangers. Elsewhere it has been shown that race may be a determinant in the appointment of doctors, particularly in psychiatry [83]. Recent evidence shows that the process may have been underway even at the student selection stage. Psychiatry more so than any other branch of medicine employs communication skills as the main tools of investigation. Access to any health care system is affected by psychological factors and the selection of patients and therapists. Culture and race are important in both instances. Any provision which fails to take account of the proximity of the facility to the work-place or residence, the opening hours, the provision of an appointment or drop in system, or particularly that the elderly migrant may not speak English would in effect be withholding a service from such individuals.

In the present paper the cultural dimension has not been emphasized. Culture describes learned behaviour affected by home, religion, ethnic group, language, neighbourhood, school and age-group. Among migrant ethnic minority groups the place of socialization will also be important to one's cultural orientation. The utilization of health care will vary according to whether the individual has been socialized only at home, in a rural or urban area – the first generation; at home as well as in the new environment for those who migrate in early adolescence – the second generation; or in the new environment only – subsequent generations. Clearly, it would be impossible for the therapist to learn the cultural parameters of well over 150 language groups in Britain, or the combinations of these with other factors mentioned. Therefore, the discipline of psychiatry should seek to enrich its communication skills by training in a general approach to culture. It will also be important to protect patient rights by introducing a code of practice on race. This should allow any patient exposed to the possibility of discrimination or insult by virtue of religion, culture, language or race to be seen for opinion and/or therapy by a therapist of similar background. A code of practice on race should assist patient and therapist and should reduce the feeling of indignity among black patients shown earlier to be overrepresented in detained populations.

Conclusion

It has been shown that deprivation factors may be crucial in describing excesses among black populations. Note has been made of the limits of epidemiological interpretation. Race and language are as important in evaluation as background factors of deprivation.

One or two conclusions can be reached. The Afro-Caribbean and Asian populations are grossly overrepresented in the worst living conditions in Britain. Indeed, it may be true that a third of these groups share these intolerable conditions with less than a tenth of the white population and this factor may be the major determinant of poor health for these people. The second consideration is the mental illness statistic as an outcome of deprivation, racism and social factors. Without these factors the mentally ill may not go to hospital. The reinforcement of stigma, the increased social distance of doctor to patient, and the poor after-care of black patients reflect lower trust in and access to the services. Staffing by race may be an issue. The third consideration is the substantial block to self-realization being created by the above-mentioned factors and the consequences in terms of child care and behaviour disturbance.

References

1 Burke, A. W. First admissions and planning in Jamaica. *Soc. Psychiatry*, **9**, 39–45 (1974)
2 Burke, A. W. Socio-cultural determinants of psychiatric disorder among women in Trinidad & Tobago. *West Indian Med. J.*, **23**, 75–79 (1974)
3 Burke, A. W. Trends in Caribbean psychiatry Part I: the problems. *West Indian Med. J.*, **24**, 218–222 (1975)
4 Burke, A. W. Attempted suicide among East Indian women in Trinidad and Tobago and in Birmingham. *Ind. J. Psychiatry.*, **17**, 207–210 (1975)
5 Burke, A. W. Physical illness in psychiatric hospital patients in Jamaica. *Br. J. Psychiatry*, **121**, 562, 321–322 (1972)
6 Burke, A. W. Trends in social psychiatry in the Caribbean. *Int. J. Soc. Psychiatry*, **25**, 110–117 (1979)
7 Varma, V. K. Present state of psychotherapy in India. *Indian J. Psychiatry*, **24**, 209–226 (1982)
8 Bhopal, R. S. (1986) The inter-relationship of fold traditional and Western medicine within an Asian community in Britain. *Soc. Sci. Med.*, **22**, 99–105

9 Johnson, M. Inner city residents, ethnic minorities and primary health care in the West Midlands. In *Health, Race and Ethnicity*, (eds T. Rathwell and D. Phillips), Croom Helm, London, pp. 192–212 (1986)

10 Donovan, J. *We Don't Buy Sickness, It Just Comes: Health, Illness and Health Care in the Lives of Black People in London*, Gower, London (1986)

11 Burke, A.W. Racism and mental illness. *Int. J. Soc. Psychiatry*, **30**, 1–161 (1984)

12 Rosenstock, I. M. Why people use health services. *Milbank Mem. Fund Q.*, **44**, 94–127 (1966)

13 Malik, F. *Asian Women and Mental Health or Mental Ill-Health*, Asha/Asian Women's Aid, Southwark (1988)

14 Townsend, P., Phillimore, P. and Beattie, A. *Health and Deprivation: Inequality and the North*, Croom Helm, London (1988)

15 Townsend, P. and Davidson, N. (eds). *Inequalities in Health. The Black Report*, Penguin, Harmondsworth (1982)

16 Brown, C. *Black and White Britain. The Third PSI Survey*, Heinemann, London (1985)

17 Black Health Workers and Patients. Group Psychiatry and the Corporate State. *Race Class*, **25**, 49–64 (1983)

18 Lumb, K. M., Longdon, P. J. and Lealman, G. T. A comparative review of Asian and British born maternity patients in Bradford 1974–8. *J. Epidemiol. Community Health*, **35**, 106–109 (1981)

19 Robinson, M. J., Palmer, S. R., Avery, A. *et al.* Ethnic differences in perinatal mortality – a challenge. *J. Epidemiol. Community Health*, **36**, 22–26 (1982)

20 Balarajan, *et al.* Patterns of mortality among migrants to England and Wales from the Indian subcontinent. *Br. Med. J.*, **289**, 1185–1187 (1984)

21 Adelstein, A. M. Current vital statistics: methods and interpretation. *Br. Med. J.*, **2**, 983–986 (1978)

22 Strogatz, D. S. and James, S. A. Social support and hypertension among blacks and white in a rural, southern community. *Am. J. Epidemiol.*, **124**, 949–956 (1986)

23 Johnson, E. H., Spielberger, C. D., Worden, T. J. and Jacobs, G. A. Emotional and familial determinants of elevated blood pressure in black and white adolescent males. *J. Psychosom. Res.*, **31**, 287–300 (1987)

24 Burke, A. W. Socio-cultural determinants of attempted suicide among West Indians in Birmingham: ethnic origin and immigrant status. *Br. J. Psychiatry*, **129**, 261–266 (1976)

25 Bentham, G. Migration and morbidity: implications for geographical studies of disease. *Soc. Sci. Med.*, **26**, 49–54 (1988)

26 Jahoda, M. *Current Concepts of Positive Mental Health*, Basic Books, New York (1958)

27 Edwards, D. W., Black versus whites: when is race a relevant variable? *J. Pers. Soc. Psychol.*, **29**, 34–49 (1974)

28 Rack, P. *Race, Culture and Mental Disorder*, Tavistock, London (1982)

29 Littlewood, R. and Lipsedge, M. *Aliens and Alienists: Ethnic Minorities and Psychiatry*, Penguin, Harmondsworth (1982)

30 Greenley, J. R. and Mechanic, D. Social selection in seeking help for psychological problems. *J. Health Soc. Behav.*, **17**, 249–262 (1976)

31 Jalali, B., Jalali, M. and Turner, E. *et al.* Attitudes towards mental illness. *J. Nerv. Ment. Dis.*, **166**, 692–700 (1978)

32 Black, J. The difficulties of living in Britain. *Br. Med. J.*, **290**, 615–617 (1985)

33 Burke, A. W. Family stress and the precipitation of psychiatric disorder. *Int. J. Soc. Psychiatry*, **26**, 35–40 (1980)

34 Saggar, S. The 1984 Labour Force Survey and Britain's 'Asian' population. *New Community*, **13**, 395–411 (1987)

35 Wing, L. Mentally retarded children in Camberwell (London). In *Estimating Needs for Mental Health Care* (ed. H. Hafner), Springer, Berlin, pp. 107–112 (1979)

36 Coard, B. *How the West Indian Child is Made Educationally Sub-normal*, New Beacon Books, London (1971)

37 Maxime, J. E. Some psychological models of black self-concept. In *Social Work with Black Children and their Families* (eds S. Ahmed, J. Cheetham and J. Small), Batsford, London, pp. 100–116 (1986)

38 Nicol, A. E. Psychiatric disorder in the children of Caribbean immigrants. *J. Child Psychol. Psychiatry*, **12**, 273–287 (1971)

39 Bagley, C. Deviant behaviour in English and West Indian schoolchildren. *Res. Education*, **8**, 47–55 (1972)

40 Rutter, M., Yule, W., Berger, M. *et al.* Children of West Indian immigrants – I. Rates of behavioural deviance and of psychiatric disorder. *J. Child Psychol. Psychiatry*, **15**, 241–262 (1974)

41 Earls, F. and Richman, N. Behaviour problems in pre-school children of West-Indian born parents. A re-examination. *J. Child Psychol. Psychiatry*, **21**, 107–117 (1980)

42 Robins, L. N. Sturdy childhood predicots of adult antisocial behaviour: replications from longitudinal studies. *Psychol. Med.*, **8**, 611–622 (1978)

43 Spearly, J. L. and Lauderdale, M. Community characteristics and ethnicity in the prediction of child maltreatment rates. *Child Abuse Neglect*, **7**, 91–105 (1983)

44 Madge, N. Unemployment and its effects on children. *J. Child Psychol. Psychiatry*, **24**, 311–319 (1983)

45 Segal, U. A. Factors affecting placement decisions of children following short-term emergency care. *Child Abuse Neglect*, **9**, 543–548 (1985)

46 Robinson, V. The achievement of Asian children. *Educational Res.*, **22**, 148–150 (1980)

47 Scarr, S., Caparulo, B. K., Bernardo, M. *et al.* Developmental status and school achievements of minority and non-minority children from birth to 18 years in a British Midlands town. *Br. J. Dev. Psychol.*, **1**, 31–48 (1983)

48 Essen, J. and Ghodsian, M. The children of immigrants: school performance. *J. Comm. Rac. Equal.*, **7**, 1–8 (1979)

49 Tizard, B., Hughes, M., Carmichael, H. and Pinkerton, G. Language and social class. Is verbal deprivation a myth? *J. Child Psychol. Psychiatry*, **24**, 533–542 (1983)

50 Cooper, B. and Gath, D. Psychiatric illness, maladjustment and juvenile delinquency: an ecological study in a London borough. *Psychol. Med.*, **7**, 465–474 (1977)

51 Porteous, M. A. Developmental aspects of adolescent problem disclosure in England and Ireland. *J. Child Psychol. Psychiatry*, **26**, 465–478 (1985)

52 Burke, A. W. A cross-cultural study of delinquency among West Indian boys. *Int. J. Soc. Psychiatry*, **26**, 81–87 (1980)

53 Burke, A. W. Determinants of delinquency in female West Indian migrants. *Int. J. Soc. Psychiatry*, **28**, 28–34 (1982)

54 Power, M. J., Benn, R. T. and Morris, J. N. Neighbourhood, school and juveniles before courts. *Br. J. Criminology*, **12**, 111–132 (1972)

55 Hall, S., Critcher, C., Jefferson, T. and Roberts, B. *Policing the Crisis: Mugging, the State and Law and Order*, Macmillan, London (1978)

56 Home Office. *Prison Statistics*, HMSO, London (1986)

57 McGovern, D. and Cope, R. The compulsory detention of males of different ethnic groups, with special reference to offender patients. *Br. J. Psychiatry*, **150**, 505–512 (1987)

58 Hitch, P. J. and Clegg, P. Modes of referral of overseas immigrant and native-born first admissions to psychiatric hospital. *Soc. Sci. Med.*, **14A**, 369–374 (1980)

59 Littlewood, R. and Lipsedge, M. Some social and phenomenological characteristics of psychotic immigrants. *Psychol. Med.*, **11**, 289–302 (1981)

60 Rogers, A. and Faulkner, A. *A Place of Safety: MIND's Research Into Police Referrals to the Psychiatric Service*, MIND, London (1987)

61 Merrill, J. and Owens, J. Ethnic differences in self-poisoning: a comparison of Asian and White groups. *Br. J. Psychiatry*, **148**, 708–712 (1986)

62 Pope, H. G. Jr, Champoux, R. F. and Hudson, J. I. Eating disorder and socioeconomic class: anorexia nervosa and bulemia in nine communities. *J. Nerv. Ment. Dis.*, **175**, 620–623 (1987)

63 Lacey, J. H. and Dolan, B. M. Bulimia in British blacks and Asians: a catchment area study. *Br. J. Psychiatry*, **152**, 73–79 (1988)

64 Holden, N. L. and Robinson, P. H. Anorexia nervosa and bulimia nervosa in British blacks. *Br. J. Psychiatry*, **152**, 544–549 (1988)

65 Crawford, F. R., Rollins, G. W. and Sutherland, R. L. Variations between Negroes and whites in concepts of mental illness and its treatment. *Ann. N.Y. Acad. Sci.*, **84**, 918–937 (1960)

66 Tien, J. L. Black mental health clients preference for therapists: a new look at an old issue. *Int. J. Soc. Psychiatry*, **31**, 258–266 (1985)

67 Giggs, J. Ethnic status and mental illness in urban areas. In *Health, Race and Ethnicity*, (eds T. Rathwell and D. Phillips), Croom Helm, London, pp. 137–174 (1986)

68 Burke, A. W. Epidemiological aspects of the repatriate syndrome. *Int. Soc. Psychiatry*, **28**, 291–299 (1982)

69 Burke, A. W. Outcome of mental illness following repatriation: a predictive study. *Int. J. Soc. Psychiatry*, **29**, 3–11 (1983)

70 Cochrane, R. Mental illness in immigrants in England and Wales: an analysis of mental hospital admissions 1971. *Soc. Psychiatry*, **12**, 25–35 (1977)

71 Dean, G., Walsh, D., Downing, H. and Shelley, E. First admissions of native-born and immigrants to psychiatric hospitals in South-east England 1976. *Br. J. Psychiatry*, **139**, 506–512 (1981)

72 Merill, J. and Owens, J. Self-poisoning among four immigrant groups. *Acta Psychiatr. Scand.*, **77**, 77–80 (1988)

73 Adelstein, A. and Mardon, C. Suicides 1961–74. Population Trends 2 (Office of Population Censuses and Surveys), HMSO, London, pp. 13–18 (1975)

74 Burke, A. W. Suicide in Jamaica. *West Indian Med. J.*, **34**, 48–53 (1985)

75 Glover, G. First admissions of native-born and immigrant patients to psychiatric hospitals. *Br. J. Psychiatry*, **150**, 882 (1987)

76 Malzberg, B. Section B: mental disease among native and foreign-born negroes in New York State. *J. Negro Education*, **25**, 175–181 (1956)

77 Carpenter, L. and Brockington, I. F. A study of mental illness in Asians, West Indians and Africans living in Manchester. *Br. J. Psychiatry*, **137**, 201–205 (1980)

78 Ineichen, B., Harrison, G. and Morgan, H. G. Psychiatric hospital admission in Bristol. *Br. J. Psychiatry*, **145**, 600–611 (1984)

79 Hitch, P. J. and Rack, P. H. Mental illness among Polish and Russian refugees in Bradford. *Br. J. Psychiatry*, **137**, 206–211 (1980)

80 Burke, A. W. Cultural aspects of drinking behaviour among migrant West Indians and related groups. In *Alcohol Related Problems* (ed. N. Krasner), John Wiley, London, pp. 179–205 (1984)

81 Ghosh, S. K. Prevalence survey of drinking alcohol and alcohol dependence in the Asian population in the UK. In *Alcohol Related Problems* (eds N. Krasner, J. S. Madden and R. J. Walker), John Wiley, Chichester, pp. 179–190 (1984)

82 Cox, J. L. *Transcultural Psychiatry*, Croom Helm, London (1986)

83 Anwar, M. and Ali, A. *Overseas Doctors: Experience and Expectations*, Commission for Racial Equality, London (1987)

84 Collier, J. and Burke, A. Racial and sexual discrimination in the selection of students for London medical schools. *Med. Education*, **20**, 86–90 (1986)

85 Fisher, G., Joseph, D. and Ward, P. Black single mothers in Brent: some issues, policies and responses – a pilot study. Black Workers Support Group Working Paper No. 2, Black Workers Support Group, Brent (1986)

Chapter 22

Ethnic factors in psychoses

Part A   A picture from Birmingham, UK

D. McGovern

Psychiatric studies of Afro-Caribbean migrants to Britain consistently report an excess of hospital admissions for psychoses (particularly schizophrenia) compared with the native population [1,2]. There is no generally agreed explanation. Those who accept the findings as real have usually supported explanations relating to selective vulnerability of migrants or to the social stresses of migration. Other authors, doubting whether true differences in morbidity exist, suggest misdiagnosis, differences in service usage or miscalculation of population data.

Early studies investigated first-generation migrants from the Caribbean, who had generally arrived in Britain between 1952 and 1964. Many of their children, born in Britain, are now adults. So far second-generation Afro-Caribbeans have received comparatively little attention. It has been anticipated that psychiatric morbidity would approach that of the native British population [3,4]. Having been raised in Britain it might be expected that use of services would be similar to local white British use and that presentation of illness or distress would be more familiar to British psychiatrists than that of their parents. Diagnosis should if anything be more accurate than in the first generation. Predictions have also been made that second-generation Afro-Caribbeans would have a more realistic appreciation than their parents of the effects of racism faced by black people in Britain. This realism might protect self-esteem and lead to lower psychiatric morbidity. To investigate psychiatric illness in the second generation a series of studies has been conducted in Birmingham and some of the results are presented here.

To establish morbidity rates in the young British Afro-Caribbean it is necessary to estimate local population size.* This is difficult because the 1981 Census did not ask the question of ethnicity. An estimate has been made however and a full description of the method used is given elsewhere [5,6]. In brief there is considerable evidence that one Census statistic: 'Persons Usually Resident in Private Household . . . by Birthplace of Head of Households' [7], gives a good approximation of the number of British-born individuals from different ethnic groups. We have used three other surveys as a check. One of these, the National

---

* See Chapter 21 for an alternative view of population size estimates

Dwelling and Household Survey [8], suggested that the Census underestimated the size of the British-born Afro-Caribbean population by 10%. It was important not to falsely overestimate admission rates so the Census figure was increased by 10%. The numbers of Afro-Caribbean migrants and white British were obtained from other Census tables.

The definition of second-generation Afro-Caribbean was enlarged to include not just those born in Britain but also young Afro-Caribbean migrants. In the 1981 Census about one-third of the Afro-Caribbeans between the ages of 16 and 29 were born in the Caribbean. These individuals are likely to have migrated as children and been raised in Britain, sharing many experiences of the British born. In many ways therefore it is valid to group them with the British born as second-generation Afro-Caribbeans. In the Birmingham studies age 30 is used to divide first- and second-generation Afro-Caribbeans, partly to coincide with Census data but also because very few of the British born were over the age of 29 in 1981, the middle year of the study. Within the 16–29 age range however the British-born Afro-Caribbeans had a lower average age than the migrants.

In one of the Birmingham studies [6] case notes were examined of first admissions to a local psychiatric hospital for 1980 to 1983. The hospital catchment area included a relatively high proportion of individuals from ethnic minorities, as approximately 5% of the entire Afro-Caribbean population of Britain reside there. Information on age, sex, ethnic group and place of birth was obtained and compared with numbers in the catchment area population. In this way age-specific first admission rates were calculated (Table 22.1). Presenting results for the sexes combined hides differences. White female rates were, as elsewhere, higher than rates for white males but young second-generation Afro-Caribbean female rates were only two-thirds of the male rate. The second-generation rates exceed those of the young whites by nearly five times. The older Afro-Caribbean migrants are only slightly in excess of the older white rate.

The proportion of admissions with a diagnosis of some sort of psychosis was estimated. Eighty-five per cent of second-generation Afro-Caribbeans had such a diagnosis compared with 46% of young whites and respectively 65% and 53% in the older groups.

All admissions were divided into four diagnostic categories: schizophrenia/paranoid psychosis; affective disorder; cannabis psychosis and 'others'. The category cannabis psychosis was included because about a sixth of Afro-Caribbean males were given this diagnosis (Table 22.2). In second-generation Afro-Caribbeans, all rates exceed those of the whites, with a threefold increase in affective disorder, a 10-fold increase in schizophrenia/paranoid psychosis and a 30-fold increase in cannabis psychosis. In the older age-group the only Afro-Caribbean excess is a fourfold increase in schizophrenia. These results suggest

Table 22.1 Number of first admissions to a Birmingham psychiatric hospital between 1980 and 1983 and annual first admission rates per 100 000 local population (sexes combined)

Age-group (yr)	Whites		Afro-Caribbean	
	No.	Rate	No.	Rate
16–29	164	62.5	82	275.2
30–pensionable age	444	82.2	34	103.5

Table 22.2 Number of first admissions by diagnosis and annual first admission rates per 100 000 local population by diagnosis (sexes combined)

	Whites		Afro-Caribbean	
Age-group (yr)	No.	Rate	No.	Rate
16–29				
Schizophrenia/paranoid psychosis	33	12.6	38	127.5
Affective disorder	42	16.0	14	47.0
Cannabis psychosis	4	1.5	13	43.6
Other	85	32.4	17	57.0
Age 30–pensionable age				
Schizophrenia/paranoid psychosis	62	11.5	16	48.7
Affective disorder	192	35.6	6	18.3
Cannabis psychosis	1	—	—	—
Other	189	35.0	12	36.6

that the diagnosis of major psychiatric illness in second-generation Afro-Caribbeans, far from showing a decrease compared to that in first generation, may actually be increasing. Of course first hospital admissions cannot be equated with the incidence of psychiatric disorder in the population at large, although it is a fairer measure of serious mental illness. In this study any filter affecting admission to hospital may actually exclude more Afro-Caribbeans than whites because a higher proportion of white admissions had less severe (i.e. non-psychotic) illnesses. Good community studies are needed to clarify this, but the careful case-finding method of Harrison in Nottingham reported later on in this chapter, with a similar difference in the rate of schizophrenia between Afro-Caribbeans and whites suggests that the differences found here may be real.

Another major doubt, however, is the validity of the case note diagnosis. A follow-up study [9] is in progress to confirm diagnosis but another study in which the case notes of the young Afro-Caribbeans and whites with a diagnosis of schizophrenia were examined found that 80% of each group conformed with a DSM III [10] diagnosis of schizophrenia or schizophreniform disorder. Moreover, the Afro-Caribbeans had longer illnesses and longer admissions.

At first glance these results seem to suggest that second-generation Afro-Caribbeans have a different and greater risk of developing major psychiatric illness than first-generation migrants. However, it is possible that the risk has remained the same for both first and second generations but has been brought forward by the stresses of belonging to a minority group so that illness first appears in a younger age-group. If this were so it would be expected that previous studies of first-generation migrants showed the same predominance of illness in the young.

There are some studies [11] which show large increases in the rate of schizophrenia in young Afro-Caribbeans compared with whites (e.g. Rwegellera [12] found an eightfold increase in inception rates of schizophrenia for Afro-Caribbeans compared with UK-born in Camberwell in 1968). However, I have been unable to find any study which reports an overall increase of admissions or such an increase in psychosis as that found in the present study. At present the hypothesis that second-generation Afro-Caribbeans comprise a separate cohort at greater risk of major psychiatric illness than the first cannot yet be refuted.

There is no obvious explanation for such an increased risk, if indeed it is occurring. Any genetic explanation would be related either to an increased risk in the country of origin or to the migrants being a selectively vulnerable group. What evidence there is supports neither of these [6]. Moreover, if Afro-Caribbeans were genetically at greater risk of developing major psychoses it might explain a continued high level of morbidity in the second generation but not an increased level.

Early environmental insults from trauma or viruses [13] have been implicated in schizophrenia and other psychoses. It is hard to accommodate such theories of aetiology with an increased risk for both second-generation Afro-Caribbeans born in the West Indies and those born in Britain. Cannabis has also been implicated in the aetiology of major mental illness and a recent Swedish study [14] suggested that cannabis intake predisposed to the development of schizophrenia. If there is an increase in Rastafarianism among young Afro-Caribbeans there might indeed be some increase in cannabis consumption, but it is by no means obvious that as a group more Afro-Caribbeans than whites take cannabis. Indeed a recent survey of teenagers [15] suggested the opposite. Clearly psychiatrists in the Birmingham hospital were sensitive to the possibility of cannabis being responsible for the altered mental state of young Afro-Caribbean patients in the study, hence the large numbers in the somewhat dubious category 'cannabis psychosis'. It would seem extraordinary if in addition cannabis were responsible for the excessive rates in other categories such as schizophrenia.

Explanations invoking social stress have usually assumed that the second generation would have decreased psychiatric morbidity compared to the first. The model of goal-striving stress has been found to be related to mental illness in West Indian migrants [16]. This model may be less relevant to second-generation Afro-Caribbeans (although it has not been tested). Nevertheless, the second generation is faced with considerable problems which can be conceptualized in different ways, e.g. relative deprivation. Unlike first-generation migrants, second-generation Afro-Caribbeans have been raised in a racist society. 'Migrant myths' of return to the Caribbean have little meaning for these 'black British' people. They have been described as having no way 'up or out' [17]. It may be that they use the 'white British' working class as their reference group more than the first generation did and so exclusion brings a greater sense of relative deprivation as regards white people with whom they have grown up, which may be stronger than that experienced by their parents.

It is possible therefore to argue that second-generation Afro-Caribbeans experience greater psychosocial stress than the first generation, but is this related to increased risk of developing major psychoses such as schizophrenia? Most British psychiatrists would probably consider that stress played a minor part in the aetiology of schizophrenia. Nevertheless, social-psychological variables such as goal-striving stress and relative deprivation have been associated with major mental illnesses in minority groups. These have been neglected in recent psychiatric research in Britain but should be included in future investigations.

The results presented here are puzzling and disturbing. Since they were first published other studies [18,19] from other parts of the country have produced similar findings. There is a need for follow-up studies to confirm diagnosis and for community studies to examine the possibility that different use of services may account for some differences. In addition, the exact measurement of population sizes will remain a problem although this will be helped if a question on ethnicity is included in the 1991 Census. Even if the results continue to be confirmed the explanation remains elusive.

References

1 Cochrane, R. Mental illness in immigrants to England and Wales. *Soc. Psychiatry*, **12**, 25–35 (1977)
2 Carpenter, L. and Brockington, I. A study of mental illness in Asians, West Indians and Africans living in Manchester. *Br. J. Psychiatry*, **137**, 201–205 (1980)
3 Bagley, C. Sequels of alienation: a social psychological view of the adaptation of West Indian migrants in Britain In: *Case Studies of Human Rights and Fundamental Freedoms*, vol. 2 (ed. K. Glaser), Nijhoff, The Hague (1975)
4 Cochrane, R. *The Social Creation of Mental Illness*, OPCS, Longman (1983)
5 McGovern, D. A. and Cope, R. V. The compulsory detention of males of different ethnic groups with special reference to offender patients. *Br. J. Psychiatry*, **150**, 505–512 (1987)
6 McGovern, D. A. and Cope, R. V. First psychiatric admission rates of first and second generation Afro-Caribbeans. *Soc. Psychiatry*, **22**, 139–149 (1987)
7 Office of Population Censuses and Surveys. Census 1981 County Report, West Midlands Part I, HMSO, London (1982)
8 Department of the Environment. National Dwelling and Housing Survey, HMSO, London (1979)
9 McGovern, D. A. and Cope, R. V. Young Afro-Caribbean and young white patients with schizophrenia. Submitted
10 *Diagnostic and Statistical Manual of Mental Disorder*, 3rd edn. American Psychiatric Association, Washington (1982)
11 Dean, G., Walsh, D., Downing, H. and Shelley, E. First admissions of native born and immigrants to psychiatric hospital in South East England. *Br. J. Psychiatry*, **139**, 506–511 (1981)
12 Rwegellera, G. G. C. Psychiatric morbidity among West Africans and West Indians living in London. *Psychol. Med.*, **7**, 317–329 (1977)
13 Crow, T. Schizophrenia as an infectious disease. *Lancet*, **i**, 819–820 (1983)
14 Andrearson, S. *et al*. Cannabis and schizophrenia. *Lancet*, **ii**, 1483–1485 (1987)
15 William, M. The Thatcher Generation. *New Society*, 21 February, 312–315 (1986)
16 Parker, S., Kleiner, R. and Needleman, B. Migration and mental illness. *Soc. Sci. Med.*, **3**, 1–9 (1969)
17 Rex, J. *Race Relation in Sociological Theory*, 2nd edn, Weidenfeld & Nicolson, London (1982)
18 Harrison, G., Owens, D., Holton, A. *et al*. Prospective study of severe mental disorder in Afro-Caribbean patients. *Psychol. Med*, **13**, 643–657 (1988)
19 Sinclair, M., Littlewood, R., Lipsedge, N. and Wood, S. First admission rates for schizophrenia in British born Afro-Caribbean population. In preparation

Part B   A perspective from Nottingham, UK
Glynn Harrison

Epidemiological research in schizophrenia is fraught with methodological problems, having a relatively low population incidence and inadequately defined diagnostic criteria. Countless studies appear to suggest that this illness varies in both incidence and prevalence between, and sometimes within, different cultures [1]. Researchers have enthusiastically scrutinized groups ranging from the Achinese warriors of Sumatra, to higher caste populations of India and small French communities in rural Canada for possible clues to aetiology. They are often met by justified scepticism over fundamental methodological errors such as size of the population at risk, reliability of diagnoses and the effects of service-related (nosocomial) factors on the number of 'cases' detected.

To clarify some of these fundamental questions, the World Health Organization mounted a major transcultural study in the late 1960s, the 'International Pilot Study on Schizophrenia' (IPSS). Although not a strict epidemiological study, considerable groundwork was undertaken: was it possible to mount international studies on this scale? How difficult, indeed how feasible, would it be to train investigators of different nationalities to use standardized instruments for measuring symptoms?

This study showed that under careful conditions of measurement, schizophrenia appeared with similar frequency in different parts of the world, with major variations in course and outcome between 'developing' and 'Western' countries. A second 'International Collaborative Study' was therefore undertaken in 1978 [2] based on sound epidemiological principles: case finding in a defined catchment area and a prospective design to include all first-onset psychoses linking 'an estimation of incidence rates to a diagnostic and psychopathological classification of cases utilizing several diagnostic criteria'.

When relatively 'broad' criteria were used, there was considerable variation in first contact incidence rates between the 12 participating centres. However, when more restrictive criteria for schizophrenia were applied to the psychoses entering the study, such as the computer-assigned S+ classification, there was little significant difference in rates. This suggested that either environmental factors play little role in aetiology or, alternatively, that such factors are very evenly distributed across populations and are fairly insensitive to cultural variation.

Studies of Afro-Caribbean migrants in the UK have had the same methodological difficulties as those experienced with other epidemiological studies. The reliability of previous findings of high rates of schizophrenia in Afro-Caribbeans (e.g. [3–6]) may be questioned on the basis of diagnostic accuracy and ambiguity, as retrospective studies based upon hospital admissions only, and difficulties in defining the size of the at-risk (or 'denominator') population*. As Nottingham had been a field centre for the 1978 WHO International Study referred to above, we decided to mount a prospective investigation of psychoses in patients of Afro-Caribbean origin, utilizing the same methodology and comparing our findings with those from the earlier 'general population' study [7].

The plan of investigation (Figure 22.1) is as follows: we attempted to contact and interview every patient of likely Afro-Caribbean origin (and a key relative), presenting to the psychiatric services for the first time from a defined catchment area, and showing symptoms of psychosis. Details of methodology and results have been reported elsewhere [8]. Forty-five patients entered the study, and in each case information about symptoms, onset and considerable background history were used to make consensus diagnoses on several internationally agreed criteria for schizophrenia, reflecting varying degrees of 'restrictiveness'. The diagnostic breakdown of patients (excluding three over age 55) is shown in Figure 22.2: cases of 'atypical' and unusual psychotic syndromes as reported by Littlewood and Lipsedge [9] were relatively infrequent; similar unusual presentations of illness occurred in the 1978–80 general population cohort of patients. We could not confirm previous suggestions of higher frequencies of paranoid symptoms among Afro-Caribbean patients [9,10], and onset for the Afro-Caribbean and general population cohorts of 'definite' schizophrenic patients was very similar.

---

* See Chapter 21 for an alternative view of general population size for young Afro-Caribbean men.

196

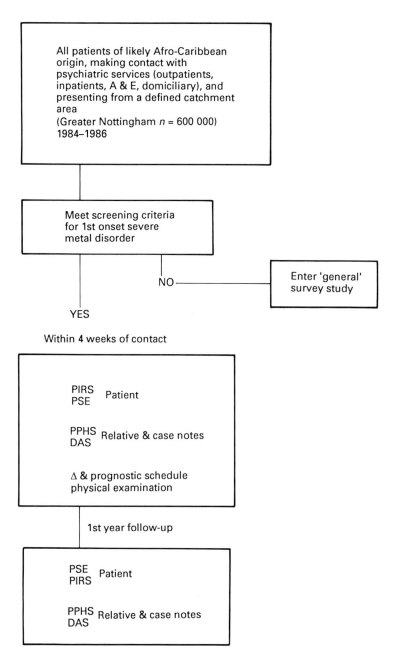

All patients of likely Afro-Caribbean
origin, making contact with
psychiatric services (outpatients,
inpatients, A & E, domiciliary), and
presenting from a defined catchment
area
(Greater Nottingham n = 600 000)
1984–1986

Meet screening criteria
for 1st onset severe
metal disorder

NO —— Enter 'general'
survey study

YES

Within 4 weeks of contact

PIRS   Patient
PSE

PPHS Relative & case notes
DAS

Δ & prognostic schedule
physical examination

1st year follow-up

PSE   Patient
PIRS

PPHS Relative & case notes
DAS

Figure 22.1 Plan of investigation. The PSE (Present State Examination) and PIRS (Psychological Impairments Rating Schedule) are standardized instruments for recording abnormal mental state phenomena. The PPHS (Personal and Psychiatric History Schedule) is a standardized guide to history data collection and the DAS (Disability Assessment Schedule) allows for a coding of social and personal 'disability', occurring as a result of mental disorder

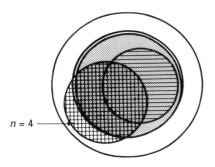

$n = 4$

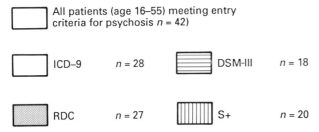

All patients (age 16–55) meeting entry
criteria for psychosis $n = 42$)

ICD–9 $n = 28$ DSM-III $n = 18$

RDC $n = 27$ S+ $n = 20$

Figure 22.2 Diagnostic classification at entry. ICD-9 (International Classification of Diseases), RDC (Research Diagnostic Criteria), DSM-III (Diagnostic and Statistical Manual) and S+ (CATEGO Computer Classification) are commonly used research and clinical criteria for the diagnosis of schizophrenia

There were striking differences, however, in calculated mean annual incidence rates for schizophrenia, based upon 'restrictive ICD-9' and DSM-III criteria (Table 22.3). To calculate the size of the denominator, that is, the population at risk, we used the 'persons usually resident in private households . . . by birthplace of head of household' statistic obtained from the 1981 Census. There are considerable difficulties here as the 1981 Census did not include questions on ethnic origin, and there are now many British-born Afro-Caribbeans. However, subsequent labour force studies, which did ask about 'likely ethnic origin' on face-to-face interview, suggested that the 'head of household' criterion was a reasonably good estimate of the size of the population of Afro-Caribbean origin [11]. Because it counts many non-Caribbeans living in such homes, it may be a slight overestimate. The rates shown in Table 22.3 are certainly distorted by changes in the age structure of the population at risk between 1981 and 1985, the midpoint of our study. Unfortunately, 5-year age bands are not available for Nottingham alone, but figures published for England and Wales suggest that, in order to take account of the shift of two 'peaks' in the age profile, it is necessary to decrease the rates of the 16–29 group by abut 20% and to increase the 30–44 age-specific rates by about 10%. Rates for British-born aged 16–29 were surprisingly high at 36.4 per 10 000. Due to major changes in the age profile between 1981 and 1985, these rates should also be reduced to about 22 per 10 000.

Apparent ethnic differences in rates of illness and other social phenomena can often be accounted for by differences in the age, sex and social class profiles of the

Table 22.3 Mean annual incidence rates for schizophrenia, restrictive ICD-9 and DSM-III diagnoses per 10 000 population

Diagnosis	Age-group (yr)	
	16–29	30–44
ICD-9		
Caribbean	29.1 (n = 20)	19.7 (n = 7)
General population	2.2 (2.0)* (n = 39)	1.6 (1.6)* (n = 20)
DSM-III		
Caribbean	17.5 (n = 12)	16.9 (n = 6)
General population	0.98 (1)* (n = 17)	1.0 (1)* (n = 13)

* Rates excluding Afro-Caribbean patients in 1978–80 'general population' sample, adjusting denominator using 1981 Census 'head of household' estimate.
Note: relatively small number of cases overall so that rates have wide confidence limits.

populations being compared. In comparing homicide rates for the black population in the USA, a stepwise elimination of racial differences may be achieved by controlling for education, purchasing power, employment status and so on [12]. For schizophrenia, it is important to recognize marked variations in 'spatial' distribution of incidence across urban areas, with higher rates in inner city, relatively deprived areas and to attempt to control for social status. Fortunately, the cohort of 'general population' patients from the 1978–80 study with which Afro-Caribbean patients are compared has been 'mapped' in small enumeration districts sharing certain socioeconomic characteristics [13]. The majority of our black patients lived in areas having relatively higher rates for schizophrenia in the general urban population, of about 3.5 per 10 000 per annum, but even when controlling for social status and urban conditions, these age-specific rates for schizophrenia in the Caribbean community remain considerably elevated, with a six- to seven-fold increase.

Allowing for difficulties in the size of denominator, and taking into account possible 'service-related' distortions in our figures, the relative size of increase in incidence rates reported here does suggest a real increase in this serious illness in the Afro-Caribbean population in Britain. Earlier suggestions that such findings could be accounted for by 'misdiagnosis' are not supported, and rates in 'second-generation' Afro-Caribbeans remain surprisingly high.

Wherever variations in rates of schizophrenia have been reported, authors have eagerly recruited their findings to support their favoured theory of aetiology. Unfortunately, the richness and profusion of speculation has not always been matched by the quality of data. We believe that findings presented here go some ways to clarifying the diagnostic debate regarding psychoses in people of Afro-Caribbean ethnic origin. While the incidence of schizophrenia is similar when comparing large urban areas in different countries, marked variations may occur within those populations, especially when comparing distinct cultural groups. These data should be interpreted with extreme caution, recognizing difficulties in establishing causal connections, and the likely multifactorial aetiology of schizophrenia. Racism is a subtle and pervasive phenomenon in society, and within psychiatry itself: Prudhomme and Musto [14] summarized a disturbing literature illustrating how racist myths have been incorporated into theoretical frameworks throughout the history of psychiatry. There has been much recent interest in the potentially 'schizophrenia-evoking' effects of discrimination and the sense of 'marginalization' that many young Afro-Caribbeans feel. Nevertheless, it is important that the debate is not over-simplified: potential biological factors, following considerable advances recently, as well as social factors, merit further investigation.

If possible, larger cohorts of patients, utilizing a similar careful methodology are required. There is much justifiable concern in the Afro-Carribean community about the quality and quantity of mental health services, especially in deprived inner city areas. Recent research [15,16] confirms a continuing pattern of higher rates of compulsory detention, more involvement of police in admissions, and less primary care in the management of mental disorders in Afro-Carribean patients. Epidemiological findings are also important in the planning and development of services, which must be more specifically targeted to the needs of the local community. Such research is time consuming and fraught with pitfalls, but may yet provide important clues in the search for the aetiology of this serious and potentially disabling condition.

Acknowledgements

This article is based upon work carried out in collaboration with Dr David Owens, Dr Tony Holton, Dr David Neilson and Mrs Daphne Boot. The study was funded by a grant from the Locally Organized Research Scheme, Trent Regional Health Authority.

References

1 Torrey, E. F. Prevalence studies in schizophrenia. *Br. J. Psychiatry*, **150**, 598–608 (1987)

2 Sartorius, N., Jablensky, A., Korten, A. *et al*. Early manifestations and first contact incidence of schizophrenia in different cultures. *Psychol. Med.*, **16**, 909–928 (1986)

3 Cochrane, R. Mental illness in immigrants to England and Wales. *Soc. Psychiatry*, **12**, 25–35 (1977)

4 Rwegellera, G. G. C. Psychiatric morbidity among West Africans and West Indians living in London. *Psychol. Med.*, **7**, 317–329 (1977)

5 Dean, G., Walsh, D., Downing, H. and Shelley, E. First admissions of native-born and immigrants to psychiatric hospitals in South-East England 1976. *Br. J. Psychiatry*, **139**, 506–512 (1981)

6 Gordon, E. B. Mentally ill West Indian immigrants. *Br. J. Psychiatry*, **111**, 877–887 (1965)

7 Cooper, J. E. Goodhead, D., Craig, T. *et al*. The incidence of schizophrenia in Nottingham. *Br. J. Psychiatry*, **151**, 619–626 (1987)

8 Harrison, G., Owens, D., Holton, T. *et al*. A prospective study of severe mental disorder in Afro-Caribbean patients. *Psychol. Med.*, **18**, 643–657 (1988)

9 Littlewood, R. and Lipsedge, M. Acute psychotic reactions in Caribbean-born patients. *Psychol. Med.*, **11**, 303–318 (1981)

10 Carpenter, L. and Brockington, I. F. A study of mental illness in Asians, West Indians and Africans living in Manchester. *Br. J. Psychiatry*, **137**, 201–205 (1980)

11 Office of Population Censuses and Surveys. Sources of Statistics on Ethnic Minorities. Population Trends, 28, HMSO, London (1982)

12 Cooper, R. Race, disease and health. In *Health, Race and Ethnicity* (eds T. Rathwell and D. Phillips), Croom Helm, London (1986)

13 Giggs, J. and Cooper, J. E. Schizophrenia, affective psychosis and the ecological structure of Nottingham. *Br. J. Psychiatry*, **151**, 627–633 (1987)

14 Prudhomme, C. and Musto, D. F. Historical perspectives on mental health and racism in the United

States. In *Racism and Mental Health* (eds. C. V. Willie, B. M. Kramer, and B. S Brown), University of Pittsburgh Press, Pittsburgh (1973)

15 Harrison, G., Ineichen, B., Smith, J. and Morgan, H. G. Psychiatric hospital admissions in Bristol 11. Social and clinical aspects of compulsory admission. *Br. J. Psychiatry*, **145**, 605–611 (1984)

16 McGovern, D. and Cope, R. V. The compulsory detention of males of different ethnic groups, with special reference to offender patients. *Br. J. Psychiatry*, **150**, 502–512 (1987)

Part C   Psychiatric hospital admissions in North London
Gyles R. Glover

Introduction

Several studies have reported an apparent excess of schizophrenia among Caribbeans in the UK even with the narrowest diagnostic criteria [1,2]. This excess is greatest in the young. Being confined to single centres, most of these include only small numbers of cases. This chapter outlines the use of larger routine data sources to study patterns in more detail, particularly changes over time.

Data

The study was based on information collected by the UK Health Department about admissions to inpatient psychiatric care. The data include admission and discharge dates, area of residence, age, sex, birthplace, legal status and diagnosis. Until recently this was called the Mental Health Enquiry (MHE).

Information systems within the British National Health Service are poorly developed and very inaccessible. However, from 1976 to 1986, the MHE information was collated and computerized centrally by the Health Department with tapes made available annually to Regional Health Authorities. With some difficulty it was possible to obtain copies of some raw data tapes for two of the London Regions, North-east Thames (NET) and North-west Thames (NWT).

The data covers only inpatient care and for the study of mental illness in ethnic minorities includes only birthplace as an index of ethnicity. It is also deficient in both quality and completeness. These are serious limitations but no other source offers the same scale of data. With a duly critical eye it therefore seems worth examination.

Population data were drawn from the 1981 Census, restricted to the parts of the regions within the Greater London boundary, and relating to ethnic minorities which are available with far greater precision than elsewhere in Britain.*

* See Chapter 21 for an alternative view of young black population size.

Age/sex patterns – a cohort effect

Figure 22.3 shows an analysis for Greater London north of the Thames for 1984/5, comparing mental hospital admission rates for Caribbean and English/Welsh born. The Caribbean rate for each age/sex group was divided by the corresponding

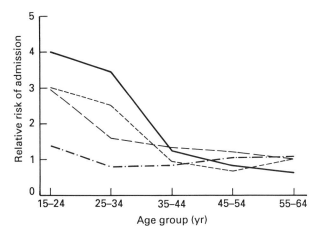

Figure 22.3 Age- and sex-specific relative risk of admission or first admission in inpatient psychiatric care for Caribbean-born people as compared to English/Welsh-born, north-east and north-west Thames regions, 1984/5. All admissions: ———, men; — — —, women. First admissions: ---, men; –·–·–·–, women

English/Welsh rate giving the relative risk. First admissions were considered separately since an individual may have many admissions but only one first admission. Population data for 1984/5 was extrapolated from the Census data for 1981 using the assumption that no net migration had occurred and that there was no appreciable difference in the death rates for the two groups.

The excess of mental hospital admissions for Caribbeans has a different pattern for the two sexes. Men under 35 were more likely to have a first admission and, by a greater margin more likely to have any admission. Older men were *less* likely to have either. By contrast, women of all ages were only marginally more likely to have a first admission, this applied to all admissions except for the youngest group who show a greater excess. Thus once admitted, young Caribbeans of both sexes were more likely to be readmitted.

A cohort effect?

An excess localized in young people could mean that the lifetime pattern of mental hospital admission of Caribbeans in the UK will prove to be different to that for native Britons. Burke's [3] observation that young men were substantially overrepresented among first admissions to Bellevue psychiatric hospital in Jamaica lends some support to this hypothesis. On the other hand the pattern could reflect a cohort phenomenon where a group of younger Caribbeans at each stage of their lives may have more mental illness than their parents.

The second part of the study attempted to distinguish between these possibilities. A similar set of figures were derived for the years 1976/7. Unfortunately data for these years was only available for one of the two North Thames regions (Figure 22.4). The most striking differences are that the peak for young men is confined to the youngest group and no peak for young women appears. This would suggest that a cohort of people, currently young, at sharply higher risk of admission is working its way up through the age-groups.

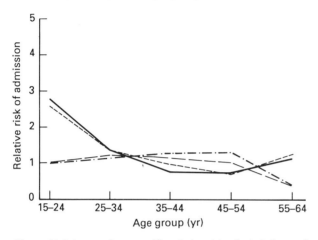

Figure 22.4 Age- and sex-specific relative risk of admission or first admission to inpatient psychiatric care for Caribbean-born people as compared to English/Welsh-born, north-west Thames region, 1976/7. Key as in Figure 22.3

A subsequent analysis of data for the NWT region for the whole decade 1976–85 classifying individuals by their year of birth confirmed that for men born in the Caribbean there was a sharp difference between those born before about 1950 and those born later. The former, and women across the spectrum had about a twofold excess of first admissions for all psychotic diagnoses and a proportionate or slightly low first admissions rate for non-psychotic conditions. The later-born men, by contrast, had about a fivefold excess of first admissions for psychotic, although not non-psychotic diagnoses. In all groups the excess for psychotic diagnoses was most marked for schizophrenia.

How reliable are the data?

These findings can be criticized on several grounds: in about 30% of cases the birthplace was omitted. However, recent work has suggested that the incompleteness is fairly random [4]. The diagnostic data are more suspect – usually obtained by clerks without consulting doctors or nurses, they should be treated with a degree of scepticism. However, it is unclear why these factors should produce the sharp cohort effect seen for men.

It might be argued that misallocation of UK-born Caribbeans to the Caribbean-born group has occurred. This would inflate the rates for the youngest group most sharply but would not explain the sex difference. However, in 80% of admission episodes in which birthplace was recorded as Caribbean, the island was specified, strongly suggesting that the individual concerned was asked.

Could restriction of the data source to hospital admissions introduce distortion, such as one group being more liable to be hospitalized for a given level of illness. It would be much easier to explain a deficit of admissions on this basis than an excess. For young men it would mean that only one-fifth of the English/Welsh-born men who develop psychotic illnesses reach inpatient treatment even if *all* Caribbeans did. This seems unlikely and it would not explain the sharp difference in older men.

Finally could the cohort effect be the result of a selective deficit in the denominator data? It is notable that in the 1981 Census Caribbean-born individuals living in the relevant area showed a sex ratio of nearly 1.4 women to each man in the age ranges 20–39. At other ages the ratio was much more explicable. With a migrant population it is impossible to specify what the sex ratio should be but at least one possible explanation is that the men were selectively underenumerated. However, recalculating the age-specific relative risks for men using the numbers of women as denominators made only a small difference to the extent of the disparities.

Discussion

These findings suggest that some feature of living in Britain induces major mental illness to an unusual extent in Caribbeans. Perhaps the explanation lies in the experience of living in a racist society and it seems most likely that the sorts of stresses to which black people are subjected, such as those perceived by young men in the 'ghettoes', account for some of the excess. However, at least a component seems to be attributable to a genuine excess of cases of schizophrenia [2], a disease increasingly recognized to have a neuropathological basis [5]. Sharp increases in incidence over short periods have been described in many situations [6], although the mechanism remains obscure.

The course of this apparent epidemic needs close monitoring to see if detailed epidemiological data can help to understand its cause. It may be even more crucial that mental health services in Britain develop to become more acceptable to the Caribbean community.

References

1 McGovern, D. and Cope, R. V. First psychiatric admission rates of first and second generation Afro-Caribbeans. *Soc. Psychiatry*, **22**, 139–149 (1987)
2 Harrison, G., Owens, D., Holton, A. *et al.* A prospective study of severe mental disorder in Afro-Caribbean patients. *Psychol. Med.*, **18**, 643–657 (1988)
3 Burke, A. W. First admissions and planning in Jamaica. *Soc. Psychiatry*, **9**, 39–45 (1974)
4 Glover, G. R. 993W: birthplace not stated or born at sea. *Psychol. Med.*, **17**, 1009–1012 (1987)
5 Murray, R. and Lewis, S. Is schizophrenia a neurodevelopmental disorder? *Br. Med. J.*, **295**, 681–682 (1987)
6 Torrey, E. F. *Schizophrenia and Civilisation*, Jason Aronson, New York (1980)

Chapter 23

Tuberculosis

M. W. McNicol

There are wide variations in the incidence of tuberculosis [1] and some of these appear to be based on race. There are historical accounts of epidemics of tuberculosis among susceptible groups characterized by race [2–6] and apparent resistance to disease as a racial characteristic in some reports [7] was noted to reverse under subsequent major stress [8]. Social and environmental factors are particularly important in determining the incidence of tuberculosis [9–11]. In none of the instances of the reputed effect of 'race' was there any control for these factors.

Natural history

In tuberculosis there are two stages, primary and post-primary. Clinical disease may occur at the time of initial infection, or after a latent interval. The younger the child when primary infection occurs the more likely is the development of disease [12]. Most post-primary disease occurs 5–10 years after the primary infection, usually associated with breakdown of apparently healed lesions rather than with re-infection. The clinical picture is modified by the specific immunity which has been acquired. The shorter the interval between primary infection and the development of post-primary disease the poorer the outcome [13]. Poor nutrition is associated with higher morbidity and mortality [14]. Chronic intercurrent infection depresses general immunity, debilitating diseases such as diabetes, leukaemia or alcoholism increase incidence as does immunosuppression either therapeutic (e.g. steroid therapy) or in consequence of disease (e.g. AIDS). Other lung diseases such as silicosis or the general impairment of lung defences due to smoking also appear to increase incidence [10,11,14,15].

The dominant influence however appears to be social and environmental. Tuberculosis is a disease of urbanization and the underprivileged. It was epidemic in the Western world in the nineteenth century, and in the past hundred years it has steadily declined. That decline has been little influenced by treatment which has only been effective in the past 25 years [11]. The influence of social class has been striking; in the UK the disease was twice as common in unskilled compared with the professional classes, a difference maintained over many years in the face of a substantial overall decline in incidence [10]. The most clearly identified social factor is overcrowding which facilitates spread [16]. The influence of under-nutrition and chronic intercurrent infection are more difficult to quantify. Stress experienced by a community is also said to be important, as evidenced by the increase in Western Europe in the 1914–1918 and 1939–45 wars [11], although it should be noted that during these times poorer nutrition, alcohol and cigarette consumption might have had a significant effect [17,18].

Measures of incidence

It is relatively easy to monitor the incidence of tuberculosis. For pulmonary tuberculosis, the commonest and most important form of the disease, even when medical facilities are primitive the diagnosis can be made accurately by simple direct smear examination of sputum. In many countries notification procedures, despite many inaccuracies [19], provide a reasonable overall picture. Mortality figures are similarly widely available and reasonably accurate [20]. In addition, the tuberculin test, a measure of hypersensitivity to tuberculin and evidence of previous infection, is relatively simple to carry out, is reproducible, and can be used for population screening to assess the prevalence of occult infection.

Race and tuberculosis

The concept of a link between tuberculosis and race was based on the apparently increased susceptibility in specific populations [2–6]. In the most susceptible, not only was the disease very common but it often ran an acute course with a high mortality. It was also believed that rural populations in Ireland and the Highlands of Scotland were particularly susceptible (quoted in [11] without supporting data). This was thought to be due to either lack of community immunity in populations not previously exposed, or to genetically determined increased susceptibility, as seen in certain selectively bred strains of laboratory animals [21]. The belief that race had a major influence on tuberculosis tended to be reinforced by the great geographical variation in incidence.

The WHO Annual Reports document compellingly the present situation about tuberculosis. The incidence in Western Europe and North America is now very low, but the disease remains almost as common as ever in the poorest countries of the world and in North East Africa, the incidence may even be increasing [1]. However, it is clear that none of these populations provides valid data for comparison and the observations are not controlled for the social and environmental factors which have a major effect on the incidence of the disease. The differences in incidence show a closer relationship with national economic prosperity than with race. Apparently highly susceptible groups such as immigrants into more prosperous countries show a progressive fall in incidence and rates come to resemble that of the host country [22,23]. Interestingly, people of (black) West Indian origin who emigrated to Britain have had rates similar to the UK-born population, probably reflecting the lower rates of the disease in the West Indies than in the Indian subcontinent [23]. In relatively prosperous countries with several racial communities such as South Africa there has been a similar fall in incidence in all races suggesting a similar pattern of response, although the absolute levels are higher in the black and least privileged group [24,25]. When social, environmental and other factors are similar any 'racial' susceptibility is difficult to demonstrate.

There is no convincing evidence from morbidity or mortality rates that variation in susceptibility due to race needs to be invoked; social and economic factors provide a more satisfactory explanation. However, there are no adequately controlled trials and there might be small racially determined differences in susceptibility which cannot at present be demonstrated. Extrapulmonary disease is a regular feature of tuberculosis among people of Indian subcontinent origin in Britain [26].

Follow-up studies on at-risk populations provide further information. The subjects are selected population groups such as long-stay hospital inmates or armed forces recruits, or are identified as being at risk by positive tuberculin tests, e.g. positive reactors in preliminary testing for BCG vaccination, or control groups in chemoprophylaxis trials. One controlled study [27] demonstrated that there was no significant increase in tuberculosis mortality in black patients in long-stay mental hospitals, although mortality in the black population in the community was four times greater than in the whites. The reports of follow-up of positive tuberculin reactors are summarized by Kushigemachi et al. [28]. Widely different rates of development of disease were noted in different races, from 29/100 000/year in the Danish [29] to 936/100 000/year in Eskimos [30]. Clearly these differences do not occur in comparable populations. A reasonably well-controlled study among naval recruits [31] which demonstrated some differences in incidence apparently based on race was not controlled for differences in the social and environmental background of its subjects, which could account for the observed differences. Moderately well-controlled studies on mixed race groups from Puerto Rico showed a marginally lower incidence of tuberculosis among the black population [32]. Kushigemachi et al. concluded that the observed differences do not support the case that there is a significant racial variation in susceptibility to tuberculosis.

Genetic studies

No characteristic genetic, including HLA, associations have been identified [33]. There is some controversy whether the incidence is greater in monozygotic or dizygotic twins [34,35], but the evidence on this point is not strong. HLA typing has not shown any characteristic pattern [36].

Conclusion

The large variations in incidence of tuberculosis currently loosely attributed to 'racial' factors are almost certainly due to social and environmental factors, and there is no convincing evidence for an effect of race of itself. As Fishberg said in 1932 [36], 'tuberculosis is not inherently a racial problem'.

References

1 Styblo, K. Epidemiology of tuberculosis. *Bull. Int. Union Tuberc.*, **42**, 5 (1978)
2 Borrell, A. *Ann. Inst. Pasteur*, **32**, 105 (1920)
3 Fergusson, R. G. *Tuberculosis among the Indian of the Great Canadian Plains*, NAPT, London (1928)
4 Turbott, H. B. *Tuberculosis in the Maori*, Department of Health, New Zealand (1935)
5 Abrahams, E. W. Tuberculosis in indigenous Australians. *Med. J.Aust.*, Suppl. 2, 23 (1975)
6 Grysbowski, S., Galbraith, J. D. and Dorken, E. Tuberculosis in Eskimos. *Tubercle*, **57**, Suppl. 4 (1976)
7 Drolet, G. J. *N. Y. Tuberc. Assoc. Bull.*, **4**, 3 (1923)
8 Rakower, I. Tuberculosis among Jews. *Am. Rev. Tuberc.*,**67**, 85–93 (1953)
9 Hart, P. D. A. and Wright, G. P. *Tuberculosis and Social Conditions in England*, NAPT, London (1939)
10 Pagel, W., Simmonds, F. A. H., McDonald, N. and Nassau, E. In *Pulmonary Tuberculosis*, 4th edn, Oxford University Press, Oxford (1964)
11 Crofton, J. and Douglas, A. *Respiratory Diseases*, 3rd edn, Blackwell, Oxford (1981)
12 Miller, F. J. W. *Tuberculosis in Children*, Churchill Livingstone, Edinburgh (1982)
13 Sutherland, L. The evolution of clinical tuberculosis in adolescents. *Tubercle*, **47**, 308 (1966)
14 Edwards, L. B., Livesay, V. T., Acquaviva, F. A. and Palmer, C.E. Height, weight, tuberculous infection and tuberculous disease. *Arch. Environ. Health*, **22**, 106 (1971)
15 Citron, K. M. and Girling, D. J. In *Oxford Textbook of Medicine* (eds D. J. Weatherall, J. G. G. Ledingham and D. A. Warrell), Oxford University Press, Oxford, pp. 5.237 *et seq.* (1983)
16 Stein, L. Tuberculosis and the 'social complex' in Glasgow. *Br. J. Soc. Med.*, **6**, 1 (1951)
17 Smith, F. E. and Palmer, D. L. Alcoholism, infection and altered host defences: a review of clinical and experimental observations. *J. Chronic. Dis.*, **29**, 35 (1976)
18 Lowe, C. R. An association between smoking and respiratory tuberculosis. *Br. Med. J.*, **2**, 1081 (1956)
19 Davies, P. D. O., Derbyshire, J., Nunn, A. J. *et al.* Ambiguities and inaccuracies in the notification system for tuberculosis in England and Wales. *Community Med.*, **3**, 108 (1981)
20 WHO Annual Reports. World Health Organization, Geneva (1985)
21 Laurie, M. B. Resistance to tuberculosis. In *Experimental Studies of Native and Acquired Defence Mechanisms*, Harvard University Press, Cambridge, pp. 118–180 (1964)
22 Sutherland, I., Springett, V. H. and Nunn, A. J. Changes in tuberculosis notification rates in ethnic groups in England between 1971 and 1978/9. *Tubercle*, **65**, 83–91 (1984)
23 Nunn, A. J., Darbyshire, J. Fox, W. *et al.* Changes in annual tuberculosis notification rates between 1978/9 and 1983 for the population of Indian subcontinent ethnic origin resident in England. *J. Epidemiol. Community Health*, **40**, 357–363 (1986)
24 Fourie, P. B. The prevalence and annual rate of tuberculosis infection in South Africa. *Tubercle*, **64**, 181–192 (1983)
25 Benatar, S. R. Tuberculosis in the 1980s with particular reference to South Africa. *S. Afr. Med. J.*, **63**, 359 (1982)
26 Innes, J. A. Tuberculosis in Asians in Britain. *Postgrad. Med. J.*, **57**, 779–780 (1981)
27 Katz, J. and Kunofsky, S. Environmental versus constitutional factors in the development of tuberculosis among negroes. *Am. Rev. Respir. Dis.*, **81**, 17 (1960)
28 Kushigemachi, M., Schneiderman, L. J. and Barrett-Connor, E. Racial differences in susceptibility to tuberculosis: risk of disease after infection. *J. Chronic Dis.*, **37**, 853–862 (1984)
29 Horwitz, O., Wilbek, E. and Erickson, P. Epidemiological basis of tuberculosis eradication. 10 Longitudinal studies of the risk of tuberculosis in a low prevalence area. *Bull. WHO*, **42**, 95–113 (1969)
30 Comstock, G. W., Ferebee, S. H. and Hammes, L. M. A controlled trial of isoniazid prophylaxis in Alaska. *Am. Rev. Resp. Dis.*, **95**, 935–942 (1967)
31 Comstock, G., Webster, R. G. and Livesay, V. T. Tuberculosis mortality in the US navy: its distribution and decline. *Am. Rev. Resp. Dis.*, **100**, 839 (1974)
32 Comstock, G. W., Livesay, V. T. and Woolpert, S. F. The prognosis of a positive tuberculin reaction in childhood and adolescence. *Am. J. Epidemiol.*, **99**, 131–133 (1974)

33 Papiha, S. S., Wentzel, J., Behjati, F. and Agarwal, S. S. Human leukocyte antigens and circulating immunoglobulin levels in Indian patients with pulmonary tuberculosis, *Tubercle*, **66**, 25–33 (1985)
34 Simmonds, B. *Tuberculosis in Twins*, Pitman, London (1963)
35 Comstock. G. W. Tuberculosis in twins: a re-analysis of the Prophit Survey. *Am. Rev. Respir. Dis.* **117**, 621 (1978)
36 Fishberg. M. *Pulmonary Tuberculosis*, Philadelphia (1932)

Chapter 24

Sarcoidosis

M. W. McNicol

It is difficult to assess the incidence or prevalence of sarcoidosis because of the lack of a simple sensitive diagnostic test and many cases go undiagnosed. Much of the reported variation in incidence could be explained by differences in the rate of diagnosis. It is widely believed that the incidence is high in some ethnic groups and rare in others, but it is unclear if these differences are significant after considering diagnostic and survey methods.

Diagnostic criteria

1. *Clinical.* Most patients are diagnosed clinically using a wide variety of tests in symptomatic patients. Clinical series are often unsatisfactory as enthusiasm may lead to overdiagnosis and underdiagnosis is common when the disease is thought to be rare [1–8].
2. *The chest X-ray* is a moderately sensitive technique in diagnosis and probably the single most useful investigation. At some time in the disease mediastinal gland involvement is invariable, usually with bilateral hilar adenopathy. Pulmonary involvement is not uncommon but may only be microscopic. More than 80% of patients have radiological evidence, usually with bilateral hilar adenopathy. Simple investigation can exclude the few other important causes of mediostinal adenopathy such as tuberculosis or lymphoma, and the remainder can generally be assumed to be due to sarcoidosis. Conventional large films and mass miniature radiography have been used [9], but such screening is now rarely undertaken as it has little place in detecting tuberculosis.
3. *Histology of biopsy specimens* confirms the diagnosis but does not help to estimate incidence. Even if there is no obviously affected tissue, biopsy of the liver, or bronchial biopsy via fibreoptic bronchoscopy is positive in over 80% of confirmed cases. Clearly these investigations cannot be widely used.
4. *The Kveim–Siltzbach test* requires intradermal injection of antigen extracted from sarcoid tissue with biopsy of the injection 4–6 weeks later. With potent antigen and good technique the Kveim test reliably confirms the diagnosis in about 80% of patients, especially in those with relatively recent onset of disease and mediastinal node involvement [7,10]. Unfortunately the test requires sophisticated technology and its epidemiological potential is limited.

There are no other useful diagnostic tests. Many other investigations can be undertaken to establish the extent or activity of the disease but they do not help in establishing the diagnosis.

Methods of assessing incidence or prevalence

1. *Based on clinical or symptomatic diagnosis.* As criteria and investigation vary widely, firm conclusions on incidence or prevalence from personal or institutional series are difficult [11]. Several reports suggest that sarcoidosis is uncommon in certain racial groups such as Indians [12] and Chinese [13], but give a high incidence in the Irish [14], the black population of North America [15] and West Indians in Europe [14]. The former probably represents sampling bias [16] but that in blacks seems to be real. Underdiagnosis is the most likely explanation for the low incidence in India and once interest in the disease had been aroused larger numbers were diagnosed, as reflected in current reports from India [6] and from Indian populations in other countries [5,8] suggesting that sarcoidosis is not uncommon, and in China [17]. Where tuberculosis is common, cases of sarcoidosis are likely to be labelled as tuberculosis: almost certainly accounting for its apparently low prevalence in underdeveloped countries. Intensity of investigation is important [18]. Even if standards of diagnosis are high, deduction on prevalence from clinical series is limited. The population from which the patients are drawn is usually ill defined and may be representative.
2. *Point surveys of diagnosed cases attending hospitals, clinics, etc.* Estimates of prevalence from diagnosed cases attending medical institutions on a single date [19] provide a better picture than single-clinic data but are still dependent on clinical diagnosis and diagnostic habit and are subject to limitations.
3. *X-ray screening of 'entire' populations* are essentially surveys of hilar adenopathy without other obvious cause, and provide prevalence estimates in Western European and North America. In mass X-ray surveys for tuberculosis in the 1950s and early 1960s, up to 60% of the population was sometimes radiographed, but because of favouring symptomatic people, sampling error could likely lead to overestimation. While at some point the chest X-ray is likely to be abnormal in a high proportion of patients, at any one time many people with active sarcoidosis have a normal X-ray. These probably represent the best estimates of prevalence; such information will decline as mass X-ray screening in developed countries is now rare. Facilities are limited in underdeveloped countries, and mass screening is no longer regarded as a useful method of finding cases of tuberculosis [20,21].
4. *Periodical medical examination of groups selected* by occupation (e.g. military personnel) [22–25] provide accurate estimates of the incidence and prevalence in the study population, but extrapolation requires caution. Selection by age, sex and exposure to environmental and other hazards may be relevant in causing the disease. Despite these reservations such studies provide useful evidence on the high incidence of sarcoidosis in certain ethnic groups.
5. *Detailed population surveys using all available diagnostic techniques* have been attempted on entire populations [26] or on persons seeking medical advice [18]. Routine health screening including a chest X-ray was regularly offered to the population of Uppsala and was taken up by 60% [26]. Using an aggressive

approach to diagnosis in the relatively stable population of the Isle of Man, Parkes *et al*. [18] confirmed that underdiagnosis is common. They increased the diagnosis rate by a factor of 5 from 3.5/100 000 to 14.7/100 000, figures generally comparable with the Uppsala prevalence rate of 19/100 000 over 15 years of age. Both series used stringent diagnostic criteria and probably provide a fair indication of prevalence, but are subject to errors from diagnosing occult forms of sarcoidosis, failure of uptake and failure to seek medical advice due to lack of symptoms.

Unfortunately the resources required prevent wide application, particularly in underdeveloped countries.

6. *Post-mortem data* on diagnosed cases is not likely to be helpful epidemiologically. Sarcoidosis is rarely fatal, between 1 and 2% of known cases dying of the disease or its complications, and routine autopsies are not sufficiently widely or carefully carried out. One post-mortem study [27] on approximately 60% of deaths in a Swedish town, suggested that the prevalence of sarcoidosis may be as high as 640/100 000. The authors included only 'certain active sarcoidosis' and excluded sarcoid reactions secondary to tumours, etc. but give only general information about their criteria. In 6706 autopsies, mainly in elderly subjects, there was evidence of 'certain active' sarcoidosis in 43 (6.4%), of whom only three had been diagnosed before death. In the remaining 40, active sarcoidosis was an incidental finding. This report is remarkable for both the high incidence and the small proportion diagnosed. Data from mass X-ray surveys carried out at the same time in Sweden show an incidence 10 times lower – 60/100 000. The very small proportion of clinically diagnosed cases (7% of the total) is not surprising as only 25–50% of patients diagnosed by chest X-ray have symptoms. These surveys emphasize the unreliability of information based on clinical diagnosis. There are no other reports confirming or refuting Hagerstrand and Linell's findings and further information would be useful to confirm the very high prevalence at an age when the incidence of the disease is past its peak.

There is therefore no satisfactory method of estimating the prevalence of sarcoidosis. Underdiagnosis is a major problem. Radiological screening, the only method currently suitable for population surveys, detects a two to four times greater number of cases than symptomatic diagnosis, but probably detects less than 10% of the total.

Present comparative evidence on racial differences in the incidence of sarcoidosis

The epidemiology of sarcoidosis has recently been reviewed by Bresnitz and Strom [20] and by Tierstein and Lesser [21]. It is also critically reviewed by James and Williams [7] and Scadding and Mitchell [10]. In general the greatest incidence is between the ages of 20 and 40 years with a slight preponderance in women. In most Western European and North American populations the prevalence of sarcoidosis is 15–30/100 000. Variations are reported within these populations, but diagnostic error or problems in population sampling are frequent. Detailed studies [16] suggest that a higher prevalence in the Irish living in England [14] is due to sampling artefact. Some evidence suggests a higher incidence in rural versus urban populations with environmental factors responsible. Familial case clusters are well recognized, but there is no good evidence of their cause, or of any genetic abnormality.

Widely varying incidences reported elsewhere (Spain, Israel, South America) again probably represent differences in diagnostic pattern.

The apparently low incidence in Indian, Chinese ,and other south-east Asian people and North American Indians may reflect underdiagnosis. Sarcoidosis, once said to be very rare in India is now diagnosed not uncommonly [6]. In emigrant Indians elsewhere it seems to be at least as common as in the local community [5,8]. A recent study in China [17] identified over 300 known cases and suggested that the incidence is underestimated. Lee et al. [28] reported eight cases in Singapore over a 10-year period, drawn from an unspecified population. Previous mass X-ray surveys of about 500 000 people had failed to detect any cases, but since 1960 a total of 14 cases of pulmonary sarcoidosis had been described and an increase in incidence was expected. The apparently low incidence in Africa may also be due to underdiagnosis. However, the difference in incidence between blacks in Africa and North America and Europe is an enigma unless it is due to increased susceptibility to environmental factors not operating in Africa (see below). However, reports from South Africa also suggest a higher prevalence and more florid disease elsewhere [29].

Sarcoidosis in North American and West Indian black populations

All sources document a high incidence of sarcoidosis in black Americans in whom the manifestations are more florid with increased extrapulmonary disease. The prognosis in prospective surveys [24] and in clinical reports [30] is less good and cannot be accounted for by occupational or environmental factors. A similar trend appears among West Indian blacks living in Britain [4,5,8,31]. James and Jones [7] also quote a high incidence in the West Indian black population in France. The incidence in Europe appears to be less than in North America (three to five times as opposed to 10 times higher than in whites), but the pattern is similar with more extrapulmonary disease, a more protracted course and a higher mortality [32].

There are a number of anomalous findings, particularly the apparently low incidence among similar populations in West Africa or the West Indies. The general setting of health care is not particularly favourable to making the diagnosis, but this does not appear to be a satisfactory explanation. In West Africa and the West Indies even in centres alerted to sarcoidosis, few cases appear to present. Jasyk [33] working in a University Hospital in Nigeria, reported eight cases with skin lesions, and was only able to find 11 previous reports of cutaneous sarcoidosis in West Africa. Following his first case in 1974 when hilar adenopathy had been present, interest had been aroused, but in the subsequent 6 years, sarcoidosis was diagnosed radiographically in only two cases, both of whom had skin disease. However, in skin clinics the incidence appeared to be 50/100 000 new attendances, a rate suggesting that sarcoidosis is commoner than immediately apparent. Newsome and Choudhuri [34] working in Nigeria reported a single case, and that this was the only one in 8 years' experience. There is little information on other racial groups except in South Africa, where the incidence appears to be lower than in Western Europe, but where the rate in blacks appears to be similar to that in North America and Europe [29]. There is little information on sarcoidosis in the

West Indies. At the University Hospital in Jamaica the disease is regarded as uncommon, although a number of cases are seen annually at the National Chest Hospital, a specialist referral centre. However estimates of incidence in the West Indian population in London suggest a prevalence of over 60/100 000 with more florid forms unlikely to escape clinical diagnosis.

It is difficult to reconcile these conflicting observations. The information from North America and Europe suggests a genuinely high incidence in blacks. The difference may be due to underdiagnosis in West Africa and the West Indies, or to an increased susceptibility to unidentified environmental factors in North America and Europe, not found in West Africa or the West Indies. It is not possible to be certain of the explanation.

Possible genetic associations

There is no general association between HLA antigen distribution and sarcoidosis, although some manifestations have been linked to HLA types, notably an association of arthropathy and erythema nodosum with B8 [35,36]. There is no association between sarcoidosis and ABO or Rh blood groups, nor with any immunological abnormality despite the evidence of an abnormal immune response in active sarcoidosis.

Conclusion

The prevalence of clinical sarcoidosis is probably around 15–30/100 000. Problems in diagnosis account for most of the minor variations around this figure, and failure to make the diagnosis probably accounts for most of the reports of low prevalences. Despite the reputedly low incidence in West Africa and the West Indies, there appears to be an increased incidence in those of black West African or West Indian origin in North America and Europe and the disease also shows somewhat different and more severe clinical features.

The true prevalence of the diseases is probably much greater than the prevalence assessed clinically, possibly by as much as a factor of 10. Such a difference adds to the difficulties of interpretation of the reported variations in prevalence.

References

1 Israel, H. L. and Sones, N. Sarcoidosis: clinical observations on 160 cases. *Arch. Intern. Med.*, **102**, 766–776 (1958)
2 Scadding, J. G. Prognosis of intrathoracic sarcoidosis in England. *Br. Med. J.*, **2**, 1165–1172 (1961)
3 Hosada, Y. *et al*. Epidemiology of sarcoidosis in Japan. In *Proceedings of the Sixth International Conference on Sarcoidosis, Tokyo* (eds K. Iwai and Y. Hosada), University of Tokyo Press, Tokyo, pp. 297–302 (1974)
4 Honeyborne, D. Ethnic differences in the clinical features of sarcoidosis in South-east London. *Br. J. Dis. Chest.*, **74**, 63–69 (1980)
5 Edmondstone, W. M. and Wilson, A. G. Sarcoidosis in Caucasians, Blacks and Asians in London. *Br. J. Dis. Chest*, **79**, 27–36 (1985)
6 Gupta, S. K., Mitra, K., Chatterjee, S. and Chakravarty, S. K. Sarcoidosis in India. *Br. J.Dis. Chest*, **79**, 275–283 (1985)

7 James, D. G. and Jones, W. W. *Sarcoidosis and Other Granulomatous Disorders*, W. B. Saunders, (1985)

8 McNicol, M. W. and Luce, P. J. Sarcoidosis in a racially mixed community. *J. R. Coll. Physicians Lond.*, **19**, 179–183 (1985)

9 Bauer, H. J. and Lofgren, S. International study of pulmonary sarcoidosis in mass chest radiography. *Acta Med. Scand., Suppl.*, **425**, 102–105 (1964)

10 Scadding, J. G. and Mitchell, D. N. *Sarcoidosis*, Chapman & Hall, London (1985)

11 James, D. G. *et al*. A world-wide review of sarcoidosis. *Ann. N.Y. Acad. Med.*, **278**, 321–324 (1976)

12 Gupta, S. K., Chatterjee, S. and Roy, M. Clinical profile of sarcoidosis in India. *Lung, India*, **1**, 5–10 (1982)

13 Bovornkitti, S. and Kangsadal, P. Sarcoidosis in Asia. In *Sarcoidosis*, Japan Medical Research Foundation, University of Tokyo Press, Tokyo, pp. 339–354 (1981)

14 Brett, Z. Prevalence of intrathoracic sarcoidosis among ethnic groups in London. *Postgrad. Med. J.*, **45**, 241 (1971)

15 Israel, H. L. and Washburne, J. D. Characteristics of sarcoidosis in black and white patients. In *Proceedings of the Eighth International Conference on Sarcoidosis* (eds W. Jones Williams and B. H. Davies), Alpha Omega, Cardiff, pp. 497–507 (1980)

16 Cumminskey, J. and Dean, G. The frequency of sarcoidosis in Ireland. *J. Irish Med. Assoc.*, **72**, 500–505 (1979)

17 Bovornkitti, S. Sarcoidosis in the Chinese. *Chest*, **81**, 132 (1982)

18 Parkes, S. A., Barker, S. B. DeC., Bourdillon, R. E. *et al*. Incidence of sarcoidosis in the Isle of Man. *Thorax*, **40**, 284–287 (1985)

19 Hosada, Y. *et al*. Case collection and diagnosis of sarcoidosis in epidemiology. In *Sarcoidosis and Other Granulomatous Disorders* (eds J. Chretien, J. Marsac and J. C. Saltiel), Pergamon Press, Oxford (1981)

20 Bresnitz, E. A. and Strom, B. L. Epidemiology of sarcoidosis. *Epidemiol Rev.*, **5**, 124–156 (1983)

21 Tierstein, A. S. and Lesser, M. Worldwide distribution and epidemiology of sarcoidosis. In *Sarcoidosis and Other Granulomatous Diseases of the Lung* (ed. B. L. Fanburg), Dekker, New York (1983)

22 Cooch, J. W. Sarcoidosis in the United States Army, 1952 through 1956. *Am. Rev. Resp. Dis.*, **85**, (5 pt 2), 103–108 (1961)

23 Hiraga, Y. *et al*. Epidemiology of sarcoidosis in a Japanese working group – a 10 year study. In *Proceedings of the Sixth International Conference on Sarcoidosis* (eds. K. Iwai and Y. Hosada), University of Tokyo Press, Tokyo, pp. 303–306 (1974)

24 Sartwell, P. E. and Edwards, L. B. Epidemiology of sarcoidosis in the US Navy. *Am. J. Epidemiol.*, **99**, 250–207 (1974)

25 Munkgaard, S. The prevalence and incidence of intrathoracic sarcoidosis among Danish draftees. In *Sarcoidosis and Other Granulomatous Disorders* (eds J. Chretien, J. Marsac and J. C. Saltiel), Pergamon Press, Oxford, pp. 245–249 (1981)

26 Hillerdahl, E., Osterman, K. and Schmekel, B. Sarcoidosis: epidemiology and prognosis; 15 year European study. *Am. Rev. Resp. Dis.*, **130**, 29–32 (1984)

27 Hagerstrand, I. and Linell, F. The prevalence of sarcoidosis in the autopsy material from a Swedish Town. *Acta Med. Scand. Suppl.*, **425**, 171–173 (1964)

28 Lee, S. K., Narendran, K. and Chiang, G. S. C. Pulmonary sarcoidosis in Singapore. *Ann. Acad. Med. Sing.*, **14**, 446–469 (1985)

29 Benatar, S. R. A comparative study of sarcoidosis in white, black and coloured South Africans. In *Proceedings of the Eighth International Conference on Sarcoidosis, Cardiff* (eds W. J. Williams and B. H. Davies), Alpha Omega, Cardiff (1980)

30 Terris, M. and Chaves, A. D. An epidemiological study of sarcoidosis. *Am. Rev. Resp. Dis.*, **94**, 50–55 (1966)

31 James, D. G. and Brett, Z. Prevalence of intrathoracic sarcoidosis in Britain. *Acta Med. Scand. Suppl.*, **425**, 115–117 (1964)

32 Neville, E., Walker, A. N. and James, D. G. Prognostic factors predicting the outcome of sarcoidosis: an analysis of 818 patients. *Quart. J. Med.*, **208**, 525 (1983)

33 Jasyk, W. K. Sarcoidosis in the West African: a report of eight Nigerian patients with cutaneous lesions. *Trop. Geogr. Med.*, **36**, 231–236 (1984)

34 Newsome, F. and Choudhouri, S. G. B. Sarcoid in a Nigerian: geographical variation of the frequency of sarcoid among blacks considered. *Trans. R. Soc. Trop. Med. Hyg.*, **78**, 663–664 (1984)

35 Neville, E. *et al*. HLA antigens and clinical features of sarcoidosis. In *Sarcoidosis* (eds W. W. Jones and B. H. Davies), Alpha Omega, Cardiff, p. 676 (1980)

36 Gardner, J., Kennedy, H. G., Hamblin, A. and Jones, E. HLA associations in sarcoidosis: a study of two ethnic groups. *Thorax*, **39**, 19 (1984)

Chapter 25

Nutritional patterns and deficiencies

P. J. Pacy

Introduction

This chapter discusses adult nutritional patterns and deficiencies in ethnic groups from the Indian subcontinent, East Africa and the Caribbean now resident in the UK. Broad categories such as 'Asians' are not appropriate, owing to the heterogeneity of such ethnic groups, but are used in places as a general term. Clustering among ethnic groups slows cultural assimilation so diets remain distinct. It is worth stressing that nearly all groups are well nourished and the major nutritional problem is obesity; only ethnic dietary problems are outlined here. The reference list provides a comprehensive source of original articles.

Migrant origins

Indian subcontinent

Initially migration from the Indian subcontinent was largely confined to men during the Second World War and the 1950s. Subsequently they financed travel for other male relatives and friends, generally from areas such as Gujarat and Punjab. The original immigrants usually provided financial and social support for the recent arrivals in distinctive communities in Southall, Leicester and Bradford and elsewhere.

In the 1960s changes in the law curtailed immigration so that new arrivals were primarily dependents of those already resident in the UK. In 1974 the mass expulsion of Ugandan (and other East African) Asians increased immigration and more recently quite large numbers of immigrants have arrived from Bangladesh.

A map of the main sites of emigration from the Indian subcontinent to the UK is shown in Figure 25.1.

Food habits are influenced by two major factors, origin and religious affiliation. Thus, people from the Indian state of Gujarat traditionally use millet in the preparation of chapatis but when resident in the UK they use wheat [1].

The three major regions in the Indian subcontinent, Hinduism, Sikhism and Islam, also play a key role in nutritional practices. These topics are discussed in Chapter 26 on specific dietary intakes.

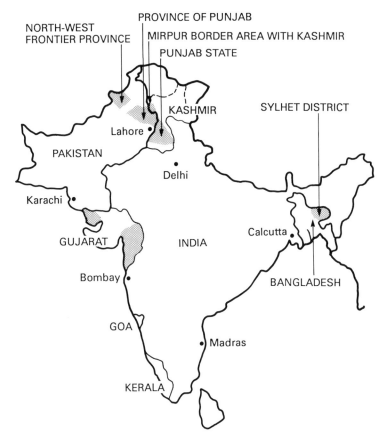

NORTH-WEST
FRONTIER PROVINCE

PROVINCE OF PUNJAB

MIRPUR BORDER AREA WITH KASHMIR

PUNJAB STATE

KASHMIR

SYLHET DISTRICT

Lahore •

PAKISTAN

Delhi

Karachi •

GUJARAT

INDIA

Calcutta •

Bombay •

BANGLADESH

GOA

Madras •

KERALA

Figure 25.1 Main emigration areas in the Indian subcontinent. Reproduced with permission from Henley, A. (1979) *Asian Patients in Hospital and at Home*, Pitman Medical, London, for the King Edward's Hospital Fund for London, p. 8

Afro-Caribbean

As with migrants from the Indian subcontinent, immigration from the Caribbean islands expanded in the early 1950s. These migrants were recruited, often after repeated visits to the Caribbean by British Ministers, into a variety of employments, mainly in inner city areas in distinctive communities such as Brixton in South-west London and Handsworth in Birmingham. The influx of immigrants from the Caribbean was also drastically reduced in the 1960s with the change in the law.

Afro-Caribbeans, like white Europeans, are broadly Christian so there is little religious reason for differences in dietary habit. Small numbers of Afro-Caribbeans, particularly those born in the UK, belong to the Rastafarian sect who are generally vegetarian.

Nutritional deficiencies

Iron

Iron deficiency has been observed in infants of Asian and Afro-Caribbean origin since 1960. Davis *et al.* [3] studied 114 infants aged from 5 to 23 months after excluding those with a positive sickle cell test. None had evidence of any parasitic infestation. Mean haemoglobin and mean corpuscular haemoglobin concentration (MCHC) levels in Afro-Caribbean children were significantly lower than in matched white children in all 3-month age-groups, being most pronounced for the 17–19-month cohort. Iron deficiency (MCHC < 30%) was significantly more frequent in Afro-Caribbean children (53.5% versus 22.4%). Unfortunately it is uncertain how representative these children were of their communities. As so often in early ethnic studies the authors felt that the differences were due to genetic rather than dietary factors but no formal dietary assessment was attempted.

A similar increased frequency of iron deficiency anaemia in Afro-Caribbean compared with local white and Irish-origin infants was reported in some 300 children aged less than 5 years attending Paddington Green Children's Hospital, London [4]. The difference was most apparent at 1–2 years, and appeared unrelated to differences of birthweight, duration of milk-feeding or past illness. By contrast to the previous publication a genetic cause for the frequency of iron deficiency was largely discounted since Irish infants had intermediate total haemoglobin and MCHC levels. The haematological variables thus matched the socioeconomic status of these ethnic groups.

A subsequent study of Afro-Caribbean and white English children from South-east London [5] confirmed this result and comparable differences have been published in America [6].

It has also been long claimed that children of parents from the Indian subcontinent are more at risk of iron deficiency than whites [7]. However, that review of children from Bradford provided no new data to confirm the authors' claims. By the 1970s the relatively high frequency of dietary iron deficiency, particularly among Pakistani Muslims, was more firmly established. These data and possible reasons are covered in references [8] to [15]. The problem among Asian children is reviewed in Chapter 29.

A campaign for extra iron supplementation in high risk groups on the lines of the Stop Rickets Campaign has been proposed. However, as a *British Medical Journal* editorial commented [16], there is currently insufficient data for this, although some would disagree in view of the apparent success of a US campaign (see Chapter 29). Nevertheless, nutritional iron deficiency appears relatively common in all adult Asian subgroups, particularly in those who are vegetarian.

Vitamin B_{12} and folate deficiency

Forty years ago a vitamin B deficiency syndrome allied to sprue was described in Gujaratis which responded to yeast, liver and other agents suggesting inadequate nutritional intake [17]. Recognition of similar dietary deficiencies (of B_{12}, folate or both) leading to megaloblastic anaemia in groups of Indian origin resident in the UK has been somewhat slower but these are now regarded as common.

Stewart *et al.* [18] reported on 12 Asian women (mean age 32 years) and a 24-year-old Irish lady with nutritional vitamin B_{12} deficiency. All the Asian women were Hindu, none ate meat, eggs or fish, one occasionally ate cheese but the only animal produce taken by the remainder was milk. Only two of the consumers drank fresh milk, the rest boiled it, a practice that may reduce the B_{12} content by 50% within 10 minutes [19]. Most had reduced bone marrow iron stores while none was considered folate deficient.

Another report on 25 Indians living in Southall, South London claimed a threefold increased prevalence of megaloblastic anaemia in their predominantly Sikh and Hindu population compared with whites [20]. However, in contrast to the previous study six had pure folate deficiency, four pure B_{12} deficiency, while seven had a mixture. All except one of the individuals were lacto-vegetarian, and again drank milk which had frequently been boiled for a considerable time. The remaining three Asians were considered to have pernicious anaemia and gastrointestinal disorders. The megaloblastic anaemia occurred at a significantly earlier age than is usually seen in whites.

The cause of anaemia was more recently assessed in a random community survey of 251 Punjabi female migrants over 11 years of age [21] (94% of those approached); 32% were anaemic, mostly due to iron deficiency, indicated by serum iron concentration below 10 mmol/litre. The authors commented that the prevalence of megaloblastic anaemia had fallen considerably since their 1971 case study [20] due to changes in nutritional habits and/or possibly gastrointestinal flora [22].

Two further hospital-based case studies have evaluated megaloblastic anaemias in Asians. Sixteen of the 22 patients from Leicester with evidence of nutritional vitamin B_{12} deficiency were women (mean age 34.8 years) and all were Hindu vegetarians, the group's mean age being 34.8 $\pm$ 11.3 years. Five had pernicious anaemia (mean age 53.6 years), one the sole Muslim Asian. Dietary intakes of total calories, protein, iron, vitamin B_{12} and folate were below those recommended. In 27 months, some 150 cases of megaloblastic anaemia occurred in Leicester, with 33% in Asians, who were three times more likely than local whites to have megaloblastic anaemia with a predominantly nutritional origin.

From North-west London, the causes of megaloblastic haemopoiesis were analysed in 138 Hindu Gujaratis (age 13 to over 80 years) between 1970 and 1984 [24]. All were lifelong vegetarians; 69% had nutritional B_{12} deficiency, only 3% had nutritional folate deficiency while 14% had pernicious anaemia. B_{12} deficiency was more common in females at each 10-year interval. Of the 20 with pernicious anaemia 13 were male, with 60% under 49 years compared with 19% among white individuals reported by Cox [25]. This frequency of pernicious anaemia was almost identical to that of white Europeans at around 128/100 000 [26], contrasting with earlier claims that pernicious anaemia was relatively uncommon in Asians [27,28]. Several other interesting findings were reported by Chanarin et al. [24]. Active tuberculous infection occurred in 12% of Hindus with megaloblastic anaemia. Fifty-six per cent of those with nutritional vitamin B_{12} deficiency and 11 (55%) with pernicious anaemia had coexistent iron deficiency. Serum calcium was low in 31% and alkaline phosphatase elevated in 26% of those with nutritional vitamin B_{12} deficiency, compared with 54% and 0% in those with pernicious anaemia. Overt clinical osteomalacia occurred in 20% of both groups. The most important conclusion from the study by Chanarin's group was their hypothesis. They postulated that the low B_{12} (cobalamin) dietary intake of vegetarian Gujaratis might impair killing of bacilli, particularly tubercle, by macrophages whose phagocytosis is cobalamin dependent [24]. If proven, at least some of the excess tuberculosis in Gujaratis may be due to a dietary deficiency rather than any genetic tendency (Chapter 23).

Table 25.1 Case reports of nutritional osteomalacia/rickets in immigrants predominantly from the Indian subcontinent

Authors	Reference	City	Individuals (no.)	Sex	Age (yr)	Period of data collection (yr)	Comments
Dent and Smith (1969)	[32]	London	4 Hindu 3 Europeans	7F	20–46	15	All vegetarian
Wills et al. (1979)	[33]	London	1 Gujarat	1M	15	Not relevant	Excellent response to reduced dietary phytic acid
Stamp et al. (1980)	[34]	London	43 Asian 2 European (both elderly female)	10M 35F	10–88	6	Number of cases did not decrease during the course of the study
Swan and Cooke (1971)	[35]	Birmingham	12 Pakistani 13 Indian	8M 17F	11–36	6	64% predominantly vegetarian. No nutritional rickets occurred in black West Indians
Clarke et al. (1976)	[36]	Newcastle	6 Hindu 7 Sikh	7M 8F	11–42	Not supplied	Healthy relatives of those with osteomalacia often had subclinical disease
O'Hara-May and Widdowson (1976)	[37]	Coventry	3 Hindu 3 Sikh 3 Muslim	9M	14–16	1–2	No dietary difference in vitamin D or calcium compared to matched non-ricketsial controls

Vitamin D and calcium

In the past nutritional rickets and osteomalacia in the UK has been confined to low socioeconomic groups and the elderly. This has changed considerably in recent years with claims of the relative frequency of rickets and osteomalacia in individuals of Indian subcontinent origin. The re-emergence of these problems was probably first described in 1962 among Pakistani Muslims from Glasgow [29], after the discovery of florid osteomalacia in two Pakistani Muslim girls and their mother. Subsequently, 11 families (two from prosperous backgrounds) were studied (35 males; 39 females), of whom 15 males and 20 females had some evidence of osteomalacia. Dietary vitamin D and calcium intakes were low in children over 5 with rickets, although those less than 5 years and most adults seemed to have adequate vitamin D intakes. The high prevalence of osteomalacia recorded was almost certainly overestimated owing to recruitment procedure, i.e. complaints of limb pains.

Over the next 25 years many similar reports were published, but with similar flaws which include small numbers, non-random selection, and no or poorly matched controls [30].

In 1963 all cases of childhood nutritional rickets at two large London hospitals over 5 years were analysed [31]: six in Afro-Caribbeans, five in Greek Cypriots, four in other ethnic groups and only one a white child. This report claimed an increased risk of rickets in immigrants compared with whites but the data did not permit such conclusions.

Case reports followed from several cities throughout the UK, particularly in more elderly individuals from the Indian subcontinent. These are summarized in Table 25.1 [32–37].

Attempts have been made to assess more formally the prevalence of nutritional rickets and osteomalacia. Thirty per cent of both Asian adults and children in Rochdale had clinical rickets compared with 4% in white children [38]. Comparable data were not available for white adults.

Later a repeat survey was undertaken [39]. Muslim Asian children ($n = 103$; age 5–18 years) but not adults ($n = 159$) showed improvement in biochemical variables of vitamin D deficiency. Vitamin D levels below 12.5 nmol/l occurred in 33% of girls and 22% of boys, in 35% of Asian men and 33% of women. Mean vitamin D concentration in both was less than in white controls. Muslim Asians from East Africa had lower levels than those from the Indian subcontinent.

Children

The problem among children has also been assessed in four main studies [40–43]. In Glasgow [40], 100 children each of African, Chinese and Scottish and 200 of Asian origin were surveyed. Florid rickets was only noted in 10 Muslim Asian, seven of whom came from a single family. A further 15 Asian, 3 African, 3 Chinese and 1 Scottish children had minimal and/or healing rickets; all belonged to social classes III and IV. Daily dietary vitamin D of less than 50 iu was recorded in 32% of Asian and 24% of Chinese but only 9% of white and 7% of African children.

Ford et al. [41] conducted a retrospective case record survey of hospital admissions due to rickets in Bradford between 1969 and 1972. Healthy randomly selected school children aged 9–16 years were venesected in May (156 Asians; 40 West Indian, 35 whites). Over 4 years, 22 Asian, 10 white but no West Indian children aged 0–3 years had nutritional rickets. In the 9–16 age-group this was confined solely to 23 Asians. In the random sample abnormalities of calcium, phosphate or alkaline phosphatase were noted in 79 Asians, 9 West Indians but in no whites. Mean ± s.e.m. 25(OH)D levels were lowest in Asians (5.23 ± 0.7 ng/ml), highest in whites (15.10 ± 0.94 ng/ml), while intermediate in West Indian children (9.59 ± 0.73 ng/ml). Forty-one per cent of Asians had very low levels (below 3.8 ng/ml).

A better designed study from Edinburgh hospital [42] compared 45 Asian boys and 62 girls (71% Islamic, 22% Sikh, 7% Hindu), randomly recruited, with 221 non-Asian children who had no evidence of rickets. All children were over 2 years and any with adverse effects on calcium metabolism were excluded. The 25(OH)D status of the Asian children was lower than the controls; Asian girls had significantly lower vitamin D concentrations than boys (18.7 ± 9.9 versus 23.7 ± 10.9 nmol/l).

The Birmingham group [43] have examined iron and vitamin D status in 144 Asian toddlers aged 21–23 months, finding low 25(OH)D levels in 40%, especially in girls and more in Muslims than others. As with most previous studies, a matched non-Asian control group was not recruited. These authors discuss their view of the effect of fortification campaigns in Chapter 29.

Adults
Vitamin D (25(OH)D) levels have been used to establish the frequency of osteomalacia in adults. 25(OH)D levels in 24 asymptomatic Pakistani immigrants in Glasgow were significantly lower than 41 aged-matched healthy white controls [44]. The same group [45] confirmed reduced levels of 25(OH)D during October and November in urbanized Pakistanis and whites with intermediate levels in rurally residing Asians from Stornoway (Outer Hebrides). These 25(OH)D levels in Pakistanis fell rapidly after settling in the UK.

Hunt et al. [1] assessed the effects of religious, dietary and social customs on vitamin D status in 81 Ugandan Asians, randomly chosen, who had immigrated to the UK in 1972. There were 14 Catholics, 18 Ismailis, 13 Muslims, 13 Sikhs and 23 Hindus. Their mean 25(OH)D level was 15.7 nmol/l, considerably lower than considered normal in whites. Blood was taken in the early autumn, with the 25(OH)D levels probably at their nadir. Twenty-eight per cent were less than 8.7 nmol/l as found in individuals with overt osteomalacia/rickets. The Roman Catholics, the most Westernized and darkly pigmented of the Asian groups, had significantly higher plasma levels and dietary intake than the other groups. Vegetarian Hindus had the lowest levels with the Ismailis, Muslims and Sikhs intermediate. No comparably matched white control group was studied.

Shaunak et al. [47] compared the vitamin D status of 60 healthy adult Hindu Asian couples with 48 healthy white hospital personnel as controls. Blood was taken in late spring. Twenty-six (22%) had levels of 25(OH)D of less than 10 nmol/l compared with none of the whites. No sex difference was observed, but marked similarities of 25(OH)D concentrations between couples were found. The duration of time in the UK and vegetarian status appeared irrelevant to vitamin D levels; Punjabis appeared more likely to have lower levels than Gujaratis.

Summary

Despite the shortcomings of these studies, their consistency firmly suggests that Asian adults and children, particularly vegetarian females, tend to have suboptimal 25(OH)D concentrations and a greater frequency of osteomalacia and rickets than whites. There are few reports in other ethnic groups, although a potentially at-risk group among Afro-Caribbeans has been highlighted. Four cases (age range 11–22 months) of florid nutritional rickets occurred in seven Rastafarian children admitted over 3 months to a Bristol hospital [48,49]: all were females. Rastafarians tend to be vegetarian although cheese is eaten (see Chapter 30). As in other cases, all four infants responded quickly to vitamin D supplementation.

What is the cause of the low vitamin D status in people of Indian subcontinent origin?

There is little doubt that the reduced 25(OH)D in 'Asian' osteomalacia represents true vitamin D deficiency. 25(OH)D levels tend to fall in this ethnic group during residence in the UK [45], but are normal on arrival [46] and in the country of origin [50,51]. Levels generally rise during the summer which may result in spontaneous healing of the disease [52,53]. Lower dietary vitamin D in vegetarians, and high fibre, low meat diets appear the most likely to lead to vitamin D deficiency [54] but alone would not cause appreciable deficiency as 90% of the 25(OH)D arises from the skin [45,55]. The increased skin pigmentation of Asians as a possible cause of 'nutritional' rickets per se is unlikely as Afro-Caribbeans with darker skins seem not to have the same problems. Indians, Pakistanis and whites all have a similar capacity to produce vitamin D in response to ultraviolet irradiation but those from the Indian subcontinent may require greater exposure for a similar response [56]. There is some evidence that rachitic children have less outdoor exposure than those without evidence of the disease [53].

Phytic acid
In several studies high dietary phytic acid, particularly in chappatis, appears to be an important cause of Asian rickets [1,54], while reducing dietary phytic acid may result in healing [33,57]. Binding of calcium by phytic acid probably prevents its absorption from the small intestine but should not cause vitamin D deficiency. However, as proposed by Heath [58], it appears that high fibre, high phytate diets bind vitamin D in the gut resulting in its excretion and thus greater vitamin requirements. This, together with possible effects of vegetarian diets on liver oxidases [59], and reduced sunlight, may result in reduced plasma 25(OH)D levels.

Value of campaigns
Programmes such as the 'Stop Rickets Campaign' have been designed to publicize the problem and success, particularly in children, has been claimed [60,61]. However, attempts deliberately to persuade Asians to eat more traditional western diets are by and large unsuccessful and culturally elitist [39,58]. Indeed, discharge rates of Glaswegian Asian children with rickets and osteomalacia fell during the 4 years before vitamin D supplementation [60,62] and similar observations were made in the Rochdale Asian population who were not supplemented [39].

Thus it is not clear whether supplementing the diet with 400 iu doses of vitamin D is as efficacious as often stated. However, it seems sensible to allow such supplements to be freely available for at-risk groups which, as shown here, means all families of Indian subcontinent origin, particularly if vegetarian.

Conclusions

What was most apparent during preparation of this chapter was the relative paucity of data on nutritional patterns and deficiencies in many of the other non-Asian ethnic groups who live in Britain. The importance of different disease patterns among ethnic groups compared with white Europeans should provide a stimulus to future research.

Asian vegetarian groups appear to be particularly susceptible to nutritional deficiencies of iron and vitamins B_{12} and D. Changing lifestyles among various ethnic subgroups, likely with each succeeding generation, may alter this. Meanwhile it appears prudent to give vitamin D supplements to 'Asians' of all subgroups at a daily dose of 400 iu. Iron supplementation is a more vexed question but certainly in lower income groups may reduce iron deficiency.

References

1 Hunt, S. P., O'Riordan, J. L. H., Window, J. and Truswell, A. S. Vitamin D status in different subgroups of British Asians. *Br. Med. J.*, **2**, 1351–1354 (1976)
2 Carlson, E., Kipps, M. and Thomson, J. An evaluation of a traditional Vietnamese diet in the UK. *Hum. Nutr. Appl. Nutr.*, **36A**, 107–115 (1982)
3 Davis, I. R., Marten, R. H. and Sarkany, I. Iron-deficiency anaemia in European and West Indian infants in London. *Br. Med. J.*, **2**, 1426–1428 (1960)
4 Oppe, T. E. Medical problems of coloured immigrant children in Britain. *Proc. R. Soc. Med.*, **57**, 321–323 (1964)
5 Pollak, M. Comparison of Rearing and Development in Three Groups of Children in South London. MD Thesis, London University (1970)
6 Sadowitz, P. D. and Oski, F. A. Iron status and infant feeding practices in an urban ambulatory center. *Pediatrics*, **72**, 33–36 (1985)
7 Hussain, M. A. and Wadsworth, G. R. Nutritional status of Asian infants. *Proc. Nutr. Soc.*, **26**, 212–218 (1967)
8 Goel, K. M., Logan, R. W., House, F. *et al*. The prevalence of haemoglobinopathies, nutritional iron and folate deficiencies in native and immigrant children in Glasgow. *Health Bull.*, **36**, 176–183 (1976)
9 Harris, R. J., Armstrong, D., Ali, R. and Laynes, A. Nutritional survey of Bangladeshi children aged under 5 years in the London Borough of Tower Hamlets. *Arch. Dis. Childhood*, **58**, 428–432 (1983)
10 Ehrhardt, P. Iron deficiency in young Bradford children from different ethnic groups. *Br. Med. J.*, **292**, 90–93 (1986)
11 Miller, V., Swaney, S. and Diehard, A. Impact of the WIC Program on the iron status of infants. *Pediatrics*, **75**, 100–105 (1985)
12 Stroud, C. E. Nutrition and the immigrant. *Br. J. Hosp. Med.*, **5**, 629–634 (1971)
13 Saarinen, U. M. and Siimes, M. A. Iron absorption in infants: high bioavailability of breast milk iron as indicated by the extrinsic tag method of iron absorption and by the concentration of serum ferritin. *J. Pediatr.*, **91**, 36–39 (1977)
14 Smith, N. J. and Rios, E. Iron metabolism and iron deficiency in infancy and childhood. *Adv. Paediatr.*, **21**, 239–280 (1974)

15 Fomon, S. J., Ziegler, E. E., Nelson, S. E. and Edwards, B. B. Cow milk feeding in infancy: gastrointestinal blood loss and iron nutritional status. *J. Pediatr.*, **98**, 540–545 (1981)

16 Addy, D. Happiness is: iron. *Br. Med. J.*, **292**, 969–970 (1986)

17 Cooke, A. B. A vitamin B deficiency syndrome allied to sprue. *Indian Med. Gaz.*, **79**, 429–437 (1944)

18 Stewart, J. S., Roberts, P. D. and Hoffbrand, A. V. Response of dietary vitamin B12 deficiency to physiological oral doses of cyanocobalamin. *Lancet*, **ii**, 542–545 (1970)

19 Banerjee, D. K. and Chatterjea, J. B. Pernicious anaemia in Asiatic Indians. *Blood*, **6**, 631–636 (1951)

20 Britt, R. P., Harper, C. and Spray, G. H. Megaloblastic anaemia among Indians in Britain. *Quart. J. Med.*, **40**, 499–520 (1971)

21 Britt, R. P., Hollis, Y., Keil, J. E. *et al.* Anaemia in Asians in London. *Postgrad Med. J.*, **59**, 645–657 (1983)

22 Albert, M. J., Mathan, V. I. and Baker, S. J. Vitamin B12 synthesis by human small intestinal bacteria. *Nature*, **283**, 781–782 (1980)

23 Matthews, J. H. and Wood, J. K. Megaloblastic anaemia in vegetarian Asians. *Clin. Lab. Haematol.*, **6**, 1–7 (1984)

24 Chanarin, I., Malkowska, V., O'Hara, A. M. *et al.* Megaloblastic anaemia in a vegetarian Hindu community. *Lancet*, **ii**, 1168–1172 (1985)

25 Cox, E. V. The clinical manifestations of vitamin B12 deficiency in Addisonian pernicious anaemia. In *Vitamin B12 and Intrinsic Factor 2* (ed. E. C. Heinrich), Enke, Stuttgart (1962)

26 Scott, E. Prevalence of pernicious anaemia in Great Britain. *J. Coll. Gen. Pract.*, **3**, 80–84 (1960)

27 Das Gupta, C. R. and Chatterjea, J. B. Pernicious anaemia in Asiatic Indians. *Blood*, **6**, 631–636 (1951)

28 Britt, R. P., Stranc, W. and Harper, C. Pernicious anaemia in Indian immigrants in the London area. *Br. J. Haematol.*, **18**, 637–641 (1970)

29 Dunnigan, M. G., Paton, J. P. J., Haase, S. *et al.* Late rickets and osteomalacia in the Pakistani Community in Glasgow. *Scott. Med. J.*, **7**, 159–167 (1962)

30 Peach, H. A review of the aetiological and intervention studies on rickets and osteomalacia in the United Kingdom. *Community Med.*, **6**, 119–126 (1984)

31 Benson, P. F., Stroud, C. E., Mitchell, N. J. and Nicolaides, A. Rickets in immigrant children in London. *Br. Med J.*, **i**, 1054–1056 (1963)

32 Dent, C. E. and Smith, R. Nutritional osteomalacia. *Quart. J. Med.*, **38**, 195–209 (1969)

33 Wills, M. R., Day, R. C., Phillips, J. B. and Bateman, E. C. Phytic acid and nutritional rickets in immigrants. *Lancet*, **i**, 771–773 (1972)

34 Stamp, T. C. B., Walker, P. G., Perry, W. and Jenkins, M. V. Nutritional osteomalacia and late rickets in Greater London, 1974–1979: clinical and metabolic studies in 45 patients. *Clin. Endocrinol. Metab.*, **9**, 81–105 (1980)

35 Swan, C. H. J. and Cooke, W. T. Nutritional osteomalacia in immigrants in an urban community. *Lancet*, **ii**, 456–459 (1971)

36 Clark, F., Simpson, W. and Young, J. R. Osteomalacia in immigrants from the Indian subcontinent in Newcastle upon Tyne. *Proc. R. Soc. Med.*, **65**, 478–480 (1972)

37 O'Hara-May, J. and Widdowson, E. M. Diets and living conditions of Asian boys in Coventry with and without signs of rickets. *Br. J. Nutr.*, **36**, 23–36 (1976)

38 Holmes, A. M., Enoch, B. A., Taylor, J. L. and Jones, M. E. Occult rickets and osteomalacia amongst the Asian immigrant population. *Quart. J. Med.*, **42**, 125–149 (1973)

39 Stephens, W. P., Klimiuk, P. S., Warrington, S. *et al.* Observations of the natural history of vitamin D deficiency among Asian immigrants. *Quart. J. Med.*, **51**, 171–188 (1982)

40 Groell, K. M., Sweet, E. M., Logan, R. W. *et al.* Florid and subclinical rickets among immigrant children in Glasgow. *Lancet*, **i**, 1141–1148 (1976)

41 Ford, J. A., McIntosh, W. B., Butterfield, R. *et al.* Clinical and subclinical vitamin D deficiency in Bradford children. *Arch. Dis. Childhood*, **51**, 939–943 (1976)

42 O'Hare, A. E., Uttley, W. S., Belton, N.R. *et al.* Persisting vitamin D deficiency in the Asian adolescent. *Arch. Dis. Childhood*, **59**, 766–770 (1984)

43 Grindulis, H., Scott, P. H., Belton, N. R. *et al*. Combined deficiency of iron and vitamin D in Asian toddlers. *Arch. Dis. Childhood*, **61**, 843–848 (1986)

44 Preece, M. A., Ford, J. A., McIntosh, W. B. *et al*. Vitamin-D deficiency among Asian immigrants to Britain. *Lancet*, **i**, 907–910 (1973)

45 Preece, M. A., Tomlinson, S., Ribot, C. A. *et al*. Studies of vitamin D deficiency in man. *Quart. J. Med.*, **44**, 575–589 (1975)

46 Stamp, T. C. B. Sources of vitamin D nutrition. *Lancet*, **i**, 316 (1980)

47 Shaunak, S., Colston, K., Ang, L. *et al*. Vitamin deficiency in adult British Hindu Asians: a family disorder. *Br. Med. J.*, **291**, 1116–1168 (1985)

48 Ward, P. S., Drakeford, J. P., Mitton, J. and Jones, J. Nutritional rickets in Rastafarian children. *Br. Med. J.*, **282**, 1242–1243 (1982)

49 Wolinski, A. P., Nakielny, R. and Duncan, A. Nutritional rickets in Rastafarian children. *Bristol. Med. Chir. J.*, **98**, 68–72 (1983)

50 Hodgkin, P., Kay, G. H., Hine, P. M. *et al*. Vitamin-D deficiency in Asians at home and in Britain, *Lancet*, **ii**, 167–172 (1973)

51 Rashid, A., Mohammed, T., Stephens, W. P. *et al*. Vitamin D state of Asians living in Pakistan. *Br. Med. J.*, **286**, 182–184 (1983)

52 Gupta, M. H., Round, J. M. and Stamp, T. C. B. Spontaneous cure of vitamin-D deficiency in Asians during summer in Britain, *Lancet*, **i**, 586–588 (1974)

53 Stamp, T. C. B. and Round, J. M. Seasonal changes in human plasma levels of 25-hydroxy-cholecalciferol. *Nature*, **247**, 563–565 (1974)

54 Dunnigan, M. G., McIntosh, W. B., Ford, J. A. and Robertson, I. Acquired disorders of vitamin D metabolism. In *Clinical Endocrinology 2 – Calcium Disorders* (eds D. A. Heath and S. J. Marx), Butterworth, London, pp. 125–150 (1982)

55 Haddad, J. G. and Hahn, T. J. Natural and synthetic sources of circulating 25-hydroxyvitamin D in man. *Nature*, **244**, 515–517 (1973)

56 Lo, C. W., Paris, P. W. and Holick, M. F. Indian and Pakistani immigrants have the same capacity as Caucasians to produce vitamin D in response to ultraviolet irradiation. *Am. J. Clin. Nutr.*, **44**, 683–685 (1986)

57 Ford, J., Colhoun, E. M., McIntosh, W. B. and Dunnigan, H. G. Biochemical response of late rickets and osteomalacia to a chapatti free diet. *Br. Med. J.*, **iii**, 446 (1972)

58 Heath, D. A. Thoughts on the aetiology of vitamin D deficiency in Asians. *Postgrad. Med. J.*, **59**, 649–651 (1983)

59 Dollery, C. T., Fraser, H. S., Davies, D. and MacIntyre, I. Vitamin D status in different subgroups of British Asians. *Br. Med. J.*, **i**, 104 (1977)

60 Dunnigan, M. G., McIntosh, W. B., Sutherland, G. R. *et al*. Policy for prevention of Asian rickets. *Br. Med. J.*, **282**, 357–360 (1981)

61 Dunnigan, M. G., Glekin, B. M., Henderson, J. B. *et al*. Prevention of rickets in Asian children: assessment of the Glasgow campaign. *Br. Med. J.*, **291**, 239–242 (1985)

62 Goel, K. M., Sweet, E., Campbell, S. *et al*. Reduced prevalence of rickets in Asian children in Glasgow. *Lancet*, **ii**, 405–407 (1981)

Chapter 26

Features of Gujarati, Punjabi and Muslim diets in the UK

S. Ganatra

In the 1981 Census, 2.3% of the total UK population was of Asian origin. Asians have migrated from four main areas of the Indian subcontinent, Bangladesh, Punjab, Gujarat, Pakistan, and also via East Africa. Their food habits are influenced by two main factors – the area from which they originate, which determines their staple foodstuff and the foods with which they are familiar, and the religious group to which they belong. This determines which foods are taboo and how and when they fast. The three main philosophies and religions of the Asian community are Hinduism, Sikhism and Islam.

Hinduism is one of the oldest religions of the world dating back to 200 BC. Hindus practise the doctrine of non-violence, hence killing of any animal is forbidden. Orthodox Hindus are strict lacto-vegetarians, not eating any type of meat, fish or eggs. Gujaratis, who make up the major part of the Hindu community in Britain, adhere to their religious laws with varying degrees of orthodoxy but regard the cow as a sacred animal so even non-vegetarian Hindus will not eat beef or any food containing beef extract. However, the products of the cow, milk, yoghurt and ghee (clarified butter), are held in high esteem. Fasting and food prohibition is an essential part of Hinduism and takes various forms from total abstinence to eating just one meal per day or eating only foods that are considered to be pure e.g. milk, fruit, yoghurt, nuts and potatoes.

In the fifteenth century Guru Nanak founded the Sikh religion. Its teachings were derived from both Hinduism and Islam. Sikhs have few dietary taboos, having rejected those of Islam and Hinduism from which they were mostly converted [1]. Sikhs in Britain are primarily from the Punjab and many have come to Britain from East Africa. Punjab is situated in North-western India, so the staple food for Punjabis is wheat [2]; rice is also eaten but not in large quantities. Butter and ghee are the fats most commonly used in Sikh cooking, with occasional use of oil. Some Sikhs are vegetarians and some of the non-vegetarians will not eat pork or beef, reflecting their Hindu and Muslim background. The meats most commonly eaten are chicken and mutton; fish is eaten very occasionally. Dairy products are important with yoghurt, buttermilk, panir (homemade cheese) and milk all consumed regularly. Pulses are a major source of protein, especially among the vegetarians.

The Muslims in the UK are mainly from Pakistan and Bangladesh with again some who migrated from East Africa. There are also Muslims from other countries (e.g. Arabs, Yemenis, Iraqis) who observe the same religious food laws but their food culture is very different. Islamic food laws are written in the Holy Book of

Koran which states that only the flesh of cloven-footed and cud-chewing animals is lawful food. It forbids the consumption of blood of any animal. All animals have to be killed by ritual slaughter by slitting the jugular vein and draining the blood (Halal meat). The Koran also forbids its follower to eat pig, carnivorous animals or birds. Alcohol is strictly forbidden. Besides abstaining from certain foods, Muslims from adolescence until old age are expected to fast for Rhamadan, the ninth month of the lunar year. The fast lasts 30 days during which no food or liquid may be taken between dawn and sunset.

The features of Bengali and Pakistani diets are very different. The Pakistanis use chapati as their staple whereas the Bengalis use polished rice; wheat is not cultivated in Bengal. The Pakistanis mainly use oil in cooking and eat more chicken or mutton. Fish, both fresh and dried, makes up a large part of the Bengali diet whereas the Pakistanis will perhaps eat more chicken and mutton.

There are customary and religious food laws laid down for pregnant and lactating women and infants. In India and Pakistan the first feed to the newborn baby is usually sweetened water, as the mother's colostrum is often considered to be indigestible and therefore harmful. In Pakistan it is believed to be poisonous because it is thought to have been in the breast since conception. Breast feeding is therefore only started 3 or 4 days after delivery. In some states in India solid foods are started as late as 18 months, and there is only one transition from a milk diet to various curries, rice and chapatis. Asian mothers confronted for the first time with a choice of Western infant foods without guidance, often adopt undesirable feeding patterns, e.g. rice pudding, egg custard or cereal rusks three times a day [3].

Particular diseases

Various researchers have looked at Asian diets in relation to coronary heart disease, rickets and osteomalacia, anaemias and low birthweight babies. In Britain the age/sex-specific mortality attributed to coronary heart disease (CHD) is considerably higher in Indian origin, than in European, men and women [4], and was found in Gujaratis, Punjabis and Muslims (see Chapter 6). The basis of the increased CHD risk in people of Indian origin is unknown. Our group at Northwick Park Hospital carried out a survey to determine how far the recognized CHD risk factors, particularly dietary fat intake, serum lipoprotein concentration and coagulant factor status (factor VII and fibrinogen) could explain the ethnic difference. Five days' weighed dietary records were collected from 20 Gujarati and 20 European men aged 45–54 years, as a representative random sample of men living in Wembley, Middlesex. The results are shown in Table 26.1.

Our results did not explain why Gujaratis were more prone to CHD than the Europeans. The percentage energy derived from fat was the same in both groups and the Gujaratis had higher P : S ratios which are in accordance with most current recommendations for coronary heart disease prevention. McKeigue et al. [5] had similar findings to ours. The plasma total cholesterol and high density lipoprotein cholesterol was similar to the control group. A suggestion was made recently that it is the oxidized esters of cholesterol in Gujarati cooking that may be important.

The prevalence of rickets and osteomalacia in Asian communities in Britain has prompted a number of surveys of vitamin D intake (see Chapters 25, 27–29) [6,7]. The Asian diet together with inadequate solar ultraviolet light radiation, genetic factors and clothing habits contribute to Asian rickets [8]. Analysis of food quality

Table 26.1

	Gujaratis		Europeans	
	Dietary analysis	% of energy	Dietary analysis	% of energy
Energy				
Kcal	2222		2677	
KJ	9325		11223	
Protein (g)	69	13	94	14
Fat (g)	95	39	115	38
Carbohydrate (g)	275	49	309	44
Total saturated fat (g)	29		46	
Total monounsaturated fat (g)	26		38	
Total polyunsaturated fat (g)	14		12	
Polysaturated: saturated ratio	0.52		0.26	

Table 26.2

	Nutrients (MJ)	
	Asians	Average for general population
Calcium (mg)	87	101
Riboflavin (mg)	0.10	0.18
Retinol equivalent (μg)	77	128
Vitamin D (μg)	0.16	0.28

purchased by Asian households among the 21 452 households in the National Food Survey between 1972 and 1974 is shown in Table 26.2. The quality of the Asian diet was much lower than the national average for riboflavin, vitamin A and vitamin D. Since the marginal vitamin D intake cannot be made up by exposure to sunlight it may be advisable to provide vitamin D supplements to vulnerable children, pregnant and lactating mothers to prevent rickets and osteomalacia.

Megaloblastic anaemia is a common problem in Hindu vegetarians. Most cases are considered to have nutrient deficiency of vitamin B_{12} and occasionally folate deficiency [9]. True pernicious anaemia is said to be rare. These problems are discussed in Chapters 25, 28 and 29.

Several studies have shown that Asian babies tend to be lighter than European babies (see Chapters 10 and 28) [10]. The mean birthweight of Hindu babies was found to be about 190 g lighter than that of European babies. The relationship between dietary intake and fetal growth was unclear but deficiencies of protein, energy, zinc and pyridoxine have been implicated.

Generally in pregnancy the energy content of a Hindu diet (which varies from a traditional lactovegetarian to Western style food) is no different from European diets [10–13]. Although 10–18% less than the recommended 2400 kcal/day, it is sufficient to support a rate of weight gain in pregnancy of 0.45 kg/week, equal to that of healthy European women [14]. By this criterion the diet can therefore be considered adequate to support fetal growth. The protein intake in the Abraham Study accounted for more than 10% of energy which again is adequate. Cambell-Brown [15] showed that zinc intake ranged from 3.1 to 16.9 mg/day with average intake least in vegetarian Hindus and most in Europeans. Average copper intakes, between 1.48 and 1.80 mg/day, were similar in vegetarians, non-vegetarian Hindus and in Europeans. No association was found between crude or adjusted birthweight and any of the measures of zinc or copper status and there was no evidence that this acted as a nutritional constraint or was the cause of slower intrauterine growth rate.

When making dietary recommendations to any particular ethnic group it is important to remember that food habits are an indicator of identity as much as dress, language or religion. Ethnic identity and cultural food habits support one another. To recommend Asians to change to a Western diet will be unsuccessful, as was seen in Glasgow and Rochdale [16,17] when they attempted to reduce rickets and osteomalacia. Food habits are patterned by family habits, cultural and religious values and rituals. Religious dietary laws influence what foods, how, when and with whom they are eaten.

References

1 Carlson, E., Kipps, M., and Thomson, J. Influences on the food habits of some ethnic minorities in the UK. *Hum. Nutr. Appl. Nutr.*, **38A**, 85–98 (1984)
2 Gopalan, C. L. and Balasubramian, S. L. *Diet Atlas of India*, Indian Council of Medical Research, Hyderabad (1969)
3 Shukla, K. Diet and culture. *Nursing (Oxford)*, **12**, 523–525 (1980)
4 Marmot, M. G., Adelstein, A. M. and Bulusu, L. Lessons from the study of immigrant mortality. *Lancet*, **ii**, 1455–1458 (1984)
5 McKeigue, P. M., Marmot, M. G., Adelstein, A. M. *et al.* Diet and risk factors for coronary heart disease in Asians in North West London. *Lancet*, **ii**, 1086–1090 (1985)
6 Ruck, N. An individual dietary survey of school children in Birmingham. *Proc. Nutr. Soc.*, **33**, 17A (1974)
7 O'Hara-May, J. L. and Widdowson, E. Diets and living conditions of Asian boys in Coventry with and without signs of rickets. *Br. J. Nutr.*, **36**, 23 (1976)
8 Wenlock, R. W. and Buss, D. Nutritional quality of foods purchased by Asian families participating in the National Food Survey. *Proc. Nutr. Soc.*, **36**, 61A (1977)
9 Hunt, S. Traditional Asian food customs. *J. Hum. Nutr.*, **31**, 245–248 (1977).
10 Abraham, R., Campbell Brown, M., Haines, A. P. *et al.* Diet during pregnancy in an Asian community in Britain: energy, protein, zinc, copper, fibre and calcium. *Hum. Nutr. Appl. Nutr.*, **39a**, 23–35 (1985)
11 Campbell, D. M. Maternal energy intake in pregnancy and its relation to maternal and fetal factors. *Proc. Nutr. Soc.*, **41**, 30A (1982)
12 Smithells, R. W., Ankers, C., Carver, M. E. and Lerron, D. Maternal nutrition in early pregnancy. *Br. J. Nutr.*, **38**, 497–506 (1977)
13 Tuttle, S. *Trace Element Requirements During Pregnancy* (eds D. M. Campbell and M. O. G. Gillmer), Royal College of Obstetricians and Gynaecology, London, pp. 47–57 (1982)
14 Hytten, F. E. and Leitch, I. *The Physiology of Human Pregnancy*, 2nd edn, Blackwell Scientific Publications, Oxford, pp. 370–376 (1971)
15 Campbell-Brown, M. Zinc and copper in Asian pregnancies – is there evidence for a nutritional deficiency? *Br. J. Obstet. Gynaecol.*, **92**, 875–885 (1985)
16 Dunnigan, M. G., Glekin, B. M., Henderson, J. B. *et al.* Policy for prevention of Asian rickets in Britain: a preliminary assessment of the Glasgow rickets campaign. *Br. Med. J.*, **1**, 357–360 (1981)
17 Stephen, W. P., Klimink, P. S., Berry, J. L. and Mower, E. B. Annual high-dose vitamin D prophylaxis in Asian immigrants. *Lancet*, **ii**, 1199–1201 (1981)

Chapter 27

Diets and food habits in the Indian subcontinent

Rachel Abraham

The vastness of the Indian subcontinent with its regional variation in climate and culture has led to dietary practices as diverse as those in Europe. The religious groups have further modified the culinary traditions and successive foreign invasions have contributed to the dietary practices – Moghul cookery brought in excessive use of ghee, the Portugese introduced chillies and the British Raj left behind the 'white loaf'. This account is a brief sketch of some of the available data from India on nutritional issues relevant to Indians living abroad. Local sources in India can be contacted for further details.

Indian diets are cereal-based, determined by what is grown in the different regions. The cereal item is the primary food and other components of the meal like lentil, vegetable and meat curries are regarded as side-dishes. The side-dishes are served in small quantities and the number included varies with income. In poorer families just a chutney is used to flavour the cereal item and in higher income groups a few curries, dhal, yoghurt, and salad are served. This fundamental difference between cereal-based Indian diets and meat, fish and cheese-based western diets inevitably affects the nutrient content. The fibre content of diets of pregnant women in India was 14.4 g/1000 kcal when compared with 10.9 g/1000 kcal for their counterparts living in Harrow, UK [1].

Fat in the Indian diet is primarily as added fat, particularly in the middle and high income groups. Safflower, coconut, groundnut, sesame, rape/mustard oils are the main cooking oils. About half of the hydrogenated fat comes from groundnut oil; the rest is cottonseed or rice bran oil. Pooled dietary survey data [2] show that with an increase in income, fat intake increases, mostly as hydrogenated fat and ghee. This results in a reduction in linoleic acid intake except in Tamilnadu where sesame seed oil is used. The extensive use of hydrogenated fat, known as 'vegetable ghee', by the upper socioeconomic groups has been confirmed by Raheja [3]. Regional differences in cooking methods and preferences for certain oils affect the fat content of the diet and the fatty acid profile. The proportion of visible fat intake is consistent through all age-groups in any of the regions monitored by the National Nutrition Monitoring Bureau (NNMB) [4]. Also, the number of families unable to afford any added fat varies between regions, a finding unexplained by income differences. Similarly, strong regional preferences affect the fatty acid content of the diet. In Gujarat and Andhra Pradesh groundnut oil is used, while in Kerala and Bengal the oils of choice are coconut and mustard respectively. Between 5% and 28% of the fat is linoleic acid (Table 27.1). The saturated fatty acid intake is exceptionally high in Kerala and Gujarat.

Table 27.1 Nature of visible fat intake in India

	Total fat (g)	Fat intake (% by wt)			
		Linoleic	Oleic	Saturates	Remainder
Andhra Pradesh	14.1	25	50	20	5
Karnataka	9.5	31	39	29	1
Kerala	21.4	4	10	85	1
Tamil Nadu	10.3	28	48	23	1
Gujarat	44.3	8	34	53	5
Maharashtra	30.7	10	37	34	19
Calcutta City	25.7	13	24	16	47
Punjab	17.0	6	27	40	27

Modified from Achaya [2].

The dietary survey [5] of the NNMB monitored trends in food consumption. In the 1970s energy intake increased in India by about 400 kcal, mainly as cereal, and the gap between the rich and poor was narrowed. Pulse, milk, vegetable, fat, oil and sugar intake remain unchanged. The growth profile of preschool children assessed during this period, in terms of weight-for-age deficit, shows a slight reduction in malnutrition.

There appear to be no marked differences in energy intake in the different regions of India (Table 27.2) among men, but among women intakes in Kerala are considerably lower than energy intakes elsewhere in India. Anthropometric studies in India show that the prevalence of obesity is higher among women, particularly in the middle income groups. Where high and middle income groups are compared there is an inverse relationship between income and prevalence of obesity. The middle income groups, in addition, have a higher arm circumference and triceps skinfold thickness than the low income groups.

Comparisons of the diets of Gujarati women in Harrow, England and Gujarat show a higher fat with a lower carbohydrate and fibre content in the former group [1] (Table 27.3). This is either due to relative affluence or to substituting high fat foods from the host culture for traditional carbohydrate-rich ones. It is interesting that the diets of Asians in Harrow are similar to that of the Indians at 'high risk' of developing coronary disease described by Raheja [3]. Their higher intake of sucrose, refined cereals with meat, fish and dairy produce, is in sharp contrast to the diet of the low-risk group with unrefined cereal and large quantities of vegetables and pulses. The traditional Indian is not 'atherogenic' but there are evidently subgroups in the population in India and presumably among emigrants whose diets differ from the prudent one.

Finally, osteomalacia, the vitamin D deficiency state common among Indian-origin people (especially women) in Europe, has been reported in North India [8,9] with 20% of cases discovered during pregnancy. Most of those that present at outpatient clinics in Punjab [8] are women of reproductive age. Although the cause may be primarily dietary, the preponderance of females presenting with the disease suggests that other factors are important.

**Table 27.2 National Nutrition Monitoring
Bureau – intake of energy per day in sedentary adults**

| State | n | Calories (kcal) | |
		Mean	s.d.
Adult males (1975–78)			
Kerala	86	1846	754
Tamil Nadu	122	2123	713
Karnataka	243	2676	948
Andhra Pradesh	159	2060	712
Maharashtra	272	2088	948
Gujarat	217	2180	779
Madhya Pradesh	145	1854	596
West Bengal	118	2030	758
Uttar Pradesh	170	2220	995
Recommended levels		2400	
Adult females			
Kerala	255	1387	534
Tamil Nadu	184	1739	593
Karnataka	301	2333	892
Andhra Pradesh	226	1798	607
Maharashtra	296	1816	684
Gujarat	226	1748	645
Madhya Pradesh	143	1777	617
West Bengal	176	1595	543
Uttar Pradesh	297	1731	778
Recommended levels		1900	

Modified from National Nutrition Monitoring Bureau
1979 Report [10].

Table 27.3 Diets in pregnancy

	Harrow Indians (n = 8.13)	Indian Indians (n = 73)	Europeans (n = 54)
Contribution to total energy from fat sources (%)	43.5 ± 5.8	33.9 ± 14.9	39.7 ± 5.5
Contribution to total energy from CHO sources (%)	44.1 ± 8.2	53.9 ± 13.1	42.1 ± 7.5

Modified from Abraham [1] and other data of the author.

References

1 Abraham, R. Ethnic and religious aspects of diet. In *Nutrition in Pregnancy* (eds J. McFadyen and J. MacVicar), Royal College of Obstetricians and Gynaecologists, London, pp. 23–29 (1983)
2 Achaya, K. T. Visible and invisible fat consumption in India and the influence of region, income and age. Part III: Quality of the fat consumed. *Ind. J. Nutr. Dietet.*, **15**, 181–191 (1978)
3 Raheja, B. S. Indians, diet and heart disease (letter). *Lancet*, **i**, 228–229 (1988)
4 Achaya, K. T. Visible and invisible fat consumption in India, and the influence of region, income and age. Part I: Availability and consumption of visible fat. *Ind. J. Nutr. Dietet.*, **15**, 120–127 (1978)
5 Rao, N. P. and Sastry, J. G. Changes in diet and nutrition in ten states in India. *Nutr. News. India*, **7**, (2), 1–3 (1986)

6 Rao, K. V., Rau, P. and Thimmayamma, B. V. S. Nutritional anthropometry of Indian adults. *Ind. J. Nutr. Dietet.*, **23**, 239–256 (1988)
7 Sood, A. K., Kappil, U. and Gupta, M. C. Epidemiology of obesity in an urban community. *Ind. J. Nutr. Dietet.*, **22**, 42–48 (1985)
8 Vaishnava, H. P. and Bizvi, S. N. A. Osteomalacia in Northern India. *Br. Med. J.*, **1**, 112 (1967)
9 Vaishnava, H. P. and Bizvi, S. N. A. Nutritional osteomalacia in immigrants in an urban community, *Lancet*, **ii**, 1147–1148 (1971)
10 National Nutrition Monitoring Bureau 1979 Report, National Institute of Nutrition, Hyderabad (1979)

Chapter 28

Nutrition of Asian children: fetus and newborn

Pamela Wharton and Brian Wharton

This chapter describes the diet of women of Indian subcontinent origin (some via East Africa), 'Asians', who migrated to and become pregnant in Britain. It discusses the nutritional problems which occur during pregnancy and in the neonatal period.

Food customs of pregnant mothers

The food customs and choices of mothers from the Indian subcontinent who live in Birmingham, England are undoubtedly strongly influenced by religion (Table 28.1). Hindus avoid beef and Muslims avoid pork. Fasting also has an effect on food intake. Many Muslim women fast throughout Ramadan; although they are allowed to postpone their fast many prefer to fast with the rest of the family.

In our Birmingham survey, main meals were generally curry – of meat, fish, pulse or vegetable – eaten with a staple, wheat or maize chappati, or rice. The traditional pattern for main meals was maintained, even by people living in Britain for many years. Breakfasts were, however, more Westernized. Cornflakes and eggs were as popular as Asian foods like paratha or punjeri (a traditional food for pregnant women, made from flour, sugar, almonds and ghee) [1].

The variety of foods depends to a large extent on who does the family shopping. In Muslim households this is mostly carried out by the men, often bulk purchasing items such as flour, potatoes and onions. They tend to choose familiar foods like imported vegetables. Hindu and Sikh women are more free to go out, do their own shopping and consequently choose a wider range of foods such as fish-fingers and beef-burgers. They were also more likely to try English vegetables such as sprouts.

Hearths in many Muslim villages consist of stones supporting a large cooking pot, with a wood fire underneath. There would usually be three hearths, one for rice, one for stew, and a third for cooking the bread. Many Asian mothers in England use only the rings on top of a gas stove, corresponding with the hearths. The oven often becomes a useful store cupboard.

Nutrient intakes

Nutrient intakes during pregnancy (Table 28.2) show that Sikh women generally eat a greater variety of foods, and the highest intakes of most nutrients, although few of them eat meat. The Hindus eat more meat, fish and chicken than the Sikhs,

Table 28.1 Food customs of mothers from the Indian subcontinent living in Birmingham by geographical area of origin

	Pakistan	Bangladesh	India: Punjab	Gujarat
Religion	Islam		Sikhism	Hinduism
Fasting	Ramadhan: sunrise to sunset one lunar month		Variable	Birthdays of deities up to 3 days per week
Foods to be avoided	Pork, non 'halal' meat and meat products Alcohol		A matter of personal choice but sometimes abstention from alcohol and beef	Beef, often all meat is excluded by choice. Sometimes fish, often eggs for women
Diet				
Staple	Wheat as chapati or paratha	Rice – generally polished	Wheat sometimes maize flour as chapati paratha or puri	Wheat maize or millet flour as chapati paratha or puri
Main dish	Predominantly lamb or chicken, some beef or goat, sometimes vegetables, occasionally liver	Fish including shellfish, or chicken or lamb, less frequently offal	Predominantly lamb, chicken or vegetable, sometimes kidneys, pork or fish	Predominantly vegetables, meat less frequently, chicken, goat or lamb, and fish
Pulses	Dahl, often with spinach, occasional use of grain flour	Occasionally	Dahl eaten regularly	Pulse mixtures
			More general use of grain flour	
Fats used	Butter or ghee		Butter oil or margarine	Ghee or oil, occasionally margarine
Vegetables				
Potato	Occasionally		Often	Often
English roots	Less frequently			Turnip, swede, parsnips used often
Others	Aubergine, okra and tropical vegetables popular and much used by all groups. Cauliflower, carrots, peas, acceptable to all groups. Cabbage and sprouts used less frequently, more popular with Sikhs and Hindus			
Fruit	Fresh fruit – apples, oranges, bananas, grapes and dates are popular			

Modified from Wharton et al. [1]

Table 28.2 Mean daily intakes of energy and nutrients during pregnancy by ethnic subgroups of Asian women

	Pakistani Muslims (n = 90)	Sikhs (n = 36)	Hindu (n = 29)	Bangladeshi Muslims (n = 10)	RDA
Energy (kcal)	1589	1800	1790	1555	2400[*]
Energy (MJ)	6.7	7.1	7.5	6.6	
Protein (g)	56	53	60	59	60[*]
Fat (g)	59	60	72	52	
Carbohydrate (g)	221	253	240	227	
Dietary fibre (g)	17	21	16	12	
Sodium (g)	1.7	2.1	1.8	1.7	1.1[‡]
Potassium (g)	1.9	2.3	2.1	1.4	1.87[‡]
Calcium (mg)	791	912	812	496	500[†fl]
Magnesium (mg)	232	256	220	143	450[†]
Phosphorus (mg)	976	1013	1017	874	1200[†]
Iron (mg)	11	12	10	9	13[*]
Copper (mg)	1.1	1.2	1.1	0.7	2[‡]
Zinc (mg)	7.3	6.4	7.2	6.7	20[†]
Retinol (µg)	320	455	368	280	750RE
Carotene (µg)	1042	1789	1877	249	
Vitamin D (µg)	0.9	0.98	1.3	1.51	10[*]
Thiamin (g)	1.07	1.21	0.97	0.51	1[*]
Riboflavine (g)	1.15	1.39	1.28	0.91	1.6[*]
Nicotinic acid (mg)	9.5	10	10	6.17	18NE[*]
Tryptophane-60 (mg)	12	11	12	12	
Vitamin C (mg)	48	45	49	16	60[*]
Vitamin B$_6$ (mg)	1.02	1	1	0.7	2.6[†]
Vitamin B$_{12}$ (µg)	2.2	2.07	2.17	3.55	4[†]
Folic acid total (µg)	116	130	114	87	500[*§]

Modified from: Wharton et al. [2]. Combined recall results from 18 to 33 weeks of pregnancy.
RDA, recommended daily amounts
RE, retinol equivalents (1 retinol equivalent = 1 µg retinol or 6 µg carotene or 12 µg other biologically active carotenoids).
NE, nicotinic acid equivalents (1 nicotinic acid equivalent = 1 mg available nicotinic acid or 60 mg tryptophan).
[*] RDA for food energy and nutrients for groups of people in the UK for women aged 18–54 years plus extra for pregnancy [27].
[†] RDA in the USA for women aged 23–50 years plus extra for pregnancy [28].
[‡] USA minimum value quoted for 'estimated safe and adequate daily dietary intake for non-pregnant adults [28].
[fl] RDA for second trimester, increases to 1200 in 3rd trimester.
[§] See Eaton, Wharton and Wharton [18] concerning accuracy of folate in food tables.

and more rice. The Muslims had lower energy intakes. The Bangladeshis eat only rice, not paratha or chappati, and had lower intakes of fruit and vegetables [2]. Figure 28.1 shows the contribution of energy from protein, fat and carbohydrate in each of the four groups. Interestingly, the diet of the Bangladeshis, although low in energy, is close to recent guidelines proposed for British diets [3,4]. The energy content of all the diets is low.

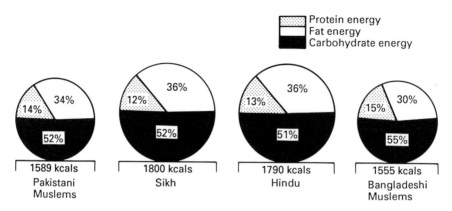

Figure 28.1 Daily energy intake: contribution from proximates. Combined recall results from 18 to 33 weeks of pregnancy; adapted from Wharton *et al.* [2]

Vitamin D intakes were very low, and many of these women did not expose themselves to sunshine. This supports the DHSS policy of offering vitamin D supplements to all pregnant women of Indian subcontinent origin.

The intake of many other nutrients was below the recommended daily amounts (RDA) in all the ethnic subgroups; intakes of zinc and pyridoxine cause concern since it has been suggested that low intakes of these nutrients may cause poor fetal growth [5,6].

Nutritional problems

Congenital malformations

Congenital malformations seem to be more common in Asian communities in this country than in Europeans. Genetic factors including consanguinity may play a role [7]. It is uncertain to what extent malnutrition may also be responsible for congenital malformations among Asians or among any ethnic groups, but deficiencies of folic acid [8,9] and zinc [10–12] have been implicated, and are now the subject of an MRC trial.

Intrauterine growth

Our Birmingham studies have led us to the following conclusion. The babies of Asian mothers are lighter than those of European mothers of similar height and parity [13], and they have anthropometric and biochemical evidence of pathological growth failure [14,15]. This is unlikely to be genetic, since in the past decade there has been a secular increase in the birthweight of Pakistani babies. Furthermore, although parental consanguinity is associated with an increase in the number of poorly grown babies, overall the effect on mean birthweight is small [16]. The secular increase in birthweight is most probably explained by environmental factors [17]. Three pieces of evidence suggest that undernutrition was one of those factors: first, food customs and low nutrient intakes suggest that some mothers could experience nutritional stress [18,19]; secondly, mothers laying down insufficient fat stores in the second trimester (i.e. showing no increase in triceps skinfold thickness in that period) had poorly grown babies [19,20]; thirdly, mothers with that evidence of compromised energy balance benefitted from a protein energy supplement and gave birth to heavier babies [21], whereas mothers who had put on sufficient fat did not benefit [22,23]; indeed there may have been an adverse affect.

Late neonatal hypocalcaemia

Convulsions due to neonatal hypocalcaemia occur where the mother has a poor vitamin D or calcium status and this condition is much more likely to occur in babies of Asian mothers. There have been three recent studies of the effect of vitamin D supplementation in Asian mothers in Britain [24–26]. Supplemented mothers had higher concentrations of plasma vitamin D and in one study gained more weight. Their babies had significantly higher plasma calcium concentrations and grew better in the first year. Symptomatic hypocalcaemis did not occur and dental enamel hypoplasia was much less common than in babies in unsupplemented mothers.

Acknowledgements

It is a pleasure to acknowledge the contribution of colleagues who have joined us in various papers quoted: [1,2,13,14,16–22]. We are grateful also to Miss Snow of the Department of Medical Illustration, Birmingham Children's Hospital.

References

1 Wharton, P. A., Eaton, P. M. and Day, K. C. Sorrento Asian food tables; food tables, recipes and customs of mothers attending Sorrento Maternity Hospital, Birmingham, England. *Hum. Nutr. Appl. Nutr.*, **37A**, 378–402 (1983)

2 Wharton, P. A., Eaton, P. M. and Wharton, B. A. Subethnic variation in the diets of Moslem, Sikh and Hindu pregnant women at Sorrento Maternity Hospital, Birmingham. *Br. J. Nutr.*, **52**, 469–476 (1984)

3 Department of Health and Social Security. *Report on Health and Social Subjects No. 28. Diet and Cardiovascular Disease*, HMSO, London (1984)

4 National Advisory Committee on Nutrition Education. A Discussion Paper on Proposals for Nutritional Guidelines for Health Education in Britain, Health Education Council, London (1983)

5 Meadows, N. J., Ruse, W., Smith, M. F. *et al.* Deficiency of zinc implicated in poor fetal growth. *Lancet*, **ii**, 1135 (1981)

6 Reinken, L. and Dapunt, O. Vitamin B_6 nutriture during pregnancy. *Int. J. Vit. Nutr. Res.*, **48**, 341–347 (1978)

7 Terry, P. B., Bissenden, J. G., Condie, R. G. *et al.* Ethnic differences in congenital malformations. *Arch. Dis. Child.*, **60**, 866–868 (1985)

8 Smithells, R. W., Shepherd, S., Schorah, C. J. *et al.* Apparent prevention of neural tube defects by periconceptional vitamin supplementation. *Lancet*, **i**, 339–340 (1980)

9 Laurence, K. M., James, N., Miller, M. H. *et al.* Double blind randomised controlled trial of folate treatment before conception to prevent recurrence of neural-tube defects. *Br. Med. J.*, **282**, 1509–1511 (1981)

10 Hambridge, K. M., Neldner, K. H. and Walravens, P. A. Zinc, acrodermatitis enteropathica and congenital malformations. *Lancet*, **i**, 577–578 (1975)

11 Brenton, D. M., Jackson, M. J. and Young, A. Two pregnancies in a patient with acrodermatitis enteropathica treated with zinc sulphate. *Lancet*, **ii**, 500–502 (1981)

12 Jameson, S. Variations in maternal zinc during pregnancy and correlations to congenital malformations, dysmaturity and abnormal parturition. *Acta. Med. Scand., Suppl.*, **593**, 21–37 (1976)

13 Wharton, B. A., Smalley, C., Millns, C. *et al*. The Asian mother and her baby at Sorrento. In *Topics in Perinatal Medicine* (ed. B. A. Wharton), Pitman Medical, Kent, pp. 141–151 (1980)

14 Fosbrooke, A. and Wharton, B. A. Plasma lipids in umbilical cord blood from infants of normal and low birth weight. *Biol. Neonate*, **23**, 330–338 (1973)

15 Wharton, B. A. Food growth and the Asian fetus. In *Obstetric Problems of the Asian Community in Britain* (eds J. McVicar and I. McFadyen), Royal College of Obstetrics and Gynaecology, London (1982)

16 Honeyman, M. M., Bahl, L., Marshall, T and Wharton, B. A. Consanguinity and fetal growth in Pakistani Moslems. *Arch. Dis. Child.*, **62**, 231–235 (1987)

17 Clarson, C. L., Barker, M. J., Marshall, M. and Wharton, B. A. Secular change in birth weight of Asian babies born in Birmingham. *Arch. Dis. Child.*, **57**, 867–871 (1982)

18 Eaton, P. M., Wharton, P. A. and Wharton, B. A. Nutrient intake of pregnant Asian women at Sorrento Maternity Hospital, Birmingham. *Br. J. Nutr.*, **52**, 457–468 (1984)

19 Bissenden, J. G., Scott, P. H., King, J. *et al*. Anthropometric and biochemical changes during pregnancy in Asian and European mothers having light for gestational age babies. *Br. J. Obstet. Gynaecol.*, **88**, 999–1008 (1981)

20 Bissenden, J. G., Scott, P. H., Hallum, J. *et al*. Anthropometric and biochemical changes during pregnancy in Asian and European mothers having well grown babies. *Br. J. Obstet. Gynaecol.*, **88**, 992–998 (1981)

21 Viegas, O. A. Ç., Scott, P. H., Cole, T. J. *et al*. Dietary protein energy supplementation of pregnant Asian mothers at Sorrento, Birmingham. II: Selective during third trimester only. *Br. Med. J.*, **285**, 592–595 (1982)

22 Viegas, O. A. C., Scott, P. H., Cole, T. J. *et al*. Dietary protein energy supplementation of pregnant Asian mothers at Sorrento, Birmingham. I: Unselective during second and third trimesters. *Br. Med. J.*, **285**, 589–592 (1982)

23 Wharton, B. A. Sorrento studies of birthweight. In Perinatal Growth: the quest for an international standard for reference (eds. B. Wharton and P. M. Dunn). *Acta Paediatr. Scand. [Suppl.]*, 319 (1985)

24 Brooke, O. G., Brown, I. R. F., Bond, C. D. M. *et al*. Vitamin D supplements in pregnant Asian women: effects on calcium status and fetal growth. *Br. Med. J.*, **280**, 751–754 (1980)

25 Cockburn, F., Belton, N. R., Purvis, R. J. *et al*. Maternal vitamin D intake and mineral metabolism in mothers and their newborn infants. *Br. Med. J.*, **281**, 11–14 (1980)

26 Heckmatt, J. Z., Davies, A. E. J., Peacock, M. *et al*. Plasma 25 hydroxyvitamin D in pregnant Asian women and their babies. *Lancet*, **ii**, 546–548 (1979)

27 Department of Health and Social Security. *Report on Health and Social Subjects No. 15. Recommended Daily Amounts of Food Energy and Nutrients for Groups of People in the United Kingdom*, HMSO, London (1979)

28 National Research Council. *Food and Nutrition Board Recommended Dietary Allowances*, 9th edn, National Academy of Sciences, Washington DC (1980)

Chapter 29

Nutrition of Asian children: infants and toddlers

Anne Aukett and Brian Wharton

Introduction

A wealth of information has recently been published on the medical and nutritional problems of children of Asian origin [1–8]. The nutritional state of the toddler and infant may well depend on the nutrition of the mother during pregnancy and lactation (see Chapter 28) [9,10] and many of their problems are also common to schoolchildren.

Patterns of infant feeding

Despite earlier reports that 'the Asian mother' adapted quickly to British infant feeding practices it later became clear that many children were fed inadequately. Probably practices were adopted which either were not fully understood or were not followed closely [3–5,11,12].

Breast and bottle

Many Asian mothers do not feed colostrum believing it to be harmful to the baby or not to be milk [8,13]. They may give sugar and water at first and start breast-feeding on the second or third day.

Many studies (Table 29.1) indicate that the majority of babies were breast-fed only for a very short time or not at all, in contrast to the feeding patterns of their previous babies born in India or elsewhere. The availability of an alternative to human milk may be the most important factor but wrong information and misconceptions about British infant feeding practices are also important. Over the last decade although the overall rate of breast-feeding in the British population has increased this has occurred much less in lower income groups and the low frequency of breast-feeding in the Asian groups may only reflect lower socioeconomic status. The general increase in breast-feeding is in part due to the increased promotional activity by health-care staff and the media, which may not have reached Asian mothers to the same extent because of language difficulties or lesser use of health-care services.

Table 29.1 Prevalence of breast-feeding

Centre	Group origin	Date of study	Age of children studied	Breastfeeding (%)		Notes/references
Bradford	Pakistani/Punjabi Muslims	1965–66	0–18 months	Birth	81	[1]
				1 week	64	
				3 months	17	
				1 year	0	
Birmingham (Sorrento)	All (Muslims, Hindus, Sikhs and Bangladeshi)	1973		6 days	26	[10] of 28% Europeans in same hospital
Glasgow	Punjabi (N India and W Pakistan) Muslims, Hindus and Sikhs	1974–76	UK born Asian born	Birth Birth	20.9 83.7 } 34%	[5]
				6 months	23	
				3 years	Some	
Wolverhampton	Rural Punjab Rural India	1976*	UK born	Birth	4	[3] of 42% previous sibs born in Asia
				10 weeks	0	
Hackney	Indian and Pakistani	1976–77	0–5 years		39 (most stopped by 2 months)	[11] of 100% breast-feeding in Asia [6]
Southall	Mostly Sikhs (Punjab)	1977		< 2 weeks	45	
				2 weeks	26	
				2 months	13	
				3 months	11	
				> 6 months	5	
Tower Hamlets	Bangladeshi	1983*		At birth	95	[12] 3 children still breast-fed at 2 years
				1 month	52	
				3 months	35	
				1 year	10	
National UK Sample		1975*		At birth	51	[35]
				6 weeks	12	
				4 months	1	
		1980*		At birth	67	[15]
				6 weeks	28	
				4 months	14	

* Date of publication

Table 29.2 Introduction of solid foods (weaning foods)

Centre	Group	Date of study	Age of children	Children on solids (%)	Notes/references
Bradford	Pakistani/Punjabi Muslims	1965–66	1–3 months	'most'	[1] Farex or Farene 50% on egg at 3 months
Glasgow	Punjabi (Muslims, Hindus and Sikhs)	1974–6	UK born 3 months	56.5	[5] 15% of all studied did not receive solids until after 1 year
			Asian born 3 months	4.7	
			UK born 6 months	88	
			Asian born 6 months	23.3	
			UK born 1 year	91.5	
			Asian born 1 year	32.6	
Wolverhampton	Rural Punjab/India	1976*	Mean age of introduction 11 weeks (6–29)		[3] of 31 weeks for previous sibs Asian born
Hackney Southall	Indian/Pakistani Punjabi (mostly Sikhs)	1976–77 1977	Later weaning i.e. after 2 months		[11] [6]
			<3 months	11	
			3 months	36	
			4 months	72	
			5 months	94	
			>6 months	100	
Tower Hamlets	Bangladeshi	1983*	2 months to 2 years	1 child only	[12] Later weaning if shorter time in UK
			3 months	51	
			6 months		
			1 year	92	
Birmingham	Muslims, Sikhs, and Hindus	1983	Mean age of introduction 23–25 weeks		[16]
National UK Sample	All races	1975*	1 month	18	[35]
			3 months	85	
			4 months	97	
		1980*	3 months	55	[15]
			4 months	89	

* Date of publication

Introduction to solids (Table 29.2)

Experience in Birmingham has shown that solids are introduced late and are often first added to cow's milk in the bottle. We agree with Jivani [4] that more difficulties are experienced in weaning Asian children than Europeans. This may be because the intermediate stage between milk and adult food involving cereals and 'junior dinners' is unfamiliar. However, the process of weaning in the Indian subcontinent, and indeed in all developing countries, is fraught with problems and danger.

Types of solids used

It is in this that Asian children differ most markedly from their European counterparts and with considerable differences between the ethnic subgroups. Many mothers stick to 'egg custard and rice', baby biscuits and other predominantly sweet foods whereas most European mothers will introduce savoury foods too. Muslim mothers will not use savoury foods because the meat they contain is not halal.

   To strict vegetarians some animal protein such as meat, fish and eggs may not be acceptable. Parents may not be able to read the contents on the labels of baby foods and hence stick to the ones they know do not contain animal produce, these are mainly the puddings. The sweet convenience foods are low in protein and iron and are often not fortified with vitamins. The child does not get used to its natural diet either; although mothers should be encouraged to give the family diet mashed up, this is not the usual practice in the Asian community [14]. Very few Bangladeshi children eat family foods by 1 year [12], but some 91% do by 2–3 years; many of these children receive only very small amounts, and convenience, mainly carbohydrate, foods remain the major constituent of the diet.

Use of cow's milk

The age of introduction of cow's milk is shown in Table 29.3. Apart from the Bangladeshis, in whom prolonged breast-feeding is the norm, most Asian families change from an infant formula to 'doorstep' milk at about 5–6 months. This is contrary to present DHSS recommendations [15] but probably very similar to European children in the same socioeconomic group. Milk provides the major part of the Asian child's diet for much longer than their European counterparts. Doorstep milk contains little iron and vitamin D.

   In our experience Asian children remain 'on the bottle' for much longer than European children, often well into the second or third year, but take other drinks such as 'pop' from cups. This reluctance to 'wean' from the bottle may well be rooted in the practice of prolonged breast-feeding which would have been the norm in their country of origin, suckling at the bottle being a 'Western' adaptation of this.

Vitamins

It is currently recommended that all children receive vitamin supplementation up to at least the second birthday and preferably until the age of 5 unless the professional adviser is confident the child receives an adequate supply from other sources. Vitamin supplements are particularly important for low birthweight infants, those

Table 29.3 Use of cow's milk

Centre	Group	Date of study	Age of children	Children on cow's milk (%)	Notes/references
Bradford	Pakistani/Punjabi Muslims	1965–66	0–18 months	9	Of those not breast-fed [1]
Wolver-hampton	Rural Punjabi/Indian	1976[*]	6 months	39	
			14 months	96	[3]
Southall	Mostly Sikhs Punjabi	1977	6 months	46	
			1 year	100	[6]
Tower Hamlets	Bangladeshi	1983[*]	6 months	7.7	[12]
			1 year	77	If not breast-fed cow's milk introduced later
Birmingham	Muslims, Sikhs and Hindus	1983	Mean age of introduction	27–31 weeks	[16]

[*] Or date of publication

who receive household milk, Asian children and those for whom other sources of vitamin D are in doubt [15]. The use of vitamin supplements among young Asians has been reported to vary between 41% and 87% [3,5,6,12]. However, these may be overestimates as in one study many mothers who said they were giving supplements did not actually have any in the house [6], and in another it was seen that many bottles remained unopened [12].

Specific nutritional problems

Growth faltering

Some children are undernourished and many show a faltering of growth around the time of weaning [4]. In the Tower Hamlets study [12] there was also a slight reduction in mean growth between 1 and 3 years.

If solids are not introduced by 9 months there may be increased difficulties in establishing full mixed feeding. The combination of late weaning and high carbohydrate intake (from mainly sweet foods) can also lead to obesity and a relatively low protein intake. The poor growth between 6 months and 2 years due to inadequate nutrition in the weaning period resembles the pattern found in malnourished children in developing countries and not the growth pattern of a genetically small race growing to its full potential. Small stature is a common cause of parental concern especially among the Bengalis [8]. However, in many cases the parents are small and the child is growing at a normal rate. These children can be easily differentiated from those failing to thrive by serial measurements. Special centile charts are not required as it is the pattern of growth and weight gain that is important; deviation from the centile lines can be seen quite well on standard charts.

Rickets

Many studies have shown an increased incidence of both florid and subclinical rickets in Asian children [6,16–21] (for details see Chapter 25). It has been suggested that this problem is decreasing and will slowly disappear when immigrants adapt to British conditions, as concluded in the DHSS report of 1980 [22]. Suggested methods of prevention include:

1. Increasing exposure to sunlight. The traditional beliefs of Purdah are not easily overcome and supplementation may provide just as much vitamin D as a British summer [16].
2. The fortification of chapati flour [6,23] and 'doorstep' cow's milk to the levels currently applied in the USA would meet the daily requirements of most children.
3. Use of fortified formulas up to 1 year and ideally beyond would provide a 'safety net'.
4. Encouraging the use of vitamin supplements: five drops of DHSS children's drops given daily from 1 month to 5 years would provide the daily requirements of vitamin D.
5. Modification of the Asian diet, e.g. replacing ghee with fortified margarine, using eggs in curry and vitamin D-rich oily fish.

In an attempt to reduce the incidence of rickets in the Asian community there have been several campaigns. The Scottish campaign was launched in 1979 and was based on the issue of vitamin D supplements on demand to children up to 18 years. There was considerable reduction in the prevalence of rickets in the postcampaign survey in 1981–82 compared with the precampaign surveys in 1978–79 [24]. A health education campaign in Rochdale [25] aiming to improve the vitamin status of Asians by encouraging dietary change did not significantly alter the consumption of vitamin D over a 10-year period. In 1981 the 'Stop Rickets Campaign' was launched by the Save the Children Fund and the DHSS [26]. This was a health education campaign concentrating on giving information about rickets and its prevention to the Asian community. Its evaluation suggests an overall increase in the knowledge of rickets as a result of the campaign but there are no data concerning the uptake of vitamin D drops. However, as a recent paper reported vitamin D levels to be low in 40% of Asian toddlers in an area of Birmingham where the campaign had been launched, there is still considerable scope for improvement [16].

Iron deficiency

The incidence of iron deficiency in Asian children varies between 26% and 40% depending on age in Birmingham [16,27], Bradford [28] and Glasgow [29]. The mechanisms are multifactorial:

1. Maternal iron deficiency in pregnancy, preterm delivery and low birthweight.
2. Lack of breast-feeding or prolonged breast-feeding.
3. Early introduction and excessive intake of unfortified cow's milk containing little iron.
4. Possible irritation of the GI tract mucosa by cow's milk leading to small daily blood losses [30].
5. Limited use of fortified baby foods and the late introduction of solids.

6. A diet consisting of few iron-containing natural foods.
7. Poor economic circumstances.

The importance of iron deficiency has recently been highlighted [31] and in particular the non-haematological consequences. Several studies have shown that anaemic children tend to have delayed development which improves when iron is given [32]. In our study [27] anaemic children, who were predominantly Asian, grew faster and more of them developed at a normal rate when they were given iron. In the USA the Women, Infants and Children Program of supplementary feeding has reduced the incidence of childhood iron deficiency [33] and some have advocated a similar programme in this country.

Conclusions

In spite of considerable interest and promotional activity in the past 10–15 years the nutritional status of Asian infants and toddlers remains poor; as many as 40% may be anaemic and 40% may be vitamin D deficient; so what of the future?

There have been several interesting innovations in care, for example, the 'Asian Mother and her Baby Campaign' launched by the Save the Children Fund and the DHSS. Pioneered in Hackney [34] this may point the way forward by involving more Asian women in health promotion. The aim is to improve attendance at antenatal clinics and encourage breast-feeding. Dietary traditions are extremely strong and advice given by health visitors may have little impact if they have no knowledge of these traditions. Rather than asking the mothers to change to 'English' foods they should be encouraged to modify their own foods to improve the nutritional content. Pictorial charts on weaning which health visitors can use would be useful as many mothers do not speak or read English.

Use of infant formulas well into the second year of life would help, as would combined prophylaxis with iron and vitamin D for the Asian baby and toddler. Child health services should be sensitive to the problems and routine child health surveillance in areas with large Asian populations should include a haemoglobin estimation.

A team approach to nutritional problems of the Asian child is needed which is both nutritionally sound and culturally sensitive. This must involve the child's parents and the Asian community as well as the health visitor, the nutritionist, and the doctor.

References

1 Aykroyd, W. R. and Hossain, M. A. Diet and state of nutrition of Pakistani infants in Bradford, Yorkshire. *Br. Med. J.*, **1**, 42–45 (1967)
2 Stroud, C. E. Nutrition and the immigrant. *Br. Med. J. Hosp. Med.*, **5**, 629–634 (1971)
3 Evans, N., Walpole, J. R., Qureshi, M. U. *et al*. Lack of breast feeding and early weaning in infants of Asian immigrants to Wolverhampton. *Arch. Dis. Child.*, **51**, 608–612 (1976)
4 Jivani, S. K. M. The practice of infant feeding among Asian immigrants. *Arch. Dis. Child.*, **53**, 69–73 (1978)
5 Goel, K. M., House, F. and Shanks, R. A. Infant feeding practices among immigrants in Glasgow. *Br. Med. J.*, **2**, 1181–1183 (1978)
6 Singleton, N. and Tucker, S. M. Vitamin D status of Asian infants. *Br. Med. J.*, **1**, 607–610 (1978)

7 Black, J. Paediatrics among ethnic minorities. Asian families I: cultures. *Br. Med. J.*, **290**, 762–764 (1984)
8 Black, J. Paediatrics among ethnic minorities. Asian families II: conditions that may be found in the children. *Br. Med. J.*, **290**, 830–833 (1984)
9 Brooke, O. G., Butters, F. and Wood, C. Intrauterine vitamin D nutrition and post natal growth in Asian infants. *Br. Med. J.*, **283**, 1024 (1981)
10 Wharton, B. A., Smalley, C., Millns, C. *et al*. The Asian mother and her baby at Sorrento. In *Topics in Perinatal Medicine* (ed. B. A. Wharton), Pitman Medical, London, pp. 141–151 (1980)
11 Marks, J. Infant feeding across culture. *Health Visitor*, **52**, 271–274 (1979)
12 Harris, R. J., Armstrong, D., Al, R. and Loynes, A. Nutritional survey of Bangladeshi children aged under 5 years in the London borough of Tower Hamlets. *Arch. Dis. Child.*, **58**, 428–432 (1983)
13 Lee, E. Asian infant feeding. *Nursing Mirror*, **160**, (21), S14–S15 (1985)
14 Dawar, A. Food for thought in work with immigrants. *Nursing Mirror*, **149**, (16) 27–30 (1979)
15 Oppe, T. E., Arneil, G. C., Davies, D. P. *et al*. *Present Day Practice in Infant Feeding. Report on Health and Social Subjects No. 20*, HMSO, London (1980)
16 Grindulis, H., Scott, P. H., Belton, N. R. and Wharton, B. A. Combined deficiency of iron and vitamin D in Asian toddlers. *Arch. Dis. Child.*, **61**, 843–848 (1986)
17 Arneil, G. C. and Crosbie, J. C. Infantile rickets returns to Glasgow. *Lancet*, **ii**, 423–425 (1963)
18 Ford, J. A., Colhoun, E. M., McIntosh, W. B. and Dunnigan, M. G. Rickets and osteomalacia in the Glasgow Pakistani community, 1961–71. *Br. Med. J.*, **2**, 677–680 (1972)
19 Dawson, K. P. and Mondhe, M. S. Nutritional rickets among the immigrant population of Bradford. *Practitioner*, **208**, 789–791 (1972)
20 Ford, J. A., McIntosh, W. B., Butterfield, R. *et al*. Clinical and subclinical vitamin D deficiency in Bradford children. *Arch. Dis. Child.*, **51**, 939–943 (1976)
21 Goel, K. M., Sweet, E. M., Logan, R. W. *et al*. Florid and subclinical rickets among immigrant children in Glasgow. *Lancet*, **i**, 1141–1145 (1976)
22 Widdowson, E. M., Elton, G. A., Exton-Smith, A. *et al*. *Rickets and Osteomalacia. Report on Health and Social Subjects No. 19*, HMSO, London, (1980)
23 Pietrek, J., Preece, M. A., Windo, J. *et al*. Prevention of vitamin D deficiency in Asians. *Lancet*, **ii**, 1145–1148 (1976)
24 Dunnigan, M. G., Glekin, B. M., Henderson, J. B. *et al*. Prevention of rickets in Asian children: assessment of the Glasgow campaign. *Br. Med. J.*, **291**, 239–242 (1985)
25 Stephens, W. P., Klimiuk, P. S., Warrington, S. and Taylor, J. L. Observations on the dietary practices of Asians in the United Kingdom. *Hum. Nutr. Appl. Nutr.*, **36A**, 438–444 (1982)
26 Save the Children Fund. *Stop Rickets Campaign*, Save the Children Fund, London (1983)
27 Aukett, M. A., Parks, Y. A., Scott, P. H. and Wharton, B. A. Treatment with iron increases weight gain and psychomotor development. *Arch. Dis. Child.*, **61**, 849–857 (1986)
28 Ehrhardt, P. Iron deficiency in young Bradford children from different ethnic groups. *Br. Med. J.*, **292**, 90–93 (1986)
29 Goel, K. M., Logan, R. W., House, F. *et al*. The prevalence of haemoglobinopathies, nutritional iron and folate deficiencies in native and immigrant children in Glasgow. *Health Bull. (Edinb.)*, **36**, 176–183 (1978)
30 Wilson, J. F., Lahey, M. E. and Heiner, D. C. Studies on iron metabolism: V. Further observations on cows milk-induced gastrointestinal bleeding in infants with iron deficiency anaemia. *J. Pediatr.*, **84**, 335–344 (1974)
31 Addy, D. P. Happiness is iron. *Br. Med. J.*, **292**, 969–970 (1986)
32 Oski, F. A. Iron deficiency – facts and fallacies. *Pediatr. Clin. North Am.*, **32**, 493–497 (1985)
33 Dallman, P. R. Iron deficiency in the weanling: a nutritional problem on the way to resolution. In *Food for the Weanling* (ed. B. A. Wharton). *Acta. Pediatr. Scand. [Suppl.]*, **323**, 59–66 (1986)
34 Winkler, F. and Yung, J. Advising Asian mothers. *Health Soc. Serv. J.*, **91**, 1244–1245 (1981)
35 Oppe, T. E., Arneil, G. C., Creery, R. D. G. *et al*. *Present Day Practice in Infant Feeding. Report on Health and Social Subjects No. 9*, HMSO, London (1974)

Chapter 30

Food type preferences and trends among Afro-Caribbeans in Britain

Jenny Douglas

Introduction

Despite a long-established Afro-Caribbean population in Britain, there have been few reports about the dietary preferences and practices of this community. A primary concern is the extent to which these, and overall nutritional status, have been affected by migration. This chapter reviews available information on Afro-Caribbean diets in Britain and reports recent research among Afro-Caribbean mothers and infants in Birmingham.

An early (1964) study of food habits among Afro-Caribbean people in London showed that families were consuming mainly Caribbean foods and dishes even in those families who had lived in Britain for over 5 years [1]. Although some English foods had been adopted these were mostly snacks or subsidiary meals such as breakfast. Later articles concentrated on the nutritional status of Afro-Caribbean children, described iron-deficiency anaemia [2]. Further research conducted in London found that malnutrition was not a feature although there was some tendency towards iron-deficiency anaemia. It was postulated to have been related to different infant feeding patterns of Afro-Caribbean children, more likely to have been breast-fed than their local white counterparts who were fed with commercial preparations of cow's milk fortified with iron.

Isolated reports of malnutrition appeared in the 1980s, including four cases of rickets in Afro-Caribbean children born in the UK of Rastafarian parents and similar cases in Canada [3,4]. At the same time reports appeared of megoblastic anaemia caused by vitamin B_{12} deficiency in Rastafarians in Jamaica [5,6]. Springer and Thomas [7] also suggested that infant feeding practices may cause malnutrition in the children of Rastafarians in Britain.

Present dietary practices of Afro-Caribbeans in the UK

A research survey established in 1983 by the Department of Social Medicine, Birmingham University and Training in Health and Race collected data on food consumption and infant feeding practices of Afro-Caribbeans in Birmingham [8,9]. The main aim was to provide reliable data on the dietary practices and to determine the risk of nutritional deficiencies. The sampling frame consisted of infants born to Afro-Caribbean women in Birmingham during specified weeks. From four samples, a total of 131 mothers aged 18–41 years were interviewed between 3 and

Table 30.1 Characteristics of Afro-Caribbean infants in Birmingham

Sample number	Age of infant at interview (months)	Infants in initial sample (no.)	Mothers interviewed (no.)	Gender of infant of mothers interviewed	
				Male	Female
1	14–26	31	29	18	11
2	22–29	29	24	13	11
3	36–80	68	56	32	24
4	22–29	30	22	13	9
Total		158	131	76	55

Modified from Kemm *et al.* [8,9].

15 months after the birth (Table 30.1). A structured interview obtained information on breast-feeding, weaning practice, sources of information about infant feeding, socioeconomic and demographic information from all mothers. Data on household food consumption patterns were obtained from 102 mothers (samples 2, 3 and 4) and food diaries were kept by 78 mothers (samples 3 and 4).

The characteristics of mothers (Table 30.2) showed 57% (75/131) had been born in the UK while the mean age of entry to the UK of the remainder was 13.2 years. Two-thirds (89/131) were assessed as being in a stable union and more than half (75/130) were receiving supplementary benefit. In the dietary survey, only six mothers reported a special diet for health reasons, while 19 mothers had a special diet for religious reasons. Meal patterns were quite similar with most households eating breakfast, few eating large meals at midday with the main meal being consumed in the evening. Traditional Caribbean meals were eaten everyday by 31%, four to five times a week by 13%, one to three times a week by 46% with only 10% reporting less than once a week. From Table 30.3 it can be seen that particular Caribbean foods were consumed frequently, e.g. cornmeal, cho-cho, green bananas, plantains, pumpkins, okra, and yam.

Table 30.2 Characteristics of Afro-Caribbean mothers* in Birmingham

Characteristic	No.
Born in UK	75
Born outside the UK	56
In paid employment	38
Unemployed	93
Has other children aged under 5	72
No other children under 5	59
In stable union	89
Not in stable union	32 (10 not known)
Receiving supplementary benefit	75
Not in receipt of supplementary benefit	55 (1 not known)
Housing	
Council housing	75
Private rented	22
Owner-occupier	35
Other	3

* Total number interviewed, 131; age range 18–41 years.
Modified from Kemm *et al.* [8,9].

Table 30.3 Number of Afro-Caribbean mothers consuming certain Caribbean foods (samples, 2, 3, 4)

Food	*Rate of consumption* (no.)			
	More than 4 times a week	*1–3 times a week*	*Less than once a week*	*Never*
Cornmeal	32	32	23	14
Yams	13	40	25	20
Sweet potato	10	26	23	43
Green bananas	9	50	31	19
Plantains	11	34	35	22
Cho-cho	5	20	18	58
Pumpkin	8	24	29	41
Okra	3	18	11	70
Rice	39	57	4	2

Modified from Kemm *et al.* [8,9].

A description of Caribbean food and diets can be found in Douglas [10]. Briefly, the main parts of traditional Caribbean meals are staples – cereals, e.g. rice, cornmeal or flour; starchy fruits, roots or tubers, which accompany meat, fish or vegetable dishes. A variety of vegetables, pulses, herbs and spices are used, frequently as 'onepot' meals, e.g. soups or rice dishes containing meat, pulses and vegetables.

Although some English foods have been adopted these are mainly convenience and snack foods such as breakfast cereals, cakes, biscuits, crisps, squashes and 'pops', sausages and hamburgers. Potato consumption was low but was replaced by rice, yams, plantains, green bananas and flour dumplings. Bread also was replaced by traditional Caribbean hard-dough bread and bun. Fish, particularly salted cod, was frequently consumed.

Infant feeding practices

Ninety-one per cent of the mothers had started breast-feeding; however, after 8 weeks this had fallen to 78% and to 34% at 3 months, while 35% breast-fed for less than 1 month. The main predictor of breast-feeding for more than 1 month was being an owner-occupier; mother's age, marital status and age of leaving school did not seem to be associated (Table 30.4).

Table 30.4 Comparison of maternal characteristics for those breast-feeding less than 1 month or not at all and those breast-feeding 1 month or more

	Breast-feeding < 1 month (n = 47)	*Breast-feeding ≥ 1 month* (n = 84)
	% (no.)	% (no.)
Owner-occupier	13 (6)	35 (29)
Receiving single parent allowance	50 (23)	30 (25)
Receiving housing allowance	54 (25)	39 (33)
Age less than 25 yr	56 (26)	46 (39)
In paid employment	22 (10)	66 (37)
Has other children age under 5 yr	50 (23)	71 (35)
Mother born in UK	61 (28)	55 (47)

In a survey by the Caribbean Food and Nutrition Institute in St Christopher-Nevis and Grenada in 1984 [11], the period of exclusive breast-feeding in both countries was very short. A review of breast-feeding practices in the Caribbean [12] suggested that exclusive breast-feeding may only last 3 or 4 months, in many instances it may last less than 1 month – and that this has been the case in the Caribbean for almost 50 years. The introduction of bottle-feeding, early weaning and supplementation were associated with the production and promotion of infant formulas after the Second World War and with the economic circumstances of many mothers. Many poorer women had to return to work and hence other relatives, friends or neighbours may look after young babies from an early age. Whether or not mothers breast-feed for longer than 1 month may be related to traditional Caribbean weaning practices which are still apparent, even in mothers born in Britain.

The same Caribbean survey [11] revealed that semi-solid foods were introduced to babies aged less than 1 month. These foods were mainly home-made porridge, e.g. cornmeal and banana, as well as commercial cereal products in the third or fourth month. Nearly half used cornmeal at weaning with other traditional foods such as green banana, plantains, sweet potatoes and pumpkin given later.

In Birmingham traditional weaning practices were continued in Caribbean households, while at the same time, British patterns of infant feeding were also being adopted [8,9]. This highlighted the need for health promotors and nutritional advisors, such as health visitors and dietitians, to be more aware of traditional Caribbean infant feeding practices to ensure that appropriate advice and information can be given. Many mothers reported that this had mostly been from their mothers and mothers-in-law, and not from general practitioners, health visitors and midwives. They would have liked more information on infant feeding and weaning.

Social and economic factors influencing food choice

Food choice in the Afro-Caribbean community is determined not only by tradition, knowledge and experience but also by social and economic factors, including availability of traditional foods and proximity to shops and markets stocking imported foods. Family size, organization and convenience will also be of great importance. In Birmingham it was very apparent that many British convenience foods had been adopted and that food advertizing had a major influence. Many imported vegetables (e.g. yam, sweet potato and plantain) are more expensive than indigenous vegetables but were consumed regularly. Thus in households with a limited income a large proportion may be spent on food. This may be a particular problem for the increasing elderly Afro-Caribbean populations where incomes may be low and for whom traditional foods serve a very important social and psychological function.

Religious factors influencing food choice

There are many different religious denominations in the Afro-Caribbean community and within each a wide range of beliefs concerning diet. Some religions are more prescriptive about diet, e.g. Rastafarians and Seventh Day Adventists.

Rastafarians believe in consuming 'ital' foods [7,13]. These are natural unprocessed foods grown and prepared without chemicals or additives. Strict Rastafarians will not eat pork or pork products; fish without fins and scales; or any fruit from the 'vine', e.g. grapes, raisins, wine. Some Rastafarians may be vegetarian or lacto-ovo-vegetarians. Many Rastafarians would avoid processed or canned foods and may not add salt to food.

Seventh Day Adventists also do not eat fish without fins or scales or pork and pork products, nor drink alcohol or drinks regarded as stimulants like tea or coffee. Many are vegetarian for health as well as religious reasons.

These religious factors may well have influenced the avoidance of certain foods by the mothers in the Birmingham survey (Table 30.5).

Table 30.5 Afro-Caribbean mothers in Birmingham avoiding certain foods

Foods	Mothers avoiding food (n = 102) % (no.)
Pork	47 (43)
Other meats	16 (16)
Fish without fins	14 (11)
Other fish	6 (5)
Salted foods	20 (20)
Canned foods	25 (26)
Eggs	13 (13)
Milk	3 (3)
Alcohol	42 (43)

Traditional beliefs about diet and health

In the Caribbean, as in all communities, there are many myths and folklore that have developed around particular foods and their effect upon health. Many are believed to have healing properties. Herbal teas are widely consumed and many are believed to have 'cure-all' properties, e.g. cerassee for hypertension, diabetes and 'bad blood' and ackee leaf tea for colds. There are many herbal remedies for minor illnesses. A considerable amount of research is presently being undertaken by the Caribbean Food and Nutrition Institute to ascertain their effectiveness; many have been found to be effective and have certainly not been found to be harmful in any way. Problems may arise where herbal remedies are used to attempt to cure chronic conditions such as hypertension or diabetes, (see Chapter 33). Particular foods such as the vegetable cho-cho and herbal teas have been thought to relieve high blood pressure, but this has not been demonstrated to be the case.

Conclusion

I have tried to give a broad overview of food choice and preference in the Afro-Caribbean community in the UK, drawing upon research conducted in Birmingham. The purpose of this chapter is to highlight areas for action by service providers, e.g. social services, health services and education, to ensure that appropriate diets are recognized and provided for the Afro-Caribbean population in all statutory organizations. Very broad guidelines about dietary practice may be useful for practitioners to the Afro-Caribbean community. However, as in any community, food choice and preference will to a large extent be governed by individual likes and dislikes.

Traditional Caribbean diets can be recommended as being sound in terms of nutritional content and balance, being high in fibre and low in saturated fats. However, nutritional problems will arise if individuals consume large quantities of fat, sugar or salt, which, in association with non-dietary factors, may lead to or aggravate hypertension and diabetes (see Chapter 34) [14]. Health promotion messages should be based upon promoting traditional Caribbean diets while at the same time recommending areas for improvement in terms of lowering fats, sugar and salt intake.

The findings of early studies highlighting nutritional deficiencies were not substantiated in the Birmingham Survey. Where nutritional deficiencies do arise they appear to be related to poverty and socioeconomic deprivation rather than culture or religion.

References

1 McKenzie, J. C. and Mumford, P. Food habits of West Indian immigrants. *Proc. Nutr. Soc.*, **23**, x/ii–x/iii (1964)
2 Martin, C. R. Child health among West Indian immigrants. *Med. Officer*, **114**, 113 (1965)
3 Ward, P. S., Drakeford, J. P., Milton, J. and James, J. A. Nutritional rickets in Rastafarian children. *Br. Med. J.*, **285**, 1242–1243 (1982)
4 Curtis, J. A., Kooh, S. W., Fraser, D. and Greenberg, M. L. Nutritional rickets in vegetarian children. *Can. Med. Assoc. J.*, **128**, 150–152 (1983).
5 Campbell, M., Lofters, W. S. and Gibbs, W. N. Rastafarians and the vegan syndrome. *Br. Med. J.*, **285**, 1617–1618 (1982)
6 Close, G. C. Rastafarian and the vegans syndrome *Br. Med. J.*, **286**, 473 (1983)
7 Springer, L. and Thomas, J. Rastafarians in Britain: a preliminary study of their food habits and beliefs. *Hum. Nutr. Appl. Nutr.*, **37A**, 120–127 (1983)
8 Kemm, J., Douglas, J. and Sylvester, V. A survey of infant feeding practices by Afro-Caribbean Mothers in Birmingham. *Proc. Nutr. Soc.*, **45**, (3) 87a (1986)
9 Kemm, J., Douglas, J. and Sylvester, V. Afro-Caribbean Diet Survey: Final Report to the Birmingham Inner City Partnership Programme (unpublished) (1986)
10 Douglas, J. Caribbean food and diets. In *Food and Diet in a Multi-racial Society*, National Extension College for Training in Health and Race, Cambridge (1987)
11 Caribbean Food and Nutrition Institute. Baseline Survey of Young Child Feeding Practices, CFNI, Kingston, Jamaica (1984)
12 Marchoine, J. J. A history of breastfeeding practices in the English speaking Caribbean in the twentieth century. *Food Nutr. Bull..*, **2**, (2), 9–18 (1980)
13 Landman-Bogues, J. Rastafarian food habits. *Cajanus*, **9**, 228–234 (1977)
14 Grell, G. A. C. Non drug therapy: diet and hypertension. *Cajanus*, **18**, 140–151 (1985)

Chapter 31

Cardiovascular disease in black and Indian origin populations outside the USA

Introduction

J. K. Cruickshank

This chapter shows how marked variation in cardiovascular disease between ethnic groups provides clues to pathogenesis (or mechanism) and to aetiology (or cause). Evidence from the USA is discussed in Chapter 7. Ischaemic heart disease (IHD) is endemic among people of Indian origin, worldwide, and is described in Part A below; a focus on the continuing rarity of IHD in Afro-Caribbeans and in West Africa follows in Part B. Part C gives an outline of cerebrovascular and renal disease and the natural history of high blood pressure is discussed in Part D.

Background to vascular mortality: ethnic contrasts in Britain

The major vascular causes of death in Britain in the 1970s, by place of birth, are shown in Figure 31.1 (see Chapter 6). Place of birth is currently the only means of identifying ethnic/'racial' origin which is not otherwise entered on British death certificates. Below the age of about 40 (birth after 1950), figures for British-born offspring of first-generation migrants merge indistinguishably into general mortality statistics.

Figure 31.1 shows that people of West Indian birth in Britain had about half the average mortality ratio for IHD of England and Wales (taken as 100), while those of Indian subcontinent birth had a 20–30% excess. Scottish and Scottish migrant rates provide interesting control groups.

The assumption that these IHD rates among West Indians in Britain reflect mortality among black (Afro-) Caribbeans may be incorrect; the much smaller number of Indo-Caribbean migrants almost certainly contributed more IHD events to the small total of deaths but would not be distinguished by place of birth. The ratios for Trinidad in Figure 31.1 support that explanation because its population is about half Indian and half African in origin; the former account for at least twice as much of the IHD rate [2]. This excess among Indo-Caribbean migrants has been noted anecdotally by the author and others over the past 6 years in North-west London.

Deaths from stroke were 2–2.5 times commoner in those born in the West Indies, with only a slight excess in Indian-born men. It is important to consider the total numbers of deaths on which these age-adjusted ratios are based. The apparent

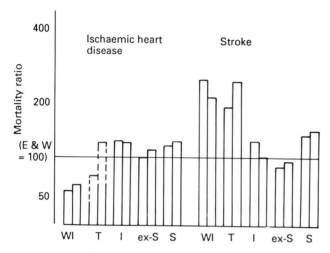

Figure 31.1 1970–78 mortality ratios for migrants from the West Indies (WI), Indian subcontinent (I), Scotland (ex-S) and home countries (T= Trinidad, 1971) and Scotland (S=1970–72) to England and Wales = 100. Adapted from Marmot *et al.* [1]

excess mortality from stroke among Afro-Caribbeans does not contribute sufficient numbers to balance their deficit in deaths from IHD, because there are so many fewer stroke than IHD deaths in Britain. Thus, the relative risk of death *from stroke* is higher in Afro-Caribbeans than in others but, perhaps due to the healthy migrant effect, their overall mortality from all causes was about 90% of the average in England and Wales. This example of competing cause of death illustrates the difference between relative and absolute excess mortality; of a total of 1961 cardiovascular deaths in Caribbean-born men in England between 1970 and 1978, even if excess (observed minus expected) deaths from hypertensive ($n = 330$) and renal disease ($n = 90$) are added to those from stroke ($n = 346$), that total of possibly blood pressure-related excess deaths ($n = 766$) about equals the overall deficit from less IHD ($n = 751$) compared with the England and Wales average. Unfortunately, similar figures for the 1980s are not yet available to allow any cohort effect (trends with time) to be assessed. As IHD is now the leading cause of death in black Americans (see Chapter 7), clearly environment, rather than genetics, is the major contributor to aetiology. The American evidence suggests that black Afro-Caribbean and African men are likely to become at risk of IHD, particularly if their smoking rates increase (see Figure 31.2) [3–5].

References

1 Marmot, M. G., Adelstein, A. M., Bulusu, L. *Immigrant Mortality in England and Wales 1970–1978*, OPCS Studies of Medical and Population Subjects No. 47, London, HMSO, (1984)
2 Beckles, G. L. A., Miller, G. J., Kirkwood, B. R. *et al*. High total and cardiovascular disease mortality in adults of Indian descent in Trinidad, unexplained by major coronary risk factors. *Lancet*, i, 1298–1301 (1986)
3 Cruickshank, J. K., Jackson, S. H. D., Beevers, D. G. *et al*. Similarity of blood pressure in blacks whites and Asians in England: the Birmingham factory study. *J. Hypertension*, **3**, 365–371 (1985)
4 Cruickshank, J. K., Beevers, D. G., Bannan, L. T. *et al*. Blood pressure and smoking habits in West Indians in Jamaica and in Birmingham in comparison with whites and Asians. *Clin. Sci.*, **60**, 32 pp. (1981)

5 Balarajan, R. and Yuen, P. British smoking and drinking habits: variation by country of birth. *Community Med.*, **8**, 237–239 (1986)

Part A   Ischaemic heart disease in people of Indian subcontinent origin

L. O. Hughes and J. K. Cruickshank

Worldwide

An increased risk of IHD appears to apply universally to migrant subgroups of Indian subcontinent origin (henceforward described as 'Asians') despite variable socioeconomic prosperity, dietary habit and duration of domicile in their adopted country. An early study in 1959 of necropsy records in Singapore found a higher incidence of IHD in Indians [1], which was also reported from East and South Africa [2,3]. Studies of two island populations, one in Fiji [4], the other in Trinidad [5], both confirmed this pattern. In Trinidad, four ethnic groups were sampled and classified on grandparental origin as white, black, mixed or Indian. The highest IHD rates were found in Indians and the lowest in blacks. HDL-cholesterol concentrations were lower, and LDL and VLDL concentrations higher in Indians than the other groups [5] (see Chapter 32), but these differences and those in smoking rates, systolic blood pressure and fasting blood glucose did not fully account for the excess *incidence* of IHD in the Indians [6,7]. Their high prevalence of diabetes (see Chapter 33) is relevant (see below 'Diabetes and IHD').

In Britain

Britain currently has the worst record worldwide for IHD without the decline reported in the USA and elsewhere [8]. An increased incidence of myocardial infarction was first reported in 1975 among predominantly Bangladeshi immigrants living in deprived areas of East London. The rate in the few black Afro-Caribbean migrants there was almost zero [9]. Hospital Activity Analysis was then used to assess ethnic differences in disease rates. Our study from Birmingham showed increased rates of myocardial infarction in Asian patients presenting to hospital in the 35–54-year age group, but a lower frequency in the older (55–64-year) age group and less than half British-born rates in men of Caribbean birth at all ages [10]. Among hospital admissions in Leicester, with ethnic group classified by surname, the odds ratio for myocardial infarction was 2.2 for Asians compared with others and was higher in the 25–44-year age group [11], also suggesting a possible cohort effect.

In England and Wales, for 1970–78, the proportional mortality ratio from IHD for those aged 20–69 was 123 for men and 119 for women born in the Indian subcontinent (Figure 31.1). Further analysis using names on these death certificates showed that the increased cardiovascular mortality occurred in all four southern Asian groups (predominantly Gujarati, Punjabi, Southerners and Muslims) resident in the UK [12]. Muslims were thought to be at particular risk, but a recent study showed similar mortality rates among diverse Asian groups in London [13].

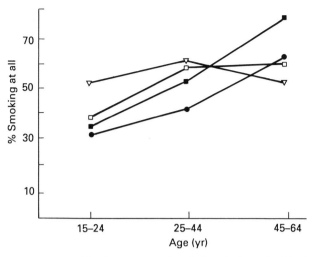

Figure 31.2 Smoking by age group (men). Results from the Birmingham and Jamaica factory studies, 1980–82 [14, 15]. Jamaican factory study: ■, Jamaicans. Birmingham factory study: ●, Asians; □, Afro-Caribbeans; ▽, whites

Risk factors similar or lower than in whites

Smoking rates have been lower in most migrant Asian populations than in whites [14–16] (Figure 31.2) with the exception of Bangladeshis [17].

In the few UK studies, *total serum cholesterol* has been lower or similar to that in non-Asians [18]. In a study of *dietary fat* intake, 7-day records of all food brought into the home were evaluated in 184 Asian households in North-west London [18]. Most were Gujarati, and vegetarian household fat intake was similar to non-vegetarians; when compared with the average British population (not actually measured) Asian households bought lower amounts of saturated fat and cholesterol but more polyunsaturated fat. A similar locally measured white control group was lacking, as it was also for the serum cholesterol values. A subsequent study of individual 5-day weighed intakes (a more accurate individual assessment which may underestimate total intake [19]) found no difference in total fat intake between white and Asian men at 38% of total calories [20] (see Chapter 26). Dietary fat intake alone in Asians seems unlikely to be the major cause of excess IHD. A suggestion that cholesterol oxides in ghee (clarified butter prized in Indian cooking) may be toxic [21] is being studied further.

Population *blood pressure* studies conclude that Asians have similar or lower values. For instance, in Birmingham, Asian factory workers had similar mean systolic and slightly lower diastolic blood pressures compared with white or black Afro-Caribbeans [14]. Systolic blood pressure was significantly lower in mainly Bangladeshi men in East London compared with others, but no difference in diastolic pressure was found [19]. These data also imply that blood pressure is not a significant factor in the excess rate of IHD in Asians.

Clotting factors (see Chapter 32 for details). There have been three studies so far on haemostatic variables (which predict IHD in whites) in UK Asians. There was no difference in factor VII clotting activity (VIIc) or fibrinogen levels between 75

Gujarati Indian and 68 white men in Miller's study, although fibrinolytic activity in Indians was marginally slower [20]. Among Bangladeshis in East London, fVIIc activity was lower and fibrinogen levels again no different than in whites [17]. Current unpublished data from one of the author's studies in North-west London (see Chapter 33, Table 33.1) also shows slightly lower mean ± s.e. fVIIc (% standard) in Gujarati men ($111 \pm 5\%$, $n = 41$) than in age-matched whites ($125 \pm 5\%$, $n = 30$). Levels in Afro-Caribbean men were lowest of all ($97 \pm 5\%$ $n = 30$), as was noted 10 years ago [22]. Fibrinogen levels were also marginally lower at 2.95 ± 0.11 g/l in Gujaratis compared with the other men (3.35 ± 0.14 and 3.33 ± 0.14 g/l respectively), again out of line with their coronary risk. Respective factor VIIc levels in women, always higher because of the influence of circulating oestrogens, were $139 \pm 8\%$ ($n = 39$), $144 \pm 12\%$ ($n = 25$) and $123 \pm 6\%$ ($n = 35$).

Diabetes and IHD

The one risk factor for IHD which is more prevalent in people of Indian origin is diabetes mellitus, particularly the non-insulin-dependent form. A higher average blood sugar in Bengali men compared with Europeans was reported in 1916 [23]. This diabetic tendency has since been demonstrated for many different Indian origin subgroups living in diverse locations [24–27] (for details see Chapter 33). Could the higher rates of diabetes account for the excess IHD in British Asians, given that other known risk factors for IHD differ little between ethnic groups? Few previous studies have addressed this question; unpublished calculations from the large Trinidad study [6,7,28] show that only some 13% of the excess IHD in those of Indian origin could be accounted for by hyperglycaemia. Much of the difference in mortality rates between Indians and Europeans could be explained by the high incidence of diabetes (19%) in Indians. However, black Afro-Trinidadians also had high rates of diabetes but the lowest rates of IHD. Cardiovascular mortality was greater in Indians than in Europeans in Trinidad, even among those with normal blood pressure and optimal fasting blood glucose concentrations [28]. This suggested that WHO-defined diabetes alone was not the responsible factor. A recent study showed excess rates of diabetes and higher serum insulin levels in an at-risk Bangladeshi community in East London compared with local whites, but rates of IHD were not measured [17].

Northwick Park Study in England

A recent study in North-west London has examined differences in the rate, severity and progression of first myocardial infarction and subsequent risk factors between consecutive Asian (predominantly Gujarati) and matched white men [29]. Rates of first myocardial infarction were over four times higher in Asians and the difference was even greater in younger men. The age profiles of the two ethnic groups were similar but Asians presented at a younger age (50.4 years versus 55.6 years (Figure 31.3)).

   The extent of myocardial damage was greater, based on higher peak creatine phosphokinase levels, and residual left ventricular function, assessed by two methods, was worse in Asians compared with matched whites. Glucose intolerance occurred in 36% of the Asian men and 11% of the white group, but the extent of

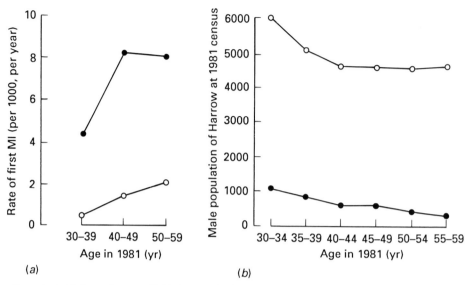

Figure 31.3 (*a*) Rate of myocardial infarction (MI) presenting to hospital (approx. half total rate for all Harrow); (*b*) Harrow male population. ●, Asians; ○, whites

myocardial damage was not greater in those with glucose intolerance than in normoglycaemics and they did not present at a younger age. *Coronary angiography was performed on 85% of the survivors*; the number of atheromatous lesions in the non-infarct-related vessels was significantly greater in Asians but was unrelated to glycaemic status. The conclusions were that coronary atherogenesis was accelerated, premature or both in Asians compared with whites. That the presence of glucose intolerance was not associated with more extensive atheroma or myocardial damage in survivors also inferred that, in Asians, a raised blood glucose in itself may not necessarily increase cardiovascular risk.

Role of insulin and C-peptide

The possible relationships between *insulin resistance, development of diabetes* and *cardiovascular risk* were examined further; 150 men surviving first infarction were compared with age- and ethnic group-matched controls randomly drawn from the general population [30]. The prevalence of diabetes and impaired glucose tolerance (assessed 2 hours after 75 g glucose between 6 months and 2 years after infarction) was 32% in Asian infarct survivors and similar at 28% in Asian controls. The rate of 15% in white patients was significantly greater than the 6% in white controls but significantly lower than in respective Asian groups. In both ethnic groups, the levels of insulin and C-peptide were significantly higher in the patients than in controls, irrespective of glucose tolerance status, and higher in Asians that in respective white groups. This suggests that insulin and C-peptide concentrations are more closely associated with cardiovascular risk than is arbitrary glucose tolerance status; if so, even apparently healthy Asian controls are at greater cardiovascular risk.

Prospective population and experimental studies have found an association between insulin levels and cardiovascular risk [31–34]. Earlier studies on survivors of myocardial infarction in the USA also reported this association [35,36]. The consistency of the epidemiological data has been disputed [37], although the Northwick Park Study outlined above answers some of the criticisms. The mechanisms by which insulin might exert its apparently detrimental influence are not clear, but fall into two broad categories: a direct effect on atherogenesis (including smooth muscle proliferation) and an adverse influence on particularly HDL-cholesterol and triglyceride metabolism [38,39]. In the Northwick Park Study Asians had higher triglyceride and lower HDL levels than whites. However, the levels of total cholesterol were higher in whites than in Asians, both in the infarct and control populations.

The total : HDL cholesterol ratio was significantly higher in patients than in controls and was highest (6.5) in the Asian patients. The triglyceride concentration correlated with the insulin concentration in white controls ($r = + 0.41$) and in Asian controls ($r = + 0.38$), but in Asian patients the association was less ($r = + 0.29$). The high insulin levels may be partly responsible for the less favourable lipid profiles found in Asians compared to whites. Thus, comparing total cholesterol concentrations *between* different ethnic groups may not be useful, as in this study, but *within* one group, the average levels may still be predictive of or related to IHD events.

The hypothesis that ineffective peripheral insulin action is a common factor in the Asian propensity to both diabetes and cardiovascular disease has been the subject of much recent research [17,26,27,30,40]. A common pathophysiological mechanism is a tempting theory and Figure 31.4 summarizes some of the established and speculative pathways involved.

Data not fully in support of the hypothesis include the elevated insulin/glucose ratios among black Afro-Caribbeans [40] (see Figure 33.3), with their low rates of

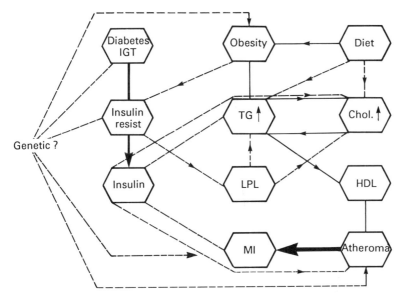

Figure 31.4 Possible interrelated origins of diabetes, myocardial infarction and atheroma. IGT, impaired glucose tolerance; TG, triglycerides; LPL, lipoprotein lipase; HDL, HDL-cholesterol; MI, myocardial infarct

IHD. However, it is possible that disturbances of insulin action may be present many years before overt IHD. The known link between body morphology (in particular central obesity) and peripheral insulin resistance suggests that the raised insulin levels in Asians may be secondary to an increased tendency to central obesity, as found in the patients above.

By whatever mechanisms, the susceptibility to cardiovascular disease of communities of Indian origin worldwide represents the single most important threat to their medical welfare.

References

1 Danaraj, T. J., Acker, M. S., Danaraj, W. *et al.* Ethnic group differences in coronary heart disease in Singapore: an analysis of necropsy records. *Am. Heart J.*, **58**, 516–526 (1959)

2 Shaper, A. G. and Jones, K. W. Serum cholesterol, diet, and coronary heart disease in Africans and Asians in Uganda. *Lancet*, **ii**, 534–537 (1959)

3 Walker, A. R. P. Extremes of coronary heart disease mortality in ethnic groups in Johannesburg, South Africa. *Am. Heart J.*, **66**, 293–295 (1963)

4 Sorokin, M. S. Myocardial infarction in Fiji. *Med. J. Aust.*, **ii**, 764–767 (1973)

5 Miller, G. J., Alexis, S. D., Beckles, G. L. A. *et al.* Serum lipoproteins and susceptibility of men of Indian descent to coronary heart disease, the St James survey, Trinidad. *Lancet*, **ii**, 200–203 (1982)

6 Beckles, G. L. A., Miller, G. J., Kirkwood, B. R. *et al.* High total and cardiovascular disease mortality in adults of Indian descent in Trinidad, unexplained by major coronary risk factors. *Lancet*, **i**, 1298–1301 (1986)

7 Miller, G. J., Beckles, G. L. A., Maude, G. H. *et al.* Ethnicity and other characteristics predictive of coronary heart disease in a developing community: principal results of the St James Survey, Trinidad. *Int. J. Epidemiol.*, in press (1989)

8 Doll, R. Major epidemics of the 20th century from coronary thrombosis to AIDS. *J. R. Statist. Soc. A.*, **150**, 373–395 (1987)

9 Tunstall-Pedoe, H., Clayton, D., Morris, J. N. *et al.* Coronary heart-attack in East London. *Lancet*, **ii**, 833–838 (1975)

10 Beevers, D. G. and Cruickshank, J. K. Age, sex, ethnic origin and hospital admission for heart attack and stroke. *Postgrad. Med. J.*, **5**, 763–765 (1981)

11 Donaldson, L. J. and Taylor, J. B. Patterns of Asian and non-Asian morbidity in hospitals. *Br. Med. J.*, **286**, 949–951 (1983)

12 Balarajan, R., Balusu, L., Adelstein, A. M. and Shukula, V. Patterns of mortality among migrants to England and Wales from the Indian subcontinent. *Br. Med. J.*, **289**, 1185–1187 (1984)

13 McKeigue, P. M. and Marmot, M. G. Mortality from coronary heart disease in Asian communities in London. *Br. Med. J.*, **297**, 903 (1988)

14 Cruickshank, J. K., Jackson, S. H. D., Beevers, D. G. *et al.* Similarity of blood pressure in blacks, whites and Asians in England: the Birmingham factory study. *J. Hypertension*, **3**, 365–371 (1985)

15 Cruickshank, J. K., Beevers, D. G., Bannan, L. T., *et al.* Blood pressure and smoking habits in West Indians in Jamaica and in Birmingham in comparison with whites and Asians. *Clin. Sci.*, **60**, 32 pp. (1981)

16 Balarajan, R. and Yuen, P. British smoking and drinking habits: variation by country of birth. *Community Med.*, **8**, 237–239 (1986)

17 McKeigue, P. M., Marmot, M. G., Syndercombe Court, Y. D. *et al.* Diabetes, hyperinsulinaemia, and coronary risk factors in Bangladeshis in East London. *Br. Heart J.*, **60**, 390–396 (1988)

18 McKeigue, P. M., Adelstein, A. M., Shipley, M. J. *et al.* Diet and risk factors for coronary heart disease in Asians in north-west London. *Lancet*, **ii**, 1086–1089 (1985)

19 Thompson, R. L., Cruickshank, J. K., Ellis, L. J., *et al.* Dietary intake of men in Wembley London by weighed inventory: comparison with national recommendations with particular emphasis on fat intake. *Eur. J. Clin. Nutr.*, in press (1989)

20 Miller, G. J., Kotecha, S. Wilkinson, W. H. *et al*. Dietary and other characteristics relevant for coronary heart disease in men of Indian, West Indian and European descent in London. *Atherosclerosis*, **70**, 63–72 (1988)

21 Jacobson, M. P. Cholesterol oxides in Indian ghee: possible cause of unexplained high risk of atherosclerosis in immigrant Asian populations. *Lancet*, **i**, 656–658 (1987)

22 Meade, T. W., Brozoric, M., Chakraborti, R. *et al*. Ethnic group comparisons of variables associated with ischaemic heart disease. *Br. Heart J.*, **40**, 789–295 (1978).

23 McCay, D., Banerjee, R. B. S. C., Ghosal, L. M. *et al*. Observations on the sugar of the blood and the sugar in the urine in varying conditions of health in Bengal. *Ind. J. Med. Res.*, **4**, 1–27 (1916)

24 Cruickshank, J. K., Beevers, D. G., Osbourne, V. L. *et al*. Heart attack, stroke, diabetes and hypertension in West Indians, Asians and whites in Birmingham, England. *Br. Med. J.*, **281**, 1108 (1980)

25 Mather, H. M. and Keen, H. The Southall Diabetes Survey: prevalence of known diabetes in Asians and Europeans. *Br. Med. J.*, **291**, 1081–1084 (1985)

26 Zimmet, P., Taylor, R., Ram, P. *et al*. Prevalence of diabetics and impaired glucose tolerance in the bi-racial (Melanesian and Indian) population of Fiji: a rural-urban comparison. *Am. J. Epidemiol.*, **118**, 673–688 (1983)

27 Omar, M. A. K., Seedat, M. A., Dyer, R. B. *et al*. The prevalence of diabetes mellitus in a large group of South African Indians. *South Afr. Med. J.*, **67**, 924–926 (1985)

28 Miller, G. J., Kirkwood, B. R., Beckles, G. L. A. *et al*. Adult male all-cause, cardiovascular and cerebrovascular mortality in relation to ethnic group, systolic blood pressure and blood glucose concentration in Trinidad, West Indies. *Int. J. Epidemiol*, **17**, 62–69 (1988)

29 Hughes, L. O., Raval, U. and Raftery, E. B. Coronary disease in Asians: an ethnic problem. *Br. Med. J.*, **298**, 1340–1345 (1989)

30 Hughes, L. O., Cruickshank, J. K., Wright, J. and Raftery, E. B. Disturbance of insulin and its action in British Asian and white men surviving myocardial infarction. *Br. Med. J.*, in press (1989)

31 Welborn, T. A. and Wearne, K. Coronary heart disease incidence and cardiovascular mortality in Busselton with reference to glucose and insulin concentrations. *Diabetes Care*, **2**, 154–160 (1979)

32 Ducimetiere, P., Eschwege, E., Richard, J. *et al*. Clinical complications of coronary heart disease according to plasma insulin and glucose levels. A further analysis of the Paris Prospective Study. In *Advances in Diabetes Epidemiology* (ed. E. Eschwege) (INSERM Symposium No. 22), Elsevier, Amsterdam, pp. 149–155 (1982)

33 Mahler, R. F. The effect of diabetes and insulin on biochemical reactions of the arterial wall. *Acta Diabetol. Lat.*, **viii**, 68–81 (1971)

34 Stout, R. W. The relationship of abnormal circulating insulin levels to atherosclerosis. *Atherosclerosis*, **27**, 1–13 (1977)

35 Tzagournis, M., Chiles, R., Ryan, J. M. and Skillman, T. C. Inter-relationships of hyperinsulinaemia and hypertriglyceridaemia in young patients with coronary heart disease. *Circulation*, **38**, 1156–1163 (1968)

36 Tzagournis, M., Seidensticker, J. F. and Hamwi, G. J. Serum insulin, carbohydrate and lipid abnormalities in patients with premature coronary heart disease. *Ann. Intern. Med.*, **67**, 42–46 (1967)

37 Jarrett, R. J. Is insulin atherogenic? *Diabetologia*, **31**, 71–75 (1988)

38 Brunzell, J. D., Porte, D. and Bierman, E. L. Abnormal lipoprotein-lipase mediated plasma triglyceride removal in untreated diabetes mellitus associated with hypertriglyceridaemia. *Metabolism*, **28**, 901–907 (1979)

39 Kissebah, A. H., Adams, P. W. and Wynn, V. Inter-relationships between insulin secretion and plasma free fatty acid and triglyceride transport kinetics in maturity onset diabetes and the effect of phenylethylguanide. *Diabetologia*, **10**, 119–130 (1974)

40 Cruickshank, J. K., Drubra, U., McDuff, J. and Mahler, R. F. Metabolic data on the epidemic of glucose intolerance and diabetes among Afro-Caribbeans, Whites and Gujaratis in north-west London. *Diabetic Med.*, Suppl. 2, **5**, 36 pp., (Abstr.) (1988)

Part B   Continuing rarity of ischaemic heart disease in Afro-Caribbeans in the West Indies and the UK, and in West Africa

J. K. Cruickshank

The West Indies

Clinical reports and reviews in the 1960s and 1970s emphasized the infrequency of clinical and autopsy evidence of IHD in Jamaica, Trinidad and other Caribbean islands, in people of black African origin. Epidemiologically, with confirmed cause of death, the data were rather weaker; indeed, in 1971 IHD was the fourth most common cause of death in Jamaica, probably because a medical practitioner could easily enter this simple category on the certificate when faced with an unexplained and unautopsied death. This is still the view of several senior local physicians.

Rarity

In Jamaica, Tulloch reported the first modern analysis of heart disease, describing admission rates, types of heart disease, clinical and autopsy details of cases admitted to the University Hospital in its first 5 years (1952–57). He was the first to detail that 'myocardial infarction is an uncommon occurrence in the Jamaican patient' ([1], p.235) Hypertension and its cardiac sequelae accounted for 34% of cardiovascular cases. There were 11 cases of 'cardiomegaly of obscure origin', an intriguing category and later possibly a distinct entity [2] but whose prevalence and real identity continued to be controversial [3].

Only 1.6% of 5251 hospital admissions had had a myocardial infarct, of which 1.1% were acute [1]. Infarcts accounted for some 3.4% of all autopsied deaths of those aged 20 years or over compared with 16% previously found by the same pathologist in Newcastle, England, at that time [4]. The similarity to other tropical African countries was clear; no clinical or autopsy cases had been seen in Kampala, Uganda, between 1951 and 1958 [5], similar to experience in Nigeria. In Ghana over a longer period, 1921–1953, 30 infarcts were found in 3645 autopsies [6]. In Jamaica, those with infarcts in Tulloch's series came from upper social groups, while the opposite was the case for entities such as syphilitic heart disease. A salutary feature of re-examining these reports from the 1950s is how little the general discussion of the aetiology of myocardial infarction has changed in 30 years. The geographical variations in serum cholesterol, if not HDL, had been noted and the possibility of increased plasma fibrinolytic activity in black populations [7] was re-documented 24 years later in the Evans County study [8].

In Jamaica, a considerable minority of 111 proven myocardial infarction cases admitted between 1968–1971 to the University Hospital were people of East Indian origin; 40% of 111 were diabetic prior to the infarct [9]. More recent hospital-based reports suggest a slight increase in IHD, particularly marked during the period of social unrest in Jamaica, 1978–79, and again, upper social groups were more frequent victims [10].

In Trinidad, the disparity between Indians and Africans was clinically apparent in the 1950s [11] and in Miller and Beckles' study mentioned previously, the relative risk of major Q waves on standardized ECGs was 3.8 times higher in Indians than Africans in the late 1970s [12]. This was confirmed by the 5–8-year all-cause and cardiovascular mortality: the Indian age-adjusted relative risks were respectively 1.54 and 2.39 times that of African men. Interestingly, their cerebrovascular mortality was also greater (1.6 times) than in Afro-Trinidadian men [13,14].

Pathology

The degree of aortic and coronary atheroma in 500 autopsy cases in Jamaica was compared first with a series in New Orleans, USA [4] and then in a four-nation study [15] which was the forerunner of the International Atheroma Project [16]. In the 1950s and 1960s, the development of aortic raised lesions by age group was similar in the USA, Jamaica and Japan but coronary lesions lagged well behind for the latter two countries, parallelling their much lower IHD rates. Complicated plaques occurred in less than 10% of Jamaican coronary vessels, even by the 8th decade, compared with up to 34% in the US group. An analysis of the effects of hypertension and diabetes showed that both conditions independently exaggerated atheroma in affected compared with unaffected patients in the same geographic pattern [17].

Evidence from West Africa

Evidence from earlier hospital reports has been mentioned and as yet the expected increase in incidence of IHD in all West African countries with 'development' does not seem to have occurred. Between 1961 and 1970 only 26 patients with myocardial infarction were seen at the University Hospital in Ibadan, Nigeria [18]. Similarly, no cases were reported among 404 patients in Zaria during 1974/75 [19]. Previous reviews report this general pattern. Up to the present day this still seems to be the case. Interestingly, compared with Jamaica in the late 1960s and early 1970s, diabetes in Ibadan, Nigeria did not seem to increase the occurrence of IHD. There were only five IHD cases in 832 patients with diabetes [20].

References

1 Tulloch, J. A. (a) Heart disease in Jamaica. (b) Some aspects of myocardial infarction in Jamaica. (c) Myocardial infarction in Jamaica: the clinical features. *West Ind. Med. J.*, **7**, (a) 169–182; (b) 235–243; (c) 244–248 (1958)
2 Stuart, K. L. and Hayes, J. A cardiac disorder of unknown aetiology in Jamaica. *Quart. J. Med.*, **32**, 39–45 (1963)
3 Miller, G. J. and Ashcroft, M. T. Reappraisal of cardiovascular surveys in Jamaica. *Br. Heart J.*, **34**, 1113–1119 (1972)
4 Robertson, W. B. Atherosclerosis and ischaemic heart disease – observations in Jamaica. *Lancet*, **i**, 444–446 (1959)
5 Williams, A. W., Ball, J. D. and Davies, J. N. P. Endomyocardial fibrosis in Africa; its diagnosis, distribution and nature. *Trans. R. Soc. Trop. Med. Hyg.*, **48**, 290–305 (1954)
6 Edington, G. M. Cardiovascular disease as a cause of death in the Gold Coast. *Trans. R. Soc. Trop Med. Hyg.*, **48**, 419 (1954)
7 Gillman, T., Naidoo, S. S. and Hawthorn, M. Fat, fibrinolysis and atherosclerosis in Africans. *Lancet*, **ii**, 696–698 (1957)

8 Dischingen, P., Tyroler, H. A. and Cassel, J. C. Blood fibrinolytic activity, social class and habitual physical activity. 1. A study of black and white men in Evans County, Georgia. *J. Chronic Dis.*, **33**, 283–290 (1980)
9 Ashcroft, M. and Stuart, K. Myocardial infarction in the University Hospital, Jamaica, 1968–1971. *West Ind. Med. J.*, **22**, 60–66 (1973)
10 Grell, G. Myocardial infarction in the University Hospital, Jamaica 1978–80. Presented at the 27th Caribbean Medical Research meeting, Nassau. (1981)
11 Wattley, G. H. Myocardial infarction in South Trinidad. *West Ind. Med. J.*, **8**, 33–36 (1959)
12 Miller, G. J., Alexis, S. D., Beckles, G. L. A., *et al*. Serum lipoproteins and susceptibility of men of Indian descent to coronary heart disease. The St James Survey, Trinidad. *Lancet*, **ii**, 200–203 (1982)
13 Miller, G. J., Beckles, G. L. A., Maude, G. H., *et al*. Ethnicity and other characteristics predictive of coronary heart disease in a developing community. Principal results of the St James Survey, Trinidad. *Int. J. Epidemiol.*, in press (1989)
14 Miller, G. J., Kirkwood, B. R., Beckles, G. L. A. *et al*. Adult male all-cause, cardiovascular and cerebrovascular mortality in relation to ethnic group, systolic blood pressure and blood glucose concentration in Trinidad, West Indies. *Int. J. Epidemiol.*, **17**, 62–69 (1988)
15 Gore, I., Robertson, W. B., Hearst, A. E. *et al*. Geographic differences in the severity of aortic and coronary atherosclerosis (US, Jamaica, South India, Japan). *Am. J. Pathol.*, **36**, 559–574 (1960)
16 Tejada, C., Strong, J. P., Montenegro, M. R. *et al*. Distribution of coronary and aortic atherosclerosis by geographic location, race and sex. *Lab. Invest.*, **18**, 49–66 (1968)
17 Robertson, W. B. and Strong, J. P. Atherosclerosis in persons with hypertension and diabetes mellitus. *Lab. Invest.*, **18**, 78–91 (1968)
18 Falase, A. O., Cole, T. O. and Osuntokun, B. O. Rarity of myocardial infarctions in University Hospital, Ibadan, Nigeria. *Trop. Geogr. Med.*, **25**, 147–154 (1973)
19 Ladipo, G., Froll, J. and Parry, E. H. Pattern of heart disease in adults of the Nigerian Savannah: a prospective clinical study. *Afr. J. Med. Med. Sci.*, **6**, 185–192 (1977)
20 Osuntokun, B. O. Hypertension in Nigerian diabetics. A study of 832 patients. *Afr. J. Med. Med. Sci.*, **3**, 257–265 (1972)

Part C   An outline of cerebrovascular and renal disease
J. K. Cruickshank

Cerebrovascular disease

Stroke, the most overt and devastating form of cerebrovascular disease, is the leading cause of death in Jamaica (see Chapter 34) and among the top causes in other Caribbean islands and in West Africa. Figure 31.1 illustrates its importance among people of Caribbean birth in England and Wales.

Between the 1930s and 1960s, cerebral haemorrhage gave way to thrombotic infarction as the primary type of pathology in industrialized countries. In Britain, Yates' autopsy and death certificate study [1] showed that the cerebral infarction : haemorrhage ratio rose due to a gradual fall over time in haemorrhagic deaths with a more abrupt rise in those from infarction. Computerized tomographic (CT) scanning methods have confirmed the continuing predominance of thrombotic over haemorrhagic strokes in non-fatal cases in England [2]. Cerebral haemorrhage is most closely related to the height of the blood pressure which, while important, is not the sole risk factor in occlusive events.

In developing countries, where reliable autopsy results were available, strokes from cerebral haemorrhage continued to predominate into the 1960s and probably later. In Jamaica in the 15 years up to 1967, 77% of 296 autopsied strokes were haemorrhagic and the remainder due to infarction, with only 10 due to extracranial emboli [3]. Hypertension conservatively defined was present in 67% of all cases and, as elsewhere, strokes occurred at a younger age in men than women. A WHO stroke register in 1973–75 showed a low rate in Ibadan, Nigeria; only clinical distinctions of type of stroke were made [4,5] which are not accurate without CT scanning or autopsy evidence [2], and under-registration occurred. Since then, stroke continues to be a major feature of clinical work anywhere in Nigeria and in all social groups [6]. Pathological studies on West African patients dying with stroke in the 1970s all showed less cerebral atheroma with a different lipid composition to that in American blacks or whites [7,8]. Recent reviews of the occurrence of stroke in black and white Americans, in both of whom there has been a major decline in cerebrovascular disease only partly related to the antihypertensive treatment [9], show that clinical and pathological types of stroke are very much less distinct between the ethnic groups in the USA [10,11]. Most of these studies have been done on selected hospital cases where it is unclear how much social/economic bias on admissions occurred [12]. Nevertheless, this is as accurate a reflection of the population pattern as is currently available; data on black Americans have been reviewed in detail elsewhere [12].

Renal disease

Dramatic differences in the incidence of end-stage renal disease are well documented in the USA [13] and have also been reviewed in detail [14]. Hypertensive renal damage is probably still the commonest cause of renal failure in American blacks. Reports of racial differences in renal vasculature in blacks and whites with essential hypertension are open to selection bias but may be relevant [15]. In the Caribbean, where the cost of replacement therapy, either as dialysis or transplantation, severely restricts its availability, malignant hypertension is a common cause of acute renal failure and moderate to severe high blood pressure also seems to be the major determinant of chronic renal disease [16].

Among Indian origin populations, the high prevalence of diabetes has led to an increasing frequency of proteinuria and nephropathy (see Chapter 33); this burden is liable to worsen but the toll from cardiovascular disease may restrict those surviving to develop renal failure. Nothing could indicate the urgency of these problems for both Afro-Caribbean and Indian-origin peoples more clearly.

References

1 Yates, P. O. A change in the pattern of cerebrovascular disease. *Lancet*, i, 65–69 (1984)
2 Sandercock, P., Allen, C., Corston, R. *et al.* Clinical diagnosis of intracranial haemorrhage using Guy's Hospital Score. *Br. Med. J.*, **291**, 1675–1677 (1985)
3 Cole, F. M. and Cole, H. L. The pattern of fatal cerebrovascular disease in Jamaica. *West Ind. Med. J.*, **18**, 202–209 (1969)
4 Osuntokun, B. O. Stroke in the Africans. *Afr. J. Med. Med. Sci.*, **6**, 39–53 (1977)
5 Osuntokun, B. O., Bademosi, O., Akinkugbe, O. O. *et al.* Incidence of stroke in an African city: results from the stroke registry in Ibadan 1973/75. *Stroke*, **10**, 205–207 (1979)
6 Iketi, V. O., Nwosu, M. C. and Nurabueze, A. C. The epidemiology of stroke in Nigerians: a study of 328 cases. *Trop. Cardiol.*, **14**, 63–67 (1988)

7 Williams, A. O., Loewerson, R. B., Lippert, D. M. *et al.* Cerebral atherosclerosis and its relationship to selected diseases in Nigerians: a pathological study. *Stroke*, **6**, 395–401 (1975)

8 Resch, J. A., Williams, A. O., Lemeicier, G. *et al.* Comparative autopsy studies of cerebral atherosclerosis in Nigeria and Senegal negroes, American negroes and caucasians. *Atherosclerosis*, **12**, 401–407 (1970)

9 Klag, M. J., Whelton, P. K., Seidler, A. J. Decline in US stroke mortality: demographic trends and antihypertensive treatment. *Stroke*, **20**, 14–21 (1989)

10 Caplan, L. R., Gorelick, P. B. and Hier, D. B. Race, sex and occlusive cerebrovascular disease: a review. *Stroke*, **17**, 648–655 (1986)

11 Maxwell, J. G., Rutherford, E. J., Covington, D. *et al.* Infrequency of blacks among patients having carotid endarterectomy. *Stroke*, **20**, 22–26 (1986)

12 Cooper, E. S. Cerebrovascular disease in blacks. In *Hypertension in Blacks* (eds W. D. Hall, E. Saunders and N. B. Shulman), Year Book Medical, Chicago, pp. 83–105 (1985)

13 Rastand, S., Kirk, K., Retsky, E. and Pate, B. Racial differences in incidence of end stage renal disease. *New Engl. J. Med.*, **306**, 1276–1279 (1982)

14 Shulman, N.B. Renal disease in hypertensive blacks. In *Hypertension in Blacks* (eds W. D. Hall, E. Saunders and N. B. Shulman), Year Book Medical, Chicago, pp. 106–112 (1985)

15 Levy, S., Talner, L., Coel, M. *et al.* Renal vasculature in essential hypertension; racial differences. *Ann. Intern. Med.*, **88**, 12–16 (1978)

16 Nicholson, G. D. Long term survival after recovery from malignant nephrosclerosis. *Am. J. Hypertens.*, **1**, 73–75 (1988)

Part D   The natural history of blood pressure in black populations in the West Indies, West Africa and the UK: a comparison with the USA

J. K. Cruickshank

Contrary to the consistent findings in the USA, average blood pressure (BP) levels among black populations in the Caribbean, West Africa and in Britain do not differ substantially from those in whites. There are difficulties with international comparisons including temperature differences between locations [1]. This section briefly reviews data available from those three areas compared where relevant with the USA (see Chapter 7).

A fourth area with considerable problems from hypertension is South Africa. Further reference to that work is not included here. Social and political conditions for non-white people render daily life so difficult that results from interethnic comparisons of BP may not be biologically meaningful or transferable to other societies. Secondly, the genetic background of black populations in the first three areas above derives from the West and West Central African states [2,3] and is quite distinct from that of black-skinned people of Southern, East Central and East Africa. An authoritative review of the South African perspective was provided by Seedat [4].

Problems of international comparison of BP studies include the quality, by modern epidemiological standards, of the available data [5]. The study sample may not be representative and there may be a lack, or impossibility, of genuine age ascertainment. Variation in conditions of measurement invalidate many studies, with errors from interobserver variation and their lack of training, use of conventional rather than random zero sphygmomanometers, consequent problems of technique, inappropriate cuff size and digit preference. The following discussion should be seen only in the light of these problems.

West Indies

The earliest prevalence studies of BP in the Caribbean were those in the US Virgin Islands [6]. Average BP levels by age group were higher for blacks than whites but social class differed markedly. A similar pattern among black residents of the Bahamas [7] was confirmed in a censused urban study there [8]. The definitive work on BP in the West Indies was the longitudinal survey of the censused community of Lawrence Tavern, a semi-rural village 16 miles outside Kingston, Jamaica [9–16]. This cohort study was the first in a black population anywhere and was started in 1958 in an MRC unit by Miall. This and Miller and Beckles' later St James study in Trinidad [17–20] are still the only two longitudinal studies in the Caribbean or Africa. Miall also surveyed an urban section of Kingston. Total response rates were over 95%, except for urban men (87%), and response rates with verified ages were over 75% for rural and 65% for urban subjects. The community was followed up for 13 years [11,12]. Following similar work by Miall in South Wales, it provided direct comparative results with those for a white European population with pressures measured by the same observer. The project supplied the original evidence on natural history of BP in the developing black world, as well as details on morbidity, mortality and glucose intolerance in this population [10–13] (see Chapter 33). Some elements of the interpretation of the former, particularly on ECG findings and the apparent prevalence of angina, became controversial [14,15].

BPs were similar to those measured in Wales [16], although the upper tails of their frequency distributions were longer in women for diastolic BP. Temperature may have been a confounding factor [1], so comparisons have to be guarded. The rural Jamaican women had higher pressures than urban, contrary to findings in West Africa [21] (see below), but similar to American studies in Evans County [22] compared with Chicago [23]. Bacteriuria and subclinical urinary infection were initially considered to result in renal hypertension in rural women but this hypothesis was not confirmed. Nulliparous women tended to have higher BPs than age-matched parous women, as found in Wales.

A detailed analysis of inheritance of BP was conducted, using the classic method of an age-adjusted score (to 35 years) [9]. Regressions of systolic/diastolic scores of first-degree relatives on those for propositi were similar to those in Wales [24] and London [25]. No evidence of bimodality was found in the frequency distributions of BP scores for relatives of the middle-aged hypertensives, although the study's power to detect it may have been too small [26]. The possibility that black populations may show bimodality of BP cannot yet be discounted.

In subsequent surveys of the same Jamaican community, the prevalence of hypertension in 53–64-year-old women had dropped from the initial 26% [16] to 10%, presumably due to regression to a lower mean. Further details of this and subsequent studies in Lawrence Tavern (reviewed by Ashcroft [12], p.10) clarify some problems. Thus, in the original 1959 survey, only those with birth certificates to verify age were reported, omitting some (with less exact age) who had lower pressures at the second 1962–63 survey, when random zero sphygmomanometers were used. (The random zero 'muddler' was actually invented in Jamaica for this study [27].) Some of these interpretation difficulties have been discussed elsewhere [28].

Other Caribbean BP studies include those more recently in St Lucia [29] and Tobago [30], the latter participating in the 'InterSalt' Study [31]. In St Lucia, 'spot' urine samples for Na^+/K^+ ratios were only marginally related to BP but because estimated K^+ intake was higher there than the only comparable study in Evans County, USA, the Na^+/K^+ ratios were lower, in line with the BPs. Langford has taken this discussion further in his hypothesis that an habitually low K^+ intake accounts for some of the high BP in poorer blacks in the southern USA [32].

The author also conducted a study of a random sample of fit working men in Jamaica in 1980 compared with those of his later Birmingham studies [33,34]. These were detailed in a thesis [28] but have not been previously published. The men were initially sampled from factory pay-rolls as in Birmingham, but it became clear that few such factories could be screened so sampling was extended to men in two other communities; one was a fishing cooperative with a list of members on the Kingston harbour front and the other a rural group of farm employees. Both these were randomly sampled from respective employee lists. Three hundred and ten men were available from these combined lists; 240 were seen (77% screened). The important feature of the Jamaican men, all of whom were working in physically active occupations, was their relative weight for height (actual over ideal weight from metropolitan standards).

In each 10-year age group this averaged 98–99% compared with the Birmingham Afro-Caribbean men whose relative weights rose from 111% at 25–34 years to 120% at 55–64 years. The respective relative weights in whites were 116–118% and in Asians 107–103% (Figure 31.5).

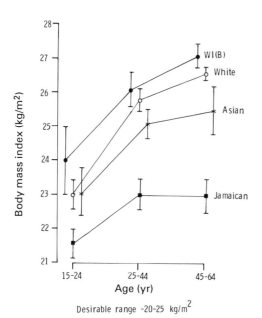

Figure 31.5 Body mass index in the Birmingham and Jamaican factory studies [*see* 28,34]

The mean (+ s.d) systolic BP was considerably lower in the younger Jamaican men, averaging 124.2 ± 15, 122.2 ± 14 and 124.4 ± 20 mmHg in the three age decades 15–24, 15–34 and 35–44 years, rising to levels similar to those in Birmingham thereafter. Diastolic BPs rose with age similarly and did not differ from those in Birmingham. A possible confounding effect from the temperature difference in Jamaica should be noted. There was thus indirect evidence that exercise, as continual heavy manual work, in factories, fishing or on farms not only contributed to a lower relative weight but also to lower (systolic) BPs which rose again once vigorous exercise ceased.

The St James' Cardiovascular Survey

This was started in Trinidad in 1977 and is unique for having carefully established ethnic status by grandparental origin [17–20]. Age-adjusted mean BPs were highest in those of African descent ($n = 460$), intermediate in those of Indian descent ($n = 367$) and men of mixed origin ($n = 239$) and lowest in the relatively few Europeans ($n = 111$). The response rate averaged 88%. Importantly, after further adjustment by analysis of variance for arm circumference, these ethnic group differences were no longer significant. If further allowance was also made for alcohol and tobacco use, mean systolic and diastolic pressures in African, Indian and mixed men were within 2 mmHg. The 3 mmHg lower average pressure in Europeans was not significant and they were in a higher socioeconomic bracket. There was a slight excess of age-adjusted combined systolic and diastolic hypertension ($\geq 160/95$ mmHg) in black men of African descent at 13% compared with 6–10% in the others. Despite this, at follow-up, the Indian men had the highest blood pressure-attributable mortality (Table 6 in [20]) which is discussed again below.

West Africa

Three studies from Nigeria illustrate the evolving BP problem in that country. The first, summarized in Akinkugbe's book based on work in and near Ibadan [21], was a rural-urban comparison in Western Nigeria; the rural area was a village conglomerate in Ibarapa district compared with an area of Ibadan. At all ages, both systolic and diastolic BPs were higher in the urban than rural subjects, in both men and women. BP levels were similar to those Miall reported in Jamaica, although rural women had had higher BPs there than urban women. BPs were considerably lower than those reported in blacks and whites in Georgia [36].

The apparent rarity of hypertensive retinopathy in Ibadan [20] remains unexplained. A recent Nigerian report has documented standard retinal lesions as found in other subjects [37]. Certainly retinopathy is widely recorded in South Africa [38], in Jamaica [39] and in the USA. Johnson measured BPs of urban subjects in Lagos [40]. Levels were again similar to those in Jamaica [9]. Thirdly, Oviasu [41] examined a northern savannah rural population among whom the prevalence of WHO hypertension ($> 160/95$) was as low as 5%, in relatively young subjects. A similar rate of 4% had been reported from rural Ghana [42].

In a much earlier project in Liberia, BPs were compared in uncensused subjects in three rural villages with those recorded earlier in the Bahamas [7,43]. BPs were considerably lower than those found in the Bahamas, or in the USA by other observers. The most recent West African results come from a large hospital-based survey in the Cameroun Republic by two observers of 2000 non-cardiological patients who were not acutely ill. In relatively young subjects (average age 41 years), the gross prevalence of 'WHO hypertension' was 15%, with higher BPs in rural subjects. An important suggestion, inadequately supported by detail or age-correction, was that BP varied between local ethnic groups: Banyanga subjects (from an area near Nigeria) had more hypertension than Bamileke people [44].

UK

There have been three reports on BP in blacks in Britain, all with relatively small numbers of subjects.

The Northwick Park Heart Study (NPHS)

This is important because of its emphasis on possible haemostatic risk factors [45]. The study examined a factory population of North-west London. There were only 48 day-shift and 38 night-shift male black workers and BPs were only significantly higher than in whites in the day shift. In 55 black women compared with 61 whites, BPs were higher but the former were also more obese by an average of 4 kg/m^2. The black group, although primarily West Indian, also included people from West Africa. Plasma renin and noradrenaline results were reported in a volunteer subgroup of workers previously in the NPHS [46]. No differences in plasma noradrenaline were found between the ethnic groups but blacks had 55% lower plasma renins than whites [47]. Urinary sodium excretion was not measured and no such study comparing ethnic groups has yet been reported from the UK.

The Birmingham Factory Study

Our study of black, white and Asian employees screened in a factory survey may be compared with a similar survey conducted by the same observer (the author) in Jamaica, referred to above. In Birmingham, 1049 factory workers aged 16–65 from a multi-ethnic workforce were screened, representing 79% of the eligible population. BP was measured sitting with random zero sphymomanometers [33,34].

Mean BPs by age decade were not significantly different among the 443 white, 172 Asian and 173 black West Indian men. Mean pressures among women were apprently higher in the blacks ($n = 101$) compared with the whites ($n = 164$), but only after 35 years of age. However, despite the use of appropriate cuff sizes for obese subjects, this difference in blood pressure among women was entirely accounted for by different body mass indices (Figure 31.6).

In a multiple regression analysis, ethnic group (being West Indian or Asian) failed to have a significant effect on either systolic or diastolic BP variance. Among 14 independent variables measured in men, age, body mass index, alcohol intake and family history of high BP made significant positive contributions to systolic BP. The same factors, with a negative effect from cigarette smoking replacing family history, affected diastolic BP variance.

The Birmingham Study suggested that, despite clinical impressions, average BPs in black men were no higher than in whites and that the female differences were

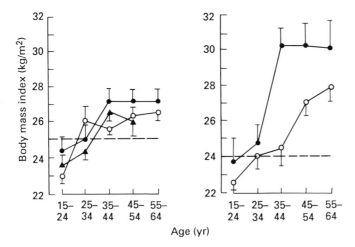

Figure 31.6 Body mass index: Birmingham factory study. Broken line = upper limit of 'acceptable' range, approx. 120% ideal weight. ●, Blacks; ○, whites; ▲, Asians. From Cruickshank *et al.* [34] with permission

due to the greater fatness of black women. A study of schoolchildren in Birmingham had similar results [48]. That conclusion was supported by the most recent British study in a sample of a North-west London inner city general practice [49]. Average BPs by age were not significantly different between blacks and whites but more blacks were being treated for hypertension.

UK/US comparison

Major studies of BP in the USA comparing blacks and whites include those by Comstock [36], in Evans County [22] and the Chicago industry and community projects [23], in addition to surveys by the National Centre for Health Statistics. The Birmingham results compared quite closely with those from the much larger Chicago projects, both in factory subjects and the use of the initial BP reading. Few differences emerged among the major variables (Table 31.1).

Table 31.1 Birmingham factory study: comparison with Chicago industry project [23] (men aged 45–64 years)

	Birmingham		Chicago	
	Whites (n = 194)	*Blacks* (n = 86)	*Whites* (n = 5604)	*Blacks* (n = 280)
SBP	146 + 24	145 + 26	143 + 21	148 + 24
DBP	86 + 15	87 + 15	74 + 12	89 + 15
Pulse/min	78 + 11	78 + 11	76 + 12	76 + 12
Rel. wt.	118 + 15	120 + 15	124 + 16	124 + 19
Cigs/day (whole group)	11 + 13	7 + 8	10 + 14	9 + 11
Alcohol (units per week)	19.3 + 24	22.5 + 32	†	†

Results shown are mean ± s.d.
† Data available but not comparable

Systolic BPs were somewhat higher in the American blacks while diastolic BPs were lower in older American whites than in either ethnic groups in the UK. American black women aged 25–44 years were much more obese at 188% of mean relative weight than the American white or Birmingham women.

A further important American study examined BP and its heredity in blacks and whites within high and low stress areas of Detroit [50–52]. BPs of black men of either age group in the low stress zone were little different from those recorded for the white men in a similar zone. Black women had consistently greater BPs than white in both 'stress' zones. The Detroit project attempted to quantify, so far uniquely, genetic compared with environmental contributions to BP in comparable censused samples of blacks and whites. Since the original series of papers, heritability estimates were found to contribute significantly, if not impressively, to systolic and diastolic BP in both blacks and whites [52].

Genes will probably not provide the answer to this public health priority although using families as a focus for prevention may be persuasive. *In vitro* markers for raised BP in blacks have been restricted so far to red blood cells [53–55] and are unlikely to offer more than measuring the BP in family members.

Prognosis of blood pressure in blacks compared with whites

A detailed discussion of this issue was presented by the author at the second meeting of the International Society on Hypertension in Blacks,[*] published elsewhere [56]. Evidence from prospective studies supports the null hypothesis that for a given level of blood pressure, individual prognosis (risk of a vascular event or death) is no different in American or other black populations than in whites. This hypothesis can be presented graphically, as shown in Figure 31.7.

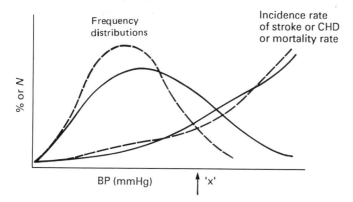

Figure 31.7 Graph illustrating hypothesis of incidence rate of stroke or CHD or mortality rate in black and white populations related to blood pressure distribution. ———, Blacks; – – –, whites

[*] Readers interested in the annual meetings of this Society, whose aims are to reduce the morbidity and mortality from hypertension in black populations by stimulating research and prevention programmes, may write to its office at: 65 Butler Street SE, Atlanta, Georgia 30303, USA.

Thus, while there are more black Americans than whites above a given cut-off value of the BP distribution, for that value event or mortality rates are no different. (From the previous discussion, the frequency distribution of BP in other black populations may be little or no different from whites.) BP should not therefore be considered 'worse' in blacks than others, but, in the USA at least, just more prevalent. Evidence from prospective studies to support the hypothesis first came from within the USA in the follow-up data of the Evans County study [57]. The report on its 20 years' results shows Kaplan–Meier survival curves indistinguishable for blacks and whites [58]. The Charleston Heart Study [59] and the 5-year mortality results from the large MRFIT study reported similar results for IHD (lower in hypertensive blacks than hypertensive whites [60]). Stroke mortality in blacks by quintile of diastolic BP in MRFIT only appeared to be greater above 90 mmHg because there were many more blacks than whites in that 'quintile' [60].

Evidence from the only two longitudinal studies outside the USA were equally persuasive. The 13-year all-cause mortality in the Jamaican Lawrence Tavern Study is redrawn from tabular data [11] (Figure 31.8). It appeared that mortality, particularly in women, did not rise significantly until BPs above 180/110 mmHg (phase IV) were reached. Analysis by logistic regression was not used but was otherwise sound. The most recent results from the St James Study in Trinidad are similar [19,20]; despite minor differences in prevalence (discussed above), attributable mortality after 8 years from systolic BP between 155 and 179 mmHg was 7.9 for black, 12.3 for Indian and still 8.2 for European men, and above 180 mmHg, 14.7, 22.8 and 15.1 deaths/1000 person years respectively.

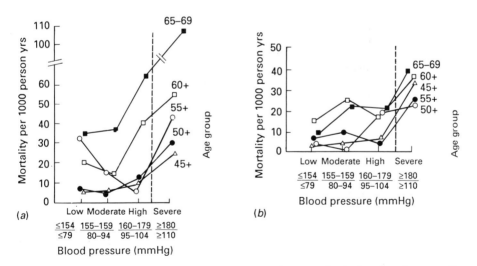

Figure 31.8 Thirteen-year all-cause mortality versus blood pressure in the Jamaican Lawrence Tavern Study [11]. (*a*) Men; (*b*) women

Thus, while hypertension prevalence is more marked in some black populations than others, with no basis for complacency anywhere, risk from high BP is no different than in other ethnic groups. Treatment needs careful attention.

Low renin status and poor response of blacks to several antihypertensive drugs

There have been other reviews of this important topic [61] but this chapter should finish with a brief summary of the limitations of current treatment for black hypertensive patients. Diuretics remain the cheapest and, in low dose, the most effective drugs in blacks. This appears to be due to their chronic activation of the plasma renin system which is otherwise much less active in blacks than whites, wherever it has been compared [47,62]. Hence other agents whose actions may depend on this system, such as β-blockers and angiotensin-converting enzyme inhibitors, have very limited effect on raised BP in blacks when used alone [63,64]. In combination with diuretics, they are useful but more expensive. This problem is not appreciated by many doctors in primary care but is clearly illustrated from our own study in diabetics [65] whose renin activity (in patients of any ethnic group) may also be suppressed.

The β-blocker metoprolol had no overall effect on either systolic or diastolic BP in black patients but once again even with the calcium antagonist the fall in BP was less than in whites (Figure 31.9). A similar result was recently reported in a randomized trial of nitrendipine and acebutolol in black patients in Zaire [66].

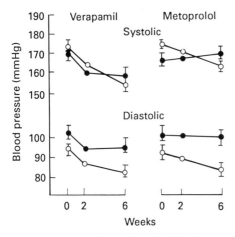

Figure 31.9 Mean (± s.e.) supine blood pressure at baseline, 2 and 6 weeks in each phase of trial. ●, Black patients; ○, white patients. Reproduced from Cruickshank *et al.* [65] with permission

Thus, choice of therapy and attention to detail of the BP results are even more important in black subjects than in other groups. With this approach and attention to broader public health measures, the morbidity and early mortality from hypertension in blacks should be controlled. Preventive efforts, while less glamorous than clinic treatments, are likely to bring the most benefit, using a team approach that is already being promoted in the Caribbean (see Figure 34.3).

References

1 Brennan, P. G., Greenberg, G., Miall, W. E. and Thompson, S. G. Seasonal variation in arterial blood pressure. *Br. Med. J.*, **2**, 919–923 (1982)

2 Patterson, O. *The Sociology of Slavery*, Grenada, London (1973)
3 Ashdown, P. *Caribbean History in Maps*, Longman Caribbean (Trinidad & Jamaica), London (1979)
4 Seedat, Y. K. Race, environment and blood pressure: the South African experience. *J. Hypertens.*, **1**, 7–12 (1983)
5 Cruickshank, J. K. and Beevers, D. G. Ethnic and geographic differences in blood pressure. In *Epidemiology of Hypertension* (ed. C. Bulpitt), Elsevier, London, chap. 5, pp. 70–88 (1985)
6 Saunders, G. M. and Bancroft, H. Blood pressure studies on negro and white men and women living in the US Virgin Islands. *Am. Heart. J.*, **23**, 410–442 (1942)
7 Moser, M., Morgan, R., Hale, M. *et al.* Epidemiology of hypertension with particular reference to the Bahamas. *Am. J. Cardiol.*, **7**, 727–733 (1959)
8 Johnson, B. D. and Remington, R. A sampling study of blood pressure levels in white and negro residents, Nassau, Bahamas. *J. Chronic Dis.*, **13**, 39–51 (1961)
9 Miall, W. E., Kass, E. H., Ling, J. and Stuart, K. L. Factors influencing the arterial pressure in the general population in Jamaica. *Br. Med. J.*, **2**, 497–506 (1961)
10 Miall, W. E., Del Campo, E., Fodor, J. *et al.* Longitudinal studies of cardiovascular disease in a Jamaican rural population. (a) Prevalence and ECG findings. (b) Factors influencing mortality. (c) Factors influencing changes in ECG. *Bull. WHO*, **46**, (a) 429–442; (b) 685–694; (c) 695–708 (1972)
11 Ashcroft, M. T. and Desai, P. Blood pressure and mortality in a rural Jamaican community. *Lancet*, **i**, 1167–1170 (1978)
12 Ashcroft, M. T. A review of epidemiological research in a rural Jamaican community. *West Ind. Med. J.*, **28**, 3–16 (1979)
13 Florey, C. du V., McDonald, J. and Miall, W. E. Blood sugar and serum insulin levels in a Jamaican community. *Int. J. Epidemiol.*, **1**, 157–163 (1972)
14 Miller, G. J. and Ashcroft, M. T. A re-appraisal of cardiovascular surveys in Jamaica. *Br. Heart J.*, **34**, 1113–1120 (1972)
15 Ashcroft, M. T. Interpretation of cardiovascular survey results in Jamaica. *West Ind. Med. J.*, **25**, 216–223 (1976)
16 Miall, W. E. and Cochrane, A. The distribution of arterial pressure in Wales and Jamaica. *Pathol. Microbiol.*, **24**, 690–697 (1961)
17 Beckles, G. L. A., Miller, G. J., Kirkwod, B. R. *et al.* High total and cardiovascular disease mortality in adults of Indian descent in Trinidad, unexplained by major coronary risk factors. *Lancet*, **i**, 1298–1301 (1986)
18 Miller, G. J., Alexis, S. D., Beckles, G. L. A. *et al.* Serum lipoproteins and susceptibility of men of Indian descent to coronary heart disease. The St James Survey, Trinidad. *Lancet*, **ii**, 200–203 (1982)
19 Miller, G. J., Beckles, G. L. A., Maude, G. H., *et al.* Ethnicity and other characteristics predictive of coronary heart disease in a developing community: principal results of the St James Survey, Trinidad. *Int. J. Epidemiol.*, in press (1989)
20 Miller, G. J., Kirkwood, B. R., Beckles, G. L. A. *et al.* Adult male all-cause, cardiovascular and cerebrovascular mortality in relation to ethnic group, systolic blood pressure and blood glucose concentration in Trinidad, West Indies. *Int. J. Epidemiol.*, **17**, 62–69 (1988)
21 Akinkugbe, O. O. *High Blood Pressure in the African*, Churchill Livingstone, Edinburgh (1972)
22 McDonough, J. R., Garrison, G. E. and Hammes, C. G. Blood pressure and hypertensive disease among negroes and whites. *Ann. Intern. Med.*, **61**, 208–213 (1964)
23 Stamler, J., Rhomberg, P., Schoenberger, J. *et al.* Multivariate analysis of the relationship of seven variables to blood pressure. *J. Chronic Dis.*, **28**, 527–548 (1975)
24 Miall, W. E. and Oldham, P. A. The hereditary factor in arterial blood pressure. *Br. Med. J.*, **2**, 75–80 (1963)
25 Hamilton, M., Pickering, G. W., Fraser, J. A. F. and Sowry, G. S. C. The aetiology of essential hypertension. 4. The role of inheritance. *Clin. Sci.*, **13**, 273–304 (1954)
26 McManus, I. C. Bimodality of blood pressure levels. *Stat. Med.*, **2**, 253–258 (1983)
27 Garrow, J. S. Zero muddler for unprejudiced sphygmomanometry. *Lancet*, **ii**, 1205 (1963)
28 Cruickshank, J. K. Blood pressure and diabetes among West Indians in Britain compared with Jamaica. *Doctoral thesis (MD)*, University of Birmingham (available on microfilm on request to the medical library) (1985)

29 Khaw, K-T. and Rose, G. Population study of blood pressure and associated factors in St Lucia, West Indies. *Int. J. Epidemiol.*, **11**, 372–377 (1982)

30 Patrick, A. L., Boyd-Patrick, H. A. and Vaughn, J. P. Cardiovascular risk factors in Tobago: comparison with other African populations. *West Ind. Med. J.*, **35**, 149–156 (1986).

31 InterSalt Cooperative Research Group. InterSalt: an international study of electrolyte excretion and blood pressure. Results for 24-hour urinary sodium and potassium. *Br. Med. J.*, **297**, 319–328 (1988)

32 Langford, H. Is blood pressure different in black people? *Postgrad. Med. J.*, **57**, 749–754 (1981)

33 Cruickshank, J. K., Jackson, S. H.D., Beevers, D. G. *et al*. Blood pressure in black, white and Asian factory workers in Birmingham. *Postgrad. Med. J.*, **59**, 622–626 (1983)

34 Cruickshank, J. K., Jackson, S. H. D., Beevers, D. G. *et al*. Similarity of blood pressure in blacks, whites and Asians in England; the Birmingham factory study. *J. Hypertens.*, **3**, 365–371 (1985)

35 Akinkugbe, O. O. and Ojo, O. A. Arterial pressures in rural and urban populations in Nigeria. *Br. Med. J.*, **1**, 222–224 (1969)

36 Comstock, G. W. An epidemiologic study of blood pressure levels in a biracial community in the southern United States. *Am. J. Hyg.*, **65**, 271–315 (1957)

37 Ladipo, G. O. Hypertensive retinopathy in Nigerians. A prospective clinical study of 350 cases. *Trop. Geog. Med.*, **33**, 311–316 (1981)

38 Seedat, Y. K. and Reddy, J. The clinical pattern of hypertension in the South African black population: a study of 1000 patients. *Afr. J. Med. Med. Sci.*, **5**, 1–7 (1976)

39 Grell, G. Clinical aspects of high blood pressure in the Caribbean. *West Ind. Med. J.*, **27**, 231–237 (1978)

40 Johnson, T. O. Arterial blood pressure and hypertension in an urban African population sample. *Br. J. Prev. Soc. Med.*, **25**, 26–33 (1971)

41 Oviasu, V. O. Arterial blood pressure and hypertension in a rural Nigerian community. *Afr. J. Med. Med. Sci.*, **7**, 137–143 (1978)

42 Pobee, J. O., Larbi, E. B., Belcher, D. W. *et al*. Blood pressure distribution in a rural Ghanain population. *Trans. R. Soc. Trop. Med. Hyg.*, **71**, 66–72 (1977)

43 Moser, M., Harris, M. and Pugatch, D. Epidemiology of hypertension: II. Studies of blood pressure in Liberia. *Am. J. Cardiol.*, **10**, 424–431 (1962)

44 Jeandel, P., Clausse, J. L., Sanga, M. and Menanga, M. Blood pressure in 2000 adults in the United Republic of Cameroun. *Trop. Cardiol.*, **14**, 71–76 (1988)

45 Meade, T. W., Brozovic, M., Chakraborti, R. *et al*. Ethnic group comparisons of variables associated with ischaemic heart disease. *Br. Heart J.*, **40**, 789–795 (1978)

46 Sever, P., Peart, W., Meade, T. W. *et al*. Ethnic differences in blood pressure with observations on noradrenaline and renin. *Clin. Exp. Hypertens.*, **1**, 733–744 (1979)

47 Meade, T. W., Imeson, J. D., Gordon, D. and Peart, W. S. The epidemiology of plasma renin. *Clin. Sci.*, **64**, 273–280 (1983)

48 DeGiovanni, J. V., Pentecost, B. L., Beevers, D. G. *et al*. The Birmingham blood pressure school study. *Postgrad. Med. J.*, **59**, 627–629 (1983)

49 Haines, A. P., Booroff, A., Goldenberg, E. *et al*. Blood pressure, smoking, obesity and alcohol consumption in blacks and whites in general practice. *J. Hum. Hypertens.*, **1**, 39–46 (1987)

50 Harburg, E., Erfurt, J. C., Chape, C. *et al*. Socioecological stressor areas. Black–white blood pressure, Detroit. *J. Chronic. Dis.*, **26**, 595–611 (1973)

51 Harburg, E., Erfurt, J. C., Schull, W. J. *et al*. Heredity, stress and blood pressure, a family set method. The Detroit project I–V. *J. Chronic Dis.*, **30**, 625–704 (1977)

52 Moll, P. P., Harburg, E., Burns, T. L. *et al*. Heredity, stress and blood pressure, a family set approach, the Detroit project revisited. *J. Chronic. Dis.*, **36**, 317–328 (1983)

53 Aderounmu, A. Relative importance of genetic and environmental factors in hypertension in black subjects. *Clin. Exp. Hypertens.*, **3**, 597–621 (1981)

54 Hilton, P. Cellular sodium transport and hypertension. *New. Engl. J. Med.*, **314**, 222–229 (1988)

55 Woods, K. L., West, M., Weissberg, P. L. and Beevers, D. G. Studies of red cell cation transport in white and black essential hypertensives. *Postgrad. Med. J.*, **57**, 767–771 (1981)

56 Cruickshank, J. K. and Beevers, D. G. Is blood pressure really 'worse' in black people? *Lancet*, **ii**, 371–372 (letter) (1980)

57 Deubner, D. C., Wilkinson, W. E., Helms, M. *et al*. Logistic model estimation of death attributable to risk factors for cardiovascular disease in Evans County, Georgia. *Am. J. Epidemiol.*, **112**, 135–143 (1980)

58 Tyroler, H. A. and Hames, C. G. Hypertension and 20 year mortality in black residents of Evans County, Georgia. In *Hypertension in Blacks* (eds W. D. Hall, E. Saunders and N. B. Shulam), Year Book Medical, Chicago, chap. 3 (1985)

59 Keil, J., Loodholt, C., Weinsuch, M. *et al*. Incidence of coronary heart disease in blacks and Charleston, S. Carolina. *Am. Heart J.*, **108**, 779–786 (1984)

60 Neaton, J. D., Kuller, L. H. Wentworth, D. and Borhani, N. Total and cardiovascular mortality in relation to risk factors and diastolic blood pressure among black and white men in MRFIT for 5 years. *Am. Heart J.*, **108**, 759–769 (1984)

61 Hall, W. D. Pharmacologic therapy of hypertension in blacks. In *Hypertension in Blacks*, (eds W. D. Hall, E. Saunders and N. B. Shulman), Year Book Medical, Chicago, chap. 13 (1985)

62 Freis, E. D., Materson, B. and Flamenbaum, W. Comparison of propranolol or hydrochlorothiazide alone for treatment of hypertension. III. Evaluation of the renin-angiotensin system. *Am. J. Med.*, **74**, 1028–1041 (1983)

63 Veterans Co-operative Study Group 1: Comparison of propranolol and hydrochlorothiazide alone for treatment of hypertension. 1: Results of short term titration with emphasis on racial differences in response. *JAMA*, **248**, 1996–2003 (1982)

64 Veterans Co-operative Study Group. Racial differences in response to low dose captopril are abolished by the addition of hydrochlorothiazide. *Br. J. Clin. Pharmacol.*, **14**, 97s–101s (1982)

65 Cruickshank, J. K., Anderson, N. McF., Wadsworth, J., *et al*. Treating hypertension in black compared with white non-insulin dependent diabetics: a double-blind trial of verapamil and metoprolol. *Br. Med. J.*, **297**, 1155–1159 (1988)

66 Lijner, P., M'Buyamba-Kabangu, J. R., Lepira, B. and Amery, A. Short term trial in black hypertensives treated with nitrendipine and acebutolol in Kinshasa. *Trop. Cardiol.*, **14**, 129–135 (1988)

Chapter 32

Ethnicity, lipoproteins and haemostatic factors

George J. Miller

The cohesion of mankind's numerous ethnic groups is conserved by behavioural patterns related to physical appearance, dress, language, religion and other beliefs. These components of ethnicity are of little direct importance for health and disease. The social interrelationships they foster, however, together with frequent inequalities in education, housing, income and employment in turn produce behavioural distinctions relevant for plasma lipoproteins, haemostatic factors, and to the risk of coronary heart disease. These contrasts include diet, alcohol consumption and cigarette smoking and, in time, changes in plasma lipoprotein and haemostatic factors.

Ethnic groups often differ genetically in physical appearances, and in the frequency of other traits such as blood groups. We do not yet know whether groups differ in the composition of gene-pools responsible for plasma lipoproteins and haemostatic factors. In some small groups factors such as inbreeding, the founder effect and random genetic drift lead to a high prevalence of an otherwise rare monogenic disorder. Examples are familial hypercholesterolaemia in Afrikaners [1] and lecithin-cholesterol acyltransferase deficiency in parts of Norway [2]. Most difficult to test is the possibility of ethnic differences in polygenic traits. The rapid expansion of molecular biology has already provided evidence: the much lower prevalence of a Sst-I restriction-enzyme polymorphism within the chromosome 11 multigene family coding for plasma apolipoproteins in Europeans than in other ethnic groups [3]. Presumably many such ethnic differences remain to be discovered, although some may represent genetic remnants of selective forces that have long passed into antiquity. These are issues for the genetic epidemiologist, who seeks to explore the distribution of genetic risk for disease in defined populations.

Neither the genetic nor the sociocultural components of ethnicity are immutable. Shorter-term fluctuations tend to be superimposed on a longer-term erosion of cultural distinctions in language, religion and dress, with blurring of genetic distinctions. Ethnic differences in plasma lipoproteins and haemostatic factors are no exceptions, and simply to catalogue them would therefore serve little useful purpose. Instead, contrasts between individuals of African, Indian, and European descent will be used to illustrate the importance of sociocultural distinctions for differences in plasma lipoproteins and haemostatic factors.

280

Plasma lipoproteins

The neonate

There have been only three comparisons of plasma lipoproteins in umbilical cord blood, in which neonates of European descent have been compared with non-Europeans. In the first two studies [4,5], black and white neonates were compared in Ohio and Louisiana, USA. The latter, larger population-based comparison found significantly lower low-density lipoprotein (LDL_{ch}) concentrations in black neonates of both sexes, and lower total cholesterol levels in black than in white male neonates. Cord blood high-density lipoprotein (HDL_{ch}) concentration was only lower in black females. In the smaller (hospital-based) study, neither HDL_{ch}, LDL_{ch} nor total cholesterol concentrations were lower in black neonates, although triglyceride concentrations tended to be higher. In the third study, Venezuelan neonates of mixed Amerindian-Spanish descent had a lower mean HDL_{ch} and a higher mean triglyceride concentration than the white neonates from Ohio, but no other ethnic differences were found in LDL_{ch} [6].

The basis of these small ethnic differences is uncertain. The fetus is not completely insulated from the mother's biology, and there must have been marked sociocultural contrasts between the parents of the groups compared. Differences between ethnic groups in the prevalence of high blood pressures [7] and diabetes mellitus [8] in late pregnancy, as well as in birthweight [9] and the stress of delivery [10], may also have contributed. There does not appear to be any study in which Indian neonates have been compared with another ethnic group.

Adulthood

Tables 32.1–32.3 present data for Jamaica [11], England [12] and Trinidad [13] in which ethnic differences in social, cultural and economic characteristics were, respectively, marked, intermediate and minimal at the time of study.

Jamaica

In Table 32.1, plasma lipoprotein concentrations are compared between businessmen in the Jamaican capital, Kingston, and farmers of the surrounding hill country. Although geographically no more than 20 miles (32 km) apart, the two groups had extremely contrasting lifestyles. The businessmen were urbanized,

Table 32.1 Plasma lipoproteins in two Jamaican communities

	White businessmen[*]		Black farmers[†]		
	Mean	s.d.	Mean	s.d.	P
Age (yr)	56.3	10.2	54.2	8.7	
Plasma cholesterol (mmol/l)					
High-density lipoprotein	1.63	0.28	2.15	0.46	< 0.001
Low-density lipoprotein	3.36	0.93	2.43	1.06	< 0.01
Total	5.74	0.80	5.02	0.88	< 0.01
Plasma triglyceride (mmol/l)	1.65	0.59	0.99	0.27	< 0.001

[*] $n = 27$.
[†] $n = 25$.

affluent, sedentary, Westernized, and for the most part of European background. The farmers were rural people who lead a physically demanding life as cultivators for subsistence and cash crops, and all but one were of predominantly African descent. The lives of these groups rarely, if ever, crossed. Mean plasma HDL_{ch} concentration was 32% higher in the farmers, while fasting triglyceride plasma LDL_{ch} and total cholesterol concentrations were respectively 40%, 28% and 12% less in farmers than businessmen. These marked group differences were probably explained partly by the greater adiposity of the businessmen and the much greater physical activity of the farmers, both of which can influence plasma lipoprotein concentrations [14,15]

London

Table 32.2 is a similar comparison of West Indian men of African descent (mainly from Jamaica) and European men in North-west London, together with a group of Indian men of Gujarati descent in the same area [12]. The West Indians arrived in England after 1955, and retained strong ties with family and friends in their country of origin. The Indians migrated mainly after 1965, coming either directly from India or via East Africa. With the influx of these people into the area, there had been an efflux of local-born residents. The Europeans remaining were predominantly from Scotland, Ireland, and continental Europe and were therefore not fully representative of the white population in England. None of those studied had married out of their ethnic group. Analysis of variance confirmed statistically significant differences in the distributions of all lipoproteins between ethnic groups. Mean HDL_{ch} concentrations were significantly increased in West Indians and those for LDL_{ch}, total cholesterol and fasting triglyceride were also lower in West Indian men than in the other groups. Overall, the differences between West Indian (African) men and European men in London were not so prominent as those between businessmen and farmers in Jamaica. Apart from low HDL_{ch}, Indian men had lipoprotein concentrations intermediate to those of West Indians and Europeans. Possible contributors to these ethnic differences were the relatively high alcohol consumption of the West Indians, and the lower ratio of polyunsaturated fat to saturated fat (P/S) in the diet of Europeans in Britain (see also Chapter 26). Alcohol tends to raise HDL_{ch} concentration [16], and a high P/S ratio may reduce serum triglyceride [17] and LDL_{ch} concentrations [18].

Table 32.2 Serum lipoproteins in men aged 45–54 years living in London

	West Indians[*]		Europeans[†]		Indians[‡]		
	Mean	s.d.	Mean	s.d.	Mean	s.d.	P[§]
Serum cholesterol (mmol/1)							
High-density lipoprotein	1.55	0.50	1.36	0.47	1.24	0.30	< 0.01
Low-density lipoprotein	2.87	1.08	3.48	1.03	3.09	0.83	< 0.01
Total	5.30	1.05	6.08	1.13	5.42	1.02	< 0.01
Serum triglyceride (mmol/l)	1.07	0.77	1.91	1.52	1.50	0.99	< 0.01

[*] $n = 24$.
[†] $n = 68$.
[‡] $n = 75$.
[§] Analysis of variance.

Trinidad

Table 32.3 summarizes the findings in men of predominantly African, Indian and European descent in a residential suburb of Port-of-Spain, the capital of Trinidad, West Indies [13]. They were all Trinidadians whose families had resided there for at least three generations, and in many cases considerably more. Their ancestral cultures had been superseded by a Trinidadian urban culture in many respects. Unlike London and Jamaica, considerable intermarriage has occurred in this community, and as many as 30% of residents were of no predominant ethnic origin (these have been excluded from Table 32.3). Analysis of variance confirmed significant ethnic differences in all lipoprotein concentrations, but the size of the differences were less than in either London or Jamaica.

Table 32.3 Plasma lipoprotein concentrations* in men of three ethnic groups in Trinidad

	African descent[†] *(mean)*	*Indian descent[‡]* *(mean)*	*European descent[§]* *(mean)*	P^{fl}
Serum cholesterol (mmol/l)				
High-density lipoprotein	1.0	0.9	1.0	< 0.001
Low-density lipoprotein	4.1	4.4	4.3	< 0.001
Total	5.7	5.9	6.0	< 0.001
Serum triglyceride (mmol/l)	1.3	1.8	1.7	< 0.001

* Age-adjusted.
[†] $n = 485$.
[‡] $n = 370$.
[§] $n = 6$.
[fl] Analysis of variance

USA

Ethnic differences in plasma lipoproteins have been reported in many American communities. In Evans County, Georgia [19] lower mean cholesterol concentrations were found in black than in white males when the community was first examined in 1960. Seven years later, this ethnic difference had largely disappeared owing to a greater increase in the blacks. Subsequent measurement showed that black men matched for age and total cholesterol concentration, had a higher HDL_{ch}, together with a lower serum triglyceride and slightly lower LDL_{ch} concentration than whites. These differences did not appear to be explained by indices of occupation, education, social class or smoking. The ethnic contrasts in LDL_{ch} and HDL_{ch} were apparent only in non-obese men, whereas that in serum triglyceride concentration was present at all levels of adiposity. In similarly matched black and white males in Cincinnati, Ohio significantly higher HDL_{ch} and lower fasting triglyceride concentrations were also found in the black group [20]. In the pooled American Lipid Research Clinics' experience [21], black males had lower LDL_{ch}, lower VLDL cholesterol, and higher HDL_{ch} concentrations between 30 and 44 years. In general, the ethnic contrasts were more marked in men than women. Indirect evidence from the American National Health and Nutrition Examination Survey for 1976–80 [22] suggested that ethnic differences in diet, cigarette smoking and alcohol consumption were probably insufficient to explain fully the higher HDL_{ch} concentration of black males in the Lipid Research Clinics population. In Texas, black adults were found to have plasma Lp(a) concentrations about twice that of white adults [23]. The meaning of this difference is obscure, but since this lipoprotein is included with LDL in the precipitation techniques for separation of lipoproteins, it is possible that true ethnic differences in LDL_{ch} are greater than those reported.

In contrast, black males of high socioeconomic status and educational attainment, who constituted a small minority of the Framingham population, were found to have a significantly lower HDL_{ch} concentration than the whites. The same pattern was found among women, and persisted even after allowance for other factors [24].

Haemostatic factors

Far fewer ethnic comparisons are available of haemostatic factors than of plasma lipoproteins, mainly because the relations of the former with coronary heart disease have received relatively little attention until recently [25,38]. Of the studies described in Jamaica, London and Trinidad, only that in London included measures of haemostatic function. Table 32.4 summarizes the findings for plasma factor VII coagulant activity (VII_c), fibrinogen concentration, dilute clot lysis time as an index of serum fibrinolytic activity, platelet count and platelet volume in men of West Indian (African), Indian (Gujarati) and European descent in the London survey [12].

Mean plasma VII_c was about 12% but not significantly lower in West Indians than in Indians and Europeans. In an earlier survey of a working population in the same region of London [26], a mean reduction of 9% in VII_c in a larger number of West Indian compared with European men achieved statistical significance, but no ethnic difference was apparent in women.

Relation of factor VII clotting activity to plasma lipoproteins and dietary fat

Factor VII_c has been shown to be correlated positively with plasma cholesterol and triglyceride concentration in a sample of the European men in this population [27]. The mean concentrations of both lipids were significantly lower in West Indian men than in European men, but similar in women of the two groups. Lower VII_c levels in association with reduced serum cholesterol concentrations in Africans as compared with Europeans has also been reported from the Gambia [28] and South Africa [29]. This probably reflects the mutual relations of these variables with dietary fat intake [30], so that ethnic differences in VII_c are most likely a consequence of group differences in fat consumption.

Table 32.4 shows that no ethnic difference was demonstrated in plasma fibrinogen concentration in the London study [12], in agreement with that found, in the larger, working population of this area [26]. In an urban–rural comparison in the Gambia, significantly higher mean fibrinogen concentrations were found in rural groups [28], probably in response to parasitic infestation. A comparison 20 years ago of the indigenous black East African population and Indians in Uganda revealed no ethnic difference in plasma fibrinogen concentration in men [31].

Analysis of variance revealed no significant ethnic difference in dilute clot lysis time in the London study (Table 32.4), although Indians had a mean time almost

Table 32.4 Haemostatic variables by ethnic group in men aged 45–54 years in North-west London

	West Indian (African)[*]		Indian[†]		European[‡]		
	Mean	s.d.	Mean	s.d.	Mean	s.d.	$P^{\S}$
Factor VII activity (% standard)	97.9	21.0	109.8	30.8	111.7	25.5	n.s.
Plasma fibrinogen (mg/dl)	299	54	304	59	326	75	n.s.
Dilute clot lysis time (h)	10.9	8.1	15.1	7.9	13.3	8.0	n.s.
Platelet count ($\times 10^3/mm^3$)	217.1	57.1	252.0	86.4	218.3	63.0	< 0.05
Mean platelet volume (μm^3)	8.33	0.97	7.95	0.94	8.38	0.97	< 0.05

n.s., Not statistically significant.
[*] $n = 24$.
[†] $n = 75$.
[‡] $n = 68$
[§] Analysis of variance.

40% greater than that of West Indians, with the Europeans having an intermediate value. A similar result for fibrinolytic activity in the latter two groups had also been found in the earlier London study [26]. In South Africa, rural Bantu men had a significantly shorter clot lysis time than urban Bantu men; differences in women were in the same direction but less obvious [32]. Bantu men of both groups had a shorter clot lysis time than South African white males, but the ethnic difference was reversed in women. Fibrinolytic activity in rural Africans in the Gambia was also found to be greater than that in several European groups [28]. In Uganda, clot lysis time was very significantly shorter among the indigenous African male than in Indian men [31] and was related strongly and positively to skinfold thickness in the Indian group [31]. These results suggested a decline in fibrinolytic activity with urbanization, possibly as a consequence of reduced habitual physical activity [33].

In contrast to the other clotting factors, significant ethnic differences were found in platelet count and volume in the London study. Indian men had a platelet count about 15% higher on average than those of West Indians and Europeans, together with a 5% reduction in mean platelet volume (Table 32.4). A lower platelet count in African than in Indian men has been reported from Uganda [31], and also in Africans in the Gambia than in several European groups [28]. Other studies support a lower platelet count in men of African descent as compared with Europeans [34,35]. Differences between West Indians and Europeans in Britain, however, are less consistent, some studies showing lower platelet counts in West Indians of one sex but not another [26,35]. The origin of these differences is unknown but similar results have been reported in cholesterol-fed atherosclerotic rabbits [36], suggesting that the ethnic differences may be acquired rather than inherited.

There have been few comparisons of platelet function across ethnic groups. In Uganda, platelet adhesiveness to glass heads did not differ between African and Indian men [31]. In London, platelet aggregability in response to adenosine diphosphate (standardized for platelet count) was found to be less in West Indians of both sexes than in Europeans [37]. Although aggregability was found to be less in smokers than in non-smokers, and less with heavier consumption of alcohol, these factors could not explain the ethnic difference.

Conclusions

These studies emphasize the value and limitations of ethnicity in epidemiology. Ethnic group differences within populations can be exploited in the search for disease causation. Consistent relations between a suspected variable and risk of disease within and between groups strengthens the evidence for a causative association. On the other hand, ethnicity is difficult to work with because, unlike age and sex, it is a complex of genetic, cultural, social and environmental factors which combine to give each ethnic group its distinctiveness. Many groups are in transition and their characteristics are changing with time. The nuances of ethnicity are difficult to assess, and need a somewhat cosmopolitan researcher to examine the issues in an objective and informed manner. Many ethnic contrasts in plasma lipoproteins and haemostatic factors are likely to diminish as cultural distinctions and socioeconomic inequalities recede into history. Some, such as the relatively low triglyceride concentration of blacks and the increased factor VIII coagulant activity reported in West Indians in London [26], suggest a role for genetic inheritance in ethnic contrasts, but this is speculative. Whether any of the differences described are relevant to cardiovascular disease rates, or merely represent forms of anthropometric contrast, will remain uncertain until the necessary prospective studies are undertaken. So far these have been confined almost entirely to plasma lipids in relation to disease in the European.

References

1 Seftel, H. C., Baker, S. G., Sandler, M. P. *et al.* A host of hypercholesterolaemic homozygotes in South Africa. *Br. Med. J.*, **281**, 633–636 (1980)
2 Teisberg, P., Gjone, E. and Olaisen, B. Genetics of LCAT (lecithin: cholesterol acyltransferase) deficiency. *Ann. Hum. Genet. Lond.*, **38**, 327–331 (1975)
3 Rees, A., Sharpe, C., Stocks, J., Vella, M. A. *et al.* DNA polymorphism in the apo AI-CIII gene cluster. Association with hypertriglyceridaemia. *J. Clin. Invest.*, **76**, 1090–1095 (1985)
4 Frerichs, R. R., Srinivasan, S. R., Webber, I. S. *et al.* Serum lipids and lipoproteins at birth in a biracial population: the Bogalusa Heart Study. *Pediatr. Res.*, **12**, 858–863 (1978)
5 Glueck, C. J., Gartside, P. S., Tsang, R. C. *et al.* Black-white similarities in cord blood lipids and lipoproteins. *Metabolism*, **26**, 347–350 (1977)
6 Nucete, H., Mendoza, S., Somoza, B. *et al.* Cord blood lipids and lipoproteins: Merida, Venezuela, and Cincinnati, Ohio. *Prev. Med.*, **9**, 667–674 (1980)
7 Parker, C. R., Hankins, G. D. V., Carr, B. R. *et al.* The effect of hypertension in pregnant women on fetal adrenal metabolism and fetal plasma lipoprotein-cholesterol metabolism. *Am. J. Obstet. Gynecol.*, **150**, 263–269 (1984)
8 Fordyce, M. K., Duncan, R., Chao, R. *et al.* Cord blood serum in newborns of diabetic mothers. *J. Chronic Dis.*, **36**, 263–268 (1983)
9 Miller, N. E., Nestel, P. J., Boulton, T. J. C. *et al.* Cord blood high-density lipoprotein concentration in 1797 births: relationship to family history of coronary disease. *J. Chronic Dis.*, **34**, 119–125 (1981)
10 Martinsen, K., Ehnholm, C., Huttunen, J. K. *et al.* Intrapartum stress lowers the concentration of high-density lipoprotein cholesterol in cord plasma. *Eur. J. Clin. Invest.*, **11**, 351–354 (1981)
11 Miller, G. J., Miller, N. E. and Ashcroft, M. T. Inverse relationship in Jamaica between plasma high-density lipoprotein cholesterol concentration and coronary disease risk as predicted by multiple risk factor status. *Clin. Sci. Mol. Med.*, **51**, 475–482 (1976)
12 Miller, G. J., Kotecha, S., Wilkinson, W. H. *et al.* Comparisons of dietary and other characteristics for coronary heart disease in men of Indian, West Indian and European descent in London. *Atherosclerosis*, **70**, 63–72 (1988)

13 Miller, G. J., Beckles, G. L. A., Byam, N. T. A. *et al.* Serum lipoprotein concentrations in relation to ethnic composition and urbanization in men and women of Trinidad, West Indies. *Int. J. Epidemiol.*, **13**, 413–421 (1984)

14 Garrison, R. J., Wilson, P. W., Castelli, W. P. *et al.* Obesity and lipoprotein cholesterol in the Framingham Offspring Study. *Metabolism*, **29**, 1053–1060 (1980)

15 Lehtonen, A. and Viikari, J. Serum triglycerides and cholesterol and serum high-density lipoprotein cholesterol in highly physically active men. *Acta. Med. Scand.*, **204**, 111–114 (1978)

16 Haskell, W. L., Camargo, C., Williams, P. T. *et al.* The effect of cessation and resumption of moderate alcohol intake on serum high-density lipoprotein subfractions. *N. Engl. J. Med.*, **310**, 805–810 (1984)

17 Chait, A., Onitiri, A., Nicoll, A. *et al.* Reduction of serum triglyceride levels by polyunsaturated fat. *Atherosclerosis*, **20**, 347–350 (1974)

18 Ehnholm, C., Huttunen, J. K., Pietinen, P. *et al.* Effect of diet on serum lipoproteins in a population with a high risk of coronary heart disease. *N. Engl. J. Med.*, **307**, 850–855 (1982)

19 Tyroler, H. A., Hames, C. G., Krishan, I. *et al.* Black-white differences in serum lipids and lipoproteins in Evans County. *Prev. Med.*, **4**, 541–549 (1975)

20 Morrison, J. A., deGroot, I., Kelly, K. A. *et al.* Black-white differences in plasma lipids and lipoproteins in adults: the Cincinnati Lipid Research Clinic Population Study. *Prev. Med.*, **8**, 34–39 (1979)

21 Tyroler, H. A., Glueck, C. J., Christensen, B. and Kwiterovich, P. O. Plasma high-density lipoprotein cholesterol comparisons in black and white populations. *Circulation*, Suppl. IV, **62**, 99–107 (1980)

22 Gartside, P. S., Khoury, P. and Glueck, C. J. Determinants of high-density lipoprotein cholesterol in blacks and whites: the Second National Health and Nutrition Examination Survey. *Am. Heart J.*, **108**, 641–653 (1983)

23 Guyton, J. R., Dahlen, G. H., Patsch, W. *et al.* Relationship of lipoprotein Lp (a) levels to race and to apolipoprotein B. *Arteriosclerosis*, **5**, 265–272 (1985)

24 Wilson, P. W. F., Savage, D. D., Castelli, W. P. *et al.* HDL-cholesterol in a sample of black adults: the Framingham Minority Study. *Metabolism*, **32**, 328–332 (1983)

25 Meade, T. W., North, W. R. S., Chakrabarti, R. *et al.* Haemostatic function and cardiovascular death: early results of a prospective study. *Lancet*, **i**, 1050–1054 (1980)

26 Meade, T. W., Brozovic, M., Chakrabarti, R. *et al.* Ethnic group comparisons of variables associated with ischaemic heart disease. *Br. Heart J.*, **40**, 789–795 (1978)

27 Miller, G. J., Walter, S. J., Stirling, Y. *et al.* Assay of factor VII activity by two techniques: evidence for increased conversion of VII to α VII$_a$ in hyperlipidaemia with possible implications for ischaemic heart disease. *Br. J. Haematol.*, **59**, 249–258 (1985)

28 Meade, T. W., Stirling, Y., Thompson, S. G. *et al.* An international and interregional comparison of haemostatic variables in the study of ischaemic heart disease. Report of a working group. *Int. J. Epidemiol..*, **15**, 331–336 (1986)

29 Merskey, C., Gordon, H., Lackner, H. *et al.* Blood coagulation and fibrinolysis in relation to coronary heart disease. A comparative study of normal white men, white men with overt coronary heart disease, and normal Bantu men. *Br. Med. J.*, **1**, 219–227 (1960)

30 Miller, G. J., Martin, J. C., Webster, J. *et al.* Association between dietary fat intake and plasma factor VII coagulant activity – a predictor of cardiovascular mortality. *Atherosclerosis*, **60**, 269–277 (1986)

31 Shaper, A. G., Jones, K. W., Kyobe, J. and Jones, M. Fibrinolysis in relation to body fatness, serum lipids and coronary heart disease in African and Asian men in Uganda. *J. Atheroscler. Res.*, **6**, 313–327 (1966)

32 Walker, A. R. P. Fibrinolytic activity of whole blood from South African Bantu and White subjects. *Am. J. Clin. Nutr.*, **9**, 461–472 (1961)

33 Fearnley, G. R. and Lackner, R. The fibrinolytic activity of normal blood. *Br. J. Haematol.*, **1**, 189–198 (1955)

34 Essien, E. M., Usanga, E. A. and Ayeni, O. The normal platelet count and platelet factor 3 availability in some Nigerian population groups. *Scand. J. Haematol.*, **10**, 378–383 (1973)

35 Bain, B. J. and Seed, M. Platelet count and platelet size in healthy Africans and West Indians. *Clin.*

Lab. Haematol., **8**, 43–48 (1986)

36 Martin, J. F., Slater, D. N., Kishk, Y. T. and Trowbridge, E. A. Platelet and megakaryocyte changes in cholesterol-induced experimental atherosclerosis. *Arteriosclerosis*, **5**, 604–612 (1985)

37 Meade, T. W., Vickers, M.V., Thompson, S. G. *et al.* Epidemiological characteristics of platelet aggregability. *Br. Med. J.*, **290**, 428–432 (1985)

38 Meade, T. W., Brozovic, M, Chakrabarti, B. *et al.* Haemostatic function and ischaemic heart disease: principal results of the Northwick Park Heart Study. *Lancet*, **i**, 533–537 (1986)

Chapter 33

Diabetes: contrasts between peoples of black (West African), Indian and white European origin

J. K. Cruickshank

This chapter compares mortality and prevalence of diabetes, available genetic work and clinical disease in four areas: in the West Indies and the Indian subcontinent, their migrants to Europe, particularly Britain, and in the black population of the USA. Such cross-nation comparisons may provide valuable clues to aetiology and to methods of control and prevention.

The primary topic is the adult-onset, non-insulin dependent type of diabetes mellitus (abbreviated to NIDDM) and its complications. Diabetes with a young onset, which is insulin dependent for life and ketosis prone (IDDM), seems to be infrequent in the West Indies and among children of migrants from both the Caribbean and the Indian subcontinent in Britain, although the published evidence is limited [1,2] (see Chapter 35). IDDM also seems to be less frequent among black Americans than whites [3,4]. Recently a third category entered the WHO classification as malnutrition-related diabetes (MRDM), based on anecdotal clinical experience rather than evidence from prospective studies [5]. There is a 'fibro-calculous' chronic pancreatitic form and another type which evolved from a small number of cases described by Hugh-Jones in 1955 [6] – Jamaican or J-type, which may perhaps be related to childhood protein energy malnutrition. These cases were followed and later partially refuted as a special form by Tulloch [7,8]. However, enough apparently atypical patients exist for the category to continue, in Jamaica reclassified as 'phasic-insulin dependence' by Morrison [9] (see Chapter 35).

Background

Chronic and vascular disease rather than infection have become the Caribbean's main health burden since the 1960s (see Chapters 34 and 35). The island nations of the West Indies thus have public health priorities quite distinct from much poorer tropical countries where infections are still rife.

Vital statistics and mortality rates for diabetes in India, particularly from the Punjab and Gujarat, from Pakistan and Bangladesh and for Indian-origin peoples in East Africa are limited. In general, high infant mortality and infectious disease remain prevalent in poorer people. Chronic disease is likely to be increasingly important, at least in the better off, some of whose relatives were migrants to Europe.

Among black Americans, chronic vascular disease with or without diabetes is the major current public health issue, unfortunately now overshadowed by AIDS.

Mortality

Afro-Caribbeans in the West Indies and in Britain

Diabetes was recognized often enough to occur in the top eight causes of death from three Caribbean islands in the 1970s. Diabetes is under-reported by up to 50% on death certificates in England and Wales [10] and under-recording may still be a problem in the Caribbean where awareness is greater but patients may not be diagnosed. We recently investigated under-recording in Jamaica from a direct inspection of all death certificates for the entire island for 1977 and 1978 (25 947 deaths). Diabetes was listed (primary and underlying causes combined) on 1695 certificates (7%). Only 66% of these had been officially recorded in the Registrar General's coding [11].

In England and Wales, perhaps due to the healthy migrant effect, total West Indian migrant mortality in the 1970s was 10% lower than the national average but proportional mortality ratios from diabetes were about four times greater than average for both men and women of West Indian birth [12] (Figure 33.1).

Although these ratios are high, total numbers of deaths were relatively low so that the overall mortality risk attributable to known diabetes is not that great for Afro-Caribbeans. Early influences pre-migration may be relevant. Deaths from coronary heart disease, so common among whites and Indians, remain low (see Chapter 31). Figure 33.1 also illustrates the remarkably high toll in deaths due to diabetes in Trinidad, whose population is half Indo- and half Afro-Caribbean (see 'Prevalence' below).

Indian migrants

In Britain, standardized and proportional mortality ratios for diabetes have been twice the national average for people born in the Indian subcontinent (Figure 33.1), who are more numerous in Britain, and among whom more work in diabetes has been done, than among Afro-Caribbeans.

Black Americans

Deaths from diabetes among American blacks are epidemic, particularly among women [13].

Prevalence

Estimates of prevalence depend on the rigour of survey methods, particularly if attempts are made to generalize from surveys in hospital attenders.

In the West Indies

Historically the 'sugar sickness' was considered rare as reported in a treatise by Rollo in 1798. A study by Brigham [14] in 1868 was an early assertion that a high

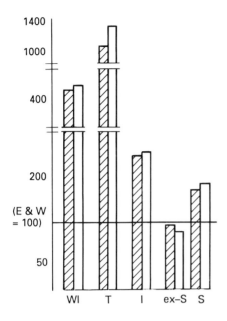

Figure 33.1 1970–78 mortality ratios from diabetes for migrants from the West Indies (WI), Indian subcontinent (I), Scotland (ex-S) and home countries (T=Trinidad, 1971) and Scotland (S=1970–72) to England (E) and Wales (W) = 100. ■, Males; □, females

sugar intake was not its major cause among indentured East Indian labourers who had been imported from the Bombay, Calcutta and Madras areas of India by British landowners to replace emancipated slaves on sugar plantations [15,16]. In 1893, diabetes mortality rates were said to be low among East Indians in Guyana [17], as they still were among the East Indian and African origin populations of Grenada and the mainly black Bahamas in 1922 [18]. A seminal book *Diabetes in the Tropics* by Tulloch in 1962 from the University Hospital of the West Indies in Kingston detailed the methodological problems and available diabetes prevalence rates then apparent to tropical clinicians worldwide [7].

Jamaica
Tulloch studied representative communities across Jamaica, half rural, half urban, with 50 g oral glucose loads if screening for glycosuria had been positive. The prevalence of diabetes was 0.9% in 1915 men and 1.5% in 2601 women (19), clearly underestimates and not updated until a later survey of volunteers with unadjusted adult rates of 6% [20]. In 1969, Florey organized a 100 g glucose tolerance screen in Lawrence Tavern, a community some 16 miles from Kingston, where a cohort study was in progress [21,22] (see Chapter 31). Two hundred and thirty-six men and 309 women were randomly sampled from the locally taken census. Only 1-h samples were taken. Compared with the 1962–64 US national survey (50 g loads), 'diabetic' results from Jamaica were generally lower in each 10-year age group, (4% > 180 mg/100 ml below 44 years and 8–10% at 45–64 years [23,24]).

Trinidad
A remarkable island-wide probability survey of 23 900 people was conducted in 1964, when those with glycosuria were tested by 50 g glucose loads. The overall age-adjusted diabetes prevalence rates were 1.4% in Afro- and 2.4% in East Indian Trinidadians [25]. To study this and the ethnic difference in coronary heart disease, Miller and Beckles established the St James study in a representative community of

Port-of-Spain [26–29]. 1500 people of East Indian and 1500 of black African origin (ethnic group defined on grandparent origin) were each challenged by 50 g of oral glucose with results adjusted to 1980 WHO criteria for 75 g loads (Figure 33.2). They have been followed for nearly 10 years.

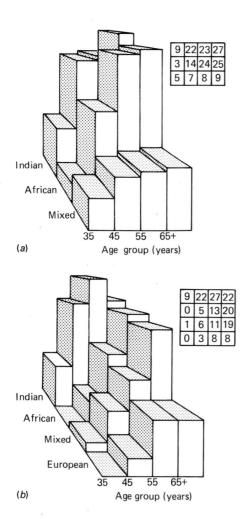

(a)

(b)

Figure 33.2 St James Survey, Trinidad. Prevalence (%) of diabetes mellitus in women (a) and men (b) by age and ethnic group

The very high rates of over 20% overt diabetes in East Indians in each age decade over 45 years of both sexes, 20% in black men and 24% in black women over 55 years, illustrate the inaccuracy of urine testing screens. Rates may have increased considerably in the 15 years since the previous Trinidad survey [25].

The Indian subcontinent and its migrants elsewhere

Ancient Hindu physicians were among the first known authors on 'honeyed urine', a disease of the plump and affluent in late nineteenth century Calcutta and Madras. Of modern studies known to the author in India, both using 50 g glucose loads, one in 1966 in Orissa produced rates in adults over 30 of 0.5–2%, these were greater in urban districts [30]. Among similarly aged outpatients in Calcutta, at least 5% was recorded depending on criteria [31]. A further national sampling study by the All India Medical Research Institute is underway. A study in a district of New Delhi has recently been compared with one among Punjabis in Britain (Figure 33.3) [32],

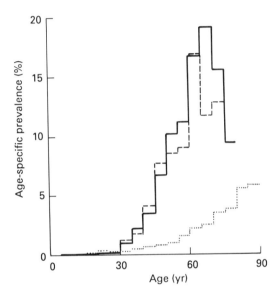

Figure 33.3 Age-specific prevalence of known diabetes. ————, Southall Indians; ·········, Southall Europeans' ————, Darya Ganj Indians. From Mather *et al.* [32] with permission

and in southern Indians in Madras [33]. In surveys of migrant Indians wherever they have moved, diabetes rates clearly exceed those of local populations. Singapore, Malaysia, Fiji, East and South Africa and Surinam and, most recently Mauritius, are all examples in addition to Trinidad [34–38].

In Britain

Within a generation of migration to Britain, the diabetes epidemic among Indian or East African-born 'Asians' became obvious, first from our 1975–79 hospital admissions survey in Birmingham [39], then in numerous other reports from Southall, West London (mainly Punjabis), North-west London and Leicester (both mainly Gujaratis) and more recently in Coventry [40]. People of Pakistani and Bangladeshi origin are not spared [41].

The most extensive study was Mather's Southall survey of *known* diabetes in West London [42]. This was based not on blood sampling but on household enquiry of known diabetics who were matched against the 1980 local census figures. Mather then collaborated with colleagues in India and a similar survey was conducted on 6878 residents in the relatively affluent Darya Ganj suburb of Delhi. Crude rates were 2.2% in Punjabis and 1.2% in whites in Southall but with marked age differences there and in Darya Ganj [43]. The dramatic differences in age-specific rates between Indians and whites in Southall but their close similarity with Indians in Darya Ganj are shown in Figure 33.3.

The age-specific rate ratio is four to eight times that for West London whites in both migrant Punjabis and the Darya Ganj.

The difference between the Darya Ganj and previous Indian results may be partly due to social class and income – over 85% of the Darya Ganj men were affluent businessmen or civil servants. Even so, 'the striking similarities' between Southall and Darya Ganj illustrate the susceptibility of Indian communities to diabetes despite internal cultural and ethnic differences; this casts doubt on a purely environmental/stress hypothesis to account for diabetes endemicity in Indian peoples abroad.

Full glucose challenge studies in Britain
The Southall results were of known cases without glucose challenge. To establish mechanisms including familial and genetic possibilities, the author is studying, by 75 g glucose challenge and WHO criteria, a population sample of Gujarati, Afro-Caribbean and white residents in a poor to medium income area in North-west London. Preliminary results to date are shown in Table 33.1

Over 50% of the Gujarati sample tested so far have 'abnormal' glucose tolerance but the rates of diabetes in the Afro-Caribbeans and of impaired tolerance in the whites are also high. These prevalence rates are associated with markedly increased insulin secretion for given levels of glucose in Afro-Caribbeans and Gujaratis compared with whites (Figure 33.4).

Table 33.1 Brent Diabetes Survey: age-specific prevalence (50–69 year olds)

	Total screened	Impaired glucose tolerance[*]	Total DM (new + known)	Age (yr)[†]	Body mass index (kg/m^2)[†]
Men					
Gujarati	55	24 (13)	29 (16)	60.5 ± 7	25.2 ± 3
White	48	25 (12)	8 (4)	63.5 ± 6	26.4 ± 4
Afro-Caribbean	51	6 (3)	29 (15)	59.1 ± 6	26.0 ± 4
Women					
Gujarati	52	37 (19)	35 (18)	61.5 ± 7	28.1 ± 7
White	51	18 (9)	—	62.3 ± 7	26.5 ± 5
Afro-Caribbean	52	19 (10)	21 (11)	57.4 ± 6	29.5 ± 4
Total	309	21 (66)	21 (66)	60.7 ± 6	27.0 ± 5

WHO criteria: impaired glucose tolerance, 2 h ≥ 7.8 mmol/l plasma glucose; diabetes, ≥ 11.1 mmol/l.
DM, Diabetes mellitus.
[*] Results shown are percentages, figures in parentheses are *n*.
[†] Results shown are mean ± s.d.

insulin secretion for given levels of glucose in Afro-Caribbeans and Gujaratis compared with whites (Figure 33.4).

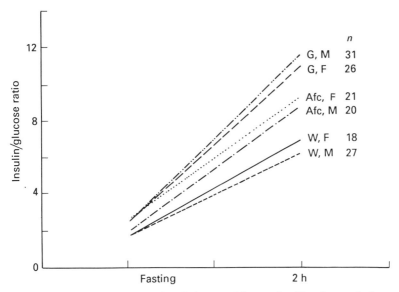

Figure 33.4 Insulin/glucose ratio by ethnic group 2 hours after 75 g glucose challenge. Sample excludes known diabetics. Afc, Afro-Caribbean; W, white; G, Gujarati; M, male; F, female

Black Americans

Prevalence of known diabetes continues to increase particularly in women. Total age-adjusted rates (and standard errors) per 1000 population for 1979–81 were 33 (3) and 45.8 (2.7) for black and 22.7 (0.7) and 23.6 (0.7) for white men and women respectively [44]. These rates rose respectively in blacks and whites from 8.3 and 5.7 at 17–44 years, to 101 and 50 at 45–64 years and to 132 and 84 over 65 years and are worse in poorer families, in cities and in those with less education (Figure 33.5). Rates have doubled in whites between 1965 and 1985 (12.5 to 24.1) and trebled in blacks (13.8 to 36.9); rates in black females have exceeded whites since 1963 but only did so in men in 1975 [44].

Genetic studies

Molecular studies using DNA restriction fragment polymorphisms (RFLPs) have led to claims by several groups for genetic markers of IDDM, NIDDM and most recently 'fibro-calculous' diabetes in the MRDM category. These have been based, sometimes tenuously, on evidence of clear heritability from family and twin studies in NIDDM, and much lower inheritance in IDDM.

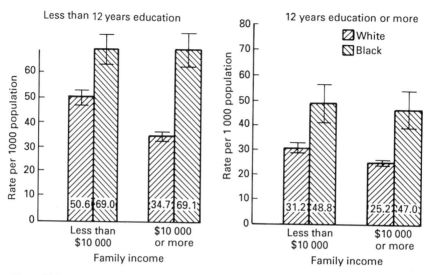

Figure 33.5 Average age-adjusted number of *known* diabetics (over 17 years)/1000, by ethnic group, family income and education; USA 1979–81. From US National Centre for Health Statistics [44] with permission

IDDM

HLA-DR3 and −DR4, or both, appear to be consistent markers across all ethnic groups, probably related to the DQ-B subregion [45,46]. Haplotype frequencies vary and may indicate genetic admixture from white gene-pools into black, with one hypothesis that admixture confers the susceptibility to IDDM [47]. However, not only are admixture estimates subject to error but DR3/4 is more closely linked with IDDM in Nigerian clinic cases (in whom admixture is unlikely) as well as in black Americans [48,49].

A recent study of IDDM cases in Afro-Caribbeans, collected from all over England because of their rarity, reported a novel DQ-B VIIc association, using RFLPs [50]. These authors had previously studied IDDM patients of Punjabi Indian origin in Britain, again with DR4 and DQB linkage [51].

NIDDM and MRDM

Efforts to establish linkage with various candidate markers (including the insulin, insulin receptor and glucose transporter genes) in RFLP studies have produced inconsistent and eventually negative results. Most control groups (e.g. in one report among black Americans [52]) have been neither randomly sampled nor had their glucose tolerance status adequately tested; as prevalence is high, many unrecognized index cases will have been considered as 'controls'. Similarly, a recent study seeking a genetic basis for MRDM (for which the evidence is scarce or non-existent given the environmental insult of malnutrition) had control groups unrepresentative of both the general population and the socioeconomic group at risk [53].

All the RFLP studies cited above are flawed by non-random sampling and, particularly for NIDDM, inadequately tested controls [54,55]. Unless considerable efforts are made to use proper community samples, the data generated may not only be meaningless but expensive enough to have diverted funds from more applied science with appropriate methodology. Prevention strategies require assaults on likely environmental promoters, whatever the genetic background. In NIDDM, families of index cases, tested and sampled from the population, provide a focus for both preventive studies and for sound genetic epidemiology.

Clinical disease

'J'-type (Jamaican) diabetes

This name was coined to describe a group of young, lean, insulin-dependent (and insensitive) but ketosis-resistant diabetics in the University Hospital Clinic in Jamaica [6]. Although much quoted this category was restricted to only 13 patients (Figure 33.6).

Two patients had ketosis and a further two were over 110% of ideal weight. Many other similar cases were described subsequently across the world in which a past history of malnutrition was suspected (although Hugh-Jones did not specify this). The 1985 WHO diabetes category, 'Malnutrition-related' (MRDM), included 'J' type as well as the more clear-cut condition of fibro-calculous diabetes, common in India and South-east Asia but not seen in the Caribbean or to any extent in sub-Saharan Africa or Ethiopia. The relationship to malnutrition of both remains

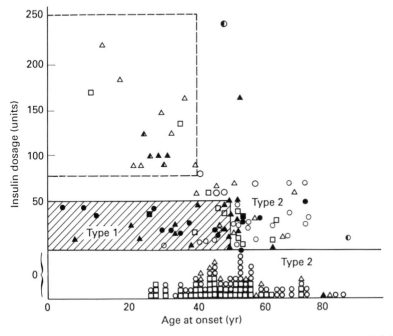

Figure 33.6 Scatter diagram relating insulin dose, at balance, to age of onset of diabetes in 198 of 215 consecutive Jamaican cases. □, Fat = + 10% or more from average weight; △, thin = − 10% or less from average weight; ○, ± 10% from average weight. Black symbols, ketosis; white symbols, no ketosis. Reproduced from Hugh-Jones [6] with permission

unclear. A recent (1988) Wellcome Tropical Institute seminar has sponsored a multicentre study to examine its existence and nature more clearly.

It is not widely appreciated that Tulloch followed up Hugh-Jones' original cases and added 11 more of his own. On long-term review, eight of these patients became ketotic; most of the remainder gained weight and soon required more usual doses of insulin and he concluded that 'J' type patients were not a separate group but Type II cases (now NIDDM) in which management was poor [8]. Nevertheless, since then in the same clinic, Morrison has followed a group of 59 patients he has termed 'phasic-insulin dependent' [9]. These patients seem to be similar to both Tulloch and Hugh-Jones' original series in being young in onset, neither overweight nor ketosis prone, and in whom insulin can be withdrawn, often for many months. The phasic pattern is heralded by frequent hypoglycaemic episodes requiring insulin dose reduction and eventually its withdrawal in some cases. Whether dietary changes have occurred simultaneously is unknown. What these patients represent in terms of pancreatic (or other) pathology remains unclear. The diagnostic labels may merely reflect a spectrum of insulin secretion and action.

IDDM (or Type I)

Classical IDDM, as noted above, appears to be infrequent in these populations. Morrison is currently aware (in 1988) of only 23 patients diagnosed below 25 years of age in his clinic of up to 2000 patients in Jamaica. Similarly, in Birmingham, England in the 1970s with a population of over 100 000 Afro-Caribbeans, no children of Afro-Caribbean parentage were known to paediatricians in its central and west districts. In Brent, North-west London over the past 5 years, from a population of some 200 000 Afro-Caribbeans, seven young Afro-Caribbeans are known to the clinic. No rates are available but the diabetic liaison sisters' impression is that the incidence is rising among these and Indian-origin children and adolescents. These anecdotes need proper evaluation and a note of caution; in our Jamaican study of death certificates with diabetes coded in 1977 and 1978, 16 deaths were recorded below 14 years and 10 deaths below 5 years (Table 4 in [11]). If incidence was equal to mortality, as age-adjusted rates, these approximate to 1.5/100 000, about eight-fold less than the incidence in Britain, which itself has a north–south gradient.

Later onset diabetes – 'NIDDM'

In the West Indies, India and in their migrant populations, the great majority of diabetics are NIDDM. The author compared 77 consecutive Afro-Caribbeans (70% from Jamaica) and 74 white patients matched for age, sex, known duration and diabetes treatment from a large Birmingham clinic in England with a random sample of 131 attenders (3 : 1 female excess) at the University Hospital Clinic in Jamaica. Some local resistance to 'the needle' and availability problems of insulin and syringes led to many fewer Jamaican diabetics being transferred to insulin despite hyperglycaemia on oral agents [2].

Combining Afro-Caribbean patients in Birmingham and the Jamaicans, only nine out of 181 (5%) had ever had ketosis and were truly IDDM, although 26 of the 208 (12%) had received insulin from diagnosis. A more typical presentation has been hyperosmolar, non-ketotic coma or pre-coma [1], often because West Indian-origin patients have taken large amounts of sweet drinks, such as

'Lucozade', as they begin to feel ill (P. Daggett, J. K. Cruickshank, D. Cohen, 1984, unpublished results).

Body mass

A striking feature of Afro-Caribbean and Indian migrants with NIDDM is the prevalence of obesity, probably more than in white patients. The failure to promote weight loss of any note following diagnosis remains a judgement on the value of typical diabetic clinics. In my study, only in the Jamaican women had there been significant falls in body weight since diagnosis. Whether this was intentional or related to chronic glycosuria is uncertain as mean glycosylated haemoglobin values were high in Jamaica at some 13% compared with 13% in Afro-Caribbeans and 11% in whites in Birmingham. The price of improved control in all these groups may be poor weight loss (and hence worse insulin 'resistance').

In Jamaica the rates of obesity were much lower than in Britain, particularly in men. Thus, as rates of diabetes in Jamaicans appear to be as high as in Britain, weight gain postmigration does not seem to be the only environmental insult to promote diabetes. Nevertheless, the Afro-Caribbean women in Britain ranked fourth in obesity if included in the 16 centres of the WHO study – only below Pima and Oklahoma Indians and Moscow women [56].

Complications

Among black diabetics

In his 1962 book, Tulloch detailed rates of standard diabetic complications. However, for any useful comparison standardized methods have to be used. The WHO study [56] compared large and small vessel disease in 14 countries but unfortunately could not include a centre of black Afro-Caribbean or African origin. The author's Jamaica/UK comparison used the same protocol and supplied some of the missing material as the only study of complications prevalence in Afro-Caribbeans in Britain [2].

Blood pressure (BP)
Measured with random zero sphygomanometers, only diastolic BP was greater in the Birmingham Afro-Caribbeans than in age-matched whites, while in Jamaica both systolic and diastolic BP were higher than in Britain because the randomly sampled patients were older. Comparative rates of hypertension were thus distorted, but in Britain and in Jamaican women over 40% were hypertensive despite treatment. As follow-up in the WHO study has shown that blood pressure, and albumin excretion above 'normal', were the most important predictors of mortality, these rates are clearly management priorities in Britain, Jamaica and worldwide.

Hypertensive treatment
Among black (Afro-Caribbean, American or African) patients, type of therapy for hypertension is critical. Several properly controlled trials in non-diabetics and a recent study by the author in diabetics, have shown that β-blockers alone are generally *ineffective*. A diuretic has to be added to achieve comparable control of

pressure to whites, probably by increasing renin activity. In my study, the calcium antagonist verapamil was effective in blacks but to a lesser extent than in whites [57]. Angiotensin-converting enzyme inhibitors are now favoured for hypertension in diabetics due to apparently beneficial effects on proteinuria and renal function. In black patients a diuretic again has to be added to achieve adequate or comparable results [58] but such studies have not been done in black diabetics.

Large vessel diabetic disease assessed in the WHO study included coronary, cerebral and peripheral vascular damage. In our study, chest pain on effort (possible angina) and previously documented myocardial infarction were significantly lower in British Afro-Caribbeans (9/76 = 12%) and Jamaicans (5/131 = 4%) than in matched whites (19/131 = 26%). Standardized electrocardiograms were not taken and have not yet been studied in black diabetics. There were no differences in crude clinical rates of loss of foot pulsation, at between 12% and 15%. More Afro-Caribbeans than whites continued to smoke. If such smoking continued, this habit alone is likely to bring coronary disease rates in Afro-Caribbeans up to those now current in black Americans.

Small vessel disease includes retinopathy and proteinuria but rates of some degree of *cataract* were 40% in both Jamaicans and Afro-Caribbeans in Britain compared with 16% of whites. The visual nuisance and handicap they cause is inadequately appreciated and treated. Hence the rates of retinopathy between Britain and Jamaica may have been underestimated but differed little. Gross proteinuria averaged about 9% in all groups at this age range. Interestingly, in a central African clinic in Zambia, cataract is also more of a threat to vision than recognized retinopathy [59].

Indian subcontinent and its migrants

The few data come from individual clinics without standardized methods, except for the Delhi clinic in the WHO study [56]. In Britain, best documented have been those from Southall, east Birmingham and Leicester. Prevalence rates of diabetic coronary disease, most difficult to standardize, have not been reported but clinical impressions are that the rates are again elevated (see Chapter 31). Average diabetes duration tends to be shorter yet both overt proteinuria and microalbuminuria appear to be commoner than in age-matched whites [60,61]. These rates have alarming implications for development of renal failure and hence dialysis and transplantation needs. However, only studies of *incidence* (i.e. numbers of new cases) rather than prevalence counts can show a greater rate of development of renal disease among Indian-origin patients.

Among black Americans

Diabetic renal disease is rife and is a leading cause of renal replacement therapy [13].

Future management and prevention

The epidemic of diabetes and hence its complications in Afro-Caribbeans, American blacks, Indians and Indian subcontinent-origin peoples is now over-stretching available resources. The incidence rates show no sign of slowing down. New strategies for management and prevention will be needed.

Prevention might initially be focused on families, where diabetes inheritance is greatest, although optimism rather than scientific proof is the only available guide. Here, efforts to restrain weight gain in youth, a 'diabetic' low-fat diet that seems appropriate for everyone, regular exercise into old age and gainful employment are the targets. Harrying of the tobacco lobby and cigarette advertizers at every opportunity seem to be the only way to cut consumption in young people. None of these standard or novel health promotion efforts (or their scientific testing) fall into the traditional role of the doctor nor can they be promoted without a team approach. Thus, the author believes a new breed of diabetic physician is required, less hospital and bed orientated but part of a team promoting care and research outside in the workplace, home and even school. Six-monthly outpatient appointments in crowded clinics are unlikely to work. Where clinic care is appropriate, the evidence that doctors are always needed (or unfortunately know what should be routine) is poor. Currently, in the UK, there are several initiatives for diabetic day centres, staffed by volunteers, organized by diabetic liaison nursing sisters and physicians. For medical care, Mather has already established mini-clinics in general practice health centres run single-handed by such liaison nurses [62]. Currently we are running a controlled trial to examine whether a clinic for NIDDM patients run by a dietitian and diabetic liaison sister without doctors achieves set standards of care and control as well or better than routine outpatients, on the hypothesis that they could do no worse [63].

The epidemic of diabetes among ethnic minority groups described here may yet force health authorities' hands so that such initiatives become routine before evidence on how they work is available. Even so, the promotion of diabetic care and prevention by the diabetic nursing specialist, dietitian, volunteer and doctor in all ethnic groups would be a welcome development.

References

1 Nikolaides, K., Barnett, A. H., Spirolopoulos, A. J. and Watkins, P. J. West-Indian diabetic population of a large inner city diabetic clinic. Br. Med. J., 2, 1374–1375 (1981)
2 Cruickshank, J. K. and Alleyne, S A. Black West-Indian and matched white diabetics in Britain compared with diabetics in Jamaica: blood pressure, body mass and vascular disease. Diabetes Care, 10, 170–179 (1987)
3 Winter, W. E., Maclaren, N. K., Riley, W. J., Clarke, D. et al. Maturity onset diabetes of youth in black Americans. New Engl. J. Med., 316, 285–291 (1987)
4 La Porte, R. E., Tayima, N., Dorman, J. S., Cruickshank, K. J. et al. Differences between blacks and whites in the epidemiology of insulin-dependent diabetes mellitus in Allegheny County, Pennsylvania. Am. J. Epidemiol., 123, 592–603 (1986)
5 WHO Expert Committee on Diabetes Mellitus. Technical Report No. 727, WHO, Geneva (1985)
6 Hugh-Jones, P. Diabetes in Jamaica, Lancet, ii, 891–894 (1955)
7 Tulloch, J. Diabetes in the Tropics, Churchill Livingstone, Edinburgh (1962)
8 Tulloch, J. and MacIntosh, D. "J" type diabetes. Lancet, ii, 119–121 (1961)
9 Morrison, E. and Richards, R. Clinical profile of diabetes mellitus in Jamaica (phasic insulin dependence). West Ind. Med. J., 34, 94–97 (1985)
10 Fuller, J. H., Elford, J., Goldblett, P. and Adelstein, A. M. Diabetes mortality: new light on an underestimated public health problem. Diabetic Log., 24, 336–341 (1983)
11 Alleyne, S. A., Cruickshank, J. K. and Morrison, E. St A. Mortality from diabetes in Jamaica. Pan Am. Health Org. Bull., in press (1988)

12 Marmot, M. G., Adelstein, A. M. and Bulusu, L. *Immigrant Mortality in England and Wales 1970–1978*, OPCS Studies of Medical and Population Subjects No. 4, HMSO, London (1984)

13 National Institutes of Health. Diabetes in black Americans. In *Diabetes in America* (ed. J. M. Roseman) (NIH Publication No. 85–1468) US Government Printers, Washington (1985)

14 Brigham, C. B. *An Essay on Diabetes Mellitus*, Press of Abner A. Kingman, Boston (1868)

15 Patterson, O. *The Sociology of Slavery; An Analysis of the Origins, Development and Structure of Slave Society in Jamaica*, Granada Publishing, London (1973)

16 Tinker, H. *A New System of Slavery*, Oxford University Press, London (1974)

17 Sen, B. C. Diabetes mellitus in British Guiana. *Ind. Med. Gaz.*, July, 241–246 (1893)

18 Hoffman, F. L. The mortality from diabetes. *Boston Med. Surg. J.*, **187**, 135–137 (1922)

19 Tulloch, J. The prevalence of diabetes in Jamaica. *Diabetes*, **10**, 286–288 (1961)

20 Morrison, E. and Alleyne, S. A. Factors related to the prevalence of hyperglycaemia in Jamaica: a pilot survey. *West Ind. Med. J.*, **29**, 90–96 (1980)

21 Miall, W. E., Del Campo, E., Fodor, J., Standard, K. *et al.* Longitudinal study of heart disease in a Jamaican rural population. (a) Prevalence and ECG findings. (b) Factors influencing mortality. (c) Factors influencing changes in ECGs. *Bull. WHO*, **46**, (a) 429–442; (b) 685–694; (c) 695–708 (1972)

22 Ashcroft, M. A review of epidemiological research in a rural Jamaican community, 1959–1975. *West Ind. Med. J.*, **28**, 3–16 (1979)

23 Florey, C. du V., MacDonald, H., MacDonald, J. and Miall, W. E. The prevalence of diabetes in a rural population of Jamaican adults. *Int. J. Epidemiol.*, **1**, 157–166 (1972)

24 Florey, C. du V. Blood sugar and serum insulin levels in Jamaica, West Indies. *Adv. Metabol. Dis.*, **9**, 65–91 (1978)

25 Poon-King, T., Henry, M. V. and Rampersad, F. Prevalence and natural history of diabetes in Trinidad. *Lancet*, **i**, 155–160 (1968)

26 Beckles, G. L. A., Miller, G. J., Kirkwood, B. R., Alexis, S. D. *et al.* High total and cardiovascular mortality in adults of Indian descent in Trinidad unexplained by major coronary risk factors. *Lancet*, **i**, 1298–1301 (1986)

27 Miller, G. J., Beckles, G. L. A., Byam, N. T. A., Price, S. G. L. *et al.* Serum lipoproteins and susceptibility of men of Indian descent to coronary heart disease. The St James Survey, Trinidad. *Lancet*, **ii**, 200–203 (1982)

28 Beckles, G. L. A., Miller, G. J., Alexis, S. D., Price, S. G. L. *et al.* Obesity in women in an urban Trinidadian community. Prevalence and associated characteristics. *Int. J. Obesity*, **9**, 127–135 (1985)

29 Miller, G. J., Kirkwood, B. R., Beckles, G. L. A., Alexis, S. D. *et al.* Adult male all-cause, cardiovascular and cerebrovascular mortality in relation to ethnic group, systolic blood pressure and blood glucose concentration in Trinidad, West Indies. *Int. J. Epidemiol.*, **17**, 62–69 (1988)

30 Tripathy, B., Panda, N. C., Tes, S. C. *et al.* Survey for detection of glycosuria, hyperglycaemia and diabetes mellitus in urban and rural areas of Cuttack district. *J. Assoc. Phys. India*, **19**, 681–692 (1971)

31 Mukerjee, A. P., Sen, S. and Dey, P. Epidemiological survey of diabetes in a mixed population of Calcutta. *J. Ind. Med. Assoc.*, **61**, 17–22 (1973)

32 Mather, H. M., Verma, H. P., Mehta, S. P., *et al.* The prevalence of known diabetes in Indians in New Delhi and London. *J. Med. Assoc. Thai.*, Suppl. 2,**70**, 54–58 (1986)

33 Ramachandran, A., Jali, M. V.., Mohan, V. *et al.* High prevalence of diabetes in an urban population in South India. *Br. Med. J.*, **297**, 587–590 (1988)

34 Zimmett, P., Taylor, R., Ram, P., King, H. *et al.* Prevalence of diabetes and impaired tolerance in the biracial (Melanesian and Indian) population of Fiji: a rural–urban comparison. *Am. J. Epidemiol.*, **118**, 673–688 (1983)

35 Marine, N., Vinik, A., Edelstein, I. and Jackson, W. P. U. Diabetes, hyperglycaemia and glycaseria among Indians, Malays and Africans (Bantu) in Cape Town, South Africa. *Diabetes*, **18**, 840–857 (1969)

36 Omar, M. A. K., Seedat, M. A., Dyer, B., Rajput, M. C. *et al.* Prevalence of diabetes mellitus in a large group of South African Indians. *S. Afr. Med. J.*, **67**, 924–926 (1985)

37 Dowse, G. K., Gareebboo, H., Zimmet, P. *et al.* The high prevalence of diabetes and impaired glucose tolerance in Indian, Creole and Chinese Mauritians. *Diabetes*, in press (1989).

38 Schaad, J., Terpstra, J., Oemrawsingh, I., Kruseman, A. *et al.* Diabetes prevalence in the three

main ethnic groups of Surinam (South America): a population survey. *Neth. J. Med.*, **28**, 17–22 (1985)

39 Cruickshank, J. K., Beevers, D. G., Osbourne, V. L., Haynes, R. *et al*. Heart attack, stroke, hypertension and diabetes among West Indians, Asians and Whites in Birmingham, England: hospital admission analysis. *Br. Med. J.*, **287**, 1108 (1980)

40 Simmons, D., Williams, D. R. and Powell, M. Prevalence of diabetes in a predominantly Asian community: preliminary findings of the Coventry diabetes study. *Br. Med. J.*, **298**, 18–21 (1989)

41 McKeigue, P. M., Marmot, M. G., Syndercombe-Court, Y. D., Cottier, D. E. *et al*. Diabetes, hyper-insulinaemia and coronary risk factors in Bangladeshis in East London. *Br. Heart J.*, **60**, 390–396 (1988)

42 Mather, H. M. and Keen, H. The Southall diabetes survey: prevalence of known diabetes in Asians and Europeans. *Br. Med. J.*, **291**, 1081–1084 (1985)

43 Verma, N. P. S., Mehta, S., Madhu, S. *et al*. Prevalence of known diabetes in an urban Indian environment: the Darya Ganj diabetes survey. *Br. Med. J.*, **293**, 423–42 (1985)

44 US National Centre for Health Statistics. In *Advance Data from Vital & Health Statistics No. 130* (eds T. F. Drury and A. L. Powell), (DHSS No: PHS 87. 1250), PH Hyattsville, Maryland (1987)

45 Keen, H. The genetics of diabetes: from nightmare to headache (editorial). *Br. Med. J.*, **294**, 917–919 (1987)

46 Kirk, R. L., Sergeantson, S. W., King, H. and Zimmet, P. The genetic epidemiology of diabetes mellitus. In *Diseases of Complex Etiology in Small Populations: Ethnic Differences and Research Opportunities*, (eds R. Chakraborty and J. E. Emoke), Alan R. Liss, New York, pp. 119–146 (1985)

47 Rodey, G. E., White, N., Frazer, T. E. *et al*. HLA-DR specificities among black Americans with juvenile-onset diabetes. *N. Engl. J. Med.*, **301**, 810–812 (1979)

48 MacDonald, M. J., Famuyiwa, O. O., Nwabuebo, I. A., Bella, A. F. *et al*. HLA-DR associations in black type I diabetics in Nigeria: further support for models of inheritance. *Diabetes*, **35**, 583–589 (1986)

49 Reitnauer, P. J., Roseman, J. M., Bargo, B. O., Murphy, C. C. *et al*. HLA associations with insulin-dependent diabetes mellitus in a sample of the American black population. *Tissue Antigens*, **17**, 286–293 (1981)

50 Fletcher, J., Mijovic, C., Odugbesan, O., Jenkins, D., *et al*. Trans-racial studies implicate HLA-DQ as a component of genetic susceptibility to Type 1 (insulin-dependent) diabetes. *Diabetologia*, **31**, 864–870 (1988)

51 Fletcher, J., Odugbesan, O., Mijovic, C., Maskay, E. *et al*. Class II HLA DNA polymorphisms in Type I (insulin dependent) diabetic patients of North Indian origin. *Diabetologia*, **31**, 343–350 (1988)

52 Elbein, S., Potwein, P., Permutt, M. A., Bell, G. I. *et al*. Lack of association of the polymorphic locus in the 5' flanking region of the human insulin gene in American blacks. *Diabetes*, **34**, 433–439 (1985)

53 Hitman, G., Kambo, P. K., Mohan, V., Ramachandran, A. *et al*. An HLA association in malnutrition related diabetes mellitus. *Clin. Sci.*, Suppl. 11, **76**, 12 pp. (1989)

54 O'Rahilly, S., Wainscoat, J. S. and Turner, R. C. Type 2 (non-insulin dependent) diabetes: new genetics for old nightmares. *Diabetologia*, **31**, 407–414 (1988)

55 Cooper, D. N. and Clayton, J. F. DNA polymorphism and the study of disease associations. *Hum. Genet.*, **78**, 299–312 (1988)

56 Keen, H. and Jarrett, J. The WHO Multinational Study of Diabetes Mellitus: macrovascular disease. *Diabetes Care*, **2**, 187–195 (1979)

57 Cruickshank, J. K., Anderson, N. McF., Wadsworth, J., *et al*. Treating hypertension in black compared with white non-insulin dependent diabetics: a double-blind trial of verapamil and metoprolol. *Br. Med. J.*, **297**, 1155–1159 (1988)

58 Weinberger,M. Veteran Administrative Co-operative Study. Racial differences in response to low dose Captopril are abolished in hydrochlorothizide. *Br. J. Clin. Pharmacol.*, **14**, 97s–101s (1982)

59 Rolfe, M. Diabetic eye disease in central Africa. *Diabetologia*, **31**, 88–92 (1988)

60 Samanta, A., Burden, A. C., Feehally, J. and Walls, J. Diabetic renal disease: differences between Asian and white patients. *Br. Med. J.*, **293**, 366–267 (see also p. 696) (1986)

61 Allawi, J., Rao, P. V., Gilbert, R., Scott, G. *et al*. Microalbuminuria in non-insulin dependent diabetes: its prevalence in Indian compared with Europid patients. *Br. Med. J.*, **296**, 462–464 (1988)

62 Honey, T. and Mather, H. M. Community diabetic clinics and the diabetes specialist nurse. *Pract. Diabetes*, **4**, 2–4 (1987)
63 Cruickshank, J. K., Thompson, R., Drubra, U. *et al.* A randomized controlled trial to develop a diatetic/diabetes nurse specialist clinic vs. routine out-patient care of NIDDM in a multiethnic community. *Diabetic Med.*, (Abstr.) in press (1989)

Chapter 34

Management of hypertension in the Caribbean: the Jamaican perspective

Gerald A. C. Grell

Introduction

Chronic diseases are now the main cause of death in the English-speaking Caribbean, and cerebrovascular and heart diseases head the list in all territories [1]. Hypertension (Table 34.1) is the single most important contributor and is the leading health issue in the region as a far more important cause of death in all Caribbean territories than in Canada or the USA (Figure 34.1).

Table 34.1 Prevalence of blood pressure in excess of 160/95 mmHg in three Caribbean populations

| Country | Age (yr) | Prevalence (%) | |
		Male	Female
St Kitts	40–49	28	45
Trinidad	45–54	30	24
Jamaica	45–54	19	34

Adapted from [24].

Aetiological considerations

Several factors, genetic and environmental, may be responsible for the high prevalence of hypertension in the Caribbean black population.

Genes
Because of the common African origins of black persons in the Caribbean and USA, similarities in their blood pressure profiles may represent the effect of inheritance, especially of the gene(s) modulating sodium homeostasis. However, Miall, *et al.* [2] concluded that single-gene inheritance could account for only a small fraction of hypertension in Jamaica; thus multifactorial environmental variables are also important.

Salt
An association between hypertension and salt intake in Caribbean islands surrounded by seawater seems a tempting hypothesis. Schneckloth's group [3] in St Kitts, showed that the average daily intake of sodium was in the range 1.0–2.6 g,

305

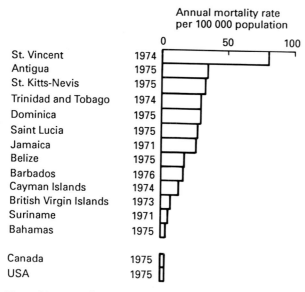

Figure 34.1 Age-adjusted death rates per 100 000 population from hypertensive disease in some of the English-speaking Caribbean compared to Canada and the USA. Reproduced from [26] with permission

levels similar to estimates in the USA. Moser [4] considered that the daily sodium intake in the Bahamas was higher than in the USA although this was never quantified. Experimental work on intracellular sodium [5] in Jamaicans indicated an increased sodium content of leucocytes in the presence of normal efflux rate constants, suggesting increased cell membrane permeability to sodium.

Parity and pre-eclampsia
In the St Kitts study [3] nulliparity but not multiparity seemed to be associated with increased hypertension, as also noted in Jamaica by Miall [2]. Subjects who had had pre-eclamptic toxaemia showed a greatly increased prevalence of hypertension when compared with women with normal pregnancies [2]. Recently, Forrester has reported a temporal relationship between leucocyte sodium content and the development and resolution of pre-eclampsia [25].

In Jamaica, where a recent detailed survey found that 26% of all maternal deaths were related to hypertensive disease [6]. As Jamaica's maternal mortality rates are some ten times greater than in Europe (even if many times lower than most developing countries), hypertensive control in pregnancy remains a major public health measure that could improve maternal death rates.

Renal problems
Fifteen per cent of Jamaican women with diastolic pressures above 110 mmHg had bacteriuria [2] and in those aged 30–60 years, with bacteriuria, blood pressure was higher than in those without.

In a study of University Hospital patients in Jamaica, 83.3% had essential hypertension and 13.3% had hypertension attributable to renal disease [7]. An even lower rate would be expected in the general population. In neighbouring

Panama, Central America, chronic renal disease did seem to contribute significantly to elevated blood pressure in the black population [8].

Stress
Some authors have attributed hypertension in Westernized populations to the 'stress' of migration into a complex urbanized environment [4]. However, agricultural workers in rural Jamaica had greater mean systolic blood pressures than city workers [2]. More recently we have shown that higher social class was associated with higher blood pressures in males while lower social class was associated with higher blood pressures in females. We have postulated that complex sociocultural factors including stress may be responsible [9].

Body mass
Obesity and higher blood pressure were associated in Jamaicans below the age of 55 years while above the age of 55 the association disappeared [2].

Clinical aspects

As elsewhere, hypertension in the Caribbean is usually asymptomatic until complications develop (Figure 34.2) [10]. Patients often present late, when target organs, especially the heart and central nervous system, are already irreversibly damaged.

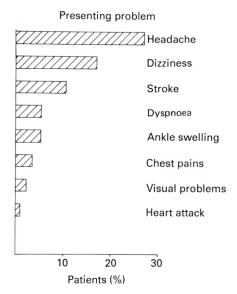

Figure 34.2 The main presenting complaints at the time of diagnosis in 170 Jamaican male and female hypertensives seen in 1980–81: percentage of patients who had symptoms. Reproduced from Grell, [10] with permission

Particular problems include case detection, early institution of therapy and compliance. In Barbados a survey of 4322 persons aged over 18 years showed that only 40% of those found to be hypertensive were previously aware of the diagnosis and only 13% were receiving medication [11]

Severe, malignant hypertension accounted for some 6.3% of all patients admitted to the University Hospital. It is the commonest single cause of renal failure requiring dialysis in all Caribbean territories [12].

Unlike Europe and North America, renal impairment, cardiac failure and stroke are more common than myocardial infarction as complications of hypertension in black Jamaicans [12] (Table 34.2). Myocardial infarction, although increasing in incidence in recent years, is commoner in persons of higher social class and in patients attending private rather than public hospitals [10].

Evidence of renal disease and ECG changes of left ventricular hypertrophy and strain (ischaemia) are found at even modest levels of blood pressure elevation [10]. Myocardial infarction was commoner in Jamaican patients with the mildest hypertension while renal failure was the commonest sequel in the most severe cases [10]. Thus, blood pressure levels alone do not establish the severity of hypertensive complications [13].

Table 34.2 The prevalence of complications in Jamaican hypertensives seen at the University Hospital of the West Indies

Complication	Prevalence (%)		
	Males	Females	Total
Renal impairment[*]	52.3	44.5	48.6
LVH on ECG	57.0	35.8	46.9
Cardiac failure	30.2	40.9	35.3
Cerebrovascular accident	24.8	29.9	27.2
Myocardial infarction	17.4	15.3	16.4
Hypertensive encephalopathy	6.0	5.1	5.6
Limb ischaemia or gangrene	3.4	2.9	3.2

Reproduced from Grell [12] with permission.
[*] Creatinine level above 150 μmol/l.

Regional perspective

While the majority of West Indians are of African ancestry with a low incidence of coronary heart disease, in Guyana and Trinidad East Indians are the co-dominant ethnic group and take with them a relatively high risk of coronary artery disease [14,15]. These ethnic differences make generalizations about regional management strategies difficult.

The Regional Caribbean Commonwealth Secretariat (CARICOM) and the Pan American Health Organization (PAHO/WHO) have attempted to standardize the management of hypertension using the structure shown in Figure 34.3. Facilities have been integrated within the framework of National Primary Health Care (PHC) services in each territory [16]. As all members of the health-care team should play some part in the overall management of hypertension, Table 34.3 has been designed for use in the Caribbean.

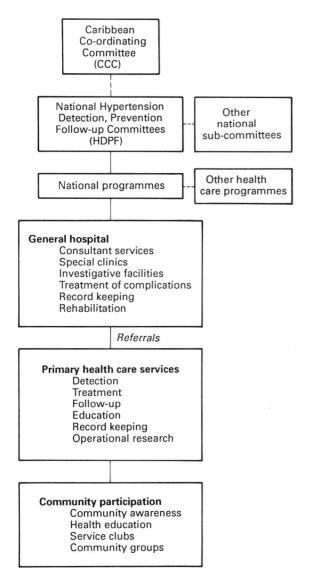

Figure 34.3 The organizational structure of services for the management of hypertension in the Caribbean. Reproduced from Grell [16] with permission

Blood pressure levels and patient risks

In 1978 Ashcroft and Desai [17] showed in a rural community in Jamaica that a significant excess mortality over a 13-year period occurred only in untreated hypertensives with blood pressure levels above 180/110 mmHg (phase IV). These epidemiological data are in contrast to findings from the USA which demonstrated that there is benefit to be derived from treating both black and white hypertensive

Table 34.3 Organization of an integrated community service for blood pressure control in the Caribbean

Responsibility	Tasks	Knowledge and skills	Supplies and equipment	Community support
Auxilliary personnel Community health workers Nutritionists and dietitians Nurses Pharmacists	History-taking BP measurement Patient education Weight and height Record-keeping Referral to nurse-practitioner or physician Public education	Knowledge of BP concepts Risk factors Complications BP measurement procedures Criteria for diagnosis and referral	BP measurement equipment Weight scale Height scale Audiovisual aids Record and referral forms	Appropriate communications system Transportation Mass media Health committees Funding for equipment
Nurse practitioners	Diagnosis Referral Patient education	As above Criteria for referral	As above	As above
Medex (Guyana)	Therapy (non-drug) Repeat prescriptions	Non-drug therapy Drug therapy	Drugs	
Clinic physicians	Diagnosis Therapy – drug and non-drug Patient and public education	As above Drug management procedures	Drugs	As above
Private physician	Referral			

patients with diastolic blood pressures above 90 mmHg (phase V) [18]. However, the cost–benefit ratio of treating such patients with mild hypertension is still being debated.

A practical working diagnosis in the Caribbean [19] is a repeated blood pressure level above 160/90 mmHg. However, individual risks and complications have to be the guidelines for drug therapy (Table 34.4). The cost of treating all mild hypertensives would be beyond the health resources of the region.

Table 34.4 Guidelines for the management of hypertension in the Caribbean

Diastolic blood pressure	Coronary risk factors	Management approach
≥ 105 mmHg	Present or absent	Drug therapy ± risk factor modification
90–104 mmHg	Present or target organ damage in evidence	Drug therapy ± risk factor modification
90–104 mmHg	Not present and no target organ damage	Careful sequential observation Non-drug therapy for initial visits Add drugs if BP continues to rise or target organ damage develops

Treatment of hypertension

Non-drug therapy

The use of drugs may be associated with side-effects and poor compliance. Their cost is also important, especially in poorer countries and poorer groups in society. Thus, non-drug therapy is a logical approach as initial therapy for mild hypertensives and as adjunctive therapy for more severe levels (Table 34.5).

Table 34.5 Non-drug approaches to the management of hypertension

Programmes	Effectiveness
1. Sodium restriction	+++
2. Weight reduction in the obese	++
3. Regular physical activity (exercise)	+
4. Relaxation, meditation, yoga	+
5. Biofeedback techniques	+
6. Avoiding cigarette smoking	+
7. Reducing excessive alcohol consumption	+
8. Potassium supplementation	+
9. High polyunsaturated/saturated fat ratio	+
10. Calcium supplementation	+/−

Drug therapy

Priorities include:

1. Diastolic pressures (phase V) above 105 mmHg.
2. West Indians with repeated casual systolic pressures over 180 mmHg.

3. The presence of target organ damage, i.e. cardiomegaly, renal impairment, coronary artery disease, cardiac failure, etc.
4. Diastolic blood pressures between 90 and 104 mmHg with associated atherosclerotic risk factors, in particular:
   (a) Diabetes mellitus;
   (b) High total cholesterol;
   (c) Heavy cigarette smoking;
   (d) Obesity;
   (e) Excessive alcohol intake;
   (f) A strong family history of hypertension and hypertensive cardiovascular complications.

Antihypertensive drugs can be grouped into several categories based on their principal site of action.

With some knowledge and experience of a few readily available agents in each category, the physician can rationalize a sequential prescription of drugs, rather than a trial-and-error or a blunderbuss therapeutic muddle. In the Caribbean, a strong case has always been presented for the step-care approach [20].

Because in general coronary artery disease is not common in blacks, thiazide diuretics are preferred as step 1 drugs. In addition, experience in Jamaica indicates that thiazides are more effective than beta-blockers alone at conventional doses [21]. Diuretics are cheap and this is always important for programmes in government clinics and hospitals. The lowest possible effective dose of thiazides should be used to minimize metabolic side-effects [22].

Current data from Europe, North America and Australia, have produced a strong preference for beta-blockers and recently calcium antagonists and ACE inhibitors as part of the therapeutic armamentarium. In the East Indian population of Trinidad and Guyana among whom coronary artery disease is common, beta-blockers are preferred as step 1 agents. In the Caribbean, methyldopa and reserpine are still widely used as they are readily available, effective, cheap and in the presence of cardiac decompensation are safer than beta-blockers. Contrary to the experience in whites, immunological abnormalities with methyldopa are rare in Jamaican black hypertensives [23].

Prazosin, captopril, enalapril and the calcium channel inhibitors, have been introduced more recently into the Caribbean as antihypertensive agents and are likely to be prescribed with increasing frequency within the step-care framework. It has often been said that the original step-care system is inflexible. However, our modified approach in Table 34.6 allows the physician several options, and is ideally suited for 'tailoring' a drug schedule to individual preferences.

Public health considerations in management

Major advances have been made in integrating the management of chronic diseases into the existing health-care delivery systems in Jamaica and the Caribbean. In developing countries, it is the inability to apply well-established technology rather than the need for current research which has been the limiting factor in solving many major health problems [16]. Chronic diseases have tended to be neglected in favour of the communicable diseases in the tropics. Data from the Caribbean over

Table 34.6 Alternative stairways in high blood pressure control to achieve individual care

Step	Alternative 1	Alternative 2	Alternative 3	Alternative 4
I	Low-dose thiazide	Low-dose thiazide	Beta-blocker	Prazosin, captopril, or nifedipine
II	Beta-blocker	Methyldopa or reserpine	Low-dose thiazide	Beta-blocker or low-dose thiazide
III	Hydralazine	Hydralazine	Hydralazine or prazosin or minoxidil*	Low-dose thiazide or beta-blocker
IV	Guanethidine	Guanethidine	Add drug acting at another site	

Alternative 1, cost-effective.
Alternative 2, use of commonly available drugs in government clinics (in the Caribbean).
Alternatives 3 and 4, for patients with coronary artery disease or coronary risk factors.
Alternative 3, for patients with renal impairment.

* A potent vasodilator, but causes intense fluid retention and hirsuitism and should be used in patients with severe renal disease in particular.

the past two decades, however, have made it clear to policy-makers that it is the chronic diseases that are now the main health issues in all West Indian territories.

Most Ministries of Health in the region have accepted the challenge and the responsibility for developing programmes to manage hypertension at a national level, and Caribbean coordination as shown in Figure 34.3 is being ensured through the appointment of regional chronic disease officers by the Pan American Health Organization office (PAHO/WHO) in Barbados [16].

An understanding of the local geography, culture and health beliefs is essential to the success of regional treatment strategies [1]. Patient and public education must be an integral part of national programmes. Adequate and continuous supplies of drugs and personnel are crucial, but budgetary and administrative constraints have to be met. New approaches, unique to a sparsely populated group of islands separated by sea but held together by a common heritage and language, need to be explored. The challenge of hypertension marks a new era of health-care delivery for the Caribbean [16].

References

1 Grell, G. A. C. Hypertension in the West Indies. *Postgrad. Med. J.*, **59**, 616–621 (1983)
2 Miall, W. E., Kass, E. H., Ling, J. and Stuart, K. L. Factors influencing arterial pressure in the general population in Jamaica. *Br. Med. J.*, **2**, 497–505 (1962)
3 Schneckloth, R. E., Corcolon, A. C., Stuart, K. L. and Moore, E. E. Arterial pressure and hypertensive disease in a West Indian negro population. Report of a survey in St. Kitts, West Indies. *Am. Heart J.*, **63**, 607–614 (1962)
4 Moser, M. Epidemiology of hypertension with particular reference to racial susceptibility. *Ann. N.Y. Acad. Sci.*, **84**, 989–994 (1960)
5 Forrester, T. and Alleyne, G. A. O. Sodium potassium and rate constant for sodium efflux in leucocytes from hypertensive Jamaicans. *Br. Med. J.*, **283**, 5–9 (1981)
6 Walker, G. J. A., Astley, D., McGaw, A., and Bernard, G. Maternal mortality in Jamaica. *Lancet*, **i**, 486–488 (1986)
7 Grell, G. A. C. Clinical aspects of hypertension in Jamaica. *West Indian Med. J.*, **27**, 231–238 (1978)
8 Taylor, C. E. Racial distribution of nephritis and hypertension in Panama. *Am. J. Pathol.*, **21**, 1031–1035 (1945)

 9 Dressler, W. W., Grell, G. A. C., Gallagher, P. N. and Viteri, F. E. Blood pressure and social class in a Jamaican community. *Am. J. Public Health*, **78**, 714–716 (1988)

10 Grell, G. A. C. Clinical Aspects of Hypertension in Black Jamaicans. MD Thesis, University of London (1983)

11 Hassell, T. Hypertensive clinic in the general population (Barbados). In *Synopsis of a Workshop on Hypertension in the Caribbean, Barbados*, 15–16 November, Abstract, p. 13 (1976)

12 Grell, G. A. C. The Jamaican hypertensive: characteristics of black patients at the University Hospital of the West Indies. *PAHO Bull.*, **19**, 265–273 (1985)

13 Tarazi, R. C. The role of the heart in hypertension. *Clin. Sci.*, **63**, 347–358 (1982)

14 Beckles, G. L. A., Miller, G. J., Kirkwood, B. R. *et al.* High total of cardiovascular disease morbidity in adults of Indian descent in Trinidad, unexplained by major coronary risk factors. *Lancet*, **i**, 1298–1300 (1986)

15 Adelstein, A. M. Current vital statistics: methods and interpretation. *Br. Med. J.*, **2**, 983–987 (1978)

16 Grell, G. A. C. Health care systems: chronic disease control in the English-speaking Caribbean with special reference to hypertension. *Trop. Doct.*, **16**, 181–184 (1986)

17 Ashcroft, M. T. and Desai, P. Blood pressure and mortality in a rural Jamaican community. *Lancet*, **i**, 1167–1170 (1978)

18 Hypertension Detection and Follow-up Programme Cooperative Group. Five year findings of the Hypertension Detection and Follow-up Programme. I. Reduction in mortality of persons with high blood pressure including mild hypertension. *JAMA*, **242**, 2562–2571 (1979)

19 Reports of Meeting of Expert Committee on Chronic Diseases (in the English-speaking Caribbean). *Strategy for the Control of Hypertension*, Part I, Pan American Health Organization, Barbados Office Publication, pp. 11–20 (1983)

20 Grell, G A. C. Clinical aspects of the management of hypertension in the Caribbean. *West Indian Med. J.*, **29**, 163–174 (1980)

21 Grell, G. A. C., Forrester, T. E. and Alleyne, G. A. O. Comparison of the effectiveness of a beta blocker (Atenolol) and diuretic (Chlorthalidone) in black hypertensive patients. *Southern Med. J.*, **77**, 1524–1529 (1984)

22 Report of Medical Research Council (MRC) Working Party on Mild to Moderate Hypertension. Adverse reactions to bendrofluazide and propranolol for the treatment of mild hypertension. *Lancet*, **ii**, 539–542 (1981)

23 Grell, G. A. C., Wilson, W. A. and James, O. Prevalence of drug-induced immunologic changes in hypertensive Jamaicans. *Southern Med. J.*, **73**, 1044–1045 (1980)

24 Grell, G. A. C. Some key issues in hypertension control in the Caribbean. In *Proceedings of the Meeting and Papers of Expert Committee on Chronic Diseases (in the English Speaking Caribbean)*, **2**, 24–28 (1983)

25 Sean, R. and Forrester, T. Relationship between leucoyte sodium content and high blood pressure during development and resolution of pre-eclampsia. *Clin. Sci.*, **76**, 199–203 (1989)

26 *Health Conditions in the Americas, 1973–1976* (Scientific Publication No. 364), Pan American Health Organization, Washington (1978)

Chapter 35

Diabetes mellitus and its management in the Caribbean

Errol Y.St A. Morrison

The populations of the Caribbean islands share a similar colonial past and are mainly of African descent. The problems of inadequate health care, education and socioeconomic stress are common to all. The estimated prevalence of diabetes mellitus ranges from 2% to 6%. Thus there should be some 600 000 diabetics in the Caribbean, with females probably being affected twice as commonly as males [1,2].

Prevalence rates are very low in the under-30-year age-group and gradually rise to a peak in the sixth decade. The average diabetic in the Caribbean spends some 10 years between the date of diagnosis and first presentation to a specialist centre [3]. It is not surprising that gangrene is still a common presenting problem [4] and the commonest complication (7% of diabetics) seen in hospital, followed in descending order, by neuropathy, 4%; retinopathy, 2% in non-hyptertensives; ischaemic heart disease, 2%; nephropathy, 1%.

Associated diseases are common especially in patients over 60 years, where hypertension is found in 53% and obesity in 45% [5]. Diabetes is a related factor in 7% of all deaths in the Caribbean.

Adequate health delivery is limited, and to most patients, inaccessible. The public health services are overcrowded, understaffed and severely restricted by lack of equipment and laboratory support. This is the real world for many practitioners, and for them, the diagnosis of diabetes mellitus cannot be based on criteria as laid down by the WHO Expert Committee. The diagnosis is most often made on the presence of glycosuria with symptoms such as polyuria, polydipsia, pruritus, infections or weight loss. Diagnosis is made even more difficult by the unavailability of blood glucose assays for the large number of diabetics who remain symptomless even with severely elevated levels of blood glucose above 22 mmol/l (400 mg/l). Another problem is the frequency of the aglycosuric hyperglycaemic syndrome, due to an elevated renal threshold when fairly severe diabetes may not be detected with urine testing alone. The prevalence of this in Jamaica has been estimated as 33% of diabetics by Hugh-Jones [6] and 42% by Alleyne et al. [3]. Despite these difficulties the ready availability of urine glucose testing is mandatory and action is needed to correct this omission.

Classical Type I diabetes ('IDDM') presenting in youth is uncommon, there currently being some 20 patients diagnosed with ketosis before age 25 in a total clinic population of nearly 2000. However, some cases may not reach hospital, as indicated by mortality figures for diabetes in this age-group, in a study of verified death certificates [7].

The clinical profile of diabetes in the Caribbean encompasses the usual insulin-treated (30%) and the non-insulin-dependent (70%) types [8] (Table 35.1). Of those patients who are insulin dependent, there is a small group, some 2% of the total diabetic population, who exhibit relative insulin resistance and require high doses of insulin ($\geq$ 90 U per day) to maintain euglycaemia. These patients frequently develop hypoglycaemic episodes, often at home. They are usually obese (body mass index > 25 kg/m^2) and are found to do quite well with a smaller dose of insulin combined with oral biguanide (metformin) therapy. They are designated as 'special' insulin dependent.

Table 35.1 The spectrum of treatments for diabetes mellitus as used in the outpatient diabetic clinic at the University Hospital, Jamaica

Treatment	Prevalence (%)
Insulin dependent/treated	13.9
Phasic insulin dependent	12.9
Special insulin dependent	1.8
Non-insulin dependent	
Diet alone	3.1
Biguanide (metformin) therapy	8.7
Sulphonylurea therapy	21.2
Sulphonylurea and biguanide combined therapy	38.4

Also becoming increasingly recognized is the clinical syndrome of phasic insulin dependence which is seen in over 10% of the diabetic population. This clinical picture is not restricted to the Caribbean and can be related in some cases to a previous history of malnutrition. Therapy is the feature which most distinguishes this syndrome. Initially, the patients require insulin in high doses (70–90 U daily) to maintain euglycaemia. Then, without any change in regimen, the patients may develop episodes of hypoglycaemia and gradually the insulin dosage can be reduced or even withdrawn. Oral hypoglycaemic agents may often then be sufficient to maintain good control, and in some cases diet alone will suffice. Periods of exacerbation, often precipitated by stress due to infections or pregnancy, or even in the absence of any identifiable stress (probably caused by a phase of increased activity of the disease process), may necessitate restarting insulin. This phase will gradually settle and after months or years a return to diet/oral therapy may be possible. An important feature of the insulin-requiring phase is that withdrawal of therapy does not result in ketoacidosis and patients may tolerate blood glucose levels in the region of 400 mg% (22 mmol/l) even up to 600 mg% (33 mmol/l) without developing symptoms. Could this picture reflect some phasic pattern of β-cell activity?

A variant of this phasic syndrome is the J-type or Jamaican-type diabetes described by Hugh-Jones in 1955 [6]. These patients are usually under 30, may have a history of malnutrition and present with abdominal pain, emaciation, hepatomegaly and painless bilateral parotid enlargement. Pancreatic calcification is rare, but may develop in later years into the picture described in many developing regions such as in India, Black Africa and the Pacific [9,10]. Research is needed on the phasic insulin-dependence group to assess insulin secretion both in the insulin- and non-insulin-requiring phases [11]. Due recognition must be given and facilities for study must be promoted to categorize the variety of syndromes, many of which may be malnutrition related. The success of any intervention programme will depend on the compliance of the patients. Compliance depends on the degree of education directed at this target group and their communities, bearing in mind the tremendous influence community opinion and folklore will have on the individual [3,11,12].

In the socioeconomically devastated countries in the Caribbean, compliance will also be influenced by availability of medication. Costs to the nation's health budget and also to the individual patient are also adverse factors.

For this reason, WHO has recently been promoting research into extracts of indigenous plants which in folklore are considered helpful treatments for a number of maladies, including diabetes mellitus. The potential savings to the country's health budget could prove cost effective and may improve compliance with treatment. Morrison and West [13,14] have been pursuing this in the Caribbean. Methods of monitoring the disease with easy-to-use and more readily accessible equipment such as blood glucose strip-meters could improve compliance. Costs are prohibitive and international agencies need to assist either centrally via government bodies or peripherally via service clubs, diabetic associations or other interested pressure groups. By such means both in the short and long term quality of life can improve for diabetics in the Caribbean.

References

1 Poon-King, T., Henry, M. V. and Rampersad, F. Prevalence and natural history of diabetes in Trinidad. *Lancet*, **i**, 155 (1969)

2 Morrison, E. Y. St A. and Alleyne, S. I. Factors related to the prevalence of hyperglycaemia in Jamaica. A pilot survey. *West Indian Med. J.*, **29**, 90–96 (1980)

3 Alleyne, S. I., Morrison, E. Y. St. A. and Richards, R. Some special factors relating to control of diabetes mellitus in adult Jamaican patients. *Diabetes Care*, **2**, 401–408 (1979)

4 Alleyne, S. I. and Golding, A. Deaths of patients with diabetes mellitus in Jamaica from 1973 to 1979. Proceedings of the Commonwealth Caribbean Medical Research Council, Scientific Meeting. *West Indian Med. J.*, **26**, 25–26 (1981)

5 Cruickshank, J. K. and Alleyne, S. A. Black West Indian and matched white diabetics in Britain compared with diabetics in Jamaica: body mass, blood pressure and vascular disease. *Diabetes Care*, **10**, 170–179 (1987)

6 Hugh-Jones, P. Diabetes in Jamaica. *Lancet*, **ii**, 891–897 (1955)

7 Alleyne, S. A., Cruickshank, J. K. and Morrison, E. Y. St A. Mortality from diabetes in Jamaica. *Pan. Am. Health Org. Bull.*, in press (1989)

8 Morrison, E. Y. St A. and Richards, R. Clinical profile of diabetes mellitus in Jamaica (phasic insulin dependence). *West Indian Med. J.*, **34**, 94–97 (1985)

9 Morrison, E. Y. St A. Calcific pancreatic diabetes mellitus. *Med. Digest*, **6**, 24–28 (1982)

10 Viswanathan, M. Pancreatic diabetes in India: an overview. In *Secondary Diabetes: The Spectrum of the Diabetic Syndrome* (eds S. Podolsky and M. Viswanathan), Raven Press, New York (1980)

11 Morrison, E. Y. St A. Diabetes mellitus in Jamaica (Guest editorial). *West Indian Med. J.*, **32**, 199–200 (1983)

12 Alleyne, S. A., and Cruickshank, J. K. The use of informal medications – particularly bush teas – in Jamaican patients with diabetes. *Cajanus*, **22**, 37–45 (1989)

13 Morrison, E. Y. St A. and West, M. A preliminary study of the effects of some West Indian medicinal plants on blood sugar levels in the dog. *West Indian Med. J.*, **31**, 194–197 (1982)

14 Morrison, E. Y. St A. and West, M. The effects of *Bixa orellana* (annatto) on blood sugar levels in the anaesthetised dog. *West Indian Med. J.*, **34**, 38–42 (1985)

Index

Accidental death, immigrants in England and Wales, 42
Acquired immune deficiency syndrome (AIDS), 159–60
Acute splenic sequestration in sickle cell disease, 133
Adolescence, behavioural disturbance in, ethnic minorities and, 180–181, 182–183
Adult T-cell leukaemia/lymphoma syndrome, 156
  prevalence in Jamaica, 164–167
Africa,
  blood pressure studies
    urban and rural East Africa, 61–68
    West Africa, 271–272
  ischaemic heart disease in West Africa, 265
African immigrants, mortality pattern in England and Wales, 45–46
Afro-Caribbeans,
  behavioural disturbance in, 182–183
  cerebrovascular disease in, 255–256
  child development in, 180–181
  diabetes in
    complications, 299–300
    mortality rate, 290–291
  dietary practices in UK, 249–254
  infant feeding practices, 251–252
  ischaemic heart disease in, 255–256
  mental illness in, 183–185, 190–203
  mortality pattern in England and Wales, 44–45
Age, at migration, and influence on disease, 14
AIDS, see Acquired immune deficiency syndrome (AIDS)
Angiographic studies, USA blacks and whites, 51–52
Antihypertensive drugs, low renin status and poor response of blacks to, 276
Aplastic crises in sickle cell disease, 134
Asian diets and food habits, 231–234
Asians,
  cancer incidence rates in Singapore, 148–149, 150
  diabetes in
    complications, 300
    mortality rate, 290
    prevalence, 290–295

infant feeding patterns of, 241–248
  breast and bottle, 241–242
  and growth faltering, 245
  and iron deficiency, 246–247
  and rickets, 246
  types of solid foods used, 244
  use of cow's milk, 244, 245
  vitamins, 244–245
  weaning, 243–244
ischaemic heart disease in, 257–263
mortality pattern in England and Wales, 44
nutrition of fetus and newborn, 235–240

Baltimore Sudden Death and MI Study, 50
Behavioural disturbance in ethnic minorities, 182–183
Beta-Blocker Heart Attack Trial (BHAT), 52
Birmingham Factory Study, 272–273
Birthweight, ethnic variation in, 89–90
Blood groups, ethnic variation in, 26–27
Blood pressure,
  and electrolytes, 64–65, 66–67
  levels of and patient risks, 309, 311
  prognosis in blacks compared with whites, 274–276
  low renin status and poor response of blacks to antihypertensive drugs, 276
  and socioeconomic factors, 65
  UK, 272–273
    Birmingham Factory Study, 272–273
    comparison with USA, 273–274
    Northwick Park Heart Study, 272
  urban and rural East Africa, 61–68
    background, 61–62
    longitudinal studies, 63–64, 65–67
    pilot studies, 62–63, 64–65
  West Africa, 271–272
  West Indies, 269–271
    St James' Cardiovascular study, 271
  see also Hypertension
Body mass,
  and diabetes, 299
  and hypertension, 307
Breast-feeding,
  Afro-Caribbean mothers, 251–252
  Asian mothers, 241–242

319